Sallie A. Brock

Richmond during the War

four years of personal observation - Vol. 1

Sallie A. Brock

Richmond during the War
four years of personal observation - Vol. 1

ISBN/EAN: 9783337826673

Printed in Europe, USA, Canada, Australia, Japan

Cover: Foto ©Andreas Hilbeck / pixelio.de

More available books at **www.hansebooks.com**

RICHMOND
DURING THE WAR;

FOUR YEARS OF PERSONAL OBSERVATION.

BY A RICHMOND LADY.

NEW YORK:
G. W. CARLETON & CO., PUBLISHERS
LONDON: S. LOW, SON & CO.
MDCCCLXVII.

To

HER

SOUTHERN SISTERS,

WHO,

IN THE CAUSE OF THE LATE

SOUTHERN CONFEDERACY,

FOR WHICH

THEIR BRETHREN YIELDED UP

THEIR LIVES—

"DID ALL THAT WOMAN EVER DARES."

IS THIS VOLUME,

HER VIRGIN EFFORT,

WITH WHATEVER THERE IS IN IT OF MERIT,

AFFECTIONATELY INSCRIBED

BY

THE AUTHOR.

CONTENTS.

CHAPTER I.
THE SECESSION OF VIRGINIA—HOW RICHMOND RECEIVED THE NEWS,   17

CHAPTER II.
THE FIRST ALARM—THE PAWNEE SUNDAY, ... 23

CHAPTER III.
GALA DAYS OF THE WAR, ... 26

CHAPTER IV.
THE GATHERING OF THE TROOPS, ... 33

CHAPTER V.
RICHMOND THE CAPITAL—SOCIAL CHANGES, ... 38

CHAPTER VI.
THE FIRST INVASION OF VIRGINIA, ... 42

CHAPTER VII.
POSITION OF THE CLERGY, ... 46

CHAPTER VIII.
THE FIRST BATTLE—GREAT BETHEL, ... 49

CHAPTER IX.
DISASTERS IN WESTERN VIRGINIA, ... 56

CHAPTER X.
THE BATTLE OF MANASSAS—ITS EFFECT IN RICHMOND. 59

CHAPTER XI.
RICHMOND A HOSPITAL—ARRIVAL OF PRISONERS, ... 65

CONTENTS.

CHAPTER XII.
Incidents of Battle, ... 68

CHAPTER XIII.
Changes in Richmond—An Evil Addition, ... 75

CHAPTER XIV.
Richmond a City of Refuge—Extortions, ... 78

CHAPTER XV.
The Close of 1861—The Hope of Intervention—Capture of Mason and Slidell, ... 81

CHAPTER XVI.
A Sad Holiday Week—Work for the Soldiers, ... 87

CHAPTER XVII.
The Fall of Roanoke Island—Disasters on the Tennessee and Cumberland Rivers—Gloom in Richmond, ... 99

CHAPTER XVIII.
Remains of Union Sentiment in Richmond—Business Changes, 101

CHAPTER XIX.
Richmond the Permanent Capital, ... 106

CHAPTER XX.
The Fight in Hampton Roads, ... 109

CHAPTER XXI.
A Growing Scarcity of Food in Richmond, ... 113

CHAPTER XXII.
Opening of the Peninsular Campaign—Magruder's Small Force, 116

CHAPTER XXIII.
Disasters to the Confederate Cause in the Southwest—The Battle of Shiloh, ... 121

CHAPTER XXIV.
Accumulating Disasters—Effect of the Fall of New Orleans, 125

CHAPTER XXV.
The Battles of Seven Pines and Fair Oaks, ... 132

CONTENTS.

CHAPTER XXVI.
Jackson's Campaign in the Valley, ... 137

CHAPTER XXVII.
Stuart's Raid, ... 140

CHAPTER XXVIII.
The Seven Days' Battles on the Peninsula, ... 144

CHAPTER XXIX.
Pope's Orders—Captures—Libby Prison, ... 155

CHAPTER XXX.
The Battle of Cedar Mountain—Northern Letter-Writing, . 158

CHAPTER XXXI.
The Provost Marshal's Office in Richmond—Incidents, . . 161

CHAPTER XXXII.
The Second Battle of Bull Run—A Woman's Stratagem, . . 163

CHAPTER XXXIII.
The Clouds Lifted, ... 166

CHAPTER XXXIV.
Return of the Confederate Congress—Women at Work in the Public Departments, ... 169

CHAPTER XXXV.
Fidelity of the Negroes, ... 177

CHAPTER XXXVI.
Lee's Invasion of Maryland—The Battle of Antietam, . . . 180

CHAPTER XXXVII.
Scenes in Richmond in the Winter of 1862-3, ... 188

CHAPTER XXXVIII.
Burnside's Campaign—Refugees in Richmond, ... 196

CHAPTER XXXIX.
Running the Blockade, ... 202

CHAPTER XL.
The Bread Riot in Richmond, ... 208

CONTENTS.

CHAPTER XLI.
Spies, ... 211

CHAPTER XLII.
Stoneman's Raid—Panic in Richmond, ... 213

CHAPTER XLIII.
Hooker's Campaign—Death of Stonewall Jackson, ... 215

CHAPTER XLIV.
Sufferings of the Wounded—Lack of Supplies, ... 225

CHAPTER XLV
The Fall of Vicksburg—Its Effect, ... 228

CHAPTER XLVI.
Lee's Invasion of Pennsylvania—Effect of the Battle of Gettysburg, ... 233

CHAPTER XLVII.
The Summer of 1863—A Woman Arrested for Treason, . . 248

CHAPTER XLVIII.
Poverty in Richmond, ... 250

CHAPTER XLIX.
Bragg's Campaign—The Battle of Chickamauga, ... 257

CHAPTER L.
Trouble with the Negroes, ... 262

CHAPTER LI.
Christmas, 1864—Opening of the New Year, ... 267

CHAPTER LII.
Confederate Currency—Fabulous Prices in Richmond, . . 271

CHAPTER LIII.
The Confederate Congress in the Winter of 1863-4, . . 274

CHAPTER LIV.
Dahlgren's Raid around Richmond, ... 276

CHAPTER LV.
The Spring of 1864—Morgan's Return to Richmond, . . . 284

CONTENTS.

CHAPTER LVI.
PROPOSED EVACUATION OF RICHMOND—REMOVAL OF THE TREAS-
URY-NOTE BUREAU, ... 288

CHAPTER LVII.
THE SUMMER CAMPAIGN OF 1864—THE BATTLES OF THE WIL-
DERNESS, ... 290

CHAPTER LVIII.
PETERSBURG, ... 299

CHAPTER LIX.
STARVATION IN RICHMOND, ... 303

CHAPTER LX.
DESTRUCTION OF THE ALABAMA—SHERMAN'S MARCH, ... 305

CHAPTER LXI.
EARLY'S CAMPAIGN—WASHINGTON THREATENED, ... 312

CHAPTER LXII.
LIFE IN RICHMOND IN 1864, ... 314

CHAPTER LXIII.
BOTH SECTIONS TIRED OF WAR—THE NEGOTIATION AT NIAGARA
FALLS — COLONEL JACQUES'S VISIT TO RICHMOND—THE
CHICAGO CONVENTION, ... 321

CHAPTER LXIV.
THE CAPTURE OF MOBILE—THE FALL OF ATLANTA—THE FALL
CAMPAIGN AROUND RICHMOND, ... 326

CHAPTER LXV.
SHERIDAN'S CAMPAIGN IN THE VALLEY—NAVAL LOSSES—RE-ELEC-
TION OF MR. LINCOLN—ARMING OF SLAVES, ... 331

CHAPTER LXVI.
HOOD'S CAMPAIGN IN TENNESSEE — SHERMAN'S MARCH THROUGH
GEORGIA—THE CONFEDERATE ARMIES DEPLETED BY DE-
SERTION, ... 336

CHAPTER LXVII.
THE WINTER OF 1864-5—WANT OF FUEL AND PROVISIONS—RO-
MANCE—PRICES, ... 340

CHAPTER LXVIII.

CAPTURE OF FORT FISHER—OCCUPATION OF WILMINGTON AND
  CHARLESTON—END OF SHERMAN'S MARCH, ... 347

CHAPTER LXIX.

MORE PEACE NEGOTIATIONS—GOVERNMENT APPEAL FOR FOOD, . . . 349

CHAPTER LXX.

FOREBODINGS OF DISASTER — SHERIDAN'S GREAT RAID AND HIS
  JUNCTION WITH GRANT, ... 357

CHAPTER LXXI.

OPERATIONS OF GRANT AND LEE—FALL OF PETERSBURG, ... 359

CHAPTER LXXII.

EVACUATION OF RICHMOND—BURNING OF THE CITY, ... 362

CHAPTER LXXIII.

VISIT OF PRESIDENT LINCOLN TO RICHMOND—THE FEDERAL GOV-
  ERNMENT FEEDING THE PEOPLE, ... 371

CHAPTER LXXIV.

SURRENDER OF LEE, ... 374

CHAPTER LXXV.

THE ASSASSINATION—CAPTURE OF JEFFERSON DAVIS—CONCLUDING
  EVENTS OF THE WAR, ... 380

CHAPTER LXVI.

LIFE IN THE OLD LAND YET, ... 388

INITIAL CHAPTER.

RICHMOND IN HISTORY.

HAD not cruel siege been laid to Saragossa, and Londonderry, and Gibraltar, and Sebastopol, they had had scarcely more than a local name, and the pages of history had not been gilded with examples of self-abnegation, sacrifice, and valor so sublime as to appeal to heaven for admiration. Heroism, patriotism, and all the nobler instincts of the human soul, are rarely developed in the bright sunshine of prosperity. The rough winds of adversity are needful to the germination of the precious seed which God has generously implanted, but chooses to bring to the budding and blossoming and fruition in his own good way. Had not the passions of man lighted the frenzied torch of war, and opened its bloody trail upon the plains of the Crimea and the waters of the Euxine, the world had never known that greatest of heroines, Florence Nightingale. Had not oppression, under specious legal pretence, trodden heavily upon America, she had not given to the world her Washington. The bloody French revolution made a Napoleon; a later revolution made another of the same great name; a still later upheaval has made a Bismarck.

With memories crowding up like trooping phantoms, some beautiful and pleasant, some taunting and derisive, our fingers are toying listlessly with a Key! It is somewhat tarnished, but the red stains are partially worn off by recent use. What must be done with it? We feel that there is something in the locked chamber that will interest us—something that the world will be wiser and better for knowing—and hesitatingly we turn the key, to reveal the secrets held by the Confederate Capital during four years of terrible civil war.

The writer, a Southern woman, tells in this volume a story of personal experiences and observations in Richmond. In beginning a series of Recollections of the War, her original intention was to give them publication through the columns of some friendly journal, but by the advice of friends, (partial, it may be,) the narrative has been so amplified as to include a much larger field than was originally intended, and is now presented as a truthful though imperfect picture of scenes of which she was personally cognizant. In opening the door of our devoted city, we do not mean to praise her, but to let the simple record tell the story of her worth. Richmond has won a place in history beside Athens and Sparta and Rome, and her heroes, like theirs, are immortal.

Acknowledgments are due to the author of the Southern history entitled "Four Years of the War," from whose pages accounts of military movements have been liberally drawn; but many incidents illustrative of the heroic endurance of the men and women of the South during the whole of their terrible ordeal are narrated from individual observation; while the singular scenes occurring in the Capital itself formed a part of the author's daily experience. She submits her work, with a sincere desire that kindly relations may be speedily restored between the lately warring sections; and asks that it may be remembered that while there is much to be forgotten, it is God-like to FORGIVE.

RICHMOND DURING THE WAR.

CHAPTER I.

THE SECESSION OF VIRGINIA—HOW RICHMOND RECEIVED THE NEWS.

TO the anxious and restless inhabitants of Richmond, the proceedings of the Virginia Convention during the winter of 1861 seemed slow, undecided, and uncertain. Separated, by the action of the other Southern States, from their former close communion with those to whom they were allied by sympathy, relationship, and interest, they chafed under the apprehension that they would be compelled to remain in the Union. Divided counsels distracted the attention of the members of the Convention; the strong party which favored immediate secession, was opposed by another which insisted upon the expediency of a compromise, and there was still another faction which bitterly resented every proposition to sever the relations existing between Virginia and the Federal Government. It was at this period that the women of Virginia, and especially of Richmond, began to play the important part in public affairs, which they sustained with unflinching energy during four years of sanguinary and devastating war. The hall of the Convention became their favorite place of resort and occasionally they engaged in political discussion before the assemblage of the members. Every prominent delegate had his own partisans among the fair sex. Every woman was to some extent a politician.

On the afternoon of the 14th of April, the news of the fall of Fort Sumter reached us by telegraph. It was received with the wildest demonstrations of delight. A hundred guns were fired, and as the reverberations were heard for miles around, the people of Richmond knew that there was some wonderful cause for joy, and those not of the city wondered whether they commemorated the victory of the Confederates at Sumter, or whether the Convention had at last passed the ordinance of secession. But the intelligence of the actual event spread rapidly; men from the adjoining country flocked to the city to hear the wonderful story; bonfires were kindled, rockets sent up, and the most tumultuous excitement reigned. All night the bells of Richmond rang, cannons boomed, shouts of joy arose, and the strains of "Dixie's Land," already adopted as the national tune of the Confederates, were wafted over the seven hills of the city.

There was little room to doubt the spirit of the people of Richmond at that time. Denunciations were heaped upon the Convention, because of its tardiness, and attempts were made to run up the Stars and Bars on the dome of the Capitol. Mothers, forgetful, in the tumult, of the restraint usually imposed upon their youthful sons, permitted them to join in the demonstrations of delight; and the boys shouted eagerly for the Southern Confederacy, and for Beauregard, the hero of Fort Sumter, and cried, "Down with the Old Flag!"

Through respect to the Sabbath, which came on the next day, these noisy demonstrations were suspended, though the subject of excitement was of too startling a character to be hushed up, even by the sanctity of the day, and was quietly discussed everywhere but in the houses of worship.

The writer of these recollections on that day crossed Mayo's Bridge, and as her eye rested on the shipping that lay at anchor in the river, she saw from the mast-heads of the vessels, floating in the breeze and sunshine, the Stars and Stripes, the old flag, under whose folds, as the ensign of her nation, she had first breathed the air of heaven. Emotions, the most thrilling yet the most inexplicable, took possession of her. Her pride in it had ever been intense ; her love for it characterized by the most sincere veneration. She questioned with herself whether she had lived to see the day when that flag, which had ever been to her the emblem of all that was great and glorious, in a free government, should become the symbol of tyranny and of oppression to the rights she held most sacred. On the next Sabbath, as she stood upon the same spot, from the mast-heads of those vessels she saw floating, not the Stars and Stripes—but the Stars and Bars. Virginia had seceded.

On the 17th of April, after sitting nearly two months, at a late hour of the night, and in secret session, the Convention of Virginia passed an ordinance of secession, while it was yet hopeful of new constitutional guaranties, and a revulsion of feeling at the North.

The resolution, which was unanimously adopted, was as follows:

"The people of Virginia recognize the American principle, that government is founded on the consent of the governed, and the right of the people of the several States of this Union, for just cause to withdraw from their association, under the Federal Government, with the people of the other States, and to erect new governments for their better security ; and they never will consent that the Federal power, which is in part their power, shall be exerted for the purpose of subjecting such States to the Federal authority."

From the secrecy which characterized the proceedings of the Convention, the people of Richmond were expecting some important results, and were not surprised at the information announced in the morning papers. Suddenly—almost as if by magic—the new Confederate flag was hoisted on the Capitol, and from every hill-top, and from nearly every house-top in the city, it was soon waving. The excitement was beyond description ; the satisfaction unparalleled. All business was suspended for the time, and the work of the moment was universal congratulation. At last Virginia was free from the obligation that bound her to a Union which had become hateful. Cannons were fired, bells rang, shouts rent the air, the inhabitants rushed to and fro to discuss the joyful event. A stranger suddenly transported to the city, without a knowledge of preceding facts, would have imagined the people in a state of intoxication or insanity.

But the grand demonstrations of delight were reserved for the evening of the 19th of April, when the whole city was magnificently illuminated, and the secession of the State celebrated by the most extensive torch-light procession ever known there. The illumination seemed so universal, that the writer, who spent the evening in walking about the city, does not remember a single building from which the gleaming of lights was not visible. A favorite form of this illumination was the Cross of the South; and if among the poor and humble, there were wanting means to illuminate grandly, a single light in the window proved that at least the inclination to rejoice was not wanting. All love for the Union appeared exhausted.

The procession, beginning its line of march on Marshall Street, rapidly swelled in numbers until, when it reached Main Street, the thoroughfare was entirely blockaded for many squares; Rockets were flashing in all directions, Roman candles darted myriads of stars, numerous bands of music discoursed the new national airs, and thousands of voices joined in the choruses. Transparencies of all sizes and descriptions, bearing significant mottoes and caricatures, were borne in the procession. Passing through Marshall and Broad Streets, and down Main Street to its terminus beyond Church Hills, the procession marched through Franklin Street, past the State Court House, and paused in front of the Ballard House, and Exchange Hotel, where enthusiastic speeches were made by various orators. The sight was novel. As far as the eye could reach down the line of Franklin Street, and over the hill, more than a mile distant, gleamed the torches, and the dim transparencies shone like illuminated squares of vapor, or gigantic fire-flies; the sounds of musical instruments growing fainter and fainter, until they were lost upon the ear, or drowned in the hum of the multitude, which now and then burst forth into the wildest hurrahs. It was impossible to mistake the sentiment which possessed the soul of the assemblage. It was not the result of a sudden ebullition of excitement, but of real emotion, long cherished.

Among the orators introduced, were one or more from Georgia, and several from North Carolina, among whom was General Ransom, afterwards favorably distinguished in the Confederate service. He came, he said, "to bring news from the Old North State, which was ready to follow the example of the Old Dominion, and had already secured every fortress belonging to her territory, with seventy-five thousand stand of arms—thus pledging herself to the cause of the South, and giving one more State to the Confederacy." This announcement called forth the wildest acclamations. Cheer after cheer rent the air. Then came another speaker, who announced the resistance in Baltimore, and described the bloody scenes which had occurred in the attempt to pass Federal troops through the streets of that city. Although this piece of information had been received several hours previously, and was commemorated on the transparencies, it was presented by the speaker with such force that renewed cheers went up, and the shouts for Baltimore were loud and long.

The orators of this occasion were introduced by a lawyer of Albemarle County, Virginia, a young man of distinguished abilities, the son of an old and prominent politician, and promising himself to make no inconsiderable figure in the political arena. In prefacing the introduction of one of Richmond's illustrious guests, excited by the enthusiasm of the moment, he declared: "I am neither a prophet, nor the son of a prophet, yet I predict that in less than sixty days the flag of the Confederacy will be waving over the White House"—alluding to the expected capture of Washington.

"Yes," exclaimed one in the crowd, "in less than thirty days!" But how feeble is human foresight, and human wisdom. The Southern cry of "On to Washington," was the complement of the Northern "On to Richmond." Uneducated in the difficult arts of war, what then seemed feasible to the glowing and enthusiastic imagination of confident hope, grew painfully less so, as instructed and bitter experience taught many that they had engaged in no mere child's play.

As we stood upon the steps of the Ballard House, entertained by a distinguished member of the Convention, while many interesting incidents of the session were discussed, allusion was made to the fact that a prominent man in that body had received from the ladies of Richmond a crown of flowers as a token of their admiration for his fidelity to the Union. Surprise was expressed, for it had been generally understood, that among the women of Richmond the secession sentiment was most warmly cherished. Pointing to a window of the hotel on the opposite side of the street, he remarked, "I am happy to enlighten you, and can explain quite to your satisfaction how the mistake originated." He continued: "You see there, two ladies?" "Yes." "Well, they are from Boston, and with them originated the compliment ascribed to the ladies of this city."

This affair, incorrectly reported at the time, gave rise to the story which appeared in the newspapers at the North, that the women of Richmond were opposed to secession. The fact was, that long before the ordinance of secession was passed by the Convention, almost every woman in Richmond had in her possession a Confederate flag—ready, at any moment, to run it out from her window.

CHAPTER II.

THE FIRST ALARM—THE PAWNEE SUNDAY.

UP to this time, we had scarcely begun to realize that war was inevitable. We had hoped against hope, until the battle of Fort Sumter was fought, that some compromise might be effected, some specific measures adopted to stay the dreaded evil. Richmond was never in a more prosperous condition. Her trade was flourishing; articles of food were abundant and cheap; the stores were well stocked with merchandise; pauperism was almost unknown; the people were independent and happy. In intelligence, morality, refinement and piety, the inhabitants compared favorably with those of any city in the Union.

On the day succeeding the night of the illumination, the city relapsed into comparative quiet; but steady watch was kept up for any hostile demonstration. Military organizations were begun, and volunteers fast filled the ranks. The Richmond Light Infantry Blues possessed some enviable historic fame. It was an organization which dated its origin prior to the Revolution of 1776, and had numbered among its ranks some of the most gallant and chivalrous of the descendants of the old cavaliers of Virginia. At this time, it was under the command of Captain O. Jennings Wise, a son of Ex-Governor Wise, and then associate editor of the *Richmond Enquirer*, which had been, since the days of the elder Ritchie, the principal organ of the Democracy of Virginia. Company F and the Richmond Greys had their ranks filled by young men generally of wealth, education and refinement, enthusiastic, brave and generous. All these companies of infantry were well drilled in military exercises, and ready to use their skill in defence of the cause which had divided the North from the South, even to the death. These companies, with the Battalion of the Richmond Howitzers, and the Fayette Artillery, composed at that time the whole military force of the city under regular organization.

It had been announced that at the slightest premonition of danger, the bell on the Capitol Square should be rung, when the military companies were to repair to their respective armories and prepare to meet any emergency. On Sunday, the 21st of April, occurred the first of a wonderful succession of Sabbath day excitements. Indeed, so common did such excitements finally become, that with few exceptions, we declared all Sunday rumors false. On this warm and balmy April day, the attendance at the different churches was more than usually large. Carefully refraining from making their pulpit discourses themes of political discussion, our clergymen nevertheless offered up the most fervent and devout prayers continually, that God, in his wisdom, might quell the surging billows of angry discord, dispose the hearts of men to peace, and stay the scourge of war; and it was noted as a singular coincidence on that day, that the peculiar lesson in the Episcopal Churches was regarded, by many, as prophetic of success to the South:—
"Yea, will the Lord be jealous for his land, and pity his people. Yea, the Lord will answer, and say unto his people, 'Behold, I will send you corn, and wine, and oil, and ye shall be satisfied therewith; and I will no more make you a reproach among the heathen, but I will remove far off from you the Northern Army, and will drive him into a land barren and desolate, with his face toward the east sea, and his hinder part toward the uttermost sea, and his stink shall come up, and his ill savor shall come up, because he hath done great things.'"

The services had proceeded until just at their close in some of the churches, and in others during the last prayer, the premonitory sound of the bell on the Square disturbed the solemnity of the hour, and awoke the people to a dread sense of danger—from what source, they could not tell.

In an instant all was confusion. The men, in the excitement, rushed pell-mell from the churches; and the women, pale and trembling with affright, clung to their sons or husbands, wherever they could—but getting no respon.

their tearful question—"What *is* the matter? What *is* the matter?"

Hasty embraces, sudden wrenchings of the hand, tearful glances of affection, and our men rushed to their armories, to prepare they knew not for what. On every female face was the pale hue of dismay; but mingled with it, the stern, unmistakable impress of heroic resolution to yield up their hearts' most cherished idols upon the altar of their country, if need be. Silently, tearfully, our women wended their way to their homes, and from every closet, the outpourings of supplicating souls, for protection to the loved ones, went up to the ear of the Eternal.

The alarm, however, was groundless. It originated in a report that the Federal sloop of war Pawnee, which had been operating in Norfolk Harbor, was making her way up James River, bent upon the destruction of Richmond. In a situation entirely defenceless, with no obstacles to prevent an easy and rapid communication with the city, either by land or water, it was by no means foolish to suppose such a plan possible, and even feasible.

On passing down Main Street, a novel sight met our gaze. The different companies of infantry were all mustered, numerous pieces of artillery of light calibre, belonging to the Howitzer Battalion and the Fayette Artillery, were drawn out into the street; almost every man carried a gun of some description, and boys, who had learned to shoot, appeared with light fowling-pieces. The ridiculous was singularly blended with the solemn and impressive. Only at the slowest pace could a carriage make its way through the crowded street, and then with much risk to the lives of the occupants, from a prospect of frightened horses.

After much deliberation it was decided to send down to a convenient position on the river, a few miles below the city, several pieces of artillery to greet the coming of the intruder. This was the first movement of the Virginia military in the late war.

As twilight gathered over the city, the faint booming of

distant cannon was distinctly heard, and apprehension of an engagement with the Pawnee was entertained; but the reports were afterwards ascertained to be only the result of a trial of the pieces. The next morning, by order of the governor, the artillery were recalled to the city, to be sent, in a very few days, to meet an emergency of greater importance.

This day has since been familiarly known to the people of Richmond as the Pawnee Sunday, and many ridiculous occurrences were the source of much subsequent amusement.

CHAPTER III.

GALA DAYS OF THE WAR.

THROUGH the management of Mr. Floyd, the South was not entirely unprepared for the emergency she was required to meet. He had succeeded in getting an order for the transfer of certain arms of an improved and valuable kind from the armories of Springfield and Watervliet to the different arsenals of the South; and with these, together with arms distributed by the Federal Government to the different States, prior to this period, and those purchased by the States and citizens, the South was not wholly wanting in the means to meet the demands of the time. But when we reflect upon the weakness of the South, her utter insufficiency, compared with the numbers and resources with which she presumed to contend, we are lost in amazement at the very inception, to say nothing of the continuation of the struggle through four long years of difficulties, that grew and thickened at every step—of impediments which arose, unlooked for, and everywhere.

The news from abroad was discouraging. Baltimore had been subdued; Federal troops were passing through daily; and many of her citizens were wending their way to Richmond.

In a very short time the population of Richmond increased in a wonderful ratio. Strange faces greeted the citizens at every turn; and the city, even at that early period, began to wear the stern and remarkable characteristics she has ever since retained. The absorbing question of the moment was that of war. The most active enthusiasm was everywhere visible. It was well that we were not then aware of our own weakness, nor that we were in want of everything but brave hearts and willing hands. We were, as a people, a living exemplification of the truth of the proverb that "Where ignorance is bliss, 'tis folly to be wise." Sanguine expectations of speedy success were entertained by many; and some doubted whether the policy of coercion would be carried out in an active engagement. It was hard to believe that we were actually plunged into the troubles we so much deprecated; that the horrent front of war was bristling before us.

The theatre of war on land was soon understood to be on our own soil. Virginia was to be the principal battle-ground of the antagonistic forces; and General Lee, who had resigned his commission as Colonel of Cavalry in the old United States Army, was placed in command of all the Confederate forces in Virginia.

Feeling that our State had become the particular object of hatred and hostility to the old government, we hastened, with all possible energy, to meet the necessities which might arise. The most active preparations for the terrible future commenced from the time that Virginia ranged herself under the banner of the Southern Confederacy. Colleges and public schools of all grades suspended operations, and our young men hastily sought instruction in the art of war. Men of all grades and professions were to be found, filling up the ranks for the coming contest. The clergyman laid aside his surplice, the lawyer his briefs, the physician his scalpel, the merchant his ledger, the farmer his plough, the artisan the tools which denoted his craft. All placed themselves in the ranks of the military, for assignment to whatever position might be best suited to them, in the defence of their country. The most lucrative employments were cheerfully abandoned, the widest fields for enterprise were unnoticed and neglected, in the spirit of patriotism which incited our population to action.

Could all this have been but from the excitement of the times—the ebullition of passion—a spurious enthusiasm? It may do for one remote from the scene of action to answer "Yes," but to an eye-witness, another solution to the mystery is evolved.

It was the bursting of the green withes with which the young giant was fettered—it was the breaking of the cords of oppression with which he had been bound—it was the undying love of Liberty—which had been re-echoed from the ancient walls of old St. John's (which gives a name to one of the seven beautiful hills of Richmond,) a legacy bequeathed by their fore-fathers, through their spokesman, the immortal Patrick Henry—"Give me Liberty, or give me death!" They felt

"To fight—
To fight in a just cause, and for our country's glory,
Is the best office of the best of men ;
And to decline when these motives urge,
Is infamy beneath a coward's baseness."

But it is useless to attempt an explanation of the motives of Virginians, at least, in the conduct of the late war—nor would we draw invidious comparison with the people of other States of the South. All were actuated by the same motives ; all were imbued by the same spirit—nor do we, by these remarks, wish any apology understood. The justice of their cause was the main-spring of their action. To them it was clear and undimmed as the cloudless sunlight; to all whose minds are unclouded by prejudice, or undarkened by fanaticism, it must appear so.

Should these lines meet the eye of any who may be disposed to give a harsh judgment, we only ask that, for a single moment, the promptings of a better principle within may be yielded to ; that a position may be taken from a

Virginia stand-point, and then make the decision. Under such circumstances we fear it not. It could only be what the brave and generous must ever award the brave and generous.

In the meantime, the uprising throughout the State had been almost universal. Military companies were speedily formed in every section of the country. Indeed, with such alacrity and zeal did the young men press forward to join in the service of the South, that the numbers seemed likely to exceed the demand. Every railroad train that arrived in Richmond bore its freight of soldiers. Very soon, from all directions around the city, the white tents of the soldiery were seen dotting the landscapes. The first regiments from the States south of Virginia, which were transported thither, were the 1st South Carolina, commanded by Colonel Gregg, and the 2nd South Carolina, commanded by Colonel Kershaw. Their entire passage from Charleston, was an ovation. Everywhere on the route, demonstrations of the most enthusiastic and flattering character greeted them. At every depot and turn-out on the railroads, crowds assembled to get a sight of the heroes of Fort Sumter. Their arrival in Richmond was greeted by the most cordial welcome, and they bore the appearance of guests at a holiday festival, rather than the stern features of the soldier. The sadder and darker side of the duties of their new profession had not become familiar. Their encampments were thronged by visitors, who wished to hear from the lips of the young volunteers, the wonderful story of the bloodless victory at Fort Sumter. The evening dress-parade attracted admiring crowds of ladies, to whom every soldier seemed a hero. It was the delight of the young South Carolinian to detail his experience in the campaign, and to give expression to the enthusiastic patriotism which swelled his youthful bosom. Hope and fancy blended around him in such a halo of glory, that disappointment or failure never found place for a moment in his imagination.

Even at that time, when the cause for which they struggled so united the people of the South, a jealous pride, and a peculiar devotion to the particular State in which they claimed birthright or adoption, were strikingly perceptible. Strangely forgetful of the common motive which brought them to Virginia, by an unfortunate selection of words it was not unusual to hear them declare they had come "to fight the battles of Virginia." This remark always provoked a ready, and often a bitter retort.

Although very nearly every woman wore a "secession badge," and a braid or rosette of palmetto on her hat, and heaped upon the young soldiers grateful and flattering attentions, she would grow indignant and strangely resentful of any remark conveying the idea that Virginia had originated the quarrel which moved the entire South, or that she needed help from other States to relieve her from the difficulty. They permitted no reflection on the Old Dominion.

An amusing incident will serve to illustrate the state of feeling sometimes engendered by this unfortunate allusion.

On an afternoon visit of a party from the city, to the encampment of the South Carolinians, one of the ladies led by the hand a beautiful little girl of some eight or ten years of age. The gracefulness and sprightliness of the child made her an object of notice to all with whom she was thrown in contact. It was not the first visit that she had made to the camp, and she was recognized by the soldiers as their "little Flora." Nothing delighted her more than to go among them laden with flowers, which she would dispense with charming grace, generally selecting, from the instinctive promptings of her generous heart, the sick, weary, or dispirited upon whom to bestow her pleasant gifts. The ladies were soon joined by several young men of the camp, who tendered their services as escorts. After discussing the probabilities and possibilities of the future, a gallant young soldier of less than twenty summers, who had recounted in an eloquent manner the scenes in Charleston Harbor, continued: "We have not only come to Virginia to fight her battles, but to take wives of her fair daughters. Will you not promise me your charming little girl?"—taking the hand of the little sprite, then disburdened of her bouquets.

"To fight Virginia's battles did you come?" exclaimed the lady, with much sarcasm and bitterness, "then indeed you should be rewarded with a wife from sheer gratitude."

The young man blushed and did not reply.

"Oh, yes," continued the excited lady, "if Virginia had been left to herself, it is not probable she would have provoked a challenge that would have called you hither as her second. But since, from her territorial position, she must stand as a bulwark between her sister States of the South and invasion, and must take upon her soil the battles of the country, I do not feel that she must be compelled to dispose of her patriotic girls as a grateful reward to their defenders. I cannot say, sir, unless you recall your ill-timed remark or qualify it by better selected language, that I can answer "yes" to your proposition. My little girl must not be yielded up as a thankful acknowledgment of services rendered. It is extremely painful to rest under obligations."

The young soldier was still mute, and the lady continued: "You appear to forget, sir, the common interest which has not only brought you hither, but has called into the field in its defence so many of our own noble young men," (pointing to a distant camp, where the Virginia soldiers were quartered.)

"Excuse me, madam," he at last ventured to reply; "I sincerely regret my *mal à propos* remark. It was indeed very foolish, when I remember the noble relation Virginia occupies to the other States of the South. I will recall it, if you please, and substitute 'the battles of the Southern Confederacy.' Will that amendment please you?"

His friend smiled. "Ah! well, then," she rejoined, "my prayer is that this unfortunate war may not continue until my little girl is old enough to dispose of to a suitor; but if so, and you can prove worthy of her in your country's service, I may consent that she shall be the prize with which you shall be rewarded. Her promise is very bright, and 'none but the brave deserve the fair.'"

She extended her hand to the soldier. He grasped it with fervor. "I thank you! I thank you!" he blushingly exclaimed; "I shall not forget your promise, and shall endeavor to prove worthy of your regard; nor shall I forget, in my extreme State pride, to be cautious in discriminating between the cause of the South and the integral parts." And venturing to kiss his little *fiancée*, he continued to the lady: "You have taught me, madam, a useful lesson."

Many amusing and striking anecdotes might be related of these times. Regardless of social distinction, or castes of society, the barriers which hedge familiar intercourse were broken down, and the man was almost forgotten in the soldier. The spirit which nerved the men to seek death at the mouth of the cannon made of every woman a heroine, and the unflinching courage with which they parted with their household gods sustained them throughout the trials, the horrors, the desolation which followed. Not only were the husband and father, the fully-grown boy yielded up, but often "little Benjamin," the youngest, the darling, the idol of the mother's heart, was called for, and cheerfully she bade him go; and if tears were shed, the boy was not made a coward by the Southern mother's weakness. Our men were brave; our women not the less so. It required even more courage to abide patiently the result of war than to face the danger and forget in the excitement of the campaign the perils incident to it.

A lady one day, while visiting an encampment of South Carolina soldiers, approached a sentinel to ask some questions, when, failing to give the desired information, he was assisted by a bright-eyed boy, in the soldier's uniform, whose fine complexion, beaming countenance and extreme youth instantly attracted her attention and interest. Turning to him she exclaimed: "How young you must be!" "I am fifteen," he answered.

"Too young for this work," the lady rejoined, kindly taking the hand of the boy; "too young—too young."

His face lighted up with pride and enthusiasm, and proudly holding out his musket at arm's length, he said,

"But, madam, my gun can shoot as hard as any man's!"

"But," continued the lady, almost overcome with emotion, "my brave boy, what said your dear mother to your becoming a soldier so young?"

"Nothing, noble lady; but she made my uniform, and she put this Testament in my pocket," exhibiting it as he spoke.

Tears filled the eyes of the woman. "My mother did not shed a tear that I could see," the boy continued.

In a very few days the regiment was ordered off. The lady saw the brave boy no more, but she never forgot him, and as often as memory reverted to that conversation, she offered up to God a prayer for the soldier boy, who, with his gun and Testament, and the remembrance of a mother who had placed upon him his uniform and armor, went forth to do battle for his country.

These were the gala days of the war in Richmond. The dire realities, the sickness, the mutilation, the sufferings, the miseries, were yet unknown. Only the glory which might accrue was shadowed forth. Absorbed in the contemplation of this, no thought was given to the darker events of the future. The shadows of coming events were not cast before, to chill the ardor of the young.

CHAPTER IV.

THE GATHERING OF THE TROOPS.

VERY soon the entire country around Richmond assumed the appearance of one vast encampment. The Central Fair Grounds, about a mile and a half above the city, were used for the camp of instruction. Thither volunteer companies were sent, the there they were drilled in the manual of military exercises, by Colonel Smith and his corps of cadets from the Virginia Military Institute at Lexington. Colonel Gillam was placed in command of the camp, and from the raw material furnished him he sent out many regiments of well-drilled soldiery. The success which crowned the efforts to tutor the soldiers spoke volumes for the excellence of our principal military academy. We were not a military people, and everything pertaining to war was to be learned. For a while after the revision of the State Constitution in the winter of 1851, the military system was abandoned, and had only been revived for a few years, through the efforts of General Kemper when in the State Legislature. Our men, of the proper age for the army, had not even the advantages of the ordinary instruction of the militia at the outbreak of the war. The raw, awkward recruit, however, soon grew soldierlike in air and bearing, under the system of training by the young cadets; and the prospective hardships and privations of a soldier's life were cheerfully submitted to by the volunteer.

The camp of instruction was a place of great interest. The blunder of the well-intentioned recruit was overlooked, in his evident desire to become a soldier, though not unfrequently the risibilities of the spectator would be excited by the amusing scenes of the drill. The recruit's hands and arms, his feet, his head, seemed to be made for some other use, or peculiarly troublesome to him in the exercise required. We were often astonished at the patience and diligence displayed by the cadets in training the recruits. Never showing weariness, they took delight in teaching the prospective soldier.

All the States of the South were represented in the camps in and around Richmond, and the striking characteristics of the people of each State were plainly distinguishable. Very soon it became easy to tell whence a regiment or company came, by the very appearance of the men.

The glowing enthusiasm of the South Carolinian was presented in striking contrast beside the cool determination of the Virginian. The fiery impetuosity of the Louisianian was vividly displayed beside the steady courage of the Arkansas man. The wild ardor of the Mississippian was visible in contrast with the active energy of the Tennesseean. The North Carolinian, the Georgian, the Alabamian, the Kentuckian, the Missourian,—each had his distinctive characteristic; while from his bold, free, independent air, the brave son of Texas was easily discovered. The world-wide fame of the Texan Ranger he brought with him to his new field of action, and throughout the war no soldiers earned a better reputation for endurance, bravery and courage than did the Texans. With them the names of McCulloch, Hayes and Chevallie were household words. The presence of General McCulloch in Richmond was to the Texan soldier the only inspiration needed to strengthen his determination and nerve his courage to greater deeds of daring. They greeted his coming with demonstrations of the wildest enthusiasm. Unhappily, he was destined soon to fall on the field of battle.

Particularly noticeable among the volunteer forces sent into Virginia was the Battalion of Washington Artillery, from New Orleans, which maintained throughout the war an honorable reputation for bravery, skill and determination. Of that splendid battalion, which gave an immediate answer to the call to arms in the South, how few are left of those who came out first to bear witness to the deeds of daring of their brave companions!

The battalion of "Tigers" from New Orleans, commanded by the intrepid Wheat, were, as their name denotes, men of desperate courage but questionable morals. They were well suited to the shock of battle, but wholly unfitted for the more important details of the campaign. Among them were many of lawless character, whose fierce passions were kept in abeyance by the superior discipline of their accomplished commander.

Major Roberdore Wheat was the son of a clergyman of

the Episcopal church. Educated under influences the most pious and refining, he was gentle, easy, graceful and dignified in society; toward the men under his command he was kind, but grave and reserved, and exacting in the performance of duty; in battle he was fiery, impetuous and resolute.

But the most remarkable corps sent by New Orleans to the war in Virginia was the battalion of Zouaves. It was composed of the most lawless and desperate material which that city could send forth. It is said that its Colonel, with the approval of the Mayor of New Orleans, established recruiting booths in the different jails there, and each criminal was given his option either to serve out his time or join the battalion. It was a strange, mixed body of desperate men of almost every nation, guilty of almost every crime, impelled by no spirit of patriotism in the defence of the country, but by the hope of being able to exercise their favorite profession of freebooting. Dressed in their striking costume of red trowsers and blue jackets, the latter adorned with fanciful embroidery, and capped by the Turkish fez, their appearance everywhere excited the greatest attention. Their bronzed complexions, countenances often disfigured by horrid scars—the marks of former desperate encounters—and the cat-like, elastic step acquired in the drill, distinguished this heterogeneous company. From the time of their appearance in Richmond robberies became frequent. Wherever a Zouave was seen something was sure to be missed. The poultry and garden stock around the city were favorite objects of depredation with these thievish soldiers.

It was common with them to walk into saloons and restaurants, order what they wished to eat and drink, and then direct the dismayed proprietor to charge their bill to the government. The hall doors of private citizens were kept rigidly locked, and the strictest watch was directed upon the Zouaves as long as they tormented Richmond with their presence.

Always finding means to effect their escape from their

barracks at night, they roamed about the city like a pack of untamed wildcats, and so clever were they in eluding the vigilance of the police, that few or none of them were brought to justice for the larcenies they committed. It was found absolutely necessary to assign them to a separate encampment, where lawlessness, strife and bloodshed became the order of the day. No man's life was safe who dared show himself within their encampment.

It was with a feeling of sincere congratulation that the people of Richmond heard at last of the departure of their terrible guests to the Peninsula, where, in the course of a few months, from death or desertion, this motley body of villains was effectually dispersed.

The troops from the northern portion of Louisiana and southern portion of Arkansas, in the vicinity of the Red River, were among the finest and most striking looking men who appeared in the city. Usually tall, brawny and muscular, bronzed by exposure and inured to the most active exercise, they were peculiarly fitted for the arduous duties of a soldier's life. Apparently incapable of fatigue, they were distinguished for their powers of endurance. In a regiment of men from the Red River section, so numerous were those of immense size, that they might have been supposed to have descended from a race of giants. Their usual height was six feet and over,—very rarely under five feet ten inches,—with massive shoulders and chests. They bore upon them not an ounce of superfluous flesh.

Florida, also, from her sparse population, furnished a creditable quota of troops, who were particularly distinguishable on the dress parade for their evident lack of military education, but after much patience and perseverance on the part of their officers they were drilled into a useful soldiery.

CHAPTER V.

RICHMOND THE CAPITAL—SOCIAL CHANGES.

IT was now found expedient to remove the seat of government from Montgomery, Alabama, which had been temporarily selected as the capital of the Southern Confederacy, to Richmond. On the 20th of May, Mr. Jefferson Davis, of Mississippi, Provisional President, arrived in Richmond. He was received with an outburst of enthusiasm. A suite of handsome apartments had been provided for him at the Spotswood Hotel, until arrangements could be made for supplying him with more elegant and suitable accommodations. Over the hotel, and from the various windows of the guests, waved numerous Confederate flags, and the rooms destined for his use were gorgeously draped in the Confederate colors. In honor of his arrival, almost every house in the city was decorated with the Stars and Bars.

An elegant residence for the use of Mr. Davis was soon procured. It was situated in the western part of the city, on a hill, overlooking a landscape of romantic beauty. This establishment was luxuriously furnished, and there Mr. and Mrs. Davis dispensed the elegant hospitalities for which they were ever distinguished. Simple and unpretending, there was nothing in his manner to offend the democratic sentiment of the people,—surely nothing to induce the belief that he meditated assuming or aspired to the prerogatives of royalty. Mrs. Davis is a tall, commanding figure, with dark hair, eyes and complexion, and strongly marked expression, which lies chiefly in the mouth. With firmly set yet flexible lips, there is indicated much energy of purpose and will, but beautifully softened by the usually sad expression of her dark, earnest eyes. She may justly be considered a handsome woman, of noble mien and bearing, but by no means coming under the description of the feminine adjective "pretty." Her manners are kind, graceful, easy and affable, and her receptions were characterized by the dignity and suavity which should very properly distinguish the drawing-room entertainments of the Chief Magistrate of a republic.

There was now work for every one to do. The effects of the blockade of our ports was very early felt. The numberless and nameless articles for which we depended upon foreign markets were either to be dispensed with or to be manufactured from our own industry and ingenuity. With a zeal as commendable as that which answered the call to arms in the South, and especially in Virginia, the people set themselves to work to meet the demands made by the exigencies of the times.

Troops continued to pour into Richmond. Regiment after regiment came, without the necessary uniform or equipments to send them to the field. Our ladies engaged to prepare them properly for the work upon which they were committed to enter.

Sewing societies were multiplied, and those who had formerly devoted themselves to gaiety and fashionable amusement found their only real pleasure in obedience to the demands made upon their time and talents, in providing proper habiliments for the soldier. The quondam belle of the ball-room, the accomplished woman of society, the devotee of ease, luxury and idle enjoyment, found herself transformed into the busy sempstress. The click of the sewing-machine was the music which most interested them, and the "stitch, stitch, stitch," from morning till night, as the ladies plied the needle and thread, was their chief employment. They very soon became adepts in the manufacture of the different articles which compose the rough and simple wardrobe of the soldier. To these, necessary for him, they took delight in adding various other articles, which taste or friendship might suggest. There were very few of the soldiers who were not furnished with a neat thread-case, supplied with everything necessary to repair his clothing when absent from a friendly pair of hands which would do it for him; a visor to shield his face from the too fierce heat of the summer sun or to protect him from the cold of winter; a warm scarf and a Havelock.

The sewing operations were varied by the scraping and carding of lint, the rolling of bandages, and the manufacture of cartridges, and many things unnecessary to mention, but which were the work of the women. The poor of the city were supplied with such employment as secured to them a plentiful support. While the demand was great for clothing for the troops, the ladies of the higher and independent classes of society would undertake nothing which might deprive those who depended upon such employment for a livelihood, nor did they choose only the lighter work for themselves while they permitted the heavier and more difficult to go to the poor; but disregarding position, they employed themselves cheerfully upon anything necessary to be done. Heavy tents of cumbrous sail-cloth, overcoats, jackets and pantaloons of stiff, heavy material, from the sewing on which they were frequently found with stiff, swollen, bleeding fingers, were nevertheless perseveringly undertaken. And when we remember that during the four long and tedious years of the war our women never for a single day shrank from the stern duties that the necessities of the times imposed upon them, and again remember the indulgences in which they were usually nurtured, and their real ignorance of the harsher phases of life, and the cheerfulness and heroism which characterized them throughout their bitter trials, our admiration exceeds our astonishment.

We have been taught to revere the memories of the noble women of 1776. We love to claim descent from those noble heroines who stood side by side with the brave men who achieved our national independence; but we glory to know that the spirit which lived in them still animates the women of our country, and that for patient endurance under the most severe trials, fortitude to meet the direst ills of life, self-sacrificing devotion to what they believe right, they were not excelled by their illustrious predecessors. And when in coming ages the records of the past shall tell the story of the sufferings of the women of the South during the four years of the late war, and the martyr-like courage with which they met and braved the "times that tried men's souls," it must be said of them, "Many daughters have done virtuously, but thou excellest them all."

In a few months the usual routine of social life in Richmond had undergone a complete change. It had become a very rare occurrence to meet a young man of the usual age for military duty in the garb of a citizen. Indeed, it became remarkable; and for the sake of their reputation, if for no other or higher motive, it grew into a necessity for our young men to attach themselves in some capacity to the army.

We were awakened in the morning by the reveille of the drum, which called the soldiers to duty, and the evening "taps" reminded us of the hour for rest. At all hours of the day the sounds of martial music fell upon our ears, and the "tramp, tramp" of the soldiers through the streets was the accompaniment. Nothing was seen, nothing talked of, nothing thought of, but the war in which we had become involved. Former distinctions were forgotten, old prejudices laid aside, in the universal interest felt in the events of the future, dimmed by the sad prospect of intestine strife. Afflictions, troubles and misfortunes make all men brothers. The high-born youth forgets his position, forgets his superiority, as he stands side by side with the humble but brave soldier who shares with him the fatigues of the march, the hardships of the camp, the shock of battle, the humiliation of defeat, or the glories of victory. Selfishness is not tolerated among soldiers. War is a leveller; and in the camp and field no man knows another save as his comrade in arms.

A little girl, who had been very exclusively reared, by force of circumstances, by a family in Richmond, though herself imbued with as much of the spirit of patriotism as could possess one so young, quite shocked at the familiarity of a soldier who had presumed to caress her, very indignantly remarked to the relative who had the charge of her, "Why, indeed! any man than wears a stripe on his pantaloons thinks he can speak to any lady!" The child had not then learned that the circumstances under which the soldier donned his uniform dissolved the barrier to introduction, and gave the soldier a right to attention from all.

CHAPTER VI.

THE FIRST INVASION OF VIRGINIA.

NO regiment was permitted to remain long in or near Richmond. As soon as the troops under instruction became sufficiently drilled in military exercises, they were transferred to positions where their services were most likely to be needed. From the spirit of determination to prosecute the war to a successful issue or perish in the contest, there were no indications that the Southern people would very readily succumb to an enemy, however powerful. The spirit of the Northern press was almost universally boastful, mocking, derisive, taunting. The rebellion at the South was regarded as a matter of such meagre import that the enlistment of volunteers for three months was considered all that was necessary to subdue the insurgents. From the superior numbers and resources of the North, it was spoken of as merely boys' play to whip the "fire-eaters" into submission. No paper fell into our hands in which the Southern people were not told how contemptibly weak they were,—what presumption it was in them to dare to oppose an enemy so potential.

The first step in the invasion of Virginia was the occupation of Alexandria by the Federal troops, on the 24th of May, 1861. This was accomplished under cover of the night, and with such secrecy and success that some of the cavalry troops of Virginia, unconscious of any danger, were surprised in their quarters and taken prisoners.

The occupation of the city by the Union forces was attended by a painfully dramatic incident, which was well calculated to teach those who invaded the soil the spirit of opposition they were destined to meet with in that State.

In the early dawn of the morning, Colonel Ellsworth, who with his Fire Zouaves had entered the town, observed a Confederate flag floating from the roof of the Marshall House, a hotel kept by one Jackson, who had a few days before placed it there, and had sworn to defend it with his life. This flag young Ellsworth had determined to secure as a prize, and making his way into the hotel, he climbed by a ladder to the top of the house and dragged down the obnoxious ensign. As he was descending, with the flag on his arm, he was met by Mr. Jackson, who, aroused by the unusual noise, sprang from his bed, and hastily donning a few clothes, armed himself with a double-barrel gun, and thus met Ellsworth and the four companions who attended him. Pointing to the flag, Ellsworth remarked, "This is my trophy." "And you are mine," responded Jackson, as, with steady and rapid aim, he discharged the contents of his gun into the heart of the young Federal commander, and the next moment sank by his side a corpse, from a bullet sped through his brain and bayonet a thrust from the hands of a soldier, and by which he was pinned to the floor.

This attempt on the part of Colonel Ellsworth is now considered to have been as rash as unnecessary. He is said to have been a young man who gave promise of military genius, and was possessed of so much grace and elegance that they won for him speedy popularity. It is sad to contemplate the sudden death of one so young and gifted, but sadder still to reflect that in Jackson's death not only a brave man was no more, but that a wife and four little children were reduced to the unprotected condition of widowhood and orphanage.

A brother of Jackson, who vowed to avenge his brother's death, afterwards became a famous scout, and if in civilized warfare the scalps of our enemies could be shown as trophies of valor, to his war-belt would have hung a number sufficient to have gratified the revenge of a savage. The soul sickens to recount such fearful stories!

Upon the occupation of Alexandria by the Federal forces, the Confederates, under the command of General Bonham, from South Carolina, fell back to Manassas Junction, on the Orange and Alexandria Railroad. These forces consisted of the first of the troops which were sent to the war in Virginia. Many of them were among those who had been engaged in the battle at Fort Sumter, with some regiments of Virginians.

In Alexandria, as in Richmond, very little of the Union sentiment remained, and much disappointment was said to have been expressed that the vanguard of the invasion was not hailed with demonstrations of pleasure, as intimations of a portion of the Northern press had predicted.

The death of Jackson excited a profound sensation throughout the entire South, and particularly in Virginia. His was the first blood shed in defence of the flag—the first shed in defence of the cause on the soil of the Old Dominion—and though afterwards her valleys were destined to run red with the blood of those who yielded up their lives upon the altar of their country, the noble heroism and patriotic example of this man were never forgotten, and many envied the death of which he died. To them it was a glorious martyrdom.

With Alexandria and Fortress Monroe in possession of the Federal Government, the most important passages into Virginia had been secured by them. General McDowell was charged with the command of the division which had been thrown across the Potomac. General Butler was in command at Fortress Monroe. The town of Hampton had been occupied, and Newport's News, at the mouth of the James River, invested by Union troops. General J. B.

Magruder, who had resigned his commission as Colonel of Artillery, in the old army, had been assigned to the command of the Confederate forces to operate in that portion of Virginia known as the Peninsula.

Taught to expect at any moment an active engagement, either with General McDowell or with Butler on the Peninsula, troops were rapidly sent from Richmond to fill up the ranks of the Confederates at both points. The most intense anxiety prevailed. All the enthusiasm which was to us augury of success, could not prevent the soul-sickening sorrow with which we bade adieu to the dear ones who were to take part in the great tragedy, for which they had been rehearsing.

As regiment after regiment passed through our streets, on their way to the theatres of active engagement, cheerful adieus were waved from every window, in the flutter of snowy handkerchiefs, and bright smiling faces beamed in blessing on the soldier—but heavy hearts were masked beneath those smiles—and as loved forms disappeared from view, and the waving of caps was no longer visible, and the cheerful shouts were lost upon the ear, and they were gone, perhaps forever! the heavy heart had added weight to its load of sorrow, to be borne henceforth, until in the grave it should sink beneath the burden, too heavy for long existence.

An old lady, the mother of several dearly loved sons, but echoed the almost universal sentiment when she said, (in a panic-stricken congregation, just emerging from church on the memorable Pawnee Sunday, before mentioned,) "War, I know, is very dreadful, but if, by the raising of my finger, I could prevent my sons from doing their duty to their country now, though I love them as my life, I could not do it. I am no coward, nor have I brought up my boys to be cowards. They must go if their country needs them."

It is a painful pleasure to recall these things; to remember the courageous fortitude which sustained those called to part under such circumstances. It is a sad pleasure to dwell upon the portraitures which hang around the walls of memory, and recall many bright and youthful faces, as the last "good-bye" was shouted from the file of the regiment, as they pressed on to what was to them the field of death, or perhaps the quick, fierce wrench of the hand, the sudden embrace, the last fond kiss, and the loved one was gone—gone forever!

The change wrought in the appearance of Richmond can only be understood by those who daily witnessed the stirring scenes which were occurring. One excitement had not time to subside before a fresh cause presented itself.

The arrival of General Beauregard, who had become the prominent hero of the people, called forth the most hilarious demonstrations of admiration for his bravery, and the most profound respect for his acknowledged genius. For a long distance, before the train of cars which bore him reached the depot in Richmond, the road was lined with crowds who pressed forward to get a look at the wonderful man of Fort Sumter. Loud cheers greeted him, bands of music discoursed the popular and now national air, Dixie, and a speech was loudly called for, as he descended from the cars. But taking a carriage in readiness, he was borne off to his hotel, followed by the crowd, keenly anxious to get a better sight of Richmond's illustrious guest. No speech could be obtained from him; his modesty equalled his bravery.

CHAPTER VII.

POSITION OF THE CLERGY.

THERE is one class of the citizens of Richmond of whom too much cannot be said in praise, to whom too much gratitude cannot be accorded. The ministers of the gospel of the different religious denominations in the city, will be held in lasting remembrance. They sustained our fainting hearts by their prayers, and example, and through the trials ever accumulating in number and heaviness, during four years of war.

Universally holding sentiments of approval, or acquiescent sympathy in the cause of the South, they carefully avoided proclaiming them from the pulpit. No flags floated from our spires ; military and religious insignia were not blended ; our churches, though simple in comstruction and material decoration, were sanctified by the presence of the Holy Spirit.

The Richmond pulpit is filled by men of a superior order of talent, of the finest and most varied style of oratory, and of unquestionable piety and integrity. In one of our parishes, the rector is earnest, zealous, devoted, unassuming. His style of oratory is vehemently eloquent, and with it is blended the urgent, pleasing simplicity of a child. Acquainted with trial and affliction from personal experience, he understands well how to temper his discourses to suit the wants and to reach the hearts of all. While the war continued, ever anxious for the safety and welfare of his eldest son, a bright, promising youth, who, from the beginning, was in the field, he preached the peaceable fruits of righteousness, and inculcated the penitent resignation which shone out in his countenance and in every act of his life.

The writer is here reminded of a period during the war, when, at his church, the regular sacrament of the Holy Communion was to be administered. It was immediately after a sanguinary engagement. The rector was absent—an unusual circumstance—and another filled his pulpit. "Where can Dr. ——— be?" was whispered from one to another, in the congregation. "He has heard," it was answered, "that his son has either been killed or dangerously wounded." A thrill of heartfelt regret and sympathy pervaded the entire concourse. With sad and gloomy interest, they listened to the clergyman who occupied the desk. The sermon was ended, and the priest was about to proceed with the preliminary exercises of the sacrament, when Dr. ―――― appeared in the chancel, and assisted in distributing the sacred emblems. The rumor was false, but the brave young man was destined in the very last engagement before the surrender of the army of General Lee, to receive a wound so dangerous that for days he hovered between life and death, and is a cripple, yet he proudly wears the scars so honorably won.

Nor was the Episcopal Church alone noted for the zeal and devotion of its clergy. The ministers of the Presbyterian, Methodist, Baptist and the Roman Catholic Churches strengthened the hands and warmed the hearts of their people by wise counsel and tender sympathy.

Early in the summer of 1862, the bishop of the diocese of Virginia—the venerable William Meade, whose attachment to the Union had been of the most indubitable character, and whose efforts had been strenuously exerted to pour oil upon the waves of angry political tumult—convinced of the justice of the reason which had impelled the South to take the position it then occupied, left as a legacy of advice to the church over which he had watched with so much solicitude—"Persevere in the separation." The act he had so long deprecated had become, as then considered, a necessity; and in reference to it, his best wishes for his beloved church were expressed.

The political bias of the distinguished diocesan of Virginia was well understood to be, at heart, with the South in her troubles, although no one saw with more bitter regret than he the disruption of the Union. It was and is still his ardent desire to preserve to the church the character for conservatism for which it had long been distinguished. Carefully abstaining from intermeddling in politics, he looked with anxious solicitude upon the struggle that told so fearfully upon the destinies of the South.

The efforts of our clergy, when called into exercise in our political affairs, were mainly directed to quelling the angry passions of the people, raging then with such fearful and determined violence. Lessons of forbearance and charity, of resignation under trials, which forced many to wander into the temptations of infidelity, were the lessons our divines were wont to teach. Although there were those among them who doffed their clerical vestments and girded on the armor of the soldier, it was not with a wish to lead in a rebellion in which was involved sin, but from a stern sense of divine direction and the whisperings of patriotism, to which conscience and an innate feeling of duty prompted and would not be stilled.

None would be so unjust, so lost to every feeling of virtue and honor, as to impute to other motives the part taken in the late war by the lamented General (Bishop) Polk, around whose memory cluster recollections too tender to breathe against a name so illustrious for all that is noble in a man, a Christian and a soldier, the slightest hint of condemnation. Nor can any one dare to whisper aught of wrong against the name or reputation of the gallant Captain (Reverend) Dabney Harrison, of Virginia, who fell at Fort Donelson, whose old father, the Reverend Peyton Harrison, after having lost three sons on the field of battle, exclaimed, "I have one more to yield up to my country, and when he is taken I will then shoulder the musket myself." "The leaders" were to be found in all classes, in all professions, and in all positions of men at the South.

CHAPTER VIII.

THE FIRST BATTLE—GREAT BETHEL.

FROM his former devotion to Virginia as his native State and the home of his ancestors for several generations, it was thought that our great military chieftain, Lieutenant-General Scott, would but prove true to his birthplace, and cast his lot with those of his own blood.

3

For a time the disappointment to which his course gave rise was keenly and bitterly felt. There were those who regarded him as Esau, who sold his birthright for a mess of pottage, and the former admiration of him as one of our statesmen, a son of the Old Dominion, a military genius and politician, (not evidenced, indeed, substantially by a very creditable vote when he was a candidate for the Presidency,) was changed into the most profound dislike,—in many instances into contempt or disgust. How far this may have been justifiable or proper, we must not pretend to judge. The devotion of the aged chieftain to the flag under which he had won all his laurels, may have rendered the Stars and Stripes to him an object of idolatry. Habit had grown to second nature with him. Indeed, when all hope had expired that he would prove a friend to the South, and particularly to his native State, it was said of him, "Ephraim is joined to his idols: let him alone."

In strong contrast to General Scott were our public men, who gave up positions of trust, honor and emolument for the precarious chances of success in the struggling cause of the South. Conspicuous among these men was the revered, the respected, the admired General Robert E. Lee, around whose name clusters all that is great and glorious as a man, a Christian, a gentleman, a scholar and a soldier.

The writer's first view of General Lee was at the camp of instruction, just above Richmond, where he was witnessing with much interest the dress parade of a splendid company of volunteers from that city. No one who has ever caught the glance of his dark, bright eyes, can forget the expression, and when it rested on this band of brave young spirits, it glowed with the generous enthusiasm of his great nature. Standing fully six feet two, and weighing upward of two hundred pounds, with no superfluous flesh, his figure is straight and erect, his chest massive, his shoulders broad, his head poised proudly. His hair, now almost silvery white, was then thickly streaked with black, giving it that peculiar shade known as iron grey. The inroads made by exposure,

THE FIRST BATTLE. 51

fatigue and misfortune upon his stalwart frame were only too visible at the close of the war; but his iron constitution well fitted him to endure the hardships to which he has been subjected.

The clouds continued to thicken and darken around us. The sullen growling of the storm approached nearer, but we had not yet experienced the shock of contending armies. From demonstrations in different sections of our State, we knew that the stillness would soon be broken by the angry clash of battle. The most serious anxiety for the safety of those nearest and dearest to us began to be felt, as day after day the time for action drew near. Our most earnest attention was directed to the Peninsula.

At Sewell's Point, eight or ten miles distant from Richmond, and opposite Newport's News, on the James River, the Confederates had erected a powerful battery, which had proved its strength and efficiency in a determined resistance to an attack by two Federal steamers. This occurred on the 19th of May, and continued for several days, and served greatly to encourage and animate our troops on the Peninsula.

The first serious trial of arms was to be celebrated in lower Virginia. On the 10th of June the contending forces came into collision at Great Bethel Church, which is on the road leading south from the village of Hampton. This was one of those primitive structures visible in almost any part of Virginia, which recall the memory of the colonial times, when the approach to these edifices was guarded by pickets to prevent interruption from hostile savages.

Here the Confederates, to the number of about eighteen hundred, under Colonel J. B. Magruder, were strongly intrenched. They were attacked by a Federal force of over four thousand, under General Pierce, of Massachusetts. The attack was received by a battery of the Richmond Howitzers, under command of the gallant Major Randolph. He began the action with a shot from a Parrott gun, aimed by himself. It was chiefly an artillery engagement, but the most striking incident of the day was the charge of the First North Carolina Regiment of Infantry, under Captain Bridges, which the young volunteers accomplished with the coolness of veterans, in the face of a terrible artillery fire; and when within sixty yards of the foe rushed on at the double-quick. Before this small but valorous band of men our enemies fell back with astonishment. They continued to fire rapidly, but in so wild a manner as to fail of effect upon our batteries. It was said that at no time during the engagement could the bodies of the Federal troops be seen by the Confederates, and the shots of the latter were mainly aimed in the direction of the glistening bayonets. For four and a half hours they continued the brisk fire of shot and shell, from six and twelve pounders, at a distance of six hundred yards only; and the loss to us from their artillery was one mule!

During all this time, it is said every shot fired by the Confederates was aimed with deliberation. The fire was always suspended whenever the forces of the enemy were not within range.

After an intermission in the assault, the Federals were reinforced by a heavy column in reserve, under the command of Major Winthrop, aid to General Butler. Those in advance deceived the Confederates by donning their distinctive badge, a white band around the cap. They also cried out repeatedly, "Don't fire!" thinking by this ruse to find our forces unprepared, and thus to accomplish their defeat. They soon, however, discovered their mistake. The brave boys from North Carolina were not so easily deceived and disconcerted. With veteran coolness they repelled the foe, and in their anxiety to make perfect work of their demolition, it was difficult for their officers to restrain them.

Terrified, and in disorder, the enemy fell back, and the final rout succeeded. Just then a bullet from the rifle of a North Carolinian pierced the breast of the brave young Federal officer, Major Winthrop, whose gallant exposure of himself in the field had made him a conspicuous target for the shots of the riflemen. Colonel D. H. Hill, who commanded the North Carolina regiment, in his official report of that engagement, says:

"Major Winthrop was the only one of the enemy who exhibited even an approximation to courage during the whole day. A contemporary remarks: 'The fact was, he had fallen under circumstances of great gallantry. He was shot while standing on a log, waving his sword, and vainly attempting to rally his men to the charge. His enemy did honor to his memory, and the Southern people, who had been unable to appreciate the courage of Ellsworth, and turned with disgust from his apotheosis in the North, did not fail to pay the tribute due a truly brave man, who without the sensational circumstance of a private brawl or a bully's adventure, was soon forgotten at the North.'"

During the entire engagement, the Confederates lost but one, a gallant young North Carolinian, Henry L. Wyatt, who volunteered to be one of four to set fire to a small wooden house, which gave, it was thought, some protection to the enemy. Running in advance of his companions, as he passed fearlessly between the two fires, he fell, pierced in the forehead by a musket ball, when within thirty yards of the house. He was the first of the Confederate dead, on the field of battle.

The result of this battle served still further to increase the confidence of the South in the ultimate success of the cause for which they were fighting. The conduct of the Confederate officers on this day is said to have been marked by the utmost coolness and bravery. That of Colonel Hill was evident from the success of his regiment. Colonel Magruder, occasionally excited and impetuous, as it is his custom to be, calmly smoked his cigar, and gave his orders with coolness and deliberation.

It was, however, received by many as another singular interposition of divine Providence in favor of the South, and the wavering irresolution and evident want of courage on the part of the Federals increased the opinion which had already gained a foothold in the minds of the people, that "the Yankees would not fight."

One of the Richmond papers, noticing the inaccuracy of aim on the part of the enemy, offered suggestions, by which, when the Southern papers found their way to the North, the foe profited.

At first, as in the engagement at Bethel, the Federals fired too low, and our men were wounded in the feet; and then they fired too high, and our men were not wounded at all. Of all of this they were informed through our tattling sheets, and it became to them "the word to the wise," as the roll of honor of the Confederate wounded and dead afterwards evidenced only too plainly.

In connection with the camp at Great Bethel Church, it is pleasant to recall an account given by a young officer of the Richmond Howitzer Battalion, of a novel religious exercise in front of that ancient house of worship.

Our army was at first rather poorly supplied with chaplains. The troops on the Peninsula were frequently served by Reverend Mr. Adams, a clergyman of the Baptist Church, who had been driven from Hampton when that village was occupied by the Federals. He was a Bostonian by birth, but had lived for many years in Baltimore as pastor of a church in that city, and thoroughly satisfied with the justice of the Southern cause, he embarked in it his talents and influence. He had already suffered much for conscience sake, having attempted from time to time to return to Hampton to visit the poor of his charge, who had been unable to leave the place, when evacuated by the citizens on the approach of the enemy. He was at last informed that any further attempt to pursue the work of the ministry, would be punished by imprisonment and he was compelled to abandon his labor of usefulness and love.

On one occasion, as this young officer informs us, Mr. Adams drove up in his buggy, in front of old Bethel Church; and finding that his congregation of soldiers would be much too large to be admitted within the building, he made use of his buggy for a pulpit, and in the open air discoursed to his immense audience. He announced as the opening hymn, the familiar one beginning:

"Am I a soldier of the Cross?"

And after reading the lines through, raised a very familiar tune, in which he was joined by a score of manly voices.

"The effect," said the narrator of the incident, "I will not attempt to describe; I have not the power of language to draw the picture."

Then kneeling in the buggy, Mr. Adams offered up a prayer fervid with the devotion of a Christian, and such as the scene before him and the necessities of the hour called forth. Then, after reading a suitable portion of the Scriptures, he announced as the theme of his discourse the passage, "Fight the good fight of faith;" and in the humble and simple eloquence which characterized his style, he exhorted his hearers to enter upon the work to which they had been so singularly called, full of the ardor of Christian faith, and in humble reliance on the assistance of God through the mercy of the Redeemer.

His audience listened attentively, impressed with the divine truths which fell from his lips. Manly emotion was visible on many countenances, and when he raised his hands and voice in prayer for a blessing on his message to the soldier, there were few hearts that were not touched, and few heads that were not bowed.

"I shall never forget," said our informant, "the impressions made upon my mind and heart by the singular services in front of Great Bethel. In the most superb edifice, where all the pomp and pageantry of the most imposing ceremonies are observed, I could never be so impressed with the beauties of the Christian religion as on this simple occasion."

Mr. Adams continued to serve as a Chaplain on the Peninsula until after its evacuation by the Confederate forces, when he was most unfortunately detained, and thus was caused his arrest by the Federals and imprisonment in the Rip Raps, where he was confined for several months, repeatedly refusing the oath which was required of him, until the weakness of human nature could no longer resist the appeals of a suffering wife and little children, who were entirely at the mercy of hostile troops, for food and shelter.

CHAPTER IX.

DISASTER IN WESTERN VIRGINIA.

THE smoke of battle had scarcely cleared away, and the shouts of victory died upon the ear, after the animating contest at Great Bethel, before the news of disaster to our forces in Western Virginia came to dampen the ardor arising from our recent successes. We were to be blessed no longer with bloodless victories. The trial of soul had begun.

The Confederate camp at Philippi had been surprised and dispersed. This disaster, as stated in the Richmond *Dispatch*, was caused by a sentinel sleeping on his post. Intimations of a contemplated attack upon the Confederate camp had been conveyed to them by two heroic women, who rode thirty miles on horseback in the night to warn them of the approach of the Federals, but too late to prevent the confusion that followed. By this misfortune to the Confederates these valorous women were cut off from their homes, and without a change of apparel were compelled to come on to Richmond, where they remained until they could conveniently return to their former places of abode.

The defeat at Rich Mountain occurred a few days after the dispersion at Philippi, and Colonel John Pegram and his entire command of sixteen hundred men were captured.

Nor with this was the measure of disaster in Western Virginia complete. General Garnett was in command of all the forces in the northwestern section of the State. With only about three thousand men he had intrenched himself at Laurel Hill; but from the well-intentioned blunders of inexperienced officers and men, and from the defeat of Colonel Pegram at Rich Mountain, he was compelled to retreat, which he managed to do in good order. Closely pressed by the enemy until he reached the second ford of Cheat River, being himself in the rear, his riderless horse announced to the vanguard that their brave commander had fallen. At Carrick's Ford, where he was killed, the enemy abandoned the pursuit, and the Confederates succeeded in forming a junction with the force under General Jackson.

Although the numbers in killed, wounded and missing were comparatively so small, this disaster was truly discouraging, as it caused the surrender of a very important portion of Northwestern Virginia, and was keenly felt as the very first check to Southern arms. Our troops had not, however, shown any failure in courage; and the fatigue endured by them in the undertaking, and the success of the retreat had not then a parallel in the history of the war. But the deepest regret was experienced at the untimely end of the gallant General Garnett. He was the first officer of high rank who had fallen in battle in the Confederate army, and his death cast the deepest gloom over the hearts of the many who loved and honored him for his bravery and nobility of spirit. He was a native of Essex County, Virginia, and belonged to an old and highly respectable family, numbering in its connection several men of distinguished talent and position. He had himself received a military education, and was thought to possess the genius which would insure him success in his profession.

There is no denying that these reverses were the cause of much anxiety to the Southern people, and for the first time a gloom spread over the souls of many whose sanguine temperaments precluded the idea of possibility of defeat to Southern arms.

But the Richmond people, although they might for a few days be bowed down by defeat, were generally reassured by the very accommodating press, which conveniently and wisely, doubtless, appropriated the proverb, "What cannot be cured must be endured;" and thus succeeded in allaying the usual discouragement and mistrust arising from petty defeats and disappointments.

We had, however, very little time to devote to the luxury of lamentation over our fallen brave, or to the sad misfortunes to our cause in Western Virginia. The sad strains of mournful music, the dull sounds of the muffled drum, as borne in the procession of the lamented Garnett, were only just lost in the busy hum of every-day life in Richmond, when our attention was called to the condition of things in a different portion of the State. Over the Potomac, and especially in the vicinity of Harper's Ferry, which had been evacuated by the Federals, the war-clouds hung heavily and ominously, and it seemed altogether evident to us that it could not be long ere the dark and sombre masses would burst upon us in the lurid lightnings and hoarse thunders of battle. We knew that somewhere in that section of Virginia would be enacted fierce scenes of sanguinary strife. July, 1861, opened upon us with a knowledge of the fact that two of the largest armies that the continent of America had ever seen were ranged in hostile defiance, and awaited with anxiety the signal to measure the relative strength of the North and South. All hearts were directed to that portion of the State over which the storm must soon break.

Our women for a time suspended the busy operations of the needle, and set aside the more expeditious and labor-saving sewing machine, to apply themselves more industriously to the preparation of lint, the rolling of bandages, and the many other nameless necessaries which the signs of the times made apparent would soon be in requisition for the unfortunates which the chances of battle would send among us mutilated and helpless. No longer the sempstress, every woman of Richmond began to prepare herself for the more difficult and responsible duties of the nurse. What pen can describe in fitting terms the history of the anxious hearts hidden behind the busy exterior, in those labors which patriotism dignified into duty, and which were lightened by cheerfulness and love? What pencil can paint the rainbow tints that glowed in the briny tear as it fell upon the snowy pile of lint which accumulated under the hands of her who had laid her heart's idol upon the altar of her country? What imagination can picture the midnight experiences of the restless, anxious ones from whose eyelids sleep had fled, as day after day and night after night brought nearer and nearer the dreaded day, which might close over in the darkness of death all we held most dear? Who can enumerate the prayers wafted on every breath, which in the humble and simple language of the publican went up continually in the cry, "Lord have mercy?"

CHAPTER X.

THE BATTLE OF MANASSAS—ITS EFFECT IN RICHMOND.

WE had not long to wait. Full soon for the anxious hearts that dreaded the precarious chances of battle came the tidings of sanguinary strife. The first movement of the "Grand Army," in the memorable "On to Richmond" programme, had been made. From the superiority of its numbers and appointments it was regarded but an easy undertaking for this body of men to open the way to the stronghold of the Confederates, and plant once more upon their Capitol the "Stars and Stripes." Nothing was omitted or forgotten in the boastings of our enemies to render us sensible of our own miserable weakness, or to discourage us in the attempt to measure strength with a foe so powerful.

On the 18th of July, on the tiny stream of Bull Run, in the essay of the enemy to force a passage, occurred the short but brilliant engagement which served only as the overture to the grand battle of the coming Sabbath, on the plains of Manassas. It was but a trial tilt, from which both armies retired to recruit their energies for the anticipated contest, which might perhaps decide the questions that had given rise to the national quarrel and the existence or non-existence of the Southern Confederacy as a distinct nationality. The gauntlet had been thrown down, the fight had begun in earnest, and the issue perhaps hung on the balance of events to be developed in the coming battle. As two lions at bay, after the first shock of encounter, pause, panting, to recover breath, so these two mighty armies, in full view of each other, paused in the horrid work of destruction, bore away their wounded, buried or removed their dead, and made ready to resume hostilities. Three days had passed since the Federals were repulsed at Bull Run.

General Scott, to whom was intrusted the plan of battle, had ordered General McDowell to advance on Manassas on Sunday the 21st of July. The quiet Sabbath morning was bright and beautiful; the quietude soon to be broken by the fierce clash of arms, and its brightness to be dimmed by the smoke of battle, and the incense rising from human blood.

An eloquent eye-witness says: "The plain, broken and wooded, bounded on all sides, as far as the eye could reach, by the azure lines of the Blue Ridge, was gay with the bright uniforms, the parti-colored flags, the glistening armor of the soldiers. The strains of music, which on any other day might have been those which called the masses together for a holiday festival, now sounded the note for the onset, and soon all was forgotten save the one desire for victory—the panting for human victims, which would decide the fortunes of the day."

"On to Richmond!" was the battle-cry of the Federals—

"Independence, or Death!" the watch-word of the Confederates.

More than once the lines of the Confederates were seen to waver. If their enemies had prudently taken advantage of this, they might have been driven ingloriously from the field. With sudden desperation, they felt themselves forced back by overwhelming odds, but, manfully contesting every inch of ground, they succeeded in circumventing the flanking columns of the enemy.

It was at this particular hour in the history of that memorable day, that General Bee, when nearly overpowered by force of superior numbers pressing cruelly upon him, pathetically exclaimed to General Thomas J. Jackson, "General, they are beating us back!" and there was given him that immortal reply, "Sir, we will give them the bayonet!" General Bee rallying his over-charged troops, cried: "See! there is Jackson standing like a stone-wall. Let us determine to die here, and we will conquer!" and the next hour yielded up his life in the sublime endeavor.

There, amid the flames and smoke of battle, the thunders of artillery, the rattling of musketry, the confusion worse confounded ever attendant upon such a scene, but a little while before he sealed his own martyrdom in the service of his country, the brave and chivalrous Bee, from the determined valor, and imperturbable coolness evinced by him on this occasion, rebaptized his companion in arms, the quiet Jackson, "Stonewall!" Not from sacerdotal hands, with the holy water, typical of the washing of regeneration, but with fire that consumes all dross, and with blood, without the shedding of which there is no remission for sins—he derived this name, which through all time must give to that of Jackson the glory of immortality; and with it will be handed down to remotest ages, that of the self-constituted priest—the martyr Bee!

For a time the weights seemed so evenly adjusted, that the balance for success scarcely rocked the beam; but the Confederates, fortunately reinforced about two

P. M., by General Kirby Smith, rallied to the charge, and soon had the happiness of seeing the enemy disorganized, and flying before their victorious columns.

The retreat became a rout. In reckless disorder, disencumbered of arms and baggage, the enemy fled in frantic confusion, as if they were chased by demons, rather than men; nor did they pause in their flight until within the friendly intrenchments of Washington they could collect their scattered courage. The result of the battle had been altogether unexpected to them. Confident of success, and as the movement was generally known in Washington, Congress had adjourned to allow its members an opportunity of witnessing the scenes of the battle-field. Visitors and camp followers of all grades and descriptions, and even some fashionable women, followed in the rank of the Grand Army to be present at the "rout of the rebels." "On to Richmond," they were bent. The idea of defeat had never been permitted to cross their minds. It was thought only necessary for the impudent rebels to come to a knowledge of the appointments of the Grand Army, and they would be dispersed like a flock of frightened sheep, or melt before their victorious legions, as in the summer sun.

We had indeed won a splendid victory; but not with little cost. Our loss was considerable, and among the number who fell, were some of our bravest and best, and the laurels of victory were entwined with the cypress. General Bee, whose death brought grief to all the South, was a native of South Carolina; a graduate of West Point, and had served with distinction in the war with Mexico; winning two brevets, the last that of captain, for gallant and meritorious conduct at the storming of Chapultepec. Georgia was called upon to mourn the death of her illustrious son, Colonel Francis S. Barton, who received his death-wound in the same charge in which the gallant South Carolinian was killed. He was chairman of the Military Committee in the Provisional Congress, which body noticed his untimely yet glorious death in a public tribute of much eloquence and solemnity.

From outward appearances in Richmond on the Sabbath of the battle of Manassas, no one would have supposed that any event of unusual importance had occurred, or was anticipated. The churches were all open, and towards them were bent the steps of throngs of worshipers. But the interior of the churches presented an aspect until late foreign to them. As the eye glanced over the concourse assembled within, one was struck at once with the great majority of females; and as here and there a well-known manly form was missed, and the question, "Where is he?" would arise involuntarily, the echoing answer from the heart was, "Where?" and a silent prayer for the safety of loved ones was uttered.

At St. Paul's Church it was noticed that Mr. Davis was absent on that day. All who knew anything of the situation of the Army of the Potomac surmised where he was, and the cause of his absence from his accustomed place on the Sabbath. He had left Richmond that morning, accompanied by his Staff, to visit the scene of conflict, at which he arrived, it is said, when the fortunes of victory for the Confederate forces seemed doubtful. But his presence along the lines infused fresh energy into the broken and dispirited troops, and wherever he made his appearance loud shouts of cheering welcome greeted him. He was there when the victory was decided, to congratulate the Generals who had conducted the mighty battle, and to thank the soldiers who had won such renown for the Confederate arms.

During the progress of these events the utmost quiet and calmness pervaded the city of Richmond. The news of the great victory was received by the Southern people with no violent manifestations of joy. To a partial observer the Confederate capital might have been considered unmoved by the stirring news. There were no bonfires kindled, no bells rung, no cannon fired, none of the parade which the event might have been expected to call forth; nor the indecent exultation which the low, vulgar and vicious might have indulged in. But, to use the language of another, "there was what superficial observation might not have apprehended and could not have appreciated,—a deep, serious, thrilling enthusiasm, which swept thousands of hearts, which was too solemn for wild huzzas, and too thoughtful to be uttered in the eloquence of ordinary words. The tremulous tones of deep emotion, the silent grasp of the hand, the faces of men catching the deep and burning enthusiasm of unuttered feelings from each other, composed an eloquence to which words would have been a mockery. Shouts would have marred the general joy. The manner of the reception of the news in Richmond was characteristic of the conservative and poised spirit of the government and people. The only national recognition of the victory was the passage of resolutions in the Provisional Congress acknowledging the interposition and mercies of Providence in the affairs of the Confederacy, and recommending thanksgiving services in all the churches on the ensuing Sabbath."

The victory had been won by too much that was sorrowful to many of our people, for others, in the forgetfulness of the moment, to shock the tender sensibilities of the mourners by exultation. Many of our bravest and best had thus early fallen; and many a youth in whom were centred the brightest hopes of fond and ambitious friends, was cut down before those hopes had their fulfillment in manhood. Many over whom the crown of early manhood had settled in dignity were consigned to the grave of the soldier, and cut off from the life of usefulness to which nature had assigned them.

The Monday succeeding the battle was as different from the preceding day as one day in mid-summer could differ from another. The warm, bright, quiet Sabbath was followed by thunder and lightning and a storm of wind and rain, which fell in such profusion that the wind seemed to drift the torrents in liquid sheets, and twist them in fitful, fantastic eddies, rarely noticeable. We remember with gratitude the heavy rain of the 22d of July, 1861, and like to regard it as especially sent for the relief of the wounded of the bloody battle of Manassas,—it matters not for what they fought, nor whence they hailed. The suffering and helpless are never enemies.

CHAPTER XI.

RICHMOND A HOSPITAL—ARRIVAL OF PRISONERS.

THE condition of Richmond for the reception of the wounded was poor indeed. Our hospital accommodations at that time are scarcely worthy to be mentioned; but these wants were amply atoned for by the generous, hospitable patriotism of the citizens, who threw open their doors and were only too happy to take into their houses, for proper care and nursing, the wounded defenders of their homes and firesides. Almost every house in the city was a private hospital, and almost every woman a nurse.

Every delicacy of the soil and season, and the treasures of the pantry and cellar, (unused then except for the sick,) were cheerfully brought forth to regale the wounded soldier. The daily watch and the nightly vigil by the couch of the suffering became the constant employment of the women of Richmond, and we cannot wonder, when we remember their ceaseless self-sacrifice and patient endurance, that there arose from the hearts of every Southern soldier a hearty "God bless the women of Virginia!"

. But there was still another class of sufferers thrown upon us by the results of the battle of Manassas, about whom, perhaps, it were as well to say nothing; but our recollections of this period would be by no means perfect could we forget or pass unnoticed those taken captive by our forces. If our hospital accommodations for the sick and wounded of our own army were inadequate, we may surely be pardoned for not having comfortable accommodations for the prisoners. Tobacco warehouses and other buildings used for similar purposes had to be made the receptacles for the men taken captive at that time; and if, as too surely must have been the case, they proved unfitted and insufficient in size to accommodate with any sort of comfort the many crowded in, by the exigencies of their singular appearance among us, it was simply because at that time no other disposition could be made of them, and surely with no design nor desire to inflict useless and cowardly torture on unarmed men, who, as prisoners of war, by all the rules of honor are entitled to due consideration as such. Any positive violation of these duties, is a violation of the holiest obligations which can exist between nations. Notwithstanding all the odium which is cast upon the Southern people for the maltreatment of prisoners, and the infamy which attaches to the names of Libby Prison and Belle Island, we learn from authority which we cannot permit ourselves to believe would be guilty of a base prevarication, that, universally, the prisoners confined in those prisons in Richmond received rations always as good as those furnished to our soldiers in the field, and often of superior quality; while the sick and wounded received the usual rations furnished the sick and wounded Confederates in the hospitals. And for the acts of cruelty accredited to the South in the treatment of prisoners, we trust that a generous public will admit the cases were exceptional and not general, and the evidence influenced by sectional feeling. It could not be supposed that the sympathies of the people, and of the women especially, would be very strikingly called forth towards those who came amongst us as invaders, nor that they would be particularly careful in seeking them out and lavishing upon them the attentions demanded by the suffering defenders of their own country.

Yet never, during the four years of the war in Richmond, even when the most unqualified success shone upon the fortunes of the Confederate cause, was there, to the mortification of the numerous prisoners who from time were marched through our streets,* any manifestations of hatred to the unfortunates, or triumph over a fallen foe, noticed by the writer.

Among the prisoners taken at the battle of Manassas and sent to Richmond, the most noted were the brave Irishmen, Colonel Corcoran, (whom we are induced now to wonder ever fought against us,) and Captain Ricketts, of the famous Sherman's Battery, (captured by the Confederates,) a most gallant and accomplished officer. Much sympathy was expressed for the latter, and this was increased by a knowledge of the fact that his faithful and devoted wife, who, having heard in Washington that her husband had lost his life in the battle, went to procure the body, but finding that he had been dangerously wounded and carried to Richmond, sought and obtained permission to join him there, where she nursed him faithfully and affectionately until he had recovered sufficiently to be removed, and finally exchanged.

In the excited and hostile feeling of the people of the South at that time, together with the distress she must have experienced in the sufferings of her husband, her position in the prison hospital, in which her husband lay, was by no means an enviable one, and called forth the deepest sympathies from many of the ladies of Richmond, who, through a feeling of delicacy, forbore the expression of it, and indeed could have done but little for her relief *

In connection with Captain Ricketts, we are amusingly reminded of the many claimants to the honor of the capture of Sherman's Battery, under his command.

So many regiments, so many companies, so many brigades claimed to have been the happy heroes who took possession of the invincible, death-dealing battery, that it has grown to quite as much a mooted question who took Sherman's Battery as who was the enviable hero that struck "Billy Patterson."

Richmond was then one vast general hospital. Our sur-

* Though our enemies say differently.

geons were kept constantly busy in the rounds of their profession, and we were told, as far as it was in their power,—except where the life of a patient was endangered by it,—they practiced the principles of conservative surgery, although much blame has been attached to the surgeons of both armies for reckless waste and sacrifice of human limbs.

Their most efficient coadjutors were the women. It is a matter of intense astonishment, when we reflect that those who had ever felt and exhibited nervous dread and sensibility at the sight of human suffering, who would faint at witnessing a bleeding wound, when duty made it apparent to them that they should tutor themselves in alleviating misery, grew strong under the painful tuition of these dreadful scenes, and became able to look upon and dress even the most ghastly wounds. The tenderness which ever accompanied their gentle ministrations made them peculiarly grateful to the suffering soldier, and rendered him many times the braver hero, when recovered and in the field again.

CHAPTER XII.

INCIDENTS OF BATTLE

WITH the many painful incidents of this battle there are connected some so beautifully touching, that with the utmost pleasure we turn from the sickening thoughts awakened by the remembrance of carnage and death to these revivals of a better nature, a holier principle within, of which every man, when not under the influence of the whirlwind of angry passion, must be in a measure possessed. After the battle is over and the dreadful work is accomplished, we find friends and foes commingling in offices of kindness, in ministrations of mercy to the wounded and dying.

Belonging to one of the cavalry companies of the Confederates there was a young man distinguished for his scholarship as well as for deep-toned piety and conscientious integrity. As he rode off the field, which to him had been the scene of much that was terrible as well as much that was sublime and glorious, he passed an enemy wounded and very near death. Raising his hand feebly, he made signs for the rider to stop and dismount. The young soldier professor (for the cavalryman occupied a professor's chair in one of the colleges of Virginia) alighted from his horse and bent over the dying man.

Gasping for breath he said, ".Stranger, do you ever pray?"

"I do," replied the Confederate.

"You see from my dress I am in the ranks of your enemies, but"—and he stretched out his feeble hand and clasped that of the man who had bent over him—"can you, will you pray for me,—will you pray for a dying man?"

"I will," answered the professor; "I know you no longer as an enemy, and even though I felt you to be one, God has given me a heart to pray for our enemies." And kneeling beside the dying Yankee, the Christian professor offered up to God a prayer that to the man before him might be granted grace and fortitude to make light and easy the passage of "the dark valley of the shadow of death," and for forgiveness and mercy on the soul which in so short a time must be in the full presence of its Maker, through the atonement of Jesus Christ the Son of the Most High.

When the prayer was ended and he looked upon the dying man, the faint breath was growing shorter and shorter, and he watched beside him until he saw the last flickering of the flame of life die away in the socket, and disposing of the body of the dead man to those who promised to give it a decent burial, being compelled to rejoin his company, he mounted his horse and rode on, a wiser, a better and a happier man, for having been able to soothe the spirit of his dying enemy.

From a Federal officer, a native of Scotland, we heard an affecting story of kindness and humanity extended to a wounded Confederate.

"On the retreat," said he, "as I pressed on rapidly, my attention was attracted to a wounded Confederate, a mere boy, who could not have been over fifteen years of age. He had a bright, beautiful countenance, though disfigured by the dust and smoke of battle. Raising his hand to attract my attention, he moaningly gasped, 'Water! water!' Not having time to stop, I took up the slight figure in my arms, and from my canteen poured down his throat some water and whiskey. Being for a moment revived, he opened his eyes, almost glazing in death, and when they rested on my uniform he cried, 'Are you a Yankee?'

"I belong to that army," I replied.

"With an imploring look, which will haunt me to my dying day, the poor boy continued, 'You are a Yankee? Will you kill me? Will you kill me?' 'No, poor boy, I will kill you no sooner than I would one of my own children; I would do you no harm. Reassured, a look of gratitude stole over his beautiful countenance, but being pressed by the pursuers, and not wishing to fall a prisoner into the hands of the Confederates, I laid my charge, which in so short a time had found a warm place in my heart, underneath the shade of a tree, and there I was compelled to leave him. He must have died, for I knew he was very near death when I held his bleeding body in my arms."

Then, as if the rushing tide of memory brought once more before his vision the countenance of the dying, youthful soldier, he murmured: "No, I can never, never forget that look bent on me as he said, 'Will you kill *me?*'" And thoughtfully shaking his head, "Such work didn't suit me, and in another department of the army, where I was not compelled to witness such scenes of suffering and bloodshed, I engaged my services."

A young man said: "I owe my life to being kicked by my gun. I had fired five rounds, and was about to fire my sixth, when the gun recoiled, and striking me directly on the nose, my head was thrown back some inches, when just at the moment a bullet came whizzing past me, and what is known as the wind of the ball deprived me of breath; but if it had not been for the force of the recoil of my gun, the ball would have passed directly through my brain." So much was he stunned by "the wind of the ball" he alluded to, that for several weeks he lay a helpless invalid, and there have been many cases of death from a similar cause, when upon the body could not be found a perceptible bruise.

There is a sad story connected with this peculiar period, of woman's devotion and man's weakness and infidelity, in which there is blended so much romance, it might, with careful illustration and embellishment, be used as the foundation upon which to build up a tale of real life, in which truth would be stranger than fiction. We cannot certifiy to the truth of it, but will only relate it as it was related to us.

At Bristow Station, very near Manassas Junction, there were sojourning numerous ladies, whose husbands and friends, fathers and brothers, perhaps, were in the army near by. Just a few days before the engagement, probably about the time of the battle of Bull Run, a young girl appeared at the hotel, plainly dressed, and having with her very mean looking baggage, but with the manners and address of a lady, and there registered an assumed name. Her appearance and manners, so much at variance, awakened the suspicion and attention of her companions, (to whose sex is imputed an undue share of these qualities,) and carefully watching her movements, they determined to ascertain something of the motives which brought her thither at that time, when only the most intense anxiety for those near and dear induced them to remain in such close proximity to the dangers which threatened them.

For several days the mystery which was connected with her increased, and added interest to her incognito. At last, after the battle was over, applying to a lady who had a list of the casualties, she, being not supplied with one, asked that the lady would read the names of the killed and wounded in a certain battalion from ——, State of ——. Heading the list was the name of Captain ——, badly wounded and removed to Richmond. Turning deadly pale, the poor young girl reeled, and would have fallen but for the sustaining arm of the lady, which was kindly thrown around her.

When sufficiently recovered, the lady said, "What is it? tell me—is this Captain —— your husband?—your lover? —or why are you so interested in him?"

She continued then, "You are not what you seem to be. I have thought so from the moment I first saw you. These coarse clothes are surely not your own. Who are you? and where are you from? and why are you here, so young, and alone?"

With kindly interest and real sympathy these questions were asked.

"Go with me to my room, and I will tell you all. It is a long story. I cannot relate it here," said the young girl.

When in the room of the unknown young girl, she began —"You are right; I *am not* what I seem. My home is in the far South, in the city of ——. I had been for some months betrothed to Captain ——, and he had urged our marriage. But I was young, and objected to it at the time, and after a while troubles arose between us. The engagement was broken off, and I pretended to be heartless and careless, until I found he was to leave me, and be exposed to all the dangers and misfortunes of war. He had seemed to neglect me, and thus incurred the indignation of my father and family. I had been forbidden to meet him, or in any wise to notice him. But I sought him, intending a reconciliation, and if he still loved me and wished me to marry him, to let him bear with him to the field of war the remembrance and love of his bride.

"I was too late. So hurriedly were the soldiers sent off to this State, he was compelled to leave with his regiment, not daring, I presume, to seek me after knowing the prohibition of my father to his house, and with no assurance from me that I shared not my father's dislike for him."

"After he left I grew very miserable. The idea of his being wounded and suffering without my being with him to minister to his distresses tortured me, and that of his probable death maddened me; and I resolved to come on, see him here, and if he still wishes to carry out our former engagement, I shall marry him.

"To accomplish what I feel to be a holy duty, I have braved the everlasting displeasure of my whole family. I was compelled to keep my determination profoundly secret to prevent the thwarting of my earnest wishes. In order to be able to secure the funds necessary for my expenses I made a confidante of a friend from whom I succeeded in obtaining a promise of secrecy, and the loan of some money, which, together with the sale of some valuables, afforded me means sufficient to meet any demands of the adventure. I also made a confidant of a female servant belonging to my father, and obtained from her the loan of the clothing and baggage you see I have with me. My real position I studiously avoided making known, resolving, if by no other means I might obtain a meeting with the man I so dearly loved, in the plain garb of a servant, and acting in that character, I would reveal my presence to him.

"Now, madam, you have heard my story, and being acquainted with it, do not say you blame me; for suffering as I have done, I could not bear reproaches for what some may term my rashness. I have dared all, and braved all; the consequences I am prepared to endure—but no reproaches."

Her listener heard her story with the sympathetic interest which ever belongs to a true woman, and promised to make such inquiries relative to her quondam lover as would be satisfactory in regard to his whereabouts, and such as, under the delicate circumstances in which the young girl was placed, *she* could not conveniently obtain, and preserve her incognito.

Ascertaining to a certainty that the captain in question

had been sent to Richmond, she also learned that he was the invalid guest of———, and that the wound, at first pronounced dangerous, was comparatively slight.

Cheered by this information, the young girl bade adieu to her newly found friend, and hastened to Richmond to be with her lover, and soothe by her presence and gentle ministrations the sufferings he endured.

Alas! for woman's devotion and man's fickleness! Cupid had played a sad game with this young devotee of Mars. Unfortunately for his old love and the better principle which should have called to remembrance "the girl he left behind him,"—the daughter of his kind host happened to be one of the most fascinating, fashionable, and irresistible belles of the rebel capital, and, caught in the rebound, the invincible "man of war," who had fearlessly faced the cannon of the enemy, cowered, and fell a victim to the bewitching charms of the fair belle of Richmond.

His attentions to her from their first acquaintance indicated that his heart was not untouched, and with a coquetry unpardonable, but which is usually the accompaniment of the recognized belle, she so encouraged his overtures, as to foster hopes that she, betrothed to another, could never crown with fulfillment.

His former *fiancée* arrived in Richmond, and from more than one of Rumor's thousand busy tongues, she learned of the cruel infidelity of the man for whom she had made such sacrifices. Broken-hearted and wretched, she carefully avoided making known to her faithless lover the fact of her presence so near him. She left for her distant home to meet the angry reproaches of her father—to bear alone the burden of her unhappiness.

CHAPTER XIII.

CHANGES IN RICHMOND—AN EVIL ADDITION.

THE decided and timely check received by our enemies in their first memorable attempt in the "On to Richmond" movement strengthened us in that city in our feelings of security, and confidence in the wisdom of the government under which we then lived, and the ultimate success of the cause for which we were engaged in war; and bright hopes of a speedy restoration to peace were entertained and freely expressed.

So strongly did these impressions enter into the feelings of the inhabitants of Richmond, and indeed of all the South, that the soldiers frequently remarked they would be sent home before frost in autumn; and even the wisest and most experienced expressed the opinion that the "backbone of the war was broken." But they sadly miscalculated the energy and perseverance of the enemy with whom we were contending. Only temporarily discouraged by defeat, it has been seen that, profiting by the lessons of experience, gained through misfortune, they began to work with redoubled energy in the prosecution of the war. It might have been supposed that the severe and unexpected chastisement inflicted by the rebels would dampen the ardor with which they would henceforth be pursued, or bring about a determination to abandon the idea of subjecting a foe that had proven so unconquerable.

The enemy's elasticity was not understood by us at the South; but we were soon taught to understand the mistake we made in our estimate of the energy of Northmen, operating through a government as determined as themselves on the subjugation of the daring rebels who had lifted impious hands against the sacredness of superior authority. (?)

We heard, with much disposition to be amused, that chafing under the defeat at Manassas, the Federal Government ment, forgetting the former prowess of our illustrious Lieutenant General, had laid him "on the shelf." General McDowell had been doomed to a measure of the public censure, and a younger, more promising, if less experienced commander, was to lead our foes to certain victory. General McClellan was placed in command of the intractable army.

Meanwhile, with the incoming of the Confederate Government, Richmond was flooded with pernicious characters. The population was very soon doubled. Speculators, gamblers, and bad characters of every grade flocked to the capital, and with a lawlessness which for a time bade defiance to authority, pursued the rounds of their wicked professions, and grew rich upon their dishonest gains. Thieving, garrotting, and murdering were the nightly employments of the villains who prowled around the city, until, by the increased vigilance of the police under the newly-appointed Provost Marshal, this alarming state of affairs was in a measure rectified.

Every man who then made his appearance in the rebel capital was by no means inspired by a patriotic principle to spend and be spent in the service of the Confederacy, but many were there for the sole purpose of subserving their own selfish and wicked ends.

For effect, all these villains donned the military dress, and for a while this was a passport to notice and respect; but growing wary of imposition, society required some other voucher to pass an unknown or suspicious individual. Guards halted every man at every corner, and unless supported by the proper credentials, a safe place was found for delinquents in durance vile, or closely watching the extent of furloughs, the idle soldiers were summarily returned to their respective regiments, or the offenders found hospitable lodgment in Castle Thunder, or Castle Godwin, and some, for flagrant offences, in the Virginia Penitentiary.

This state of things, though much to be deprecated, and extremely annoying, was not unexpected from the beginning, and taking into consideration the great variety of character and purpose which constituted the floating population of

Richmond, acts of high-handed outrage were comparatively few, and more noticeable to the resident population on account of the high tone of morals that had characterized the place in former times.

There was another class of whose presence we were from the first often warned, who were to be held in much greater dread than the thieves and murderers—the garrotters and assassins who infested the city. They did not make the midnight hour the time for their operations, nor the rope and the gag the means by which they secured the money and valuables of their victims; but they chose the open daylight for their operations, under specious pretexts got admittance into society, sought and obtained office under the government, duped the highest officials, obtaining through that means important information, and then, in the secrecy of the midnight hour, by successful stratagem, and by bribery, or perhaps with the use of the ever-ready gag and rope, ran the blockade, and conveyed to our enemies the secret designs of the government. This, we have been told, was the plan of operation.

Spies were there who for gold were ready at any moment to deliver the city into the hands of our enemies. We felt it, we knew it, and there were those who censured the government for culpable carelessness and neglect in not ferreting out these dangerous characters, and bringing them to justice for their treachery. But whether or not the consequences were dreaded by those in power, there were very few who were apprehended and brought to prompt punishment. The most lamentable feature in this case was that some who were innocent, might fall, or perhaps did fall, under suspicion.

CHAPTER XIV.

RICHMOND A CITY OF REFUGE—EXTORTIONS.

RICHMOND had already become a "city of refuge." Flying before the face of the invader, thousands sought within its hospitable walls that security they could not hope to receive in exposed and isolated places. Tales of suffering were even then the theme of thousands of tongues, as the homeless and destitute crowded into our city for safety and support. The usual hotel and boarding-house accommodations were found altogether insufficient to supply comfortable places of sojourn for the great numbers demanding sympathy and shelter. From the first day that war was declared against the South, Richmond was taxed to the utmost extent of her capacity to take care of the surplus population that accumulated within her limits.

Many of the citizens received and entertained these wanderers; but many, by the suspension of the ordinary business pursuits of the city, were so reduced in income that it became an impossibility for them to extend to such numbers the assistance which a native kindness and generosity prompted.

From the extraordinary influx of population, and the existence of the blockade, which prevented the importation of supplies in proportion to the demand, we were compelled to submit to the vilest extortions by which any people were ever oppressed. It was first observed in the increased prices placed upon goods of domestic manufacture. Cotton and woolen fabrics soon brought double prices, even before there was a general circulation of the money issued by the Confederate Treasury. The wisest laid in supplies sufficient to stock a small shop, and had enough to last during the entire war; but an overwhelming majority, unsupplied with means to use providently, waited for each day to provide for the peculiar wants of the day, and at length suffered for the simplest necessaries of life.

A lady in conversation with a friend, as early as May, 1861, said, "If you need calico, you had better purchase at once, for our ninepence goods have gone up to sixteen cents, and very soon we shall have to pay twenty-five cents. Our ten cent cotton domestics are now retailing at sixteen cents, and before the end of June it is said to be doubtful whether there will be any left in Richmond, and if any, we shall have to pay three prices." Could she have have foreseen the time when for a yard of the goods in question she would have to pay as many dollars, and later still twice the amount in dollars, she would indeed have urged her friend, who was incredulous to the truth, to purchase supplies sufficient for a number of years.

The same fact was observable in regard to imported articles of food. The extraordinary increase in price was first noticeable in that demanded for coffee. An old lady, one of the most famous of the many distinguished housewives of Virginia, in great astonishment, said in August, 1861: "Only think! coffee is now thirty cents per pound, and my grocer tells me I must buy at once, or very soon we shall have to pay double that price. Shameful! Why, even in the war of 1812 we had not to pay higher than sixty cents. And now, so soon! We must do without it, except when needed for the sick. If we can't make some of the various proposed substitutes appetizing, why, we can use water. Thank God, no blockade can restrict the supply of that. That, at least, is abundant, and given without money and without price."

Could this conscientious economist then have foreseen the cost of the berry for her favorite beverage at fifty dollars per pound, she would not grudgingly have paid the grocer his exorbitant demand of fifty cents.

During the existence of the war, coffee was a luxury in which only the most wealthy could constantly indulge; and when used at all, it was commonly adulterated with other things which passed for the genuine article, but was often so nauseous that it was next to impossible to force it upon the stomach. Rye, wheat, corn, sweet potatoes, beans, groundnuts, chestnuts, chiccory, ochre, sorghum-seed, and other grains and seeds, roasted and ground, were all brought into use as substitutes for the bean of Araby; but after every experiment to make coffee of what was not coffee, we were driven to decide that there was nothing coffee but coffee, and if disposed to indulge in extravagance at all, the people showed it only by occasional and costly indulgence in the luxurious beverage.

Tea, sugar, wines, and all imported liquors, increased rapidly in expense as the supply grew scarce, but not in the same ratio as coffee, which had been in universal use at the South—the low price at which it had been purchased, and its stimulating and pleasant effects making it agreeable, necessary and possible for even the poorest to indulge in its use.

The leaves of the currant, blackberry, willow, sage, and other vegetables, were dried and used as substitutes for tea by those who could not or did not feel justified in encouraging the exorbitant demands of successful blockade runners and dealers in the article. When sugar grew scarce, and so expensive that many were compelled to abandon its use altogether, there were substituted honey, and the syrup from sorghum, or the Chinese sugar cane, for all ordinary culinary purposes. The cultivation of the latter has become a very important consideration with the agriculturists of the more northern of the Southern States, being peculiarly adapted to the soil and climate, and furnishing a cheap and excellent substitute for the syrup of the sugar cane of the Gulf States and the West Indies.

With an admirable adaptation to the disagreeable and inconvenient circumstances entailed upon us by the blockade, the necessary self denial practiced by the people was in a spirit of cheerful acquiescence, and with a philosophical satisfaction and contentment that forgot the present in a hopeful looking for better and brighter days in the future.

Cheerfully submitting to inconveniences, and deprived

from the first of the usual luxuries and many of the necessaries of life, the people were buoyed up with the hope and belief that their sufferings would be of short duration, and that an honorable independence and exemption from the evils which surrounded them, would soon compensate amply for the self denial they were called upon to practice. The remembrance then would be rather glorious than disagreeable in the reflection that they, too, had shared the travail which wrought the freedom of their country.

If there were any who sighed after the flesh-pots of Egypt, the sighs were breathed in the silence of retirement, and not where the ardor of the more hopeful could be chilled by such signs of discontent.

There was, however, a class in Richmond who very ill endured the severe simplicity and the rigid self-denial to which they were compelled to conform in the Confederate Capital. Gradually and insidiously innovations were permitted, until at last the license tolerated in fashionable society elsewhere grew to be tolerated somewhat in Richmond, and in the course of time prosy Richmond was acknowledged "fast" enough for the fastest.

CHAPTER XV.

THE CLOSE OF 1861—THE HOPE OF INTERVENTION—CAPTURE OF MASON AND SLIDELL.

IT was with painful regret that we were driven to notice the indifference manifested in reference to the campaign in Western Virginia, and with equal sorrow that we were compelled to discover the undue estimate placed upon the moral effects of such engagements as that at Leesburg. From the fierce valor and maddened determination of the Southern troops in that battle, and the unaccountable weakness of the enemy, many considered the former invincible, and an overweening confidence took possession of their

4*

minds, in the absolute certainty of success to the Confederate arms. In the same proportion they were disposed to depreciate the courage of their foes, and underestimate their powers of endurance and determination.

The year of 1861 was drawing to a close. Autumn had been long protracted. No one can forget the unusually delightful weather of that season in the beautiful State of Virginia. Finer we had never seen. The skies were bright, the air soft and balmy, the Indian summer much earlier and much longer protracted than usual, throwing over the earth its beautiful, dreamy haze, and inviting to the voluptuous enjoyment said to be awakened by the soft airs and warm blue skies of Italy. Dissociated with the startling fact that we were in the midst of war, which rested over our souls as an incubus of blackest horror, we should have experienced perhaps, in full measure, the *dolce far niente* of Eastern romance. But we could not, by closing our eyes and ears merely, and by breathing the delightful fragrance of the air, shut out from our hearts the gaunt, grim spectre.

The one prominent idea, in which all others were absorbed, was the war. In the social, the literary, the religious and the scientific circles of Richmond, war, and the necessities arising from it, were subjects upon which all minds were turned. There seemed no time, no thought for anything else.

A celebrated artist laid aside his palette and pencil, and occupied himself with experiments in fulminating powder, but, by carelessly neglecting proper caution, lost his life by an explosion.

An excellent chemist, who would have been invaluable to the government, thoughtlessly smoked a cigar in his laboratory, as he was preparing a powerful detonating compound, and was blown to pieces by an explosion that occurred from a spark from the cigar. His mangled body was found, in parts, many yards from the scene, and the building in which he operated was completely shattered.

Very early in the war, another gentleman, after a series of

successful experiments, lost his life in an explosion that effectually destroyed the building in which he was operating, and injured several persons in the vicinity.

Those who occupied themselves in this dangerous business seemed to be lamentably careless. In the spring of 1863, in a laboratory on one of the islands in the river, where a number of females were employed, through the carelessness of some of the employees in handling some matches, a most terrific explosion occurred, and a number of women were killed. Their bodies were so torn and mutilated that in many instances they could not be identified, and, withal, were charred until they were perfectly black. These were some of the freaks of death, in its carnival held in Richmond during the war.

The quiet along the lines of the Potomac was considered by many as auspicious of good to the South. They were impressed with the opinion that the enemy did not advance during the fine weather, when the roads were good and an opportunity for a movement "On to Richmond" so favorable, on account of mortal fear of the foes with whom he should have to contend. Some of our newspapers inclined to this opinion, industriously circulated it through the press, and encouraged a spirit of security and apathy on the part of the people and military. The warning voice of the Richmond *Examiner* was too little heeded, and the caustic and stinging yet useful words from the ready and vigorous pen of the lamented editor, and the well-meant and timely reproaches and denunciations of certain of the living, were unheeded and derided by those who did not wish to accredit the truth, that the calm in the outward appearance of our "sea of troubles" was only on the surface. Underneath, the waves rolled in all their mighty fury, to lash themselves into violence when rocked by the winds of the future. Challenge after challenge failed to bring into an engagement the "Young Napoleon," and our Army of the Potomac had to content itself with heavy skirmishing along the lines, without being able to provoke a general action.

The quiet was broken in December by an episode in which was taught a useful lesson to those who encouraged no thought of defeat to the Confederate arms, although our forces at Drainesville were the victims of a deception that could not be justified by the rules of civilized warfare. It occurred on the 22d of the month. About 2,500 of our men encountered a force of the enemy greatly superior in numbers, and being encumbered with a train of wagons for foraging purposes, after fighting desperately were compelled to retreat, with a loss of several hundred in killed and wounded. They then ascertained that the fighting qualities of the enemy had sensibly improved under the tuition of General McClellan, and that the raw troops under his management were no longer to be despised or contemned. Of the frightened material that had so ingloriously retreated at Bull Run, he was making soldiers who proved their claim to the title and character, in the fearlessness and courage with which they entered the fight at Drainesville.

From the beginning of the war hopes had been entertained that foreign powers would interfere, so far, at least, as to bring about the recognition of our government by France and England, and by that means raise the blockade so rigidly enforced against us. From day to day, and from month to month, we were entertained with the near approach of this desirable notice by the two most powerful nations of Europe, and it had the unfortunate effect of decreasing the sentiment of self-reliance at the South, and causing her to look for help from extraneous sources, when a determination to conquer a peace and prove herself entitled to the favorable consideration of the powers from which she expected recognition, was the course that would have been dictated by a wisdom unblinded by conceit or confidence in her own abilities.

Towards the close of the year, doubts arose in the minds of people of intelligence, as to the prospect of the much-desired notice. In Richmond, the press began to discourage the idea, and counseled against the indulgence of a hope destined to be unfulfilled; arguing that a bold independence would insure success, and give us a right to demand justice and friendship from foreign governments.

It was thought that England, in consideration of her interests in the cotton and tobacco of the South, and France from her interests in the tobacco, with the prospect of distress at home among the operatives who lived alone by the manufacture of those articles, would be compelled to abandon a policy of neutrality, and recognize the Southern Confederacy as one of the family of nations. But the unwillingness of those powers to enter into a war across the ocean prevented them from giving the desired countenance to the cause of the South. They preferred to support their starving working class at home to engaging in war abroad.

The selfishness and heartlessness of their course towards the South awakened the most intense dislike in the minds of the people for those countries which were seemingly quietly looking on, while a strong power was preparing to crush a rebellion to which they felt they were driven by a system of oppression as cruel as it was unnecessary.

The raising of the blockade was the one desire which operated to turn the hopes of the Southern people upon help from England and France. If that was effected and intercourse opened with the outside world, there seemed to us a much brighter prospect. They, however, grew to learn that such hopes were groundless, and contented themselves with the disappointment.

About this time (in the month of December) an event occurred which again raised the hopes of the South, in a prospect of foreign intervention and a release from the blockade.

The Commissioners deputed by the Confederate government respectively to France and England, having successfully run the blockade at Charleston, in a Confederate vessel, arrived safely at Havana, a neutral port, and took passage on the British mail steamer, the "Trent,' for an English port. When but one day at sea, and while in the Bahama Channel, this steamer was brought to by a shotted gun from the Federal steam frigate "San Jacinto," and boarded by an armed boat's crew, sent out by the commander of the vessel, Commander Wilkes, under the immediate command of Lieutenant Fairfax, who demanded the delivery of the persons of the Commissioners, Messrs. Mason and Slidell, with their secretaries, Messrs. Eustis and Macfarland.

Claiming the protection of the British flag, they refused to leave the vessel, except by actual force of arms, when the Federal lieutenant declared it was his purpose to use force if resistance was persevered in. The "Trent" being an unarmed vessel, all efforts at resistance were hopeless, and the Confederate Commissioners were surrendered under a distinct and passionate protest against a piratical seizure of their persons under a neutral flag. When the news of this outrage reached Richmond, it was welcomed as one of the most fortunate phases that could have been developed for the cause of the South. Confident that the British government, in all its majesty, would resent this unparalleled insult to its flag, and, from the exultation of the North over the capture of the ambassadors, not dreaming they would be delivered up at the demand of Great Britain, it was deemed a most singular interposition of Divine Providence, that in a manner so strangely unexpected was operating in our favor.

The unhesitating surrender of the Commissioners by Mr. Seward, when they were demanded of him, as the Federal Secretary of State, by the British government, dashed all our hopes of good fortune from this circumstance, and we were thrown back to look to our own resources alone for help.

More than once there were rumors that a French fleet rested in Hampton Roads, at the mouth of the James River, and we were foolish enough, connecting these reports with a knowledge of the fact that vast quantities of tobacco owned by the French government were known to be stored in Richmond, to credit the falsehoods. So ready were we to catch at the faintest shadow of hope which promised us independence and peace, that we gave credence to many ridiculous reports, and as deceitful as ridiculous.

Alone and unaided by any help from abroad, save irregular assistance from England in vessels and munitions of war, occasionally run in through the blockade, we waged for four years, successfully, against an enemy amply supplied with everything necessary to subdue us, a war in which with us everything was wanting but "brave hearts and willing hands," and, we must add, a self-sacrificing spirit, which alone sustained us under hardships the most bitter, trials the most cruel, oppressions the most unmitigated, with the dreadful knowledge that unaided we must suffer; shut in by the most rigid blockade, unsympathized with and uncared for as a nation by the outer world

CHAPTER XVI.

A SAD HOLIDAY WEEK—WORK FOR THE SOLDIERS.

AS the year 1861 drew to a close, the weather, which in autumn had been so unusually fine, grew rainy, snowy and disagreeable. It was never intensely cold, but chilling rains and frequent snows, melting almost as quickly as they fell, rendered the season more unhealthy and uncomfortable than the clear, stinging atmosphere that quickens the circulation of the blood, raises the spirits in proportion, and makes winter rather delightful than unpleasant. The industrial operations of our women were now chiefly devoted to knitting for the soldiers. Mothers and grandmothers, who in the days of their youth had learned the valuable use of knitting-needles, gave lessons to the younger women of our country, who, through the triumph of mechanical skill in the manufacture of hosiery, had been left untutored in this branch of domestic female industry.

It was delightful to watch the busy fingers of our dear old matrons, as they deftly wove the yarn through and through the shining steel needles, making cheerful music by the winter evening's fireside, as the soldiers' socks grew under their skillful manipulation. It was amusing to behold the patient industry with which the young girl, who had "never thought to knit," caught the manipulations from the dear old hands, and the look of patient perseverance with which, when transferred to her own, the thread would wind in and out, oh! how slowly, over the needles; and with what delight, after days of toil, she would triumphantly hold up for examination the rude, ill-shapen garment, called "a soldier's sock." Many a merry laugh has been provoked as the grotesque thing was submitted for critical examination. Evenings at home, formerly spent in gayety and social amusement, were made pleasant and useful in the labors of love and duty which prepared comfortable hose for the soldier, or a warm visor or a fancy colored scarf, which, under the patronage of kind old Santa Claus, found their way to the Christmas-bag in the soldier's tent.

Although it had become expedient to curtail numerous expenses, to retrench in this necessary, or to abstain from that, kind friends at home could not permit the sacred festival to pass by without some evidence of the former delightful manner in which it had been observed. If we sat down at a board less cheerful, or less bountifully provided with creature comforts, care was taken that our own dear ones in the field should not realize it.

An extra turkey, a rosy ham, a jar of pickles, a jug of eggnogg, or a large golden pound-cake were carefully prepared, secured in a strong box, into which found their way nameless other articles of cheer and comfort, and intrusted to the patron saint of Christmas, who rarely failed to make his way amid whizzing balls and crashing, bursting shell, to the white tent, with the luxurious dinner for the young soldier who was debarred from taking it at the homestead board.

The Christmas season in Virginia has ever been one of the

most genial hilarity and delight. After the church services of Christmas day the remainder of the old year is devoted to merry-making. Dull care is thrown to the winds, and old hearts grow young, and young hearts grow glad at the happy festival. The faithful domestics are absolved from regular employment, and come in for their share of the Christmas bounties. An extra shawl, a bright plaid kerchief, a pair of gloves, or the cast-off clothes from the abundant wardrobe of the masters and mistresses, showed they were not forgotten when this delightful time came round for the interchange of presents; and many times the heart of the kind mistress was gladdened by the simple offering of a faithful slave, from the hoarded-up savings of months, to purchase for her the "Christmas gift."

Never before had so sad a Christmas dawned upon us. Our religious services were not remitted, and the Christmas dinner was plenteous as of old ; but in nothing further did it remind us of days gone by. We had neither the heart nor inclination to make the week merry with joyousness when such a sad calamity hovered over us. Nowhere else could the heart have been so constantly oppressed by the heavy load of trouble as in Richmond, and the friendly congratulations of the season were followed by anxious inquiries for dear boys in the field, or husbands or fathers whose presence had ever brought brightness to the domestic hall, and whose footsteps were music to the hearts and ears of those to whom they were so dear.

As the rushing tide of recollection surged over the soul, and the brightness of past happy days of peace came back to us, to mock us with delights fled forever, we could not close our eyes to a picture that reflected so much brightness; but as we followed the course of thought down the stream of time, with a bitter revulsion that well nigh stopped the pulse-beat at the fountain of life, the awful realities of our present opened up before us in the clouds, and darkness, and hail, and storm, and tempest of sanguinary warfare. All before us seemed a wilderness, through which our feet, bleeding, bare and torn, must travel; but faith in the righteousness and ultimate success of our cause was to us the "pillar of cloud by day" and the "pillar of fire by night," to guide us, like the wandering tribes of Israel, through the desert to the land of promise that our National Independence bounded.

New Year's day was bright, balmy and beautiful as spring. The first day of the year has never been observed in Richmond as one of public reception for ladies, and of visiting for gentlemen. The usual arrangements of the household under the *régime* of slavery, would have forbidden such a custom. Christmas week was an undisputed holiday for our domestics. Those who owned their servants could not, by time-honored and regularly established usage, claim regular duties from them, and New Year's day usually found a Southern housewife altogether unprepared for entertaining friends, and intently engaged in the rearrangement and reconstruction of the *ménage* upon something like a basis of comfort and order. Therefore New Year's entertainments never became popular under the "old *régime.*"

It had been, however, from time almost immemorial, a custom with our Governors. Members of the Legislature, officials of the government, and any gentlemen who desired, were expected to pay their respects to his Excellency, and to drink his health in champagne, apple-toddy, whiskey-punch, or egg-nog.

Governor Letcher received, as usual, on the return of the anniversary that ushered in the year 1862. His guests were welcomed with the broad, good-humored hospitality and dignified courtesy which ever distinguished this gallant son of Virginia. Minus champagne, through the rigid effects of the blockade, the giant punch-bowl was filled with the steaming beverage, the smell of roasted apples betrayed the characteristic toddy, and through the crystal cut-glass gleamed the golden hue of the egg-nog, to regale the guests of the Governor.

As may be supposed, on this occasion Bacchus asserted his

triumph over Mars, and the devotees at his convivial shrine were many of them oblivious, happily, to the sterner mandates of the God of War.

The President of the Confederacy, for the first time since its existence, struggling into national life, had his New Year's reception. The officers ; civil, naval, and military, the members of Congress and the State Legislature, and admiring crowds of less note, pressed forward to testify their admiration and esteem of the first President of the South. With the ease, grace, dignity and gentleness peculiar to him, Mr. Davis received his guests, to all of whom he had something cheerful to say—some pleasant reminiscence to revive, and some graceful, genuine compliment to offer. There was in him none of the rigid austerity, the repulsive hauteur with which persons of position, sometimes attempt to overawe those less favored by fortuitous circumstance. A beautiful incident, illustrative of the kindly simplicity which characterized him in society, is related of this reception:

A preacher of the Methodist Church, famed as much for his singular eccentricity as for his strength of mind, without a precedent in the customs of fashionable society, took with him to the reception of President Davis his three little children, to place in their youthful minds, (as he said,) an ever pleasant remembrance. This appearance with his little ones, occasioned much amusement for the guests of the President. When he was presented to his Excellency, and in turn presented his children, Mr. Davis, neglecting other and more pretentious guests, devoted special attention to the pleased little ones, and when after a friendly talk with each of them, and their father with them, they were about to retire, he said, "Not yet, not yet, Mr. D.," and ordered his own little ones to be brought from the nursery to entertain his juvenile guests, and declared that no tribute of esteem ever paid him had touched him so nearly, or was more gratefully received, or was more complimentary than this singular notice by the Methodist minister.

In nothing did Mr. Davis show more genuine amiability, more true nobility of character, than in the notice he never failed to bestow on children. Every one can remember, who lived in Richmond, to have seen him many times riding on horseback with one of his little ones in his lap, and the great pleasure it seemed to afford him to give pleasure to a child. His mode of life, always simple and unostentatious, made it easy to approach him; and a sure road to his heart was ever found by the widow and the orphan.

As the year of 1862 dawned upon us, it was not spanned by the rainbow-tinted arch of future happiness to us as a nation, nor did roseate clouds of peace and comfort reflect the sunshine of prosperity; but though dark, threatening, thunder-charged clouds hung over the future, the vision, quickened by anxiety, caught the light ahead which led to peace, to independence; and Hope stood by, and with her syren song lulled the weary mind to repose as she pointed onward and whispered, " Liberty !"

It was a singular fact, but from actual observance we assert the truth, that from the 1st day of January, 1862, until the middle of March, there were not two consecutive days of fine weather. There was never any extreme cold, but alternate snow, and sunshine, rain, and hail, and sleet, and mud, and all things disagreeable in the weather of winter. We had none cold enough to freeze the water sufficiently to gather ice for use in summer, and with the necessity for it which was apparent, it was the cause of much real anxiety, and the suffering in consequence is one of the saddest remembrances of the summer of 1862.

Our army suffered terribly from the effects of the winter, and necessary exposure in the camp and field. The mortality among the troops in Virginia was terrible, and very unwillingly acknowledged by those to whom the truth was unacceptable. Pneumonia, pleurisy, rheumatism, catarrhal fevers, and other diseases of the lungs swept the men off by scores, unaccustomed as they were to the hardships of the field. The Army of the Potomac was more healthy than that of the Peninsula. There the miasma brought on the most distressing agues and fevers—often the precursors of other diseases which soon brought the soldier to his grave.

In a private way all was done in Richmond that could be done to provide for the wants of the sick in the army. Our commissariat was never judiciously managed, and there was great suffering which might have been relieved or alleviated by more careful attention to food for the sick. For this purpose delicacies were preserved and hoarded up by the women of the South, and in Richmond the suffering from inappropriate diet was slight compared with that endured by the soldiers away from the city. In many instances, doubtless, neglect of precautionary care and attention to the health of the army should be considered culpable, but we are unwilling to attach blame to responsible persons when the extenuating circumstances are not understood.

Soldiers from the Peninsula told rare stories of misery. They would tell of lying down upon as dry a spot of earth as they could find, to awake in the morning and discover themselves almost submerged in water. Only the most vigorous could endure this exposure, and the constitutions of many were shattered in consequence. A young man said: "I once laid down to sleep, wrapped head and ears in my blanket, without my cap, but awaking in the night I stretched out my hand, and raising my cap to my head, I deluged it with the water that had fallen while I slept."

But they were cheerful. Enduring hardship, disease and suffering with uncomplaining heroism, declaring they could endure much more for the independence they were seeking.

It is easy to imagine the moral courage, the heroic bravery with which the soldier is inspired on the field of battle, where the sublimity of excitement would glory in courting death; but we have yet to learn the secret of cheerfulness and fortitude when it comes in the stealthy breath of the pestilence, and cuts down its victims silently but not less surely than the sabre thrust or the Minié ball. Truly, to the soldier death in the camp is more awful than on the field of battle; in his tent than breasting the foe.

CHAPTER XVII.

THE FALL OF ROANOKE ISLAND—DISASTERS ON THE TENNESSEE AND CUMBERLAND RIVERS—GLOOM IN RICHMOND.

FROM the gloomy prospects with which the new year opened upon our military condition, we had no hope to build upon for successfully conducting the war but the unflinching patriotism and the steady enthusiasm of our soldiers. Peace only awaited us through our own perseverance, unaided by extraneous influences.

The results of the campaign in Missouri were discouraging. The end of the affair of the "Trent" had quite extinguished all hope of foreign interference. The talk of an exhausted treasury at the North was silenced by the knowledge that millions of money and almost numberless armies were being raised to prosecute the work of our subjugation. Our privateers were accomplishing very little for us upon the high seas, murmurs of dissatisfaction were distinct towards the government, the Cabinet was unacceptable to the masses of the people, the means of living were becoming more and more scarce day by day, articles of food and clothing were diminishing through the existence of the blockade, and those left to us were held at such a figure that constant retrenchment in expenses and sacrifice of the commonest necessaries of life were constant. The health of our armies was of such a character as to awaken the most intense anxiety; our soil was being covered with the graves of thousands of our best and most promising young men; yet no word of failure in the cause for which we were striving was heard; no thought of submission found vent in language, but "unaided we can conquer a peace" was the expression which raised the spirits of those over whom the shades of despondency were beginning to hover. Was it an infatuation, or were we given over to believe a sophistry that was to work our ruin? Let it be accounted for in any manner it may be, the patriotic principle which buoyed up a people depressed by such external circumstances and such internal distresses, reaches a degree of sublimity, of grandeur, which cannot be described in the meagre gift of language possessed by those who would fain give it the proper coloring.

During the month of January nothing of importance to our cause was observable in the Army of Virginia, but the operations of General Jackson and his famous Stonewall Brigade in the vicinity of Winchester. Under such a leader we feared very little for their honor or success. His presence served as an electric influence upon the brave fellows under his command, and deeds of the fiercest daring were inspired by this singular man. Fatigues were endured, hardships laughed at, and successes achieved, marvellous to relate.

From the West discouraging news came to us. On the 17th of January we were defeated in the battle of Mills Springs, in Kentucky, and our brave young Zollicoffer was killed. Flushed with success, our enemies in that region prepared for still further triumphs. Yet this defeat engendered no moral results unfavorable to the Confederate cause. It was not felt in Richmond as a matter for very sincere regret, because, perhaps, of the unaccountable political position of Kentucky, and the distance from the more important operations of the Confederate army. Our attention was now mainly directed to Roanoke Island, on the coast of North Carolina, situated between Croaton and Roanoke Sounds, and commanding an entrance to each of these channels. After the abandonment of Forts Hatteras and Clark, (shortly after the State seceded to the Confederacy,) and the fortifications of Oregon Inlet, this island became one of the most important positions on the coast. It was the key that unlocked all of the northeastern portion of North Carolina, and the rich back country in the rear of Norfolk and Portsmouth, and prevented an approach of the enemy upon those cities. From these advantageous circumstances it was considered next in importance to Fortress Monroe.

It was now threatened by a Federal fleet under General Burnside, of immense proportions and ably commanded.

Brigadier General Wise had been placed in command of the military district in which this important position was included, under the superior command of General Huger, of South Carolina, commanding the department of Norfolk.

Finding the defences wholly inadequate, General Wise made known to the government the utter uselessness of attempting to hold the island unless efficient aid was rendered him in the improvement and perfection of the defences, and supposed to be wholly within the means of the government to supply. Again and again he applied for help, for proper reinforcements, and it is reported he used no very measured or polite terms as to the certain fate of himself and his command, if such assistance was not secured to him. But his entreaties were cruelly neglected.

The attack on the island was made by the fleet of the enemy on the 7th of February. General Wise was at the time confined to his bed by sickness, at Nagg's Head, four miles distant, and entirely unable to command in person. The immediate command then devolved on Colonel Shaw, of the North Carolina State troops, who, after a brilliant and energetic defence, and when no prospect was left him but the utter annihilation of his forces, surrendered the island and the army under him.

When this information reached Richmond, with it came slanderous reports in regard to Colonel Shaw, who was charged with treachery in yielding up his army, and was said to have been wrapped in the Union flag and congratulated by the Federal commander upon the successful manner in which he had accomplished the purpose with which he had charged himself. Very soon, however, these falsehoods were refuted, and the blame of the failure charged upon other parties, who refused with indifference the urgent requests of General Wise, and neglected the repeated forewarnings with which he admonished the government of the insecurity of his position, and the fierce remonstrances against any attempt to hold it unaided by heavy reinforcements of men and abundant supplies of armament and ammunition.

The orders of the Secretary of War, Mr. Benjamin, were peremptory, and with all the pride of military etiquette and the indignation of one superior in judgment, Wise obeyed, yet without a public murmur, and undertook the unfortunate mission which ended, as he had predicted, in defeat.

Although foreseen by him, his distress, when the tidings of the battle were borne to him, was said to have been inconceivable, and heightened by the fact that his own noble son, the gallant young captain of the Richmond Light Infantry Blues, had fallen.

The body of this amiable young officer, in whom Virginia felt all the natural pride over offspring so illustrious, had fallen into the hands of the enemy, but was treated with all the respect merited by one so worthy, and was surrendered, on application, to his broken-hearted father. On the arrival of the remains at Portsmouth, all the bells of the city tolled the requiem of the young hero,—and there his father was permitted to gaze on his placid countenance, and the still form, in the rigid beauty of death. His emotions were said to be uncontrollable, and melted all who witnessed the sight. Unable to restrain himself, he bent over the loved figure, and taking in his one of the cold hands of the departed, exclaimed: "My noble boy, you have died for me! You have died for me! You have died for your father!" Large tears rolled down the cheeks of the statesman warrior, "He died for me—he died for me!" and he then fell insensible to the ground.

The devotion of Captain Wise to his father, was understood to be of a most remarkble character, and partook rather of the tender self-sacrificing nature of a daughter's love, than the less sensitive and more independent tone of a son's attachment. Ever jealous of the honor and reputation of his father, he had more than once openly resented attacks reflecting on a name dearer to him than his own life.

Never was there a sadder funeral in Richmond than that which commemorated the death of Captain O. Jennings Wise. St. James's Church was crowded to its utmost capacity, to give room to the numbers that succeeded in getting into the church, and crowds were assembled on the outside, and remained standing during the services, although the ground was saturated with mud and water from the melting snow. A long retinue of carriages, conveyed the mourning family, and the numerous friends of the deceased. The principal dignitaries of the General and State Governments attended on horseback; the Mayor and City Council, and a vast procession of citizens, the old members of the Richmond Blues, and all the military in the city, with arms reversed, and bands of music, with muffled drums, swelled the funeral cortege, and followed the hearse, in which was placed the coffin containing all that was mortal of that brave young son of Virginia, draped in the banner of his State, and the Confederate flag, in whose defence he had so gallantly lost a life so precious to his friends, his city, his country! The windows and sidewalks of Richmond were densely crowded with spectators of this mournful pageant, and tears of heart-felt sorrow flowed unrestrained, as we watched the sad train that bore the hallowed remains to their quiet resting-place, in our beautiful cemetery at Hollywood.

The gurgling, never-ceasing music of the river, and the winds as they whisper through the trees, and the birds singing amid the branches, are the endless requiem over the grave of this young patriot of Virginia, the ever-lamented O. Jennings Wise. But his memory will live in the hearts of his countrymen, until the children and grandchildren of the Southern soldier shall take up the story to tell their descendants of the deeds of daring and glory inspired by this brave young commander.

THE FALL OF ROANOKE ISLAND.

The fall of Roanoke Island produced the most profound sensation in Richmond. Somebody was in fault—who was it? It remained for the public to decide. Surely not General Wise. His protest against holding the island under such circumstances was fully understood and duly appreciated; therefore he was readily acquitted of all blame. The slanders which sought to tarnish the reputation of Colonel Shaw, providentially in command of the Confederate troops there, were too soon refuted to be brought into consideration, and the charges of the inefficiency and want of courage in the soldiers engaged in the battle were disproved almost as soon as scandalously whispered, and the eyes of the people turned upon the government. After an investigation of this serious misfortune by Congress, the blame was fastened on our Secretary of War, who alone appeared responsible for this defeat, which might have been avoided if he had paid practical attention to the predictions and remonstrances of General Wise, after he had made a personal observation of the position, and reported prospects more than once or twice to the Secretary.

The hearts of the people were sadly torn by this disaster. Mr. Benjamin was not forgiven. His neglect seemed culpable, yet we had the mortification to behold his promotion to a position of higher grade, though at the time of less vital importance to us. This act on the part of the President, in defiance of public opinion, was considered as unwise and arbitrary, and a reckless risking of his reputation and popularity, with a sensible compromise of the unbounded influence before possessed by him.

Although no complaints of want of efficiency as Secretary of State were made against Mr. Benjamin, he was ever afterwards unpopular in the Confederacy, and particularly in Virginia. We had scarcely recovered from the shock of this disaster, the sad funeral procession of the lamented O. Jennings Wise had barely faded upon our vision, when news arrived of misfortune to our arms in the West, on the Tennessee River. Fort Henry, an important position near the boundary line of Kentucky and Tennessee, on the east bank of the river, had been yielded up to the enemy. It was under the command of General Tilghman, and in the department of General Albert Sidney Johnston, and was attacked by an expedition of gunboats on the 6th of February. After a gallant resistance, when all hope of successfully holding the fort had become exhausted, under circumstances of the greatest bravery and fortitude, General Tilghman hoisted a white flag, pathetically remarking, "It is in vain to fight longer. Our gunners are disabled, our guns are dismantled, we cannot hold out five minutes longer." The fortress was surrendered, and he and his brave little garrison of forty men were taken prisoners.

This event, coeval with the disaster at Roanoke Island, filled the hearts of the Southern people with gloom and sorrow. Richmond groaned under this fresh weight to her burden of grief. Quickly treading on the heels of this misfortune, intelligence was received that our enemies were preparing for a visitation to Fort Donelson, on the Cumberland River—a position of much greater importance to the Confederate cause, and much more strongly fortified than Fort Henry had been.

From day to day, as the news of the battle of Fort Donelson reached us in Richmond in straggling items, we were encouraged to hope for success there, and anon our hopes were doomed to disappointment; but when the full and correct account was brought, the effect was like a stroke of paralysis. In mute despair we listened until the heart grew sick, and grim war seemed unendurable, and a long, bitter cry for peace once more took possession of the soul, but with it still a resolve for no peace if to be purchased by ignoble submission.

Again arose the question: Who is in fault in this defeat? At one hour General Johnston received news of a victory, at another, a defeat. Somebody was again to blame—who is it? where is he, that the indignant Confederate public may heap on the base head of the originator of this terrible blow the deserved punishment? Who is the scapegoat? This defeat at Donelson involved the surrender of Nashville. A train of misfortunes followed, and the guilty parties were ferreted out by public indignation.

CHAPTER XVIII.

REMAINS OF UNION SENTIMENT IN RICHMOND—BUSINESS CHANGES.

FOR the first time since the beginning of the war, we became conscious of the remains of Union sentiment in Richmond. We had imagined it quite exhausted, or, if any had entertained it after the beginning of our troubles, the sufferings of the people, who were entirely irresponsible for political disagreements, had brought all to a compromise of affection for a government that could so coolly tolerate human misery. But at that period, when success perched unmistakably on the "Old Flag," when the fortunes of the Confederacy seemed to be waning, the spirit that walked in the darkness left its testimonials to be revealed in the light of day.

On the walls of buildings at various street corners were read such inscriptions as these: "Union Men to the Rescue!" "Now is the time to rally around the Old Flag!" "God bless the Stars and Stripes!" "What has become of Providence?" "Providence has forsaken its pinks!" and many other taunts, that convinced we had traitors among us.

Numbers of persons were suspected, and several arrests effected, the most important of which was that of John M. Botts, of Virginia, whose incomprehensible neutrality was thought, in the opinion of his old worshippers, by no means to compromise the *amor patriæ* he professed. It is not left for man to judge,—it has been decreed in the Book of Books that "to his own conscience he standeth or falleth." A successful whiskey dealer and manufacturer, and a German butcher in the First Market, were conspicuous among the number suspected. Caucuses of the Union men were said to be held nightly somewhere, and detectives were kept on the track, but through cowardice or otherwise they considered "discretion the better part of valor," and very soon the excitement subsided, and indeed there never was serious cause for alarm.

These demonstrations increased the bitter feeling against those who invaded our territory. The most dreaded, the most hated of all beings was the "Yankee." Social feelings and the ties of consanguinity were lost in the political whirlwind which bore away every other feeling in its course.

Little boys on the streets discussed politics with the ardor of men grown up, and treasured revenge for those who oppressed their fathers. Little girls learned to dread and fear the Yankee above all tame or wild animals, and amusing lessons were often gleaned by those who paid attention to the innocent sports of the children.

A little boy, who had been brought up in town, was carried by his mother on a short visit to the country, and while indulging in a stroll in the woods near the house at which she was stopping, got on his leg one of those tenacious and troublesome insects known by us as ticks. Any one acquainted with the nature of these bugs will remember that, when once they stick to the flesh, they bury their head in, and continue to draw blood until full, and then drop off. They are altogether disgusting. This little fellow had rubbed and pulled in vain at his "pet tick" for some moments after he discovered it, and when at last he succeeded in pulling off the objectionable vermin, he held it up between his fingers, and with an expression of droll malignity, and provoking the laughter of all present, exclaimed : "Ah! you're a Yankee!"

Two lovely little girls, whose parents were of Northern birth, were frequently reproached by their little playmates for "being Yankees." On one occasion, when in the room of a lady who very much loved little children, she was attracted to a rupture among a little party who had begged permission to be allowed to have a play there.

An incorrigible little girl cried out : "There, now, you have broken my doll, you horrid little Yankee!"

The elder of the children of such reproachful origin ran at once to the kind lady for sympathy, and laying her head on the knee of her friend, with tearful eyes and quivering lips, said : "I can't help where I was born!" But her younger sister, in more courageous three-year-old dignity than her sister of five, exclaimed : "You are bad! you are bad! I shan't pay wid you any more; I shan't pay any more!" whereupon a four-year-old Baltimorean, a magnificent specimen of Young America, lifted himself triumphantly, and looking after her as she ran to the door, cried out: "Ginny, I always thought you were a Yankee, and now I knowth it, for that ith a *real Bull Run!* Now I knowth it; now I knowth it. Ah, Ginny!"

The child is truly the father of the man, and these simple anecdotes will serve to illustrate the sentiments of the people more clearly, perhaps, than the expressed opinion of the older and more careful.

Later, a little girl of five years old, who had witnessed the arrest of her father, under the orders of General Pope, (when in command of the Department of the Rappahannock,) compelling all male citizens to take the oath of allegiance to the Federal government, or be sent out of the lines, and whose terror of the Yankees had been increased until the child considered them more fearful than bears or lions, was in the dressing-room of a young lady, her aunt, and watching, with all the interest of a little girl, the dinner toilette of the lady, and seeing a braid of hair upon the table at which she stood, took it up, and handling it very roughly, attracted the attention of the aunt, who exclaimed: "Put that down, child, you will ruin it; see how you have already tangled it."

"Whose hair is it, auntie?"

"Mine," replied the lady.

"Did it grow on your head?" queried the curious child.

"No, it did not."

"Well, whose is it?"

"Mine, I tell you; I bought it."

"Well, but whose head did it grow on?" persevered the child.

"Oh, I don't know," answered the lady; "it is dead folks' hair," (rather mischievously.)

"Dead folks' hair? Well, I would not wear it,—I wouldn't wear dead folks' hair."

And very superstitiously dropping the hair, the child left the room, looking over her shoulder at her aunt, as if she thought she was committing a sacrilege by adorning herself with the hair of one dead. But the child was not silenced altogether. Two days afterward, coming into the room of her aunt again when the dinner toilette was made, her attention was directed to the objectionable braid. Climbing up in a chair and watching with interest the hair as it was coiled on the back of the head of the lady, she said:

"Auntie, did you say that was a dead person's hair?"

"Yes, and what of it, now?"

"I wouldn't wear it."

"Why, child?"

"Because, *it might be* a Yankee's!"

Amused, her aunt had to suspend the operations of the toilette for a few moments to indulge in a hearty laugh, when she replied: "I think it very probable, as it came from a Yankee town; but I shall wear it, nevertheless." The lady's prejudice did not prevent her from making use of an article which contributed so much to heighten her beauty, although its belongings were questionable.

Great economy was at that time practiced in expenditures for dress. Staple articles had grown exceedingly scarce, but there still remained in the stores large quantities of fine goods, rich silks, laces, etc., and the merchants, supposing there would be but little demand for such articles, were willing to sell at the usual prices, and even, in some instances, at or below cost. Some of our ladies wisely at that time invested in fine goods at a much lower price than the most indifferent fabrics commanded at a period twelve months later.

Merchants from all parts of the Confederacy removed their stores to Richmond, and in February of 1862 there was sold at auction, by a firm from Augusta, Georgia, the finest stock of silks, laces and other delicate and rich articles, that had ever been exhibited in the city.

One could almost have imagined being in a strange city, from the signs over the doors of the shops. Old establishments had closed out or had entered into other branches of business, and new firms placed their names before the public. Israel and David, and Moses and Jacobs, and Hyman and Levy, and Guggenheimer and Rosenheimer, and other names innumerable of the Ancient People, were prominent, instead of the old Anglo-Saxon which had designated the most important business firms of Richmond.

The war was a harvest to that class of our population. Claiming no distinctive nationality, and with the wisdom usually displayed by them in financial concerns, their investments were of such a character that many of them at this time are the capitalists of Richmond, and must be the future Rothschilds of the South. They were not found, as the more interested of the people, without the means to purchase food when Confederate money became useless to us from the failure of our cause. They were much abused for extortion, but surely they were quite equalled by many who should have set them an example worthy of imitation among our own people.

CHAPTER XIX.

RICHMOND THE PERMANENT CAPITAL.

THE permanent government of the Confederate States was established on the 22d of February, 1862.

The birth-day of the "Father of his Country" was the one set apart for the advent of the established government of our infant nation. It was anticipated with the most interested feelings over the whole south, and for days previous visitors, to be present at the inaugural ceremonies of our first (and last) President, crowded into the city from all parts of the country. Carriages were engaged a week beforehand to convey persons to the Capitol Square, and hired at the most extraordinary prices.

The weather had been precarious for some days, and on the morning of the 22d the rain fell in torrents, and the streams and the gutters were like the flowing of little rivers. Yet the friends of the President, and the curious crowds of residents and strangers in the city, were not to be deterred from witnessing the scene of the inauguration by the rain and mud, which was in some places so deep as almost to render the crossings impassable.

The square of the Capitol was crowded with a dense throng of old and young—men, and women, and children— soldiers and citizens—mingled with carriages and umbrellas, dripping hats, and cloaks, and blankets, and oil-cloths, and draggled skirts, and muddy boots, and all other accompaniments of mud and rain upon such a dense mass of human beings in the singular panorama of the occasion.

A covered platform had been erected just underneath, or beside the Washington Monument, where the brazen image of "the Father of his Country" looked down upon this singular sight in the capital of his native State, seeming to watch with interest the novel proceedings—with his arm outstretched to shield the platform beneath, and his finger pointing southward. It seemed to us, of the hopeful class, significant.

Very few heard the inaugural address. The pattering of the rain on the carriages and the umbrellas, would have prevented the sound of the human voice from reaching our ears—but the sight alone of his Excellency, and his gestures, always dignified, satisfied those who caught not a word that fell from his lips. .With patient enthusiasm, they remained until the ceremonies were over, and retired to their homes—the gentlemen to prepare for the reception at the house of our President, and the ladies—who were not fortunate enough to have a carriage, to doff garments wet and muddy, and to anticipate pneumonia and the many nameless evils held up before us as bugbears by the profession who make their living from the aches, and pains, and miseries of others.

Never was there a man put into power so nearly by public acclamation as Mr. Davis. So well satisfied did the southern people feel that he was the man for the place, that no other was mentioned as his competitor for office.

The charge that he was placed in the position he occupied by a few factionists is not true, and when we hear him spoken of as the "Leader of the Rebellion," we can only regard him as the constituted head of a people who, to a certain extent, were all more or less leaders.

We could not, with our feeble pen, nor would our inclination cause us to venture upon a work so presumptuous, as to attempt a vindication of the relation of Mr. Davis to the rebellion in the South; but the commonest, faintest dictates of jusẗce and humanity should control public opinion towards a man only responsible for his position by virtue of the talents with which he was endowed by God himself. His statesmanlike abilities had long been acknowledged in the Senate of the United States. He possessed an enviable reputation for genius in the peculiar profession of politics, and openly, manfully, and independently he has avowed the sentiments that found an echo in the hearts and voices of the Southern people, and made him available for their cherished purposes. Let justice be done by a corrected public opinion; and the ex-President of the "so-called Southern Confederacy " will stand acquitted before his present most unforgiving opposers—before even those most uncompromising enemies, who would fain assist him to the ignominious death of a malefactor. On the head of the whole Southern people let the blame rest, who for their sins, if sins they must be considered still, have been scourged enough already, in the misery, desolation, and death through which they have been passing until late, and not upon the head of one alone, their unfortunate chief representative. In the name of righteousness, justice and mercy, we of the South would ask this—and that no more be added to the cruel burden of sorrow, which we will admit, if necessary, but only for the sake of argument—in our rashness, we brought upon ourselves.

The administration of Mr. Davis was never wholly acceptable to the people. The nearly arbitrary power conferred upon him placed in his hands almost exclusive control of our military affairs, which were managed in such a way as to irritate some of our most accomplished and best informed generals. His refusal to concede anything to the people in their wishes in regard to changes in the cabinet, to whom, from seeming inefficiency, Mr. Mallory, Secretary of the Navy, and Mr. Benjamin, Secretary of War, had become exceptionable, was the fruitful source of unpopularity. That he made mistakes we all must admit. But the question is—who, in the trying position of ex-President Davis, would have done better?—who as well? He has been charged by some as using his office to put down and elevate whom he chose. Perhaps so. We are not prepared to censure him. General Randolph of Virginia was appointed to fill the vacancy in the War Department, an appointment that was immensely popular, and under which success once more dawned upon the Confederate arms. About the same time the confidence of the people was strengthened by the appointment of General Robert E. Lee by the Confederate Congress to the position of commanding general—a rank created by the demands of our situation, and which, after being vetoed by the President, was afterwards consented to, but so modified by him that General Lee, as commanding general, should "act under his direction."

CHAPTER XX.

THE FIGHT IN HAMPTON ROADS.

A FEW weeks of quiet supervened, and under the immediate shadow of the now firmly constituted government, we of Richmond were watching here and there, towards the North, and West, and South, for the next turn of the military wheel, which might reveal a fresh excitement. A true history of the war as it appeared in Richmond from this date, would be of a calm to-day and storm to-morrow—clouds and sunshine—if only enough of the sunshine to reveal behind the clouds a streak of the "silvery lining."

The uselessness of our navy was to be no longer a reproach to us. Mr. Mallory's skill and exertions were to receive at least a measure of reward. Hampton Roads, at the mouth of James River, and in which, in days gone by, brilliant naval engagements had taken place, were once more to have their waters ruffled by the ploughing keel of the man-of-war, and to reverberate the thunders of artillery from the engines of destruction. "On the morning of the 8th of March, the Virginia, (formerly the Merrimac,) left the navy-yard at Norfolk, accompanied by the Raleigh and the Beaufort, and proceeded to Newport's News to engage the enemy's frigates the Cumberland and the Congress, their gunboats, and their shore batteries. The Confederate squadron was under the command of flag-officer Buchanan, (a Marylander by birth, and accomplished in his profession). It consisted of the Virginia, the Beaufort, the Raleigh, the Patrick Henry, and the Teaser, carrying in all twenty-seven guns.

On passing Sewell's Point Captain Buchanan made a

speech to his men. It was brief and to the point. "My men," said he, "you are now about to face the enemy. You shall have no reason to complain of not fighting at close quarters. Remember you fight for your homes and your country. You see those ships. You must sink them. I need not ask you to do it. I know you will do it."

On steamed the mysterious looking craft, like an immense turtle swimming on the surface, and puffing out vapors of fiery breath. Straight up to the Cumberland she went, and as if to satisfy her revenge for the former mischief perpetrated by her in the Navy Yard at Norfolk, when within proper distance sent a terrible visitor from her guns to salute the mystified crew, on the deck of the enemy's vessel she so closely assailed. Then, with a terrible crash on the starboard bow, she saw the reeling vessel slowly settling to disappear beneath the dark waters forever.

She next turned her attention to the Congress, which poured upon her iron sides a furious shower of shell, that bounded off without indenting her armor, and opening upon this frigate, sent such a visitation of carnage and dismay, that very soon her colors were hauled, and a white flag at half-mast run up.. The Beaufort, ran up alongside to take possession of the vessel, and secure the officers and crew. Lieutenant Parker, commander of the Beaufort, received the flag of the Congress, and her surrender from the commander, William Smith, and Lieutenant Pendergrast, with the side-arms of these officers.

After delivering themselves up as prisoners of war, they were permitted to return to the Congress, to assist in the removal of the wounded to the deck of the Beaufort; but notwithstanding they had pledged themselves to return to the Beaufort, and had left their swords as a pledge, they never returned! Although two white flags, raised by her own crew, had been hoisted by the Congress, and were flying in full sight, a perfidious fire was opened upon the Beaufort from the shore batteries. Captain Buchanan noticed this, and determining that the Congress should not fall again into the hands of the enemy, he said: "That vessel must be burned." The suggestion was immediately responded to by Lieutenant Minor, who volunteered to take command of a boat for that purpose. A deadly fire was opened upon him, wounding him and several of his men. When the commander of the Confederate squadron observed this, he recalled the boat, and opened a fire of hot shot and incendiary shell, which soon destroyed the ill-fated Congress.

The explosion of the magazine of the Congress was heard at Norfolk, and the illumination extended for a vast distance over the waters, signalling to the anxious people the news of the wonderful victory.

In the fire from the shore Captain Buchanan was wounded in the thigh, by a Minié ball, and being too much disabled to continue in command of the vessel, it was transferred to Lieutenant Catesby Jones, with orders to fight her as long as the men could stand to the guns.

She was then attacked by the Minnesota, the Roanoke and the St. Lawrence, all of which, after awhile, were driven under cover of the guns at Old Point. On Sunday she engaged the Monitor (Ericsson battery.) It is said to have resembled an immense "cheese-box," of midnight hue, which, like a thing of darkness, moved about with spirit-like rapidity, and from its size, and the quickness of its movements, gained, at one time, an apparent advantage over the invulnerable Confederate iron-clad.

The Minnesota again joined in the fight, and the Monitor here and there poured its fire into the Virginia; but after a while, a column of smoke shot up above the Minnesota and she withdrew, disabled, and riddled with shot from the contest. The Virginia thrice silenced the fire of the Monitor, once brushed her, and narrowly missed the opportunity of sinking her with her prow, when, declining further action, the Monitor retired from the contest, and the victorious Virginia steamed back to Norfolk amid shouts of victory.

The news in Richmond was electrifying. Our despised navy was brought into enviable notice, and had the honor of constructing a man-of-war, superior to any that had ever been engaged upon any waters. There is no record of an affair so brilliant. For days, this glorious engagement filled all hearts and minds. Nothing else was talked of, until murmurs began to arise that instead of one such vessel, we might have had many.*

The excitement in the North was quite as great as with us, and in Europe the utmost interest grew out of the wonderful achievements of the Confederate iron-clad, and a new impetus was given to naval architecture, by our infant Confederate Navy.

Shortly after this, the convenient help of the ladies of Richmond was demanded in the manufacture of sand bags. For many days the operation went on, and thousands of bags were sent to General Magruder, to assist in the fortifications at Yorktown. He was menaced by the Federal fleet, and with his small army, to contend against the overwhelming numbers which at any moment might be landed, his situation caused much uneasiness.

Had his weakness been fully understood by the enemy, he must have fallen a victim to superior strength. Our hands and hearts and prayers were employed for the safety of the little band that lay in immediate range of the guns from the gunboats, which could be brought to bear upon the Army of the Peninsula.

---

* A clerk in the Navy Department, returning to his boarding-house, after eleven o'clock of the night when the news reached Richmond, was so elated that he passed from door to door in the house to see if any one still was awake to share the joy of the news he had heard. It was too much to endure alone.

CHAPTER XXI.

GROWING SCARCITY OF FOOD IN RICHMOND.

DURING all this time, extortion had increased in Richmond, until the complaints of the people grew loud and terrible. Articles of food, absolutely necessary to sustain life, had gone up in price, until it was thought a necessity to legislate upon the traffic. General Winder, the Provost Marshal of the city, in order to remedy the evil, laid a tariff of prices on all articles of domestic produce, but did not legislate upon groceries, liquors, and articles imported from abroad.

The consequence was, the markets were so ill supplied that they had almost as well been closed.

It was next to an impossibility to procure a dinner at all. The meats were so indifferent as scarcely to be fit for food, and fish became the staple article. To secure these, it was necessary to send to market for them before the break of day, and frequently, then, the crowd that pressed around the fish-market was so dense that many were compelled to leave without anything for a dinner, except potatoes and poor beef, and the market men declared the people might "*starve!*"—they would bring in no more supplies until the tariff was withdrawn, or the sale of imported articles regulated in a manner to protect *them* likewise from imposition. They argued, if they were forced to pay the exorbitant demands for sugar, tea, brandy and other articles from abroad, they had a right to charge similar prices for their meats, poultry, butter and vegetables, or they would not sell them. The greatest inconvenience arose from the want of such articles of food as were in the power of hucksters to control. Butter and eggs were never seen, and the fishmongers grew tired of the annoyances to which they were continually subjected by their hungry patrons, and refused to keep up a supply.

Finding our situation so deplorable, and soliciting relief, through a committee of citizens appointed to wait upon the

Provost Marshal, the tariff was raised, and the merchandise of the hucksters again flowed into our markets. From that time until the end of the war we were entirely at their mercy. Being wholly dependent upon them for so much that was essential to existence, they charged what prices they pleased for their merchandise, and we were forced to pay them or abstain from many necessary articles of food altogether. As if to recompense themselves for time and money lost to them while the tariff was enforced by military authority, they doubled the old prices on their merchandise, and where the people groaned under the extortion before, they found the burden so much increased that the groaning was doubled in proportion.

Fishmongers ran up the prices of the piscatorial tribe to such a degree that it became no longer needful to send a servant to market before the dawn of day for a pair of shad or a rockfish for dinner, for so few could afford the luxury that the supply was greater than the demand.

Butter dealers tempted the appetites of their customers with huge rolls of golden, fragrant butter, at the moderate price of one dollar per pound, increased from forty cents before the tariff existed.*

However, as the spring advanced and vegetables became more abundant, the prices declined to a small extent, but not the spirit of extortion. That was unmitigated, and was one of the greatest annoyances to which we were subjected.

While we were engaged in the manufacture of sand bags for General Magruder, and battling against the growing extortion in Richmond, the news from the West came to us in

---

* We were amused to see a sagacious looking old gentleman put on his spectacles and peer curiously at a beautiful print of butter, as it stood on the table of a dealer. After a satisfactory investigation of the choice article, when asked by the polite merchant: "Will you take this, sir?" he replied: "Oh, no, no! I only wished to see what kind of butter it could be to be worth one dollar per pound." Two and a half years later the delicious article would have readily commanded twenty-five dollars per pound!

straggling parcels, and often of the most untrustworthy character.

Anxiety for the fate of the commands of Generals Price and Van Dorn increased the unhappiness of the people. We felt that in Price, Van Dorn, McCulloch, McIntosh, and in the poet-lawyer, General Albert Pike, we possessed a tower of strength in the distant West against the advance of Generals Curtis and Sigel, in command of the enemy's forces, and a confidence of success buoyed up our spirits.

But from the battle of Elkhorn, in Arkansas, there was borne to us intelligence that added two leaves more to the chaplet of mourning for heroes gone. Our brave, invincible, indefatigable Texas Ranger, the gallant McCulloch, and McIntosh, of scarcely less far-famed courage, fell victims to the fury of our enemies.

The gallant old grey-haired warrior of the West was wounded, but in that engagement wrote in characters indelible his name—"*Hero.*"

We read from the pen of an accomplished historian of the South : "Nor is this all the testimony to the heroism of General Price, on the famous battle-fields of Elkhorn. Some incidents are related to us by an officer of his conduct in the retreat, that show aspects of heroism more engaging than even those of reckless bravery. In the progress of the retreat, writes an officer, 'every few hundred yards we would overtake some wounded soldier. As soon as he would see the old General he would cry out, 'General, I am wounded!' Instantly some vehicle was ordered to stop, and the poor soldier's wants attended to. Again and again it occurred, until our conveyances were covered with the wounded. Another one cried out, 'General, I am wounded!' The General's head drooped upon his breast, and his eyes, bedimmed with tears, were thrown up, and he looked in front, but he could see no place to put his poor soldier. He discovered something on wheels in front and commanded : 'Halt! and put this wounded soldier up. I will save my wounded if I lose my whole army.' This explains why the old man's poor soldiers love him so well."

CHAPTER XXII.

OPENING OF THE PENINSULAR CAMPAIGN—MAGRUDER'S SMALL FORCE.

ALTHOUGH from time to time our attention was diverted to the operations of our army in the South and West, our interest centred more immediately on the operations of the Army of Virginia. The spring had dawned upon us, and with the opening of the fine weather active military movements were expected. / Closely watching the designs of the enemy, our sagacious and accomplished General Joseph E. Johnston, in command of the Army of the Potomac, was preparing to evacuate the lines of defence held by him since the victory at Manassas. Anticipating "a change of base" for General McClellan, in the programme of the movement "On to Richmond," he had been quietly removing the army stores, (which had accumulated vast quantities,) and with such skill and address that his designs baffled the wisdom of many of his men to understand. When he had accomplished all this, he prepared to move his army unencumbered.

His soldiers were astonished, and not less the enemy, to whom this unexpected event was made known by the smoke of the soldiers' huts, which had been fired by our army. Baffled in his plans of strategy, the enemy was compelled to make still further changes, and thus was delayed the active opening of the campaign. Every day's delay gave to us an advantage, and proved a hindrance to the successful operations of the enemy.

But with the desertion of the lines of the Potomac the valley of Virginia was not left uncared for. We knew that it was nobly defended by our invincible "Stonewall," who was operating in the neighborhood of Winchester. Near this place, on the 23d of March, occurred the battle of Kernstown. Colonel Ashby, with his fearless cavalry, covered the retreat of our army, and, as on many other occasions, by his reckless bravery and daring exploits, made himself the terror of our foes.

When the town of Winchester was occupied by the Federals, maddened at the thought that it should become the possession of his foes, he remained until the streets began to fill with hostile soldiers, and when they had advanced to within less than two hundred yards of where he sat on his horse, he waved his hat, cheered for the Southern Confederacy, and dashed off at full speed for the Valley Turnpike. Finding his way intercepted by only two of the enemy's pickets, he drew his pistol, shot one, and dragged the other from his horse, terrified and a prisoner, into the Confederate lines.

In the Valley of Virginia, where the name of Stonewall Jackson is repeated with a reverence which approaches to worship, the name of this young cavalier of Virginia is everywhere a household word, and every one has a story to tell of his bravery and daring.

In personal appearance Colonel Ashby was not prepossessing. He was small of stature, delicate in constitution, and was remarkable for his long, black silken beard and glittering black eyes. His manners were reserved, polished, and characterized by the extreme modesty of the Southern gentleman. Pious and devout in his religious experience, there was in him a mixture of the most refined gentleness and conscientiousness with courageous enthusiasm. Instead of the stalwart frame of the relentless adventurer, with which imagination might picture this dashing young cavalier, the small, delicate figure, and the refinement of manner which belonged to him, made him still more remarkable. It is said that when he gave his most daring commands he would gently draw his sabre and wave it around his head, and then his clear-sounding voice would ring out the simple, thrilling words: "Follow me!"

When inspired by such a leader, together with the electrifying influence of our beloved Stonewall Jackson, we wonder not that the Army of the Valley of Virginia performed prodigies of valor and feats of heroism unparalleled in the history of the war. Jackson and Ashby,—"though dead yet shall they live," as long as there are brave hearts to recognize the deeds of brave men, and honest hearts to do justice to true patriotism.

> "Whoever with an earnest soul
> Strives for some end from this low world afar,
> Still upward travels, though he miss the goal,
> And strays—but towards a star!"

Were we dealing in fiction, and wished a model of all that was excellent, all that was noble, all that was heroic, all that was simple in Christian faith and sublime in Christian excellence, we should turn to the memories of Stonewall Jackson, in the hearts of the brave men of the Valley Campaign, and such a character as imagination never portrayed would stand out from the pages of our manuscript, for "truth is stranger than fiction," and we who lived where the names of Jackson and Ashby were as familiar as our own, need go no further on the pages of the history of the mighty dead for our models for heroes.

With sickening anxiety our hearts were turned towards the little band of men that defended the Peninsula. Numbering less than eight thousand effective troops, they were holding a strip of land between two rivers, from either of which the enemy poured upon them from their gunboats an almost continuous fire. The question of evacuation was brought up before a council of war of the officers in command. The necessity seemed imperative, and the decision to leave the Peninsula was urged by all except one, who declared his preference to die in the intrenchments to giving up a position so valued by him. He was sustained by General Magruder, who determined to hold the place until reinforced by General Johnston, and even then until compelled to evacuate or to surrender.

We have listened to details of the campaign of the Peninsula from the lips of the hero of Bethel, until, catching the rare enthusiasm of the brave old man, we felt that to die in such a cause was a death to be sought for. We have ever felt that justice was not done to General Magruder by the Confederate government, perhaps because his plans, thwarted at the very moment which to him was auspicious of good, prevented the development of the genius which might have shown him capable of much greater deeds than those achieved at Bethel. After this decision his men stood in the damp trenches—the shells flying over them almost unceasingly, making the air resound with their terrific rush, and crashing and bursting like terrible lightning —resolved to await reinforcements or to die there!

From General Magruder himself we learned that with his little force of eight thousand he so deployed his men that he kept at bay the enemy, who brought against him an army of perhaps a hundred thousand, until the arrival of reinforcements from the army of General Johnston covered the retreat from the Peninsula.

The day of the passage of the Army of the Potomac through Richmond will long be remembered by those who were then in the city. It was known that they were on their way to the Peninsula, and for days they had been expected to march through the streets of the capital. The greatest interest and excitement prevailed. The morning was bright and beautiful in the early spring, balmy with the odors of the violet and the hyacinth, and the flaunting narcissus, the jonquil, and myriads of spring flowers threw on their parti-colored garments to welcome the army of veterans as they passed.

From an early hour until the sun went down in the West the steady tramp of the soldier was heard on the streets. Continuous cheers went up from thousands of voices; from every window fair heads were thrust, fair hands waved snowy handkerchiefs, and bright eyes beamed "welcome!" Bands of spirit-stirring music discoursed the favorite airs,— Dixie's Land, My Maryland, the Bonny Blue Flag, and other popular tunes—and as the last regiments were passing we heard the strains of "Good-Bye," and tears were allowed to flow, and tender hearts ached as they listened to the significant tune. Soldiers left the ranks to grasp the hands of friends in passing, to receive some grateful refreshment, a small bouquet, or a whispered congratulation. Officers on horseback raised their hats, and some of the more gallant ventured to waft kisses to the fair ones at the doors and windows. We shall never forget the appearance of General Longstreet, the sturdy fighter, the obstinate warrior, as he dashed down Main street surrounded by his splendid staff.

Through other streets poured our cavalry, under their gallant chieftain, the pink of Southern chivalry,—the gay, rollicking, yet bold, daring and venturous "Jeb." Stuart. As we saw him then, sitting easily on the saddle, as though he was born to it, he seemed every inch the cavalier. His stout yet lithe figure, his graceful bearing, his broad, well-formed chest and shoulders, on which was gracefully poised his splendid head, his bright, beaming countenance, lighted up with a smile as pleasant as a woman's, his dark red hair and flowing beard, with his lower limbs encased in heavy cavalry boots, made up the *tout ensemble* of this brave son of Maryland. His genial temperament made him the idol and companion of the most humble of his men, and his deeds of daring and heroic courage made him respected as their leader.

As they swept through our streets on that beautiful morning, with their horses in good order, their own spirits buoyant and cheerful, many of them wearing in their caps bouquets of the golden daffodils of early spring, cheered on by the ringing sounds of the bugle, we thought never to see them pass again with worn-out horses and weary, listless spirits, as they spurred on their broken-down steeds; but so it was.

Twelve months had added another cycle to the age of time. Twelve months made cruelly long by suffering;

twelve months into which had been compressed the events of an age, of many ages to some generations; twelve months since the first gun upon Fort Sumter signaled the commencement of the bloody war; twelve months since the sun of peace had set in darkness or had fled our country. Her gentle presence seemed further off than when first upon the walls of Sumter the hot shell poured their fiery shower. The thirst for blood was not quenched. Upon the red altar of war the ill-fated victims were being laid, and all around the earth drank up the warm stream from human sacrifices.

CHAPTER XXIII.

DISASTERS TO THE CONFEDERATE CAUSE IN THE SOUTHWEST—THE BATTLE OF SHILOH.

THE first anniversary of the battle of Fort Sumter was signalized inauspiciously for the Confederate cause. Fort Pulaski, the principal defence of the harbor of Savannah, had surrendered to the Federals after a brief bombardment. The news was altogether unpleasant and unexpected, as from day to day we received intelligence that the surrender of that fortress was wholly improbable. In a very few days we heard of the surrender of Fort Macon, an important fortification commanding the entrance to Beaufort harbor, on the coast of North Carolina.

About this time we were also discouraged by the news from the Southwest. We were entirely unprepared for disaster on the waters of the Mississippi. Looking forward to success in that direction, the capture of Island No. 10 was a terrible blow to us, and a source of undisguised triumph to our enemies. Their victory was decisive, and from no battle-field had such fruits been gathered by them as from this island in the Mississippi.

In the meantime, from the movements of the enemy on the Tennessee River, it became evident that from that direction we might prepare to hear of another and more extensive battle than had been fought since the commencement of the war. General Beauregard had concentrated all the forces under his command at and around Corinth, a small town situated at the junction of the Memphis and Charleston and the Mobile and Ohio Railroads, about ninety miles east from Memphis. General Albert Sidney Johnston, the Commander-in-Chief of the Army of the West, had taken up a line of march from Murfreesboro, Tennessee, to form a junction with General Beauregard. This army was increased by several regiments from Louisiana, two divisions of General (Bishop) Polk's command from Mobile and Pensacola, and in numbers and appointments, and in the great names of the commanders of this army, it was one of the most magnificent the Confederates ever had in the field.

They were opposed by General Grant, whose victory at Fort Donelson had raised him into favor with the government under which he served. Awaiting reinforcements from General Buell, who was expected to unite with him, General Grant was not disposed to fight, but General Beauregard determined if possible to push him to an issue.

Retarded by the condition of the roads from getting his artillery in position, General Buell was compelled to delay the attack, which inspired Grant to hope that the anxiously expected aid from General Buell would arrive in time to afford him the necessary assistance. The rain and the muddy condition of the roads prevented Beauregard from coming up with the enemy until Saturday evening, the 5th of April. The morning of Sunday, the 6th of April, was to usher in the scenes of another memorable battle, near Shiloh Church, a rude log chapel, in the vicinity of Corinth.

We will not pretend to describe the scenes of this battle as the news came to us in Richmond. The Confederates sustained the character for valor that they had displayed with rarely an exception, from the first gun that was fired at the opening of the war. Their advance and their irresistible attack were compared by General Beauregard, in his official report of the battle, to an "Alpine avalanche." Our men acted with determined coolness and bravery. Our officers displayed the most reckless courage, and even led the men into the very hottest of the fire, and to the mouth of belching cannon. But, as if to satisfy public opinion and wipe out a shadow which had unjustly rested upon his irreproachable name from our defeat at Fort Donelson, General Albert Sidney Johnston, upon whom the hopes of the whole Confederacy hung, bravely exposed his precious life, and fell as he was leading a charge upon the third camp of the enemy.

The wound was inflicted by a musket ball upon the calf of the right leg, and was not at first considered by him as mortal. We read: " Soon after receiving it he gave an order to Governor Harris, who was acting as volunteer aid to him, who, on his return to General Johnston in a different part of the field, found him exhausted and reeling in his saddle. Riding up to him, Governor Harris asked: 'Are you hurt?' To which the dying hero answered: 'Yes, and I fear mortally;' and then, stretching out both hands to his companion, fell from his horse and soon expired. No other wounds were discovered on his person."

The day was already secured in victory to the Confederates, but the death of the brave commander was prudently kept from the army. Amid the cheers of victory this glorious chieftain breathed his last.

The fruits of the victory were to us immense in prisoners, arms, ammunition, means of subsistence, and all things which go to make a victory complete. We had engaged a greatly superior number of stalwart fighting men from the West, and the captured Federal General Prentiss readily admitted to General Beauregard: "You have whipped our best troops to-day."

General Beauregard established his headquarters at Shiloh, and our troops were ordered to sleep on their arms in the camp of the enemy from which they had driven them. "But," says a writer, "the hours which should have been devoted to the refreshment of nature were spent by the troops in a disgraceful hunt after the spoils." The temptation presented by the rich camp of the enemy was more than weak human nature could resist, and the most disgraceful demoralization attacked our army, which had just won the honors of heroes on the bloody field of battle, and degraded the soldier into the plundering brigand. General Beauregard abandoned, unfortunately, the pursuit of the enemy when he arrived at the river, at which it is said Grant could but ill conceal his exultation, and being reinforced by Buell and General L. Wallace with not less than 33,000 fresh troops, prepared to resist the dreaded assault, expected on the succeeding day. At an early hour in the morning the fighting was resumed, but after repeatedly repulsing the overwhelming reinforcements brought against them, the Confederates were driven back, and General Beauregard determined to withdraw from a contest so unequal, and secure for himself the victory of the preceding day. So admirably was the retreat conducted that the enemy did not attempt to follow, and although our success was defeated on that day by the superior numbers of the enemy, the result of the engagement reflected gloriously on the South.

But to our chaplet of mourning was added another leaf. No death was more sadly lamented than that of General Albert Sidney Johnston. Our grief was heightened when we learned that his death might have been averted by prompt and proper surgical attention. It is hard in some cases to submit with resignation to the will of Providence! His military record was untarnished by an act of dishonor, cowardice or inefficiency, and the South felt she had lost one of her bravest, one of her best, one of her most praiseworthy men. In reckoning the lost jewels of this battle the South can count not only General A. S. Johnston, but General Gladden, of South Carolina, Governor Johnston, of Kentucky, Captain Monroe, the son of the venerable Judge Monroe, of Kentucky, Colonel Williams, of Memphis, Colonel Blythe, of Mississippi, and thousands of lesser lights, but dear to some riven heart, which bled afresh under this new and heavy trial.

CHAPTER XXIV.

ACCUMULATING DISASTERS—EFFECT OF THE FALL OF NEW ORLEANS.

AFTER this time, for many months, there was a rapid succession of startling events. Outwardly, Richmond seemed stoically calm, but her great heart heaved and surged like the smothered fires of a volcano. The fall of New Orleans was the next event of importance borne to us with the marvellous swiftness of unwelcome tidings, to call up to the surface the deep throbbings of national sorrow. It was as unexpected as mortifying and discouraging. The wise heads of Richmond had not hesitated to declare the most unlimited confidence in the defensible condition of the Crescent City. It was pronounced impregnable.

The effect of the fall of New Orleans was felt immediately in Richmond in the increased prices charged for such articles of food as were brought from that section of our country. At once the price of sugar was enormously increased, and other groceries were made to share in the exorbitant charge upon that article. We were helpless victims to extortion. A fortunate speculator, having in store a vast quantity of salt when our troubles commenced, grew rich from the sale of this article alone, and was afterwards facetiously styled "Lot's wife." Closely following upon the distressing news of the fall of New Orleans, (by which we lost command of the navigation of the Mississippi, and the rich valley dependent upon it, from the mouth of the river to Memphis,) occurred the evacuation of Norfolk, with its splendid navy-yard, the destruction of the Virginia, and immediately afterwards, the evacuation of the Peninsula, and the blasting of the most cherished hopes of General Magruder and his little army of veterans. Our skies were darkening. Mobile and Charleston were in a perilous condition, and Richmond menaced by one of the largest armies the world ever saw. We were now fully awake to an appreciation of the terrible crisis.

So rapidly succeeded these events that it is wonderful we could endure such an accumulation of ill-luck, or better, such unforeseen disasters in the providential events of the war. The evacuation of Yorktown was accomplished by the Confederates on the third and fourth days of May, and the place was occupied by General McClellan. On the day following occurred the battle of Williamsburgh, caused by an attack of the Federals on the rear-guard of the army of General Johnston. The retreat from Yorktown, decided upon in a council of war of the commanding officers in the Confederate army, after the reinforcement of General Magruder by General Johnston, was admirably conducted, and withdrew our forces to the intrenchments around Richmond, the more conveniently and successfully to operate against the immense army brought against us by McClellan. The battle of Williamsburgh, though engaging so few comparatively of our forces, was one eminently successful to the Confederates. Longstreet's division, which brought up the rear, was engaged from sunrise until sunset, and succeeded in driving back the enemy, capturing three hundred and fifty prisoners and nine pieces of artillery, and leaving on the field, of the killed and wounded, at least three thousand of the enemy. During the night following it resumed its march towards Richmond, evacuating the town of Williamsburg, under the necessity of leaving our killed and wounded in the hands of the enemy.

On the seventh of May an ineffectual attempt was made by the enemy to land at Barhamsville near West Point.

On the 10th occurred the evacuation of Norfolk—decided upon as a military necessity—to bring the forces under the command of General Huger to the more needful position around Richmond. It was accomplished without a blow, and came upon the unsuspecting inhabitants of that city with the effect of a tornado from a cloudless sky. The scenes of the evacuation are said to have been thrilling beyond description. The citizens fled in every direction, in every conveyance that could be secured to take them beyond the lines of the enemy.

The medical director of the Confederate army was warned of the approach of the Federals only in time to gallop on horseback out at one direction while the Federal army was marching into the town from another.

The destruction of the Virginia was the most unexpected and distressing of this series of disasters which came upon us so rapidly at this period of the war.

This invincible iron-clad had become, from her brilliant achievements in the naval engagement in Hampton Roads, the pride of the South. Her loss to us is said to have been of greater importance than if ten thousand men had perished on the field of battle.

The evacuation of Norfolk had been predetermined more than a week before its accomplishment. Mr. Mallory, the Secretary of our navy, had made a visit to the city to superintend the removal of certain naval stores, and yet gave no instructions as to the disposition of this important vessel, properly called the Iron Diadem of the South.

At the time, or about the time of these occurrences, General Magruder was sick at Westover, on James River, and being impressed with the probability of the destruction of the Virginia, addressed a letter to Mr. Mallory, giving some advice, and offering some suggestions as to the disposition which might be made of the Virginia; and fearing lest Mr. Mallory might not be impressed by advice once tendered, arose, after retiring at night, sick and disheartened, lighted a candle, and wrote again, urging the necessity of preventing the destruction of this admirable vessel. As the sequel proved, the suggestions were unheeded, to the mortification of General Magruder, and the injury of the whole Confederacy.

She was destroyed under the immediate orders of her commander, Commodore Tatnell, on the morning of the 11th of May, in the vicinity of Craney Island.

He alleged that he had been betrayed into the necessity of destroying the vessel by firing her magazine, upon the misrepresentations of his pilot, who at first assured him they could, after lightening her so that she would draw less water, carry her to within a safe distance from Richmond—but who, after she had been lifted so as to render her unfit for action, declared that they could not carry her beyond the Jamestown flats, up to which point the shore on either side was occupied by the enemy. This statement, however, has been denied by the pilots, and it is due them to make known facts, which if not noticed, would leave a reflection on their courage and loyalty. At any rate, in the dead hour of the night, in haste, in obedience to the command of the Commodore, the ship was put ashore, the crew landed on Craney Island, the train set to her magazine, and this noble vessel, worth to us more than fifty thousand men in the field, was blown to the four winds of heaven, and the naval approach to Richmond left wholly unguarded.

How far the government may have been responsible for this act of madness, (as it then seemed to us,) we cannot pretend to say; but we do know that no measured censure was heaped upon the persons responsible for the wanton destruction of what was so invaluable to us in the conduct of the war. The surprise and indignation of the people seemed unappeasable, in the threatening aspect of affairs which then hovered over us. The destruction of the Virginia occurred at five A. M., on the 11th of May.

It is fair, from all the facts stated in reference to it, to suppose that it was predetermined. Mr. Pollard, in his history of the war, says: "During the morning of the same day, a prominent politician in the streets of Richmond was observed to be very much dejected. He remarked that it was an evil day for the Confederacy. On being questioned by his intimate friends he declared to them that the government had determined upon, or assented to the destruction of the Virginia, and that he had learned it from the highest sources of authority in the Capital."

At that time, as there was no possibility of knowing by telegraph of the destruction of the vessel, that took place at five o'clock that morning, it is presumable, at least, to infer that the act had been decided upon, or assented to, by the government under certain contingencies.

There never was a period of more alarming excitement than this in Richmond during the entire war, until the time of the ultimate evacuation of the city. The lines of the Chickahominy were invested by the enemy. The Valley of Virginia, filled by their forces, threatened Richmond in that direction. The defences on the river were as yet untested, and the obstructions in the channel were untried, and feared to be ineffectual to prevent the approach of the flotilla of gunboats that threatened us from the James River, and from which we felt we had the most to dread.

The hasty adjournment and dispersion of the Confederate Congress had no tendency to reassure us. The members were hastily leaving a place so dangerously menaced. The State Legislature, whose action taught a useful lesson to the government, passed a resolution declaring their intention to reduce the city to ashes rather than permit it to fall into the hands of the enemy, or to suffer the terrors and destruction of bombardment. An appropriation was made for the removal of the women and children of the indigent of the inhabitants, and every sign betokened the purposed destruction of the city if attacked by the gunboats.

Citizens were leaving by hundreds in all directions, and in all manner of conveyances. Baggage-wagons, heaped up with trunks, boxes and baskets, were constantly rattling through the streets. Houses were left deserted, or occupied by the more courageous refugees, who were glad to secure a temporary home. Business was suspended, and the only consideration of the people was the means of flight, if it became absolutely necessary. It was known that the family

6*

of the President had been sent to Raleigh, North Carolina, and those of our citizens who bravely determined to remain if allowed, or to leave at the last moment, kept their trunks packed, and all things ready for flight at a moment's warning. Some of the officers of the government, seized with the gunboat panic, decamped with the flying populace. We have never known such a panic. Our only chance for safety depended on the half-finished fort at Drewry's Bluff, which mounted four guns, to impede the progress of the much-dreaded Monitor and the terrible gunboats. We had then very few torpedoes in the channel, and they could not be relied upon. The suspense was terrible, and beyond description. Pale dismay sat on every countenance, and hearts were well nigh bursting at the misery of our situation. To add to our wretchedness the waters of James River were so high that it was feared the obstructions would be swept away by the current. But a more alarming feature was noticeable in the ominous-looking boxes that were brought out of the offices of the different departments, containing the archives of the government, and marked for Columbia, South Carolina. It was evident to a casual observer that a removal of the government was contemplated.

The question, Where shall I go? was the one that possessed the minds of the citizens. The approach to Gordonsville was threatened, and the only safe retreat seemed on the south side of Richmond, and we knew not how long we should be safe in that section of the Confederacy. On the morning of the 13th of May, the fleet of the Federal gunboats opened an attack on our fortification at Drewry's Bluff. The sound of the guns in hostile action was for the first time heard in Richmond. Various reports were in circulation in the city, and the most intense anxiety prevailed. While the excitement was at its height, an extraordinary scene occurred. In an accidental meeting of the citizens in the City Hall, at the enthusiastic call of the crowd, impromptu addresses were delivered by the Governor of Virginia and the Mayor of the city, in which they pledged themselves to the citizens against the surrender of Richmond. The Governor was peculiarly warm in his expressions, and the Mayor declared that rather than, at that time, surrender the city founded by his own ancestors, he would resign the office of the mayoralty, and though bending under the approach of three score years and ten, he would shoulder the musket himself in defence of the capital. These declarations were received with wild, ringing shouts by the citizens. Nor were they the demonstrations of the mob. In the audience were some of the most wealthy of our population, who declared they would fire their own beautiful residences, in preference to delivering up the city to our foes, and the most reliable of the men of Richmond were ready to apply the torch to the Capitol, and to blow the statue of the Father of his country to atoms, rather than see them in the hands of the invader.

Night brought the news of a signal victory; the flotilla had been compelled to retire from the contest with our shore batteries, and quietly dropped down the stream, satisfied of the impracticability of the water route to Richmond.

The reaction of joy upon the minds of the people was quite as intense as the suspense and agony had been in proportion terrible. Once again we breathed freely, and pursued the usual avocations of business, until the next turn in the enginery of war should place us in the midst of a fresh agitation.

In regard to General McClellan's skill in military affairs, we are only prepared to say that until the final surrender of the city, the most serious danger that threatened us, was from the strategy which threw him in front of Richmond, and sent his terrifying gunboats to frighten us from our homes in May, 1862.

CHAPTER XXV.

THE BATTLES OF SEVEN PINES AND FAIR OAKS.

WE had passed through a truly trying ordeal, and when tidings came that all the danger from the much dreaded gunboats had been prevented by their signal repulse at Drewry's Bluff, the reaction of joy upon the minds of the nervous and delicate was quite as overpowering as the intensity of anxiety. Our noble women, who had bravely borne the terrible trial, with pale, rigid features, and eyes unmoistened by refreshing tears, gave vent to feelings drawn out in such torturing tension, in prayers of thankfulness to a Supreme Deliverer, and their pent up tears flowed in the unrestrained measure of gratitude.

But there was little time to give to rejoicing. Along the lines of the Chickahominy, within sight of Richmond, with hostile intent, lay two great opposing armies, and we well knew that the collision of battle must soon shake the very foundations of the city. Taking a useful lesson from its unprepared condition for the comfort of the sick and wounded of the previous encounter, vigorous endeavors were made to meet the necessity of the demand. The first consideration that brought into exercise the untiring energies and industry of our ladies, was in the preparation of couches for the wounded. In these labors of duty there were no weary hands, and now there was no time to lose. Impending dangers warned us of necessary exertions to meet, if not to avoid them, and even the hours of the day of rest, the Holy Sabbath hours were again devoted to labors with the sewing machine and needle, in the manufacture of bed-ticks for the hospitals. In these assemblages of our ladies, when the startling occurrences of the last few weeks were discussed, the unprecedented flight of Congress and certain of the chicken-hearted officials of the government received a merited share of ridicule. "Self-preservation is the first law of nature," and "the better part of valor is discretion," were the favorite aphorisms applied to the swift-footed legislators and the flying officials. But we had not long to discuss the harmless flight of our law-givers and government officers, before the crash of strife riveted our attention.

> "Then shook the hills with thunder riven,
> Then rushed the steeds to battle driven,
> And louder than the bolts of Heaven
> Far flashed the red artillery!"

On the 23d of May, the Confederate forces were defeated at Hanover Court House, about twenty miles above Richmond on the Central Railroad of Virginia, by the Federals under General Fitz John Porter, but it was reserved for the 31st of May to bring so closely upon us the rush and shock of battle as that the hills on which our city is built, shook with the reverberations of cannon, as though an earthquake were undermining the foundations. The windows in the buildings rattled, and from exposed points, where the hum of business did not disturb the sound, the whir and whiz of the musketry were like the sound of a mighty rushing wind, with furious showers of hail.

The weather was cloudy and dull, and a rain had been falling, when at about two o'clock in the afternoon, the heavy booming of artillery notified us that the struggle for human life had begun. It was awfully grand! As peal after peal broke upon the still, humid atmosphere, and the glorious sublimity of the scene was present in imagination, it was sadly overpowered by the crushing knowledge, that with each note of the battle-music, were intermingled the groans of wounded and dying fellow-creatures, whose lives were the sacrifice to the mad fury of political ambition. Let those whose fancy delights to revel in such phases of the sublime, to whom the shock of crashing armies is possessed of terrible fascination, live, as has lived the writer, in a beleaguered city, where for days and weeks was heard almost incessantly the dread music of artillery, and every breath of air inhaled, was mingled with the vapor of war, and then let them reflect, at every sound which awakens in them the indescribable thrill of ecstasy, that some human being is deprived of the life that bounds so delightfully in their pulses, that some heart is quivering in the death agony, and they will be satisfied to experience no more the ecstatic emotion purchased at a price so dear to some unfortunate fellow-mortal.

On this afternoon, on the field of Seven Pines, this dreadful scene in the monstrous life-drama was enacting. The reverberations of cannon ceased not until the darkness of night fell to hide from each other the furious combatants. It was at this hour that our accomplished General, Joseph E. Johnston, was wounded. After having successfully attacked the van of McClellan's army, and driving it back more than two miles, through its own camp and from its intrenchments, he was struck by a fragment of shell. But the day had been gained, and an utter rout of the enemy was only prevented by the unaccountable tardiness of General Huger, who failed to bring his division in position to operate effectively. It had been a bloody afternoon's work. We had lost more than four thousand men in killed, wounded and prisoners, and the acknowledged loss of the enemy was over ten thousand, besides ten pieces of artillery, six thousand muskets, and various other spoils. On the morning of the 1st of June the enemy made a demonstration of attack upon our lines, but were driven back by the dashing gallantry of Colonel Godwins, of the Ninth Virginia regiment, who, with intrepid daring, far in advance of his command, cheering his men to the onset, was wounded by a Minié ball in the leg, and in a moment after had his horse shot under him, which, in falling, crushed the hip of the fearless rider. At last reinforcements came up, and the enemy were repulsed. This engagement is known as the battle of Fair Oaks. It occurred on the Sabbath.

Many of the wounded had been conveyed to the city on the previous evening, but on that day ambulances were driven in all directions over the city, bearing as their freight the mutilated victims of the battle. We had no longer to congratulate ourselves on the erring aim of our enemies. The numbers who were borne to us with shattered limbs, torn by crashing shell or crushed by the more certain if less horrible Minié ball, told unmistakably that our enemy had improved in marksmanship.

Our hospital arrangements were much increased, and had greatly improved during the time that had supervened since the battle of Manassas, which had found us so ill prepared to take care of those who suffered in our cause. But they were still very defective. Private houses, which had been left tenantless by the frightened occupants, who had fled during the existence of the gunboat panic, were many of them impressed for hospital purposes. But so short a time had been left for preparation, that the sick and wounded, in some instances, were brought into houses which alone possessed the friendly shelter of the roof and walls to accommodate the sufferers. On the evening of the battle of Seven Pines we saw men wounded and bleeding brought into private hospitals, only opened a day or two before that time, in which there was neither bed, nor pillow, nor food, nor surgeon, nor nurse, nor cook, nor anything but the bare floors to receive their shattered, aching limbs. Their wants were supplied in a few hours by the citizens, who cooked and sent refreshments, beds, pillows and blankets, water, soap, and all that could for the time relieve the helpless sufferers. Surgeons were procured, and kind and tender women bathed the bleeding wounds, washed from the hair and beards of the soldiers the stiffened mud and gore, and administered refreshments and restoratives to the worn-out, weary, dying men. Kindly words were whispered which strengthened the fainting spirit, and tears of sympathy coursed the cheek of woman as she bent over the couch, and served as a healing balm to the bleeding wound, and a life-infusing spirit to the brave fellows who had fought for their wives, their children, their homes.

On this evening, as a kind woman bent over the stalwart

figure of a noble Georgian, and washed from his hair and beard the stiffened mud of the swamps of the Chickahominy, where he fell from a wound through the upper portion of the right lung, and then gently bathed the bleeding gash left by the Minié ball, as he groaned and feebly opened his eyes, he grasped her hand, and in broken whispers, faint from suffering, gasping at every breath, "I could—bear—all—this—for myself—alone—but my—wife and my—six little—ones," (and then the large tears rolled down his weather-beaten cheeks,) and overcome he could only add, "Oh, God! oh, God!—how will—they endure it?" She bent her head and wept in sympathy. The tall man's frame was shaking with agony. She placed to his fevered lips a cooling draught, and whispered: "Think of yourself just now; God may raise you up to them, and if not, He will provide for and comfort them." He feebly grasped her hand once more, and a look of gratitude stole over his manly face, and he whispered, "God bless you! God bless you! God bless you! kind stranger!"

Our summer's work had begun. The daily rounds at the hospitals, from dawn till night were performed by the ladies of Richmond, to whom those sad duties, though so painful, were the chief delight. In no other way did they feel that they could properly testify their gratitude to the soldiers who were periling their lives for the safety of the women of their country. Nobly, cheerfully and perseveringly were these duties performed. All day they would sit amid the sickening odors of the hospital, fan the fevered brow, and bathe the gaping wound, and read from the book of life, and whisper words of strength and hope to the despondent, and point with the finger of faith to the glories of the upper world, where no more strife shall ever enter, where the battle-cry is never heard, to the poor soldier as he approached the "dark valley of the shadow of death." It was woman's duty to minister thus to the suffering and dying, and to place upon the breast of the youthful unknown hero the flowers of summer, to be borne with him to his last resting-place in the burial-ground of the soldier,—love offerings of national gratitude.

The casualties in the battle of Seven Pines did not extend largely to our prominent officers. Much concern was felt for the condition of General Johnston, but a few days developed signs of recovery for him, and we were comforted.

Conspicuous in the fight at Seven Pines was the daring impetuosity of the troops from Louisiana. Maddened by the thought of the tyrannical rule of Butler, they rushed into the fight with the battle-cry,—" Butler and New Orleans!" and again would ring out : "Boys, remember Butler!" and with the shock of a hurricane they drove before them the opposing foe. When the battles were over, on the field occupied by the enemy was found hanging on the branch of a tree a Louisiana soldier, on whose breast was fastened a placard, with the ominous words : " No quarter for Louisianians."*

The thunderings of cannon had ceased, the shower of Minié balls no more fell upon the heads of our soldiers, and we were permitted to peep beyond the bars of our siege prison for a little distance into the óuter world.

CHAPTER XXVI.

JACKSON'S CAMPAIGN IN THE VALLEY.

WE must leave, for a little time, the Confederate capital and its surroundings to look after our indomitable Jackson in his operations in the Valley, and ascertain what he did for our security in Richmond.

We left him in March retreating up the valley from Kernstown, to find him in May routing the army of Milroy

---

* We have since heard from a Federal officer that the "black flag" was raised against them on that day.

at McDowell, fearlessly moving on his little army against General Banks at Winchester, who had come among us with all the confidence and assurance of a conqueror, and driving him ingloriously from his stronghold with such success that the Federal commander wrote to the authorities at Washington, when on the opposite side of the Potomac, "There were never more grateful hearts in the same number of men, than when at midday on the 30th of May we stood on the opposite shore." He had already on the 23d of May driven the Federals from, and taken possession of Front Royal.

Carefully guarding the prisoners and spoils, we find him hastily retreating up the Valley from Winchester, preventing the junction of General Fremont and General Shields, engaging the enemy at Harrisonburg, (where we lost our gallant knight, the noble Ashby,) and then hastening on with his reliable compeer, General Ewell, to fight Fremont and Shields at Port Republic, and Cross Keys in Rockingham County, and on the 8th and 9th days of May routing their forces, driving them across the Shenandoah, where they drew up in line of battle, awaiting, in impotent idleness, further pursuit from our worn out and exhausted forces.

Finding it altogether impracticable to scale a Stonewall, when protected with a *chevaux de frise* of rebel muskets and bayonets, Fremont took up his line of retreat towards Winchester, and abandoned the idea of the need of his assistance to General McClellan at Richmond.

This brilliant campaign was accomplished with but a small force, but they were under the most superior discipline, and inspired by the bravery and example of the bravest and best of men. A gifted historian writes:—

"This famous campaign must, indeed, take a rank in the history of the war unrivalled by any other in the rapidity of its movements, and in the brilliancy of its results, accomplished with the means at its command. Its heroic deeds revived the hopes of the South, and threw the splendor of sunlight over the long lines of the Confederate host. By a series of rapid movements, which occupied but a few weeks, General Jackson had, with inferior numbers, defeated successfully four generals, with as many armies, swept the Valley of Virginia of hostile forces, made the Federal authorities tremble in their capital, and frustrated the combination by which the enemy had purposed to aid General McClellan, and environ Richmond by immense converging armies."

Jackson was then prepared to bring his invincible little army to the immediate defence of the capital.

But from the brilliant achievements of this campaign another leaf was added to our chaplet of mourning. Ashby was no more! The brave, gallant, daring young cavalier of Virginia had fallen! Our drink was mingled with weeping, and the mourning wreath was growing heavy. Ah, how heavy! It is not within the power of our pen to do justice to a character so nobly spotless. All the elements that combine to make and embellish a character, truly pure and great, were possessed eminently by this young man. His name, his deeds are immortal. They are a precious legacy to Virginia, to the South. His glorious renown their youth may emulate. Cut down, alas! in the blossomed beauty of a manhood that would have ripened into such perfection.

> "The good die first,
> But they whose hearts are dry as summer dust
> Burn to the socket!"

Peace to thy ashes, young hero! We would not awaken thee from thy dreamless slumber, and behold the throes of agony that would tear thy soul, by the defeat of the cause which inspired thee to such deeds of daring. We would not wish that thy bright beaming glance should take in the now wasted, but once beautiful and happy Valley of the Shanandoah, over which thy milk-white steed bore thee on to world-renowned feats of heroism. We would not have thy brave, yet gentle heart riven by sight of the bare chimneys, the blackened walls, the desolate homesteads, all along the pathway of the invader! We would not have thee tortured by the groans of the widowed, the childless, the orphaned! Virginia, thy cherished mother, is a widow and weeps for her children! Rest, under the unfading wreath, woven by thy chivalry, over which Fame has flung her immortal light, to gild with its lustre the pages of all the future.

> "Soldier, rest! Thy warfare o'er,
> Sleep the sleep that knows no breaking,
> Dream of battle-fields no more,
> Days of conflict—nights of waking!"

With the exception of the famous Black Horse Company, our Confederate Cavalry had thus far done very little to entitle them to distinguished notice. Mounted on good horses, which they managed with the ease and skill of Centaurs, being trained, many of them from boyhood almost constantly in the saddle, they were a gay, rollicking set, petted and fêted wherever they appeared. The orderings of the war had been such as to leave undeveloped the powers they were destined to bring into action, in a career of brilliancy and dashing heroism. The time had at last come when they should redeem their reputation from certain reproaches cast upon it, and loom up into enviable notice upon the Confederate horizon.

CHAPTER XXVII.

STUART'S RAID.

ON the 12th of June, when the battles of Seven Pines and Fair Oaks began to be spoken of as "things that were," General Stuart sallied out with his well-mounted horsemen, to make a reconnoissance in the rear of the enemy. Inspired by the novelty of the adventure, and burning with purpose high and animated, these bold Southern cavaliers dashed on across the Chickahominy, through the grounds of the enemy in Hanover and New Kent counties, destroying their camps, dispersing their forces, and making their way around to the vicinity of the White House, on the Pamunkey River, intercepted a train of cars, (and by shooting the engineer, they nearly succeeded in capturing the train,) and destroyed millions of dollars' worth of stores belonging to the enemy, thoroughly acquainted with his position. All this they accomplished, besides the capture of hundreds of prisoners, mules and horses, with the loss of only one of their number, the brave and gallant Captain Letoni, of Essex County, Virginia. While nobly leading a charge he fell, pierced by five bullets.

From the journal of an officer on General Stuart's staff we read, "At the same time we had destroyed the enemy's communication, burned property to the amount of millions, captured hundreds of prisoners, horses and mules, and put the whole Federal army in fear and consternation.

"We were warmly greeted everywhere on our return, and every sort of honor was paid to General Stuart's name. This ovation was extended to officers and men, and wherever any one who had taken part in this famous expedition was seen, he was besieged with questions, gazed at as a hero, and entreated to relate his own adventures and the story of the ride.

"The Richmond press teemed with praises of General Stuart and his followers, and even the journals of New York did not fail to render homage to the conception and execution of the bold enterprise."

Of the death of Captain Letoni, General Stuart, in his official report of the Pamunkey expedition, says: "The next squadron moved to the front under the lamented Captain Letoni, making a most brilliant and successful charge upon the enemy's picked ground, and after a hotly-contested hand-to-hand conflict, put him to flight, but not until the gallant Captain had sealed his devotion to his native soil with his blood."

The burial of Letoni is beautifully portrayed in an extract from a private letter:—"Lieutenant Letoni carried his brother's dead body to Mrs. Brockenborough's plantation an hour or two after his death. On this sad and lonely errand he met a party of Yankees, who followed him to Mrs. Brockenboroughs, and stopping there told him that as soon as he placed his brother's body in friendly hands he must surrender himself a prisoner. Mrs. Brockenborough sent for an Episcopal clergyman to perform the funeral ceremonies, but the enemy would not let him pass.

Then, with a few other ladies, a fair-haired little girl, whose apron was filled with white flowers, and a few faithful slaves, who stood reverently near, a pious Virginia matron read the solemn and beautiful burial service over the cold, still form of one of the noblest gentlemen and most intrepid officers of the Confederate army. She watched the sods heaped on the coffin lid, then sinking on her knees in sight and hearing of the foe, she committed his soul's welfare and the stricken hearts he had left behind him, to the mercy of the All Father. *Latane*

The fate of the lamented Latoni is touchingly described in verse by the pen of the gifted poet J. R. Thompson, of Virginia, and we copy it in full, as commemorative of the noble devotion of the women of the State, and of the ruthless cruelty of the enemy :

> "The combat raged not long, but ours the day;
>   And though the hosts had compassed us around
> Our little band rode proudly on its way,
>   Leaving one gallant comrade glory-crowned,
> Unburied on the field he died to gain,
> Single of all his men amid the hostile slain.
>
> One moment on the battle's edge he stood,
>   Hope's halo like a helmet round his hair—
> The next beheld him dabbled in his blood,
>   Prostrate in death, and yet in death how fair!
> Even thus he passed through the red gate of strife,
> From earthly crowns and palms to an immortal life.
>
> "A brother bore his body from the field,
>   And gave it unto strangers' hands that closed
> The calm blue eyes, on earth forever sealed,
>   And tenderly the slender limbs composed:
> Strangers, yet sisters, who with Mary's love,
> Sat by the open tomb, and weeping looked above."

"A little child strewed roses on the bier—
    Pale roses, not more stainless than his soul,
Nor yet more fragrant than his life sincere,
    That blossomed with good actions—brief but whole.
The aged matron and the faithful slave
    Approached with lowly feet the hero's lowly grave.

"No man of God might say the burial rite
    Above the 'rebel,'—thus declared the foe
That blanched before him in the deadly fight,
    But woman's voice in accents soft and low
Trembling with pity, touched with pathos, read
    O'er his hallowed dust the ritual for the dead.

"'Tis sown in weakness, it is raised in power,"
    Softly the promise floated on the air,
And the sweet breathings of the sunset hour
    Came back responsive to the mourner's prayer.
Gently they laid him underneath the sod,
    And left him with his fame, his country, and his God.

"Let us not weep for him whose deeds endure;
    So young, so brave, so beautiful, he died
As he had wished to die;—the past is sure,
    Whatever yet of sorrow may betide
Those who still linger on the stormy shore,
    Change cannot harm him now, nor fortune touch him more.

"And when Virginia, leaning on her spear,
    Victrix et vincere, the conflict done,
Shall raise her mailed hand to wipe the tear
    That starts as she recalls each martyred son,
No prouder memory her breast shall sway
    Than thine, our early lost, lamented Letoni."

This expedition of General Stuart served to excite a spirit of adventure in his men. It gave a fresh impetus to the cavalry service, and the brilliant, dashing exploits of General "Jeb" Stuart and his gallant horsemen, became, from that time, famous in the annals of the war.

CHAPTER XXVIII.

THE SEVEN DAYS BATTLES' ON THE PENINSULA.

FROM its relative local position in the heart of Virginia, the principal theatre of the war, Richmond was the point of the greatest strategic importance in the Southern Confederacy. Its capture would necessarily involve the surrender of the State to our enemies, and drive us into a more insecure position in one or the other of the States farther south. From its political importance as the seat of government, the surrender of Richmond would also so weaken the confidence of the people that a speedy demoralization might be expected, and all hope of triumph in the cause of the South, in consequence, extinguished. The capture of our capital was, therefore the most cherished aim of the Federals—the security of Richmond the all-important object of the Confederates. To secure their ends the rival governments left no means unapplied.

The Federal army, furnished with all that was needful to compass the destruction of a weaker foe, was declared to be, in all its appointments, "ready and complete." It was still knocking at the gates of Richmond. The repulse of the gun-boats and the defeat at Seven Pines had not sufficed to drive it from the vicinity of the Rebel Capital. The trepidation of our government had subsided, nor was this alone calculated to reassure the fainting courage of the people. Rising superior to temporary misfortune, we felt in the name of our great Commander-in-Chief a talisman of security, and our faith in the noble ardor and sublime fortitude of our soldiery, triumphed over the trembling apprehensions of the government.

At this period a council of war was held in Richmond. Nobly prominent in this memorable caucus stood our beloved chieftain, General Lee. Sustaining him were Generals D. H. Hill, A. P. Hill, Longstreet, Wise, Magruder, Branch, Ripley, Anderson, Whiting, and Huger; while calmly looking, with the strange, indomitable courage settling on his grave impenetrable face, was our immortal Stonewall Jackson.

The question under consideration was whether Richmond should be surrendered to the young Napoleon, with his invincible host, or defended even to its altars and its firesides. The latter was agreed upon, the means for its accomplishment decided, and the members of this remarkable caucus adjourned to meet next amid the thunder, and smoke, and storm of conflict. This occurred on the 25th of June.

On the afternoon of that day, just before sunset, the writer of these pages stood upon the roof of the Capitol, and unassisted by the use of glasses, saw on all sides, as far as the eye could reach, the encampments of the soldiery, in waiting for the most furious contest of arms ever then expected on this continent. The immediate proximity to the terrible theatre upon which were so soon to be enacted scenes appalling in fearfulness, wrought in her soul emotions indescribable. No thought of fear or danger possessed her. Her faith in the triumph of what she conscientiously regarded to be the right, made failure altogether improbable; nor did a dream of glory thrill her spirit, but a dire deprecation of the dreadful means for the purchase of victory. As in childhood she asked, why must wars ever come? Beneath her lay the white tents of the mighty host, dotting the landscape like snow-flakes in winter. In a few days this mighty host might be dispersed and wandering like a frightened flock. As she stood, and gazed, and thought, she turned to a friend, and asked, "When will the battle begin?" The words had only just escaped her lips, when the distant boom of the cannon disturbed the stillness of the afternoon, and then in rapid succession, somewhere along the lines the oft repeated "boom! boom! boom!" furnished a reply for the gentleman, and he exclaimed, almost in a whisper, "The ball is opened! the skirmishing has commenced!" From the depths of her soul she prayed, "Lord have mercy!"

It is said that the Emperor Napoleon I., in the days of the French Revolution, when a mere stripling, and an interested witness of the exciting scenes of the French capital, remarked of the noise of artillery, "That shall be my music."

On the morning of the 26th of June, just as the day dawned, we were awakened by the dreadful music which gave such exquisite delight to the Emperor. At Mechanicsville, a few miles distant from our city, all day the battle raged, and when the twilight came on, and the wounded were arriving, and we asked for tidings from the field, we heard of a terrible fight. But "Jackson is in the rear of the enemy, and all is well." Sleep fled from the eyelids of many. There were none of us who had not friends, the nearest and dearest, exposed to the dreadful hazards of battle, and we could give no time to repose when our hearts were torn with apprehensions for their safety.

By day-break on the morning of the 27th, the dreadful music once more filled our ears, and some of us, unable to find diversion in our more immediate surroundings sought quiet retreats in the suburbs of the city to listen to the sounds of conflict. As we stood on Maury Hill, in the extreme western part of the city, the roar of artillery seemed interminable, and the rattling of musketry like a shower of hail.

Again all day the battle raged, and when the night came on, and friends, wounded, were brought in, the tidings came again, "All is well!" The battle at Gaines's Mill had been won by the Hills and General Longstreet, who had defeated Fitz John Porter, and had driven him beyond the Chickahominy.

We were, however, in a perilous situation. General McClellan had succeeded in posting a portion of his army on the side of the Chickahominy next to Richmond, and the dislodgment of it was a matter of the most profound importance. But the talismanic words which found expression on every tongue kept us reassured. "Jackson is in their rear," "Stonewall is behind them," and we looked forward with calm though intense interest for the developments of the coming day. On the 28th and 29th occurred the battle of the Peach Orchard. The famous flank movement of General

Jackson, and the furious charge of Stuart's cavalry swept everything before them with the fury of the whirlwind. The attack upon the Federals was terrible—the carnage dreadful. The enemy fell back across the Chickahominy, and the battle was gloriously victorious to the Confederates!

Night brought the news to us in Richmond, and closed in mercy over the horrid scenes of carnage and strife. "All is well," was once more the tidings, and our hearts, though grateful, were lifted up in prayer to God, to stay the tide of blood. The next morning was the Sabbath. We understood that the enemy were retreating. The clouds were lifting from over Richmond, and we prayed, "If it be Thy will, oh God, drive from us our enemies, but let no more blood be shed." But it was not to be so. On that morning our forces engaged those of General McClellan at Savage's Station, on the York River Railroad, where they attempted to break through our lines, and were, to use an expression of one of their men, (taken prisoner,) "mowed down," and they left to continue a retreat, which was beginning to appear to them a hopeless one.

The sounds of artillery were growing fainter and fainter to us in the city, as the enemy were driven further and further away from Richmond, and we knew that "all" for us continued to be "well."

By daybreak on Monday morning the pursuit of the enemy was resumed, and on that day occurred the engagement at Frazer's Farm. It rivalled in the terror of its details any battle of the series of the previous days. Our forces were almost wholly unsupported by artillery, and worn out and exhausted by their long continued fighting. General Hill's division had wrought prodigies of valor, but were at one time driven back, which revived the courage of our enemies, and for a while they made a bold stand. General Hill, noticing the temporary advantage to the enemy, rode rapidly up to the position of his brigade, and cheered them on encouragingly. Catching inspiration from his gallant conduct, they loudly caught up the cheers of their General, and rushed fiercely on the foe. Supposing they were heavily reinforced, the Federals paused, and this long continued fight concluded in the winning of the field by the Confederates. The morning of the succeeding day brought to us in Richmond the tidings of the battle of Frazer's Farm. It was evident to us that the fighting could not continue much longer. The enemy were retreating to seek the friendly cover of their gunboats, and the chief object of the fight of that day would be to prevent and cut off the retreat, and thus capture the army of McClellan. The utmost anxiety prevailed in the city. The faint booming sounds of the cannon signalled that they were much further off. Yet the issue was not decided, the interest was not diminished.

Early on the morning of the 1st of July the fight was renewed by General Magruder. It is said that on no day previous had the fighting been so terrible, or confined to so small a space. There the enemy were strongly fortified, and our forces, few in number, anxiously hoping for reinforcements, charged across an open field, upon belching batteries, under a sheet of flame from artillery. In this fight General Magruder was accused of great rashness, and many declared that he was under the intoxicating influence of ardent spirits; but whether from this cause the lives of so many of our men were sacrificed, or the want of proper reinforcements, or the superior skill displayed by General McClellan in the management of his retreat, it was safely effected, and under cover of his gunboats, on which the army took passage, the siege was raised, and the capital of the Confederacy relieved from the presence of its dangerous visitors, and once more the sunlight of prosperity shed its lustre on the Confederate cause.

To the master mind that conceived the brilliant plan which brought to us success, be all credit given; nor be much less accorded to the wonderful men who always made the flank movement in the right moment, and in the rear of the enemy wrought the distress to him which brought to us the victory. The actions of our officers were determined and irresistible, and it seems wonderful that so few mistakes were made through such a long and protracted series of the hottest engagements. Public opinion reflected rather severely on General Magruder and General Huger. It was said if Magruder had been less rash, and Huger less tardy, the Federal army had never reached the security of their gunboats.

But one thing now appears evident: had General McClellan received proper reinforcements, he might never have been compelled to retreat, and had he been less skillful as a commander, he could not have saved his army from capture. It has ever since been regarded at the South as one of the most masterly retreats in the records of military history. We of Richmond are only too fully aware who it was that gave us the greatest cause for alarm, and shook most seriously the foundations of the rebel capital. And when we remember the superior advantages of General Lee's position, the immense numbers under his command, and the numerous reserves never under fire during the seven days' fight, our admiration for the skill and generalship of the Federal commander is unqualified.

Undisguised regrets were expressed at the failure of the Confederates to secure the army of the Federals, but a feeling of intense thankfulness, too deep for words, went up to God from hearts so long kept in anxiety during the bloody scenes around our city.

The seven days' battles around Richmond left us enough to do. We had neither the time nor inclination to make merry over the triumphs of our arms. There were no noisy jubilations over this succession of victories. There were no bells rung, no cannon fired, no illuminations, no indecent manifestations of exulting victory over our enemies. Prisoners were not insulted in our streets. Captured Generals were allowed on their parole to walk unmolested through the city; but there was a deep undercurrent of intense gratitude, which was not uttered in measured phrases, but which beamed from every countenance, which was felt in the thrilling pressure of the hand, which was seen in the tear that sparkled in the eye of woman, which was read in the cheerful serenity which brooded over the late heaving and terrified city, and the gradual hum of business, which took the place of the thunders of battle.

But not wholly was business suspended during the entire time. The more thoughtful, and those with whom self respect triumphed over the extortionate greed of Mammon, suspended their usual occupations, and devoted themselves to the relief of the helpless sufferers nightly crowded into our city from the battle-fields. The labors of the hospitals admitted no recreation. Duties to the sick and wounded and dying were performed by many of our noble women, while their hearts ached with a fresh thrill of agony at every repeated sound of the cannon. Selfishness is inherent in human nature. They were keenly alive to their own peculiar troubles, while none the less actively were their sympathies called forth towards the helpless strangers they attended. We had all dear ones to think of, to be anxious for; but every soldier was our brother, and distinctions were forgotten when their suffering was to be alleviated.

Richmond suffered heavily in the loss of citizens in these battles. There was scarcely a family that had not some one of its numbers in the field. Mothers nervously watched for any who might bring to them news of their boys. Sisters and friends grew pale when a horseman rode up to their doors, and could scarcely nerve themselves to listen to the tidings he brought. Young wives clasped their children to their bosoms, and in agony imagined themselves widows and their little ones orphans. Thoughtful husbands, and sons, and brothers, and lovers, dispatched messengers to report their condition whenever they could, but, alas! the worst fears of many were realized.

Conspicuous amongst the dead of Richmond was the young Colonel of the Fourth Texas regiment. He had won honorable distinction in Italy, under Garibaldi. News arrived of his instant death on the field, and his heart-broken family sat up to receive his body until after the hour of midnight ; but when it arrived, and "he lives " was told his mother, the reaction of joy almost deprived her of being. She could not realize it. The revulsion was too great. He spent a few days of mortal agony, and then a sad, mournful procession of heart-broken friends and relatives, and the riderless horse of the young warrior, announced, ah! how sadly, that Richmond's gallant son, Colonel Bradfute Warwick, had fallen!

A horseman rode up to the door of one of our houses on —— street, and cried out to the anxious mother : "Your son, madam, is safe, but Captain —— is killed!" On the opposite side, on the portico of her dwelling, a fair young girl, the betrothed of Captain ——, was said to have been sitting at the moment, and thus heard the terrible announcement!

Every family received the bodies of the wounded or dead of their friends, and every house was a house of mourning or a private hospital.

The clouds were lifted, and the skies brightened upon political prospects, but death held a carnival in our city. The weather was excessively hot. It was midsummer, gangrene and erysipelas attacked the wounded, and those who might have been cured of their wounds were cut down by these diseases.

Our hospitals were loathsome with the bloated, disfigured countenances of the victims of disease, rather than from ghastly wounds. Sickening odors filled the atmosphere, and soldiers' funerals were passing at every moment. Frequently they would be attended by only one or two of the convalescent patients of the hospitals, and sometimes the unknown dead would be borne to the grave, with only the driver of the hearse or cart to attend it.*

---

* One of the grave-diggers at a soldiers' cemetery said to the writer, when speaking of this time, (at a subsequent period,) "We could not

The mournful strains of the "Dead March," and the sounds of the muffled drum, betokened an officer *en route* for "the city of the dead," but these honors could not be accorded the poor fellows from the ranks. There were too many of them passing away—the means for costly funerals were not within our reach—yet were not our hearts less saddened by the less imposing cortege that was borne along with the private nor by the rude coffin in the cart, slowly wending its way unattended by friends, to the soldiers' cemetery. Mothers and sisters, and dear friends came from all parts of the South, to nurse and comfort dear ones in our hospitals, and some, alas! arrived to find a husband, brother, or son already dead or dying, and had the sad companionship of the dead back to their homes.

Our best and brightest young men were passing away. Many of them, the most of them, were utter strangers to us; but the wounded soldier ever found a warm place in our hearts, and they were strangers no more. A Southern lady has written some beautiful lines, suggested by the death of

---

dig graves fast enough to bury the soldiers. They were sometimes brought and put out of the hearse or cart, beside an open grave, and we were compelled to bury them in turn. Frequently we were obliged to leave them over night, when, sometimes, the bodies would swell, and burst the coffins in which they were placed, so slightly were they made. Our work was a horrible one! The odor was stifling. On one occasion, one of our grave-diggers contracted disease from a dead body, which he buried, that came to him in this terrible condition, and he died from it in less than twenty-four hours. After that we were almost afraid to continue our business, but then the soldiers must be buried, poor fellows!"

We listened to this horrible account as we stood on the hillside, and saw the hillocks innumerable, that marked the graves of our soldiers. A little girl, who visited the cemetery, on returning to the city said:— "Why, grandma, the soldiers' graves are as thick as potatoe-hills!" And she saw only a moiety of the many which crowded the hillsides around our city, for this was an extension of Hollywood cemetery only. There were several cemeteries especially laid out for the soldiers, and they were soon all filled with the mounds that marked the soldier dead.

a youthful soldier in one of our hospitals. So deeply touching is the sentiment, and such the exquisite pathos of the poety, that we shall insert them in our memorial of these sad times. When all sentiment was well nigh crushed out, which courts the visit of the muse, these lines sent a thrill of ectasy to our hearts, and comfort and sweetness to the bereaved in many far off homes of the South. Of "Somebody's Darling," she writes :—

> "Into a ward of the white-washed halls
> Where the dead and the dying lay ;—
> Wounded by bayonets, shells and balls,
> Somebody's darling was borne one day.
> Somebody's darling so young and so brave,
> Wearing yet on his sweet, pale face,
> Soon to be laid in the dust of the grave,
> The lingering light of his boyhood's grace.
>
> "Matted and damp are the curls of gold,
> Kissing the snow of that fair young brow ;
> Pale are the lips of delicate mould,
> Somebody's darling is dying now!
> Back from his beautiful, blue-veined brow,
> Brush the wandering waves of gold ;
> Cross his hands on his bosom now,
> Somebody's darling is still and cold !
>
> "Kiss him once, for somebody's sake,
> Murmur a prayer, soft and low ;
> One bright curl from its fair mates take,
> They were somebody's pride, you know.
> Somebody's hand hath rested there,
> Was it a mother's, soft and white ?
> Or have the lips of a sister fair,
> Been baptized in their waves of light?
>
> "God knows best! He has somebody's love,
> Somebody's heart enshrined him there ;
> Somebody wafted his name above,
> Night and morn on the wings of prayer.
> Somebody wept when he marched away,
> Looking so handsome, brave and grand!
> Somebody's kiss on his forehead lay,
> Somebody clung to his parting hand.

"Somebody's watching, and waiting for him,
　Yearning to hold him again to her heart,
And there he lies—with his blue eyes dim,
　And his smiling, child-like lips apart!
Tenderly bury the fair young dead,
　Pausing to drop o'er his grave a tear;
Carve on the wooden slab at his head,
　' *Somebody's darling* is lying here!'"

Were we to begin to recount the thrilling scenes of the hospitals, we should never know where to stop. They are graven on our hearts with a pen of iron, dipped in the blood of heroes and martyrs. They can never fade from memory as long as stand the fair hills of Virginia, made uneven by the mounds which cover the mouldering remains of the soldier. The picture is ours, through all time and down the endless lapse of the ages of eternity. The month of July of 1862 can never be forgotten in Richmond. We lived in one immense hospital, and breathed the vapors of the charnel house.

But we walked not in darkness wholly—there gleamed light ahead. Faint glimmerings of future peace and independence, threw over our hopes faint streaks of their welcome dawn.

Our arms had been gloriously victorious, our enemies had been severely chastised, "the Grand Army of the North" had been driven back by our invincible forces, their arrogant boastings had been quieted for the time, and we vainly hoped we had, so worthily commended ourselves to the notice of foreign nations as to compel honorable recognition. We craved not this favor from the sympathy our condition might excite, but felt that we might expect and demand it for meritorious worth. We hoped that the severe chastisement inflicted on our enemies would dampen the pursuit of our subjugation, and bring to us the desired peace, and liberty! Alas! we sadly miscalculated the action of our friends across the ocean, and the energy and perseverance of our enemies. The snake was not killed, it was only "scotched," and very little time was left us to contemplate the security temporarily brought to us by the sacrificing of the lives of so many fellow-creatures.

CHAPTER XXIX.

POPE'S ORDERS—CAPTURES—LIBBY PRISON.

WHEN General Pope was placed in command of the Federal army, he issued an order, requiring "that all commanders of army corps, divisions, brigades, and detached commands, will proceed immediately to arrest all disloyal male citizens within their lines, or within their reach in rear of their respective commands. Such as are willing to take the oath of allegiance to the United States, and will furnish security for its observance, shall be permitted to remain at their homes, and pursue in good faith their accustomed avocations; those who refuse shall be conducted South, beyond the extreme pickets of this army, and be notified that if found again anywhere within our lines, or at any point in the rear, they shall be considered spies, and subjected to the extreme rigor of military law. If any person having taken the oath of allegiance above specified, be found to have violated it, he shall be shot, and his property seized and applied to the public use."

By another order of Brigadier General Steinwehr, of Pope's command, it was proposed to hold under arrest the most prominent citizens in the districts occupied by the enemy, as hostages, to suffer death in retaliation for the shooting of Yankee soldiers by "bushwhackers," by which term was meant the citizens of the South who had taken up arms to defend their homes and families.

These orders were intended mainly to frighten our men into submission and to require an oath which involved the perjury of themselves, or the exposure of their wives and children to ruthless hordes, devoid of all principles of manliness, courage, or bravery.

In the county of Spotsylvania, about twenty miles above Fredericksburg, there lived a physician, a man of some influence, who had quietly followed the practice of his profession, but who, nevertheless, exerted all the influence of which he was possessed, in behalf of the South. Through the misrepresentations of the spies who prowled around the country, he was arrested under the charge of being a captain of guerrillas, and was taken from his home on a Monday morning, before breakfast, by a detachment of Federal cavalry. He was commanded, under pain of death, not to look back at his weeping wife and little children, who stood on the portico of his dwelling. Thus rudely and insultingly treated, he was carried to their encampment outside of Fredericksburg, and when he made his appearance under so close a guard, was surrounded by a mob who cried, "Hang him! shoot him!" "Hang him! shoot him!" Some came to tear him from his horse for that purpose, and could only be restrained by the most energetic remonstrances and threats from their officers. "If I am to die," he said, "I am not willing to be sacrificed without a hearing," and he demanded to be carried before General King, who then held command of Fredericksburg. He was accordingly carried into the town, and not being able to get an audience with the commanding general, he was thrown into a granary devoted to prison purposes, with not a mouthful to eat— there to await the pleasure of the general, and perhaps death from the bullet, or on the gallows.

After a hearing from General King, and upon the testimony of other prisoners, taken from his neighborhood, one of whom implored on his knees that the prisoner's life might not be taken on the false representations of spies, the doctor was released on parole, and sent under an escort beyond the extreme limits of General Pope's lines. His agony at the thought of his young wife and three little children left unprotected in the immediate vicinity of lawless soldiery, increased the unhappiness of his own situation. He returned to his home to find it actually deserted. A faithful negro servant had conveyed his mistress and her children, and all the domestics of the establishment to a place of safety beyond the Federal lines, and out of reach of further persecution from their enemies. The doctor came on to Richmond, and the first use made of him by the government, was to place him as surgeon in the Libby Prison, where, in a very few days, he greeted some of his former persecutors.

We very fully understand, when we approach the history of this building, that we are treading upon dangerous ground. If retaliation might have been pardonable in any case, it surely would have been so in the case of the surgeon of the prison. That he did not retaliate is proved by the fact that he made friends of his former foes, and still retains many pleasant memorials of gratitude from the very men who sought his life. An Irish surgeon, who took his degree in Dublin, left with him a case of superior surgical instruments, as a testimonial of his kindness, humanity and skill, and more humble soldiers pressed upon him simple mementoes of their gratitude for unmerited consideration. Having been familiarly associated with some of the surgeons who operated at this prison, the writer is not prepared to give credence to the monstrous stories of cruelty and oppression said to have been practiced upon the men who were crowded into it by the fortunes of war.

To attempt to vindicate the reputation of the Libby Prison, would, however, be a useless undertaking. It would be like whispering to the deaf adder.

In connection with the Libby Prison and the doctor of whom we have spoken, it may be added that it was then an easy matter to procure "greenbacks" from the prisoners. They were willing to sell their money for Confederate currency at par, or to enter into an exchange of currency. Being many of them only three months' men, and well supplied with blankets, they frequently sold them at prices much lower than those demanded in Richmond. The doctor availed himself of this opportunity to procure blankets for the use of his servants. Having invested in a large number of excellent ones, he sent them to his home where his little children, pleased with the appearance of the large, warm coverings for the winter, spread them down in the nursery for carpets to play on; but much to the dismay of the careful nurse, and to the disgust of the mother, they were found to be filled with the usual vermin of the camp. This experiment put a stop to the doctor's speculation in Yankee blankets.

CHAPTER XXX.

THE BATTLE OF CEDAR MOUNTAIN—NORTHERN LETTER-WRITING.

THE clouds of battle had scarcely been lifted from Richmond, when Stonewall Jackson, with his unconquerable little band, appeared in the vicinity of Gordonsville. On the 8th of August, at Cedar Mountain, near the boundary line between Madison and Culpepper counties, he again encountered General Banks, the total rout of whose army was only prevented by timely reinforcements under General Pope. Pope himself was compelled, however reluctantly, to turn his back upon General Stonewall Jackson, and made a safe retreat for a time to the north bank of the Rappahannock, in a few days to have his movements again intercepted and his blustering silenced on the classic field of Manassas.

It would be useless to recapitulate many of the acts of this campaign of General Pope. It can hardly be denied that it was a failure in everything which might have advanced the success of the cause for which he fought, and that it was abundantly successful only in the lawless impressment of provisions, the demoralization of slaves, (hundreds of whom were induced to leave their homes and follow the

Federal army,) the cowardly maltreatment of unarmed men and heaped-up insults upon defenceless women.

Leaving our army apprehending and intercepting the plans of the enemy, we will take a retrograde step, and notice the style of literature which flooded Richmond from the battle-fields. We are not a relic-hunting people, and take but little pleasure in mementoes which awaken such painful memories. Very few of us treasured trinkets gathered up from the field or from the *débris* of the camp; but amid the scenes of the hospital and the sterner duties which called into action our talents as sempstresses, nurses and caterers to the sick and wounded, we would sometimes amuse ourselves with the literature captured in the knapsacks of our enemies.

Some rare specimens in the province of letter-writing came under our notice. In them the rules of orthography were wholly ignored. Grammar and rhetoric were allowed neither part nor lot in the compositions, and the much-vaunted common school system of the North was by no means favorably recommended in the epistolary intercourse of the rank and file of the Federal army. Occasionally we were refreshed with something that was readable,—something in which sentiments of purity, morality and religion were expressed; but generally, from awkward, ignorant, illy-adjusted compositions, we read only coarse, vulgar abuse of the South, in which the "rebels" were denounced as being but little better than fiends incarnate, and meriting only a death on the gallows.

In some of these letters from our Northern sisters, the rebel women came in for a large share of vituperation. An excessive fear was sometimes expressed lest the "brave boys" might lose their hearts with the fair women upon whom they frequently took peculiar delight in making war.

But while these cases were not exceptional, they were not universal. Some of the most beautifully touching epistles, the emotions of pure and cultivated minds, were found in the knapsacks of the soldiers in the hostile army. When we were fortunate enough, in the immense heaps of trash, to find such gems, though fidelity to the Union was the burden of their politics, we were not excited to indignation by unqualified abuse of the South and ignorant denunciations of a people of whom they knew but little.

If we must judge of a nation by its literature, the North had a most unfortunate representation in the letters of the rank and file of its army.

Touching mementoes of friends far away were frequently found in the knapsacks brought to us. A miniature, a lock of hair, a faded flower, a bow of ribbon, would whisper to our hearts a pleasant story. Sometimes, when our feelings were chilled, when our hearts were hardened and we were forced to consider those who oppressed us so heavily as scarcely possessed of human attributes, we were softened by these evidences of a better principle, and the thought would arise : " They are at least men, and must at one time have had hearts."

We hardly dare allude to the fact, that now and then we found that the morocco case contained the miniature of a woman in whose veins ran a darker stream than that which tints the complexion of the Caucasian. At that time there were so few of the troops of the Corps d'Afrique that our most tenderly awakened sympathies, excited by the fair face of the friend of the Yankee soldier, would be overcome by disgust at the thought that any could carry with him the sable shadow, and this disgust was intensified when, in more than one instance, beside the dark lady, was shadowed forth the likeness of a soldier in the uniform of the Federal officer. Must an apology be made? These are delicate subjects, and we approach them charily, but our details would not be complete were we to pass them unnoticed. All along our route there are shoals and quicksands, and we ought to be careful that we are not sunk in the one or stranded on the other. The sea upon which we sail is dangerous ; but with Truth for our pilot we have boldly thrust out our bark, and should not fear the consequences.

CHAPTER XXXI.

THE PROVOST MARSHAL'S OFFICE IN RICHMOND—INCIDENTS.

AN unforeseen annoyance arose in the frequent disruptions which occurred between our Provost Marshal, General Winder, and the Examining Board of Surgeons, through whom the soldiers in a state of convalescence received furloughs. It was not unfrequently the case, when a convalescent soldier succeeded in procuring from his surgeon a certificate upon which to ground an application for a furlough, and when not in a condition to return to his regiment for service in the field, that he was kept in Richmond, confined to the hot, impure air of the city, because General Winder had quarrelled with the Board, and there was no authority delegated to examine into and decide upon his case. We can recall a great number of times when the poor sufferers were disappointed in this manner, but will mention only the cases of two young men, one of whom was from Virginia, and the other a young Mississippian, who afterwards signally distinguished himself for bravery. These young soldiers held certificates from their surgeon, of wounds that incapacitated them for military duty for a time, and entitled them to a furlough for sixty days. The Board had dissolved, they could get no examination, and there they were, sweltering in the heat of summer, breathing the impure air of the city, and wilting day by day, as a plant deprived of earth and moisture. They had sought all the aid, political, religious and military, that they could bring to bear upon their applications, to no effect. At last a lady friend, alive with sympathy for their condition, and worn out with their repeated disappointments, said to them:
"Give me your certificates; *I'll* see that you shall have a furlough."

"How will you manage it?" said private W——, (later, General W——.)

"I shall beard the lion in his den."

"What do you mean?"

"Never mind; will you give me your certificates?" said the lady.

"Yes—it can do no harm; but we have grown hopeless," they both exclaimed.

The lady took the certificates, and seeking the companionship of another lady and the escort of a friendly clergyman, she at once visited the office of the Surgeon General, (Dr. Moore,) presented the claims of her adopted convalescents, and laid the certificates before him for his adjudication. Reading carefully the valuable documents, he indorsed the applications, sent them down to Adjutant General Cooper for his approval, and the lady had the intense satisfaction to take them back to the disheartened soldiers, granting a furlough for sixty days, from the highest medical authority under the government. Surprise took the place of gratitude for a few moments in the hearts of the poor soldiers, but when they could find words to express themselves, they exclaimed: "Well, one woman is worth five hundred men at any time,"—"when furloughs are to be obtained," she added. Accepting the compliment only with her amendment, she allowed them to express their thanks.

We may here remark, in reference to Surgeon General Moore, there were few men in authority under the Confederate government who had a more irreproachable record, though there were few more difficult to approach. Devoted in his attention to his peculiar business, he was polite and courteous, though so remarkably sententious that his manner was mistaken for unfeeling indifference. A simple statement of business always received from him correct notice, though he never tolerated unnecessary preamble. The wise rules of business which we find in the house of almost every man of business, were those required by him of all who called upon him to transact business.

The character of Dr. Moore can best be understood from the high esteem in which he was held by the clerks in his office. Scrupulously exacting of them the strictest performance of duty, it was so well regulated as to make it a pleasure, while the slightest neglect of duty, we are told, was never permitted to pass unnoticed by him.

CHAPTER XXXII.

THE SECOND BATTLE OF BULL RUN.—A WOMAN'S STRATAGEM

BUT little more than thirteen months had left their records on the pages of history, and again on the fields of Manassas, where the enemy had received his first signal repulse in his "On to Richmond," were the camp-fires lighted. From every hill-top they were blazing, and once more we were destined to try the steel of the foemen. Not satisfied with the previous chastisement received on this bloody ground, they had persevered until at the gates of the principal stronghold of the rebels they had knocked loudly and clamorously for admittance, to be repulsed yet more signally, and still undaunted by defeat they had taken up the programme of the "On to Richmond," devised by the wisdom of General Scott, and disappointed in by General McDowell, to attempt an improvement suggested by the light of experience in the route. We were given but little time to talk about and reflect upon the glorious succession of victories which had driven the persevering invader from our very doors, when the thunder and smoke, the din and confusion of battle, again shook the hills of Virginia. It was not enough that at Bull Run, Manassas, and Ball's Bluff—at Seven Pines and Fair Oaks—at Mechanicsville, Gaines's Mill, Coal Harbor, Peach Orchard, Savage's Station, Frayser's Farm, and Malvern Hill, (around Richmond,) and at Cedar Mountain, as well as at other points on our soil, the bones of the enemy were piled in huge heaps, and that their shed blood and decaying bodies were enriching the hillsides—it was not enough that they had seen their armies melt away before the furious fire of the rebels, like snow in the sunshine—but once more, on the same plateaus where first they were dispersed like frightened sheep, they determined to make the bold attempt to wrest from the Confederates the victories won in a score of battles, and plant again the "stars and stripes" on the "rebel" Capitol.

By referring to a history of this period, we read: "The results of General Lee's strategy were indicative of the resources of military genius. Day after day the enemy were beaten, until his disasters culminated on the plains of Manassas. Day after day our men maintained their superiority to the enemy. The summer campaign had been conducted by a single army. The same toil-worn troops who had relieved from siege the city of Richmond, had advanced to meet another invading army, reinforced not only by the defeated army of McClellan, but by the fresh corps of Burnside and Hunter. The trials and marches of these troops are extraordinary in history. Transportation was inadequate, the streams which they had to cross were swollen to unusual height, it was only by forced marches and repeated combats they could turn the position of the enemy—and at last succeeding in this, and forming a junction of their columns in the face of greatly superior forces, they fought the decisive battle of the 30th of August—the crowning triumph of their toil and valor.

"The route of the extraordinary marches of our troops presented for long and weary miles the touching pictures of the trials of war. Broken-down soldiers, (not all stragglers,) lined the road. At night time, they might be found asleep in every conceivable attitude of discomfort—on fence rails, and in fence corners—some half bent, others almost erect—in ditches, and on steep hill-sides, some without blanket or overcoat. Day-break found them drenched with dew, but strong in purpose; with half rations of bread and meat, ragged and bare-footed, they go cheerfully forward. No nobler spectacle was ever presented in history. These beardless youths and gray-haired men, who thus spent their nights like the beasts of the field, were the best men of the land, of all classes, trades and professions. The spectacle was such as to inspire the prayer that ascended from the sanctuaries of the South, that God might reward the devotion of these men to principle and justice, by crowning their labors and sacrifices with that blessing which always bringeth peace."

In connection with the battle of the Cross Keys, we are just here reminded of an amusing stratagem of a rebel lady to conceal her age and charms from the enemy, who held possession of her house. She says: "Mr. K., you know, was compelled to evacuate his premises when the Federals took possession, and succeeding in making good his escape, left me there, with my three little children, to encounter the consequences of their intrusion upon my premises. Not wishing to appear quite so youthful as I really am, and desiring to destroy, if possible, any remains of my former beauty, I took from my mouth the set of false teeth, (which I was compelled to have put in before I was twenty years old,) tied a handkerchief around my head, donned my most slovenly apparel, and in every way made myself as hideous as possible. The disguise was perfect. I was sullen, morose, sententious. You could not have believed I could so long have kept up a manner so disagreeable; but it had the desired effect. The Yankees called me "old woman." They little thought I was not thirty years of age. They took my house for a hospital for their sick and wounded, and allowed me only the use of a single room, and required of me many acts of assistance in nursing their men, which under any other circumstances my own heart-promptings would have made a pleasure to me. But I did not feel disposed to be compelled to prepare food for those who had driven from me my husband, and afterwards robbed me of all my food and bed-furniture, with the exception of what they allowed me to have in my own room. But they were not insulting in their language to the "old woman," and I endured all the inconveniences and unhappiness of my situation with as much fortitude as I could bring into oper-

ation, feeling that my dear husband, at least, was safe f
harm. After they left," she continued, "I was forced t
out into the woods, near by, and with my two little
pick up fagots to cook the scanty food left to me." Tl
the story of one of the most luxuriously reared wome
Virginia, and is scarcely the faintest shadow of what r
endured under similar circumstances.

CHAPTER XXXIII.

THE CLOUDS LIFTED.

THE rapid changes of the fortunes of the Confede
and the contrast to the forlorn and hopeless situatic
which we were placed so short a time before, dispelled
gloom that had loomed over us in the brilliant prospec
future success.

The most sanguine hopes were entertained of a sp
termination to our difficulties, and a prosperous peace.
latter only to be desired with liberty. It seemed al
within our grasp. Little more than three months
passed since we had seen Richmond surrounded by
"Grand Army," our government quaking, and ready to
up the capital, our people discouraged and frantically fl
in all directions for safety, all classes demoralized, save
trusty army—now, we had not only beheld the mighty
of the enemy driven from its strong position, at our
doors, but beaten back across the Potomac, and the cor
of our enemies inviting to invasion from the conque
armies of the "rebels."

It seemed almost impossible for us to realize the cha
The clouds were breaking on all sides, they had been]
from Richmond, and an incubus so heavy that it had
nigh crushed out the life of many of us, had been l
from our hearts; and when after making this review,
the strangeness and security of our situation were

understood, and the terrible dangers warded off by the valor, the courage, the invincible determination of our foot-sore, weary and ragged army, that had in so short a time wrought such prodigies—our hearts went up in a universal "Great God, I thank thee! The Lord alone omnipotent reigneth!"

The close of the summer found the soil of Virginia free from the hostile tread of the invader. With the news of the defeated armies of the enemy that threatened us on the north of Richmond, there came to us at the same time, information of the successes of General Loring in Western Virginia. Meeting and repulsing the enemy at Fayette Court House, driving him back to Cotton Hill, which he was also forced to abandon, and still further on, dislodging him at Kanawha Falls, and capturing immense stores of provisions and ammunition, our victorious forces pushed on to Charleston, which they found in flames, and the inhabitants terror-stricken at the treatment received at the hands of the enemy. In a short time the beautiful Valley of the Kanawha was free from the incursions of the hostile troops, and his towns on the Ohio were threatened by our forces.

In the recovery of the Valley of the Kanawha, we regained the possession of one of the richest and most valuable sections of our state. With salt enough within its limits to furnish a supply for this whole continent, and which had previously sold for scarcely a farthing per pound, while we were at that time paying for it in Richmond the sum of one dollar and fifty cents per pound.*

Very soon in Richmond, and all parts of Virginia, these successes were made available in supplying the wants of the people, in an article so necessary to their sustenance

---

* It was when the Kanawha Valley was in the possession of our enemies, that the speculator before referred to, who had on hand a large supply of this article, took advantage of the necessities of the people, and made his fortune.

and comfort. We were no longer compelled to pay to the extortioners the exorbitant sum of one dollar and fifty cents per pound, but the state drew supplies of salt for the citizens, which was furnished to them at the rate of a pound per head per month, for each individual at five cents per pound. This was a vast improvement upon the price we had paid of late.

As the opposing forces now stood, the South had just cause for congratulation, the North for mortification. More had been in a short time accomplished by the South, than perhaps any people in the world had ever achieved. With a population of only eight millions, three millions of which were slaves, tampered with, and rendered disloyal and dissatisfied with their relation to the whites, at every point at which our enemies could get access to them and bring them under their control, we had for more than eighteen months successfully resisted a people of a population of twenty-three millions of residents, and with a teeming influx of emigrants daily landing on their shores, with which to recruit their exhausted ranks, without the necessity of drawing heavily upon the native population. The North was well supplied with manufactories of all descriptions to furnish materials for carrying on a war, while her ports were open to all the world, and she, in turn, had access to every country on the globe, through her commercial intercourse, inviting to competition and assistance in all the arts pertaining to the improvement of implements of warfare: there was, therefore, nothing in the material for conquest that was not within her reach.

The South, on the other hand, with only a few insignificant manufactories for arms and other implements necessary for warfare, shut out from all the world by a rigid blockade, through which only, with risk and danger, we could get any assistance from abroad, with our troops poorly armed, badly clad and still more badly fed, with no navy to compete with the thousands of vessels belonging to the North, which ploughed the trackless ocean, and brought wealth to our enemies, unassisted by any power from abroad, replete alone with the high purpose which nerved her to the contest, placed in the hands of her ragged troops arms of any and every description, and with these they had dared to oppose, and had successfully driven from our soil, the overwhelming hosts which vainly thought to crush us in the onset.

Victory after victory perched on the Confederate banners, and imperishable laurels wreathed the brow of the South.

CHAPTER XXXIV.

RETURN OF THE CONFEDERATE CONGRESS—WOMEN AT WORK IN THE PUBLIC DEPARTMENTS.

THE Confederate Congress, which had adjourned about the time that the gunboat panic took possession of so many of the people of Richmond, convened again in a "called session" in August. With unfeigned courtesy we welcomed back this illustrious body; but they were subjected to the most unmerciful twittings for the fleetness of foot they had exhibited when Richmond was so alarmingly threatened. These unpleasant allusions were received with laughable grace, the best they could summon to aid them in apology for so frantically "*skedaddling*," (to use a Western slang term,) when General McClellan had his army planted around the Confederate Capital.

To the pungent but not unamiable taunts that would sometimes assail these honorable gentlemen from their fair friends in Richmond, they would reply in the golden aphorism (which the ladies claimed to have been captured from themselves) "Discretion is the better part of valor," or rather, the ladies would reform, "Self-preservation is the first law of nature," with the added assurance that in case of another threatening demonstration, *they* would "keep guard" over the Congress while sitting.

That this illustrious body of Confederate legislators were not insensible to, nor unappreciative of the charms of the women of the capital, is proved by the fact that more than one was consoled in his lonely estate by having conferred on him the hand of a Richmond lady.

The hearts of our grave senators and representatives were not invulnerable, and Cupid kept up a lively business in the "Rebel Capital." They were not armed with "coats of mail" against the charms of the ladies of Richmond, but alas! the fair ones were driven to the mortifying consciousness of their defective magnetic powers, when a distant cloud of Federal dust betrayed the threatened approach of our incorrigible enemies.

No better armed against Federal bullets than the arrows of the god of Love, they borrowed for their heels wings from Mercury, and practiced the admirable, but not very courageous precept that,

"He who fights and runs away,
May live to fight another day."

It is usual to depreciate our public men. It seems to be altogether forgotten that the universal suffrage advocated in our country, must ever engender a spirit of demagoguism in our politicians; forbidding the development of our best talent, and putting into power those who will most readily yield to the outside pressure, and pander to the politics of the majority. Our Congress was accused of being distinguished for its weakness, for its entire want of statesmanship, kept in mortal terror, it was said, by the autocratic rule of our chief magistrate, and acting with unpardonable timidity, when the most urgent necessity for promptness and energy was apparent. Upon these points we must leave the superior wisdom of the well-informed to decide; we do not feel prepared nor willing to sit in judgment on the actions of unfortunate politicians, whose reputations are handled always unmercifully, tossed to and fro like feathers on the wind.

We do know that there were many in the Confederate councils who had made for themselves a worthy and an honorable name, who had come down to us from the old United States Congress with an enviable prestige which was not lost by their trial in the Confederate Congress. In the delegations from our own noble State, there were those well known in the history of our country, as beacon lights of superior mental lustre, to whom we might look in the darkness that enveloped us, and ask, "Watchman, what of the night?"

We know that in the legislative halls of the Confederate Capitol, there were men from all parts of the South whose patriotism had been tested by trials so conclusive, that we dare not raise against them the finger of reproach, and reject with scorn imputations that reflect disparagingly upon them. With us was repeated the old story, burdened with complaints against our representatives, and never for a moment did we charge ourselves with the slightest portion of the grave responsibilities of their position.

But in the Confederate Congress there was one character so unique, that it would be a matter of the merest impossibility for any pen less gifted than that of Dickens to do full justice to it in all its phases. The most incomprehensible of all incomprehensibilities, the most nondescript of the nondescript was this honorable gentleman.

Possessed of undoubted mental capabilities, we find him from the time of his advent into the Southern Congress, attacking at will any and every one connected with the government, from the President to the lowest official, warring upon every department alike, with a hardihood and effrontery as admirable as astonishing. Battling with the Commissary General, the Secretary of the Navy, the Army and the Treasury, hurling his thunderbolts, red hot with righteous indignation against men who abused and lived upon government emoluments, bullying the members of

Congress, provoking quarrels with whomsoever he chose, disturbing the peace of that body by his noisy invectives—he was unsparing in the manner as in the matter of his language, and often threw in the teeth of his Congressional contemporaries the most violent and bitter denunciations. Possessed of no apparent amiability himself, he seemed altogether oblivious of the existence of such a quality in the breast of any other human being. He was considered a "firebrand" in the old Congress, and brought with him his ancient reputation into that of the Confederacy.

He appeared to be a privileged member, and was allowed to rant on and fire here and there at will, only too happy for an opportunity for a grand explosion. At last, after nearly four years of such desultory warfare, we find him provoking a quarrel with a certain member of the House, of so irate a character that said member, (we regret to record,) followed him to the chamber of his wife, and could only be prevented from inflicting chastisement upon the gray-haired old offender by the strenuous efforts of other members, and the screams of the frightened lady. But when he had seemingly "fired his last round," and from the obvious disapprobation of all parties, found "Othello's occupation gone," he came up "among the missing." In his attempted escape to Washington, he was arrested by Confederate detectives at Fredericksburg and returned to the tender mercies of the outraged authorities of the Confederate government.

By no means disconcerted at this *contretemps*, he boldly delivered himself of his reason for this unwonted infidelity to the government he had so industriously threatened and served. Tired of waiting for the dawn of a better day, and ever disposed towards peace (?) he had, self-commissioned, determined to make his way to Washington to negotiate for peace with the Federal government. Finding it impossible to subdue the indomitable spirit of this incorrigible man, the Southern Confederacy was glad to let him depart in peace, with the kindly injunction of Uncle Toby to the fly.

But we are anticipating his hegira by more than two years. It was amusing to watch the shade of angry resignation that would steal over the faces of the members, and of vexation that would mantle the brows of visitors to the hall of the House of Representatives, when, upon almost every bill introduced, they were condemned to listen to the ever ready tirade of invective that seemed always to pour from the lips of this remarkable man. With a reputation for talent superior or equal to that of any man in that body, his speeches, which might have been spirited and interesting, were usually quarrelsome and disgusting. "Take him all in all," he was a man without a parallel.

His fault-findings, however, were not without cause. There was much to displease us in the operations of the government. Our financial interests were unfortunately managed. By the action of Congress, authorizing, time after time, an increase in the circulation of currency, upon a basis so insecure as our monetary system, the country was flooded with money, the public debt accumulated alarmingly, and the paper issued by the Confederate Treasury depreciated in a ratio almost unprecedented in the fiscal history of any period or nation. In the report of the President to the first permanent Congress, he represented our financial condition as one of safety—one for which we had just cause for congratulation; but twelve months had not elapsed when our paper currency was held at a discount of one thousand per cent., and it continued to increase in worthlessness, until, when the war terminated, its gold value was only a cent and a mill in the dollar.

But these disagreements, however unfortunate for us as a nation, were providentially overruled for the benefit of many. In various offices under the government, and particularly in those of the Treasury Department, the services of females were found useful. Employment was given and a support secured to hundreds of intelligent and deserving women of the South, who, by the existence of the war, or other misfortunes, had been so reduced in the means of living as to be compelled to earn a support. The Treasury Note Bureau, in which the greatest number of women were employed, was under the supervision of experienced and gentlemanly clerks, and no place in the Confederate Capital was more interesting or attractive than that where these fair operatives were engaged in signing and numbering Mr. Memminger's Confederate bills. The duties were pleasant and profitable, and so much sought after by those in need, that hundreds of applications were placed on file by women to whom it was impossible to furnish employment.

It sometimes required considerable diplomacy and influence to secure an office under our Government, and their fair friends made ample use of the members of Congress, the clergy and the military, for reference as to social position, qualification, worth, and need for such assistance.

A visit to Mr. Memminger, whose stolid and apparently unsympathizing face ever produced an unpleasant impression on the beholder, was sometimes undertaken by a woman more courageous than her sisters, to be attended with nervous apprehension when in his sight, and often by weeping when the ordeal was over. Few could endure the cold phase: "If I find your case more worthy of notice than others I will regard your application favorably," when their hearts were aching under trials so bitter that their drink was mingled with weeping, and their nights restless with the agony of the thought, "How am I to live?" But notwithstanding the cold exterior of Mr. Memminger, he was not wanting in that warmth of soul that opens with sympathy for misfortune; but it became extremely difficult for him to discriminate between the applicants, when they were so numerous, and their claims to notice so well substantiated.

From the Treasury Department, the employment of female clerks extended to various offices in the War Department, the Post Office Department, and indeed to every branch of business connected with the government. They were in all found efficient and useful. By this means many young men could be sent into the ranks, and by the testimony of the chiefs of Bureaus, the work left for the women was better done; for they were more conscientious in their attendance upon their duties than the more self-satisfied, but not better qualified, male *attachés* of the government offices.

For offices in the War Department, an examination of qualification for business was required. This, in itself, was extremely simple, but sufficiently formidable to deter many from seeking employment that required such a test of efficiency. The applicants were expected to show a thorough acquaintance with the primary rules of arithmetic, and some knowledge of fractions; but under the circumstances in which many timid ladies were examined they could scarcely tell whether or not two and two make four, or how many thirds there are in a whole. These examinations, therefore, could not be considered a test of qualification, for there were some so much frightened by the trial that, losing all self-possession, they gave up in despair. The experiment of placing women in government clerkships proved eminently successful, and grew to be extremely popular under the Confederate government.

Many a poor young girl remembers with gratitude the kindly encouragement of our Adjutant General Cooper, our Chief of Ordnance, Colonel Gorges, or the First Auditor of the Confederate Treasury, Judge Bolling Baker, or Postmaster General Reagan, and various other officials, of whom their necessities drove them to seek employment. The most high-born ladies of the land filled these places as well as the humble poor; but none could obtain employment under the government who could not furnish testimonials of intelligence and superior moral worth.

When our Congress reassembled in August, very differently did our own political skies appear from what they did when it adjourned in the spring previous. They were now spanned by the rainbow-tinted arch of future prosperity. The heavy clouds of war seemed to be breaking up on all sides. The radiant image of Peace, obscured from our vision by only trifling impediments, was ready once more to shed her beams of brightness over our beautiful Southern land.

But we could not rely fully on appearances, which (as the result has proven) might be only illusory. We could not relax our diligence, we could not give up to voluptuous ease and idle enjoyment, so long as we had fathers, brothers, husbands and friends yet in the field, bearing the heavy musket and knapsack, and sleeping on the bare earth, and exposed to the rains and dews of night, living on coarse, hard fare, and subjected to the thousand discomforts of the soldier's life During its session in the spring, Congress had passed a bill for increasing the size of the army by conscription. It was now considering what classes might be exempt from military duty by the requirements of the law.

Our army had hitherto been almost wholly filled up by volunteers, who had rushed in at the very commencement of the war. It could not be sustained by volunteer troops. Other expedients were required to fill up the ranks depleted by death or mutilation. To avoid military duty, many whose insatiate thirst for wealth overruled all instincts of patriotism, were satisfied to avoid the conscription by the purchase of substitutes to do their fighting for them, and others laid to their souls the flattering unction of duty performed, and stilled perhaps the whisperings of conscience, while they pursued the busy rounds of trade, and grew rich upon the necessities of their fellow men. There are some of us who can recall the beautiful tribute paid to Virginia by Walter Preston, in his famous speech in Congress on the Exemption Bill. It breathed all the spirit of patriotism, yet plainly indicated the difficulties that still hedged our way, and to be found mainly in the spirit and temper of our own people. We had afterwards reason to regret that the exceptions to the classes of exempts were not more numerous, or that our men, many of them, could not see more glory in honorable warfare than in the dangers and excitements of blockade-running to Baltimore, though in the dangers and excitements of the field they could not so readily and successfully line their pockets with riches.

Our railroads were now all in working order, patched up of such materials as we had on hand, but the supplies of provisions came over them in abundance, and there was no lack of edibles in Richmond, except in groceries and such articles as were received by foreign importation. A great change had become visible since the spring, when we suffered from the tariff placed on certain articles of home production, by our Provost Marshal, General Winder, when we scarce knew from day to day how we should provide for the wants of the morrow; and our situation was greatly better than when our railroads were all cut on the north of Richmond, and supplies could not be forwarded to the city. Although the prices were inflated until they were marvellously high, there was no lack of money for the purchase of creature comforts, and we failed not to give God sincere thanks for the wonderful deliverance wrought in a few short, but terrible months.

CHAPTER XXXV.

FIDELITY OF THE NEGROES.

THERE is an inherent pride in personal responsibility, and this was fully exemplified in the test of the negro during the war. It was a matter of infinite gratification with him to take care of his mistress and the little ones, while his master was absent in the field. The duties of rearing and of training the children of a Southern family were always proudly shared by the domestics known as "house servants." In almost every Southern household there was the "mammy," the "daddy," and aunties and uncles of the senior servants, who received these appellations from the affection and respect in which they were held by the members of the white family to which they were attached.

We might cite numerous instances of the fidelity of negroes that came under our notice, but will only refer to one, illustrating the deep attachment of which the negro is capable, and the just sense of responsibility which takes hold of his mind.

A young soldier from Georgia brought with him to the war in Virginia a young man who had been brought up with him on his father's plantation. On leaving his home with his regiment, the mother of the young soldier said to his negro slave: "Now, Tom, I commit your master Jemmy into your keeping. Don't let him suffer for anything with which you can supply him. If he is sick, nurse him well, my boy; and if he dies, bring his body home to me; if wounded, take care of him; and oh! if he is killed in battle, don't let him be buried on the field, but secure his body for me, and bring him home to be buried!" The negro faithfully promised his mistress that all of her wishes should be attended to, and came on to the seat of war charged with the grave responsibility placed upon him.

In one of the battles around Richmond the negro saw his young master when he entered the fight, and saw him when he fell, but no more of him. The battle became fierce, the dust and smoke so dense that the company to which he was attached, wholly enveloped in the cloud, was hidden from the sight of the negro, and it was not until the battle was over that Tom could seek for his young master. He found him in a heap of the slain. Removing the mangled remains, torn frightfully by a piece of shell, he conveyed them to an empty house, where he laid them out in the most decent order he could, and securing the few valuables found on his person, he sought a conveyance to carry the body to Richmond. Ambulances were in too great requisition for those whose lives were not extinct to permit the body of a dead man to be conveyed in one of them. He pleaded most piteously for a place to bring in the body of his young master. It was useless, and he was repulsed; but finding some one to guard the dead, he hastened into the city and hired a cart and driver to go out with him to bring in the body to Richmond.

When he arrived again at the place where he had left it, he was urged to let it be buried on the field, and was told that he would not be allowed to take it from Richmond, and therefore it were better to be buried there. "I can't do it," replied the faithful negro; "I can't do it; I promised my mistress (his mother) to bring this body home to her if he got killed, and I'll go home with it or I'll die by it; I can't leave my master Jemmy here." The boy was allowed to have the body and brought it into Richmond, where he was furnished with a coffin, and the circumstances being made known, the faithful slave, in the care of a wounded officer who went South, was permitted to carry the remains of his master to his distant home in Georgia. The heart of the mother was comforted in the possession of the precious body of her child, and in giving it a burial in the churchyard near his own loved home.

Fee or reward for this noble act of fidelity would have been an insult to the better feelings of this poor slave; but when he delivered up the watch and other things taken from the person of his young master, the mistress returned him the watch, and said: "Take this watch, Tom, and keep it for the sake of my dear boy; 'tis but a poor reward for such services as you have rendered him and his mother." The poor woman, quite overcome, could only add: "God will bless you, boy!"

To allude to an institution which is without the prospect of or a wish for its resurrection, would be like opening the grave and exhibiting the festering remains of our former social system; but we cannot forbear extracting from an evil—and only evil morally, not necessarily involving sin—many a beautiful lesson from the relation in which it was held by us. Our slaves were most generally the repositaries of our family secrets. They were our confidants in all our trials. They joyed with us and they sorrowed with us; they wept when we wept, and they laughed when we laughed. Often our best friends, they were rarely our worst enemies. Simple and childklike in their affections, they were more trustworthy in their attachments than those better versed in wisdom. For good or evil, in his present altered condition the negro has the warmest sympathies of his former master, and ever in him will find a "friend in need," who will readily extend to him the hand of kindness and generous affection.

CHAPTER XXXVI.

LEE'S INVASION OF MARYLAND—THE BATTLE OF ANTIETAM.

BY this time the theatre of active military operations had been changed. General Pope, with all his boasted skill and bravery, although assisted by McClellan, Burnside and Hunter, had been powerless to prevent the onward progress of the rebels. General McClellan had resumed chief command of the Federal army.

Leaving Arlington Heights to the right, General Lee crossed the Potomac into Maryland. Having in view the seizure of Harper's Ferry, and designing to test the spirit of the Marylanders, he also threatened Hagerstown, throwing Governor Curtin into the wildest alarm, and animating Baltimore with the hope of emancipation from the thraldom under which she restively groaned. To accomplish his purposes he began a series of brilliant manœuvres, directed mainly towards Virginia, and finally culminating in the battle of Boonesboro' Gap. There the Confederate forces engaged overwhelming odds, but, stubbornly contesting the ground, for a while they gave way under mighty pressure, until the timely arrival of reinforcements under General Longstreet gave them renewed strength. They refused to retreat, and the day was decided by their gaining nothing, though, comparatively, they lost nothing.

From this engagement Virginia counted another illustrious son among the dead. General Garland, a young man of the brightest promise, while endeavoring to rally his men under a galling fire from the enemy, was pierced by a musket ball in the breast, and died upon the field.

While the action of Boonesboro' was in progress, and the enemy attempting to force his way through the main pass on the Frederick and Hagerstown road, the capture of Harper's Ferry was accomplished by the army corps of General Jackson. This occurred on the 14th of September. It seemed only necessary for the genius of Jackson to have part in the combinations of the Confederate programme for success to follow. A writer of the time says: "The extent of the conquest is determined by the fact that we took eleven thousand troops, an equal number of small arms, seventy-three pieces of artillery, and about two hundred wagons. The force of the enemy which surrendered consisted of twelve regiments of infantry, three companies of cavalry, and six companies of artillery. The scene of the surrender was one of deep humiliation to the North. It was indeed a repetition of the revolutionary glories of Yorktown, to see here the proud, gaily-dressed soldiers of the oppressor drawn up in line, stacking their arms, and surrendering to the ragged, barefoot, half-starved soldiers of liberty."

On the 17th of September General Lee had retired to unite his forces, as far as possible, to confront the still advancing legions of the enemy, and then occurred the engagement at Sharpsburg, or Antietam. Here, with an acknowledged force of only about forty thousand men, when the battle commenced, he encountered McClellan with an army of not less than one hundred and fifty thousand men, one hundred thousand of whom were trained soldiers, disciplined in camp and field from the beginning of the war. The battle was a furious one. Many times the Confederates were driven back by the pressing numbers that seemed likely to overwhelm them, but encouraged by the daring example of their officers, they wholly performed their duty. A Federal officer writes: "It is beyond all wonder how such men as the rebel troops can fight as they do. That those ragged wretches, sick, hungry, and in all ways miserable, should prove such heroes in fight, is past explanation. Men never fought better. There was one regiment that stood up before the fire of one of our long range batteries and of two regiments of infantry, and though the air around them was vocal with the whistle of bullets and the scream of shells, there they stood, and delivered their fire in perfect order."

Were we disposed to answer the questions involved in this generous remark of the Federal officer, we might say, the courage which nerved these "ragged, hungry wretches" was found in the cause for which they fought. When "Liberty" is the watchword, therein is an element that strengthens the arm, that emboldens the spirit, that makes the hero!

"'Tis conscience that makes cowards of us all," and the Southern soldier—the Rebel, as he was proud to be termed—in his struggle for the birthright inherited from his forefathers, who too had rebelled and periled their lives for the cause of freedom, was troubled with no reproaches in the defence of his "life, his fortune and his sacred honor." It is but a poor compliment now to tell us that our noble men fought with a degree of devotion worthy of a better cause, when it was alone the overwhelming resources of our enemies that compelled them to yield up a cause dearer to them than life. Let our enemies say what they will of us, but let the name of Liberty be sacred from the profanation of unholy lips.

The day closed in a drawn battle—General Jackson on the same ground held by the Confederates in the morning, and General Burnside clinging closely to the bridge that spanned the Antietam River, afraid to give up the position, for on it hung the issue of the day. The victory to the Confederates was lost by the want of reinforcements to enable us to get possession of the bridge, but other portions of the field were theirs. The loss was immense, and not greater than that of the enemy. But added to other losses, we mourned the sad fate of two of our officers, who had distinguished themselves for great bravery. To the mourning chaplet of the South was added a leaf for Brigadier General Starke, of Louisiana, and one for Brigadier General Branch, of North Carolina, and with them we wept for many brave and gallant officers of inferior rank, and thousands of not less noble if less distinguished spirits from the common soldiery.

The enemy claimed the victory, but abundant evidence of its doubtfulness is found in the fact that they failed to follow up the attack on the broken lines of the Confederates, and permitted General Lee to recross the Potomac on the following day without an attempt at molestation or hindrance, and to secure a position on the opposite side at Shepherdstown. He then made a feint to follow him up by advancing a portion of his troops across the river, in which they were signally repulsed by General A. P. Hill, and pushed into the stream, which was perfectly blockaded by wounded and drowning men in an attempt to escape. It is also certain that this pretence of victory cost McClellan his command. Charges preferred against him were sustained by the official testimony of the Federal Commander-in-Chief, General Halleck, and resulted in the displacement of General McClellan and the elevation of General Ambrose E. Burnside of Rhode Island, who was also destined to feel the steel of the Rebel Lee.

That it was the intention of General Lee, in crossing the Potomac, to hold and occupy Maryland, is proved by his proclamation, issued at Frederick, offering protection to all Marylanders who might come into his lines; and that he was induced to return into Virginia, not by the stress of defeat in any single battle, but by force of circumstances, to which, in the Southern heart it is painful to refer, making the campaign in Maryland on the whole a failure, we are also compelled to admit.

But though in the main unsuccessful, it was not barren of usefulness to our cause. At the same time his intention of a mere predatory incursion into the territory of the enemy, as accredited to him by some who would fain defame a spotless name, could not have entered into designs which involved interests greatly superior to the dash and chivalry of a raid. Though these virtuous designs failed of perfect accomplishment, yet our army gave further illustration of their valor, and the reverse to their arms at Harper's Ferry, without a parallel in the history of the war, had inflicted on the enemy a loss in men and material far greater than our own losses, and in retreating into Virginia left to them neither provisions nor spoils, as evidences of the successes claimed.

The New York *Tribune* declares, in reference to the barren results claimed by the Federals from this campaign; "He leaves us the *débris* of his late camp, two disabled pieces of artillery, a few hundred stragglers, perhaps two thousand of his wounded, and as many more of his unburied dead. Not a sound field-piece, caisson, ambulance or wagon, not a tent, box of stores, or a pound of ammunition. He takes with him the supplies gathered in Maryland, and the rich spoils of Harper's Ferry."

The *Tribune* is honest, and further states that his defeat, if defeat it may be considered, is mainly attributable to the failure of the Marylanders to sustain the Confederate cause as they promised, and in inducements held out by them, and that General Lee's retreat across the Potomac was a masterpiece of strategy.

We had long been accustomed to listening to the cry from oppressed Maryland, from down-trodden Baltimore, "Come over and help us!" To Virginia their hands were outstretched, and imploringly they besought release from their Federal shackles. Maryland had charged upon Virginia's tardiness in the commencement of the war her own miserable condition. Our hearts bled, and remorse seized upon our souls when this reproach greeted us in Richmond. "Look at my own dear oppressed State! Give her but half a chance, and you will learn where will be the heart of Maryland in this struggle." They were ready to stake their lives on the action of Maryland.

> "Thou wilt not yield the Vandal toll,
> Maryland! my Maryland!
> Thou wilt not crook to his control,
> Maryland! my Maryland!
> Better the fire around thee roll,
> Better the shot, the blade, the bowl,
> Than crucifixion of the soul—
> Maryland! my Maryland!"

This refrain was caught up on all lips; the sentiment found echo in all hearts; and we felt like sending up loud "Hosannahs!" when there came a time to enfranchise the spirit of our beloved and commiserated sister. We rejoiced to know that crushed Maryland could throw off her iron fetters, and array herself under the star-crossed banner of her hope for redemption.

The disappointment when, in response to the proclamation of our Commander-in-Chief, a few hundred stragglers came timidly into our lines, was too keenly felt in Richmond to avoid expression in rough language, much as was deprecated the wounding of the feelings of the sensitive. There was a sensible revulsion of sympathetic feeling for Maryland in Virginia, and for a time the blatant boasts of some, unnaturally excited and offensive, were silenced. Yet scarcely with sufficient cause did Mr. Vest, of Missouri, piqued, doubtless, in his personal experience, deliver himself of a speech in the Confederate Congress, in which he unmercifully contrasted the actions of the Marylanders with those of Missourians in the South, to the reproach of the former. When a bill passed Congress including straggling Marylanders in the conscription, the beautiful and pariotic words of "My Maryland," were most amusingly travestied:

> "Conscribers' heels are at thy door,
> Maryland! my Maryland!
> So off to Baltimore we'll go,
> Maryland! my Maryland!
> We can't stay here to meet the foe,
> We might get shot and killed, you know;
> But when we're safe we'll brag and blow,
> Maryland! my Maryland!"

There is now no possibility of mistaking the throbbing of the great heart of Maryland. It was with us if not of us, and its sympathy with our destitution and misery has sublimely shown the throes it endured in the agony of separation. An apology for the failure of the people to join the standard of General Lee, to which they had been invited, and through which they had been assured protection, may be readily given in the explanation that he occupied a section of the State known to contain among its population the most violent Union men of Maryland—a population far from representing the popular feeling of the State—and that a meeting in Baltimore, though only forty-five miles from the Confederate lines at Frederick, could have been easily suppressed, as the city lay under the immediate shadow of two immense fortresses, the guns of which, in a few hours' time, could reduce it to destruction. Strongly guarded as it was by Federal pickets, it was no easy matter for the men of Baltimore to effect an escape to the Confederate army.

However, this was not at the time so understood generally at the South. In reference to it a writer says, "It is true, the South could not have expected a welcome in these counties, (the counties occupied by General Lee,) nor a desperate mutiny for the Confederacy in Baltimore, but it was expected that Southern sympathizers in other parts of the State, who so glibly ran the blockade on adventures of trade, might as readily work their way to the Confederate army as to the Confederate markets, and it was not expected that the few recruits who timidly advanced to our lines, would have been so easily dismayed by the rags of our soldiers, and by the prospects of a service that promised equal measures of hardship and glory."

In the bitterness of defeat and humiliation, asceticism and unamiability must be excused, and an appreciation of the same writer conceived, when he continues: "The army which rested again in Virginia had made a history that will flash down the tide of time a lustre of glory. It had done an amount of marching and fighting that appears almost incredible, even to those minds familiar with the records of great military exertions. Leaving the banks of the James river, it proceeded directly to the lines of the Rappahannock, and moving out from that river, it fought its way to the Potomac, crossed that stream, and moved on to Fredericktown and Hagerstown, had a heavy engagement at the mountain gaps below, fought the greatest pitched battle of the war at Sharpsburg, and then recrossed the Potomac again into Virginia.

"During all this time, covering the full space of a month, the troops rested but four days. Of the men who performed these wonders, one-fifth of them were barefoot, one-half of them in rags, and the whole of them half famished."

Remembering that Richmond was indeed the Confederate barometer, as well as the heart and brain of our young, aspiring nation, we must struggle to confine ourselves as closely as possible to the city and its surroundings, yet shall be compelled occasionally to wander into other portions of the Confederacy in order to ascertain the reflex influence on the Capital.

At this time there was a lull in the war in Virginia. By appointment of our Executive, the 18th of September had been set apart for special thanksgiving to Almighty God for the merciful deliverance from our enemies, and for the success that had crowned our arms. The occasion was universally observed; and just here it is proper to remark that, amid all the striking vicissitudes of the late war, the Christian integrity of the masses of the Southern people changed only to add a brighter and brighter lustre to the religion of Christ. The most remarkable devotion characterized the people, and prayers and thanksgivings were uttered in spirit as well as in name.

On the 19th General Lee recrossed the Potomac, and his army rested once more on the soil of Virginia. For some time there was quiet along the lines, undisturbed except by the dashing movements of General Stuart and his cavalry. By these little seems to have been intended, unless to show with what ease incursions could be made into Maryland and Pennsylvania, and the admirable good-breeding of the Southern chivalry, in contrast to the universal indignities heaped upon the innocent and helpless in the predatory incursions of our enemies. The treatment of the women of the South by certain of the Federal soldiery will present a black page in the records of the boasted civilization of this age and country.

From Kentucky the intelligence was truly depressing. It was difficult for us to understand how she could submit to her forced and unnatural position of "armed neutrality." We were exasperated at the lawless violence that reigned in Missouri, and discouraged at the prospect in Mississippi, yet upon our hopes there could have been placed no extinguisher as long as the sunlight of prosperity irradiated the prospect of peace and independence in Virginia.

CHAPTER XXXVII.

SCENES IN RICHMOND IN THE WINTER OF 1862–3.

AS the war went on, a marked change was made in the educational interests of the South. For a certain number of pupils, the teachers of schools were exempt from military duty. To their credit be it recorded that few, comparatively, availed themselves of this exception, and the care of instructing the youth devolved, with other added responsibilities, upon the women of the country. Only boys under the conscript age were found in the schools; all older were made necessary in the field or in some department of government service, unless physical inability prevented them from falling under the requirements of the law. Many of our colleges for males suspended operation, and at the most important period in the course of their education our youths were instructed in the sterner lessons of military service.

Female schools were supported as best they could be where there was a lamentable scarcity of books, and where the expenses of education were so great that only the most wealthy could afford to give their daughters the advantages of a liberal course. Such were the difficulties that hedged the way to mental cultivation, that it seemed, in many instances, almost a matter of impossibility to pursue any regular plan of education for girls.

The operations of the Richmond Female College were suspended, or rather, the building was given up for hospital purposes, and the excellent institution of Mr. LeFebvre was entirely broken up; but the Southern Female Institute, a first-grade seminary, under the supervision of Mr. Lee Powell, the fine school of Miss Pegram, St. Joseph's Academy, and other institutions under the patronage of the Catholic Church, were sustained. Though the encouragement to these schools was thoroughly liberal, so heavy were the expenses that it was almost impossible to keep them in successful operation.

There was also a sad want of school-books. The stock on hand when the war commenced soon became exhausted, and there were no new ones to supply the consequent demand. Very few came to us through the blockade. Books were the last consideration in that eccentric trade. Inconveniences arose at every step to impede the progress of education in the Confederacy. School-books which had long before been cast aside as obsolete, and banished from the shelves of the library, and hidden away to moulder in dark closets, were brought to light, and placed in the hands of children, from which to add to the stock of ideas, in the process of youthful development.

There was no time for authorship or compilation, and publication was conducted under such serious disadvantages, and at such enormous cost, that it grew to be almost impossible.

There was a pitiable scarcity of paper. Our newspapers presented as singular a variety in appearance and size as in the character of the sheets. Some afforded a double, some a single sheet, and the most important of the dailies were issued on a half-sheet of coarse paper, and sometimes on a poor quality of brown paper. Our epistolary correspondence was carried on upon such paper as before the war we should have considered indifferent for wrapping purposes. Not unfrequently letters were replied to in the same envelope in which we had inclosed our missive, but carefully unsealed, turned, and the superscription addressed on the inside.

But our philosophical men were as well satisfied to pen the glowing inspirations of patriotism on their Confederate paper, as they would have been to have inscribed them on the best vellum-post: and the Southern maiden was as well content to pen a billet-doux to her soldier lover on the coarse, rough sheet, that blotted at almost every touch of the pen, and to inclose the precious document in the rude Confederate envelope of turned wall paper, as if she had written her love on the softest, tiniest sheet of French note, and the seal to the enameled envelope had been a silver dove, bearing in its beak a scroll, on which was lettered a line of melting French or Latin. We gloried in our national simplicity, and looked to a peaceful release from the inconveniences of the moment.

Amusements were almost entirely abandoned. Our only

theatre had been destroyed by fire; and the exhibitions at the Varieties and the heterogeneous shows and performances at the Metropolitan Hall, failed to attract the better class of the Richmond public. Our women, who during the day, watched beside the couch, and made up clothes for the soldiers, would often at night, get up concerts for their benefit. Little children added their mite to the soldiers' fund, by hoarding up their trifling sums, originating fairs, and selling refreshments. Such were some of the means of virtuous endeavor.

But while these brilliant examples of the spirit of true patriotism were noticeable in our city, there were some, and I regret to record, not a few, who made use of this time of urgent necessity, to amass riches, which could only be accompilshed at the expense of all the nobler principles that should have actuated a people. That no man could make money fairly and honestly, under the painful circumstances in which we were placed, is a fact too well understood to need much argument to substantiate. A distinguished officer in the Confederate Army, who had served in an honorable capacity in the war with Mexico, said, "I should think there are very few men who will be willing, after this war, to acknowledge that they served the Confederacy as a commissary or quarter-master." Such constant use was made of the funds of the government in outside speculations, by those connected with the commissary and quartermaster's departments of the army, that the wealth acquired in that way, or the sudden riches of those men, ever excited suspicions of foul play.

The same officer—a lawyer of fine ability—remarked: "It would be well when the war is over, for the assessment of the taxes on the property of persons then and before the commencement of the war, to be compared, and all above a legitimate gain to his means, under all the circumstances by which we are surrounded, should be confiscated to the use of the soldier, who loses by the neglect of his business, while at work for his country. No man can honestly and conscientiously amass wealth at this time." And yet there were those who were before poor, now purchasing fine estates, driving fine horses, rolling in the finest coaches they could procure, and faring as sumptuously as our market would allow, while others were growing poorer and poorer, retrenching in expenditures, doing all they could, and giving all they had to spare for the support of the cause in which the interests of the South were so fully involved.

When the autumn came on, the store-houses which had been occupied for hospitals throughout the summer, were cleared of their patients, and cleared up for other uses, and although we groaned under the blockade that hindered the importation of goods into our country, these buildings were all more or less filled with articles run in on the under-ground route, and frequently overland, under the pretext of bringing in medicines, wines, etc., for the use of the Confederate Government. On almost every square in the business portion of Main Street, there was an auction-house, and we could seldom walk down that street without seeing numerous red flags of the auctioneer, or passing a motley crowd of Jews and Gentiles eagerly desirous to purchase their stock for the retail trade. Stopping a moment, we could hear the stentorian voice of the seller, as he cried, "This beautiful article (perhaps a flimsy piece of cotton domestic, or a five cent calico) going at such a price. Shameful! going at such a sacrifice, only —— *dollars* per yard. It is, I assure you, gentlemen, an outrage upon my better judgment to be compelled to sell it upon such terms! Will no one give more?—I say will no one make a better bid on this valuable article?—going!—once!—twice!—three—times!" and down would come the gavel of the auctioneer, and the gratified purchaser would be cogitating the immense percentage he should realize in the retail. It was said not unfrequently to have been the case, that the wholesale merchants of these stocks of blockade goods, had their "*by-bidders*," and if a price unsatisfactory to their avarice or cupidity could only be obtained, they were sold to these fictitious purchasers, to be resold at an early day, at a price far exceeding that offered at the previous sale. Had these dishonest proceedings been confined to articles of taste or luxury alone, we could better have endured the impositions and extortions for which we had no redress; but when, for the bare necessaries of life, we were at the mercy of these relentless persecutors, the curse became so heavy that we groaned and writhed under it.

The remark of a lady, "After the war is over, the parvenues of the time will roll by in their splendid carriages, and throw the dust of their insolence in the faces of the old aristocrats," was quoted by many, and the prospect for such a state of things seemed altogether probable.

In the stores of the jewellers there were never finer diamonds exhibited in Richmond. The sellers were not usually those who had been long established there, but new shops were opened, in which were displayed splendid gems, fine watches, and various other articles which gave rise to the question, "Where did they come from?". They were, however, sold, and the fortunate purchasers made wise investment of their Confederate money in diamonds and other gems. The excuse offered for all this was always found in the depreciation of the currency, which continued until the inflation of the prices on articles of food and clothing, put it quite out of the power of the masses to live in any sort of comfort. As yet, when spoken to on the subject of peace by submission, we were laughed at, and the noble reply, "We can endure much more before we are prepared to submit dishonorably," was that which came from the lips of those who were subjected to these additional distresses.

That the depreciation of the currency was brought about or greatly assisted by the insane spirit of speculation which possessed the people, is true beyond the power of refutation, and the valueless money was only made the apology for the continued frauds that were practiced on the government and the people.

It was, however, resisted by many, who were impotent to correct it. The indulgence in extravagances, and even the purchase of necessary articles of clothing, were abandoned by the better thinking and more patriotic class of our inhabitants. It was not in the power of the ladies of Richmond to manufacture their domestic dresses, as did the ladies in other parts of the South, but they became proficient in making their carefully kept wardrobe (by judicious turning and mending, and careful brushings and cleansing,) appear quite as well as they wished in the situation in which we were placed. Luxurious dressing was altogether given up, but for neatness, taste, elegance and refinement, even under the Confederate dress, the Southern women would compare favorably with those who never for a moment were shut out from the world of fashion and indulgence.

Our gentlemen appeared under their home-made hats, their homespun coats, or well-worn broadcloth, brushed until the threadbare appearance indicated the length of time in which it had been in service, or better, the coarse Confederate grey, was the fashionable dress of the Southern gentleman.

It was not in the power of our people to cultivate the caprices of fashion, nor to indulge in wanton luxury or extravagance, to be clad in scarlet or fine linen, nor to fare sumptuously every day, but they cultivated the better graces of the heart, the refinement of benevolence and Christian charity, and laid by useful lessons of economy and contentment, and became philosophers under the bitter chastisement of most cruel adversity. The cheerful fortitude with which the people of the South endured the numberless ills entailed upon them by the course of war bids us hold them up as brilliant examples of virtuous patriotism and heroic contentment.

> "The brave unfortunate are our best acquaintance;
> They show us virtue may be much distressed,
> And give us their example how to suffer."

The literature of the time was almost wholly connected with the all-engrossing topic of the war. Histories of battles and sieges, of successes and defeats, of dangers by land and sea, were those with which the Confederate reader was usually entertained. But in our miseries and misfortunes we were frequently cheered by merciful visits from the muses, who, picking their way through the blockade, and running the gauntlet of lines of battle, and ignoring whizzing balls and bursting, crackling shell, would sing a lullaby to anxious fears, or inspire strains of patriotism. The war poetry of the South would do credit to and would be proudly claimed by any nation.

Romance was little indulged. There were neither the time nor the means for it. The appearance of "Macaria," from the eloquent pen of Miss Evans, of Mobile, was a welcome exception to the literature of the times. A few books straggled to us through the blockade. Joseph the Second and his Court, and Victor Hugo's Les Misérables, afforded us the most pleasurable recreation and enjoyment, and added a charming variety to our reading. A few original novelettes appeared, but there was little literary endeavor. Mental improvement was pursued under difficulties wellnigh unconquerable.

A remarkable change had become evident in the agricultural interests of our people. As the raising of cotton in the more southern States had been superseded by the cultivation of the then more important crops of wheat, corn, oats, rye, and potatoes, for the use of man and beast, so in Virginia the "nauseous weed," so long a source of wealth to her planters, was made to yield place to the cereals which furnished bread for the people and the army. In many sections of our country, from which the slaves had been driven or seduced to leave, the plowing and reaping, the hoeing and planting, were performed by men over the conscript age, assisted by the women, the delicate daughters of ease, whose faces the "winds of heaven" had never been permitted to "visit too roughly;" and these labors, made compulsory by cruel misfortune, were performed with cheerfulness, and in no craven spirit of submission, or longings for luxurious indulgence heard in a sigh for the "flesh-pots of Egypt."

CHAPTER XXXVIII.

BURNSIDE'S CAMPAIGN—REFUGEES IN RICHMOND.

ALTHOUGH no State of the South had been exempt from the scourge, Virginia had borne the brunt of the war. Wherever the foot of the invader had been pressed, it left its mark in desolation. Along the Potomac River scarcely a dwelling remained to indicate that that fair region had once been the abode of one of the happiest, most refined and intelligent communities in our country, but charred monuments of destruction betokened the work of the incendiary and the despoiler.

We had enjoyed for an unusual length of time a season of calmness, but it was not to continue much longer. Our enemies were not satisfied to depredate alone upon our northern border. The cry: "On to Richmond!" again awoke an echo from our fancied security. A change of programme had been effected. Discarding the beaten track of his unfortunate predecessors, General Burnside charged himself with the destruction of the rebel capital in the usual "ten days," but by a different route. Through Fredericksburg, though by a feint in the direction of Gordonsville, he expected to deceive his formidable rival, and thus secure the shorter road to Richmond and the attainment of the desired end, by crossing the Rappahannock at that city, under the impression that General Lee had thrown a large portion of his force down the river and elsewhere, and had thus weakened his defences in the front. How fatally this mistake told upon his enterprise, is inferable from the unwilling retreat he was compelled to make across the

Rappahannock, and the immense heaps of dead left behind him to testify to the failure of his movement. On the night of the 10th of December the enemy began to throw his bridges across the Rappahannock. On the night of the 11th the cheers from the troops announced that the work was completed, and it only remained for the two armies to take such position as they could best obtain for the dreadful work ahead of them. Already the bombardment had commenced. Hundreds of families, remaining there until the last moment, now fled for their lives from the homes that had sheltered them. There they were, in the cold of winter, wandering, houseless, hungry and wretched, they knew not whither, seeking safety wherever they could find it, and many following the track of the railroad until they found shelter from the freezing cold, and were out of sight if not of sound of the missiles of destruction that were desolating the homes from which they had been forced under such cruel circumstances.

On the morning of the 13th of December, as the sun rose and dispersed the fog that had settled over the mutilated remains of old Fredericksburg, it revealed the Confederate troops under arms and awaiting the attack from the forces of Burnside. Their batteries were all in position, and soon the belching fire, and smoke, and death, and carnage, and conflict of battle shook the hills that surrounded the ancient town. Our enemies fought perseveringly, but against them the two Hills were operating; Stonewall Jackson was forcing them with his unconquered band of heroes ; General Longstreet was coolly trying their steel ; General Early was successfully telling upon them a story of dismay, and General Stuart was redeeming his promise to "crowd 'em" with artillery. The attack on Mary's Heights, committed to the task of General Meagher, with his brave Irish troops, left a sad witness, in the piles of his dead, of his failure to secure this strong position of the Confederates. The fighting was principally with artillery. Again and again the enemy rallied under the sure and steady fire of the "rebels," but were finally driven back in despair, and pushed into the town by our infantry.

The day was won. Victory once more perched on the banner of the Confederates, and the utter rout of the army of General Burnside was only prevented, perhaps, by the failure on the part of the "rebels" to attack his forces on the next day, while they remained in Fredericksburg, without affording them time to attempt to recross the river. This they accomplished on the following night, unmolested—and the army that had seemed in the very jaws of destruction quietly reorganized on the shore opposite the town, which to many had appeared as inevitably the scene of their utter demolition.

Again at this place was repeated the old story of a barren victory. A powerful check had been given to the enemy, but no more than a check. He had succeeded perfectly in withdrawing the army that had seemed in the grasp of capture.

A Southern historian says: "The story of Fredericksburg is incomplete and unsatisfactory, and there appeared no prospect but that a war waged at awful sacrifices was yet indefinitely to linger in the trail of bloody skirmishes. The victory which had only the negative advantage of having checked the enemy, without destroying him, and the vulgar glory of having killed and wounded several thousand men more than we had lost, had been purchased by us with lives though comparatively small in numbers, yet infinitely more precious than those of the mercenary hordes arrayed against us."

Besides large numbers of brave men from the ranks, and numerous subordinate officers in this battle, we lost two distinguished brigadier-generals. They were General Thomas R. R. Cobb, of Georgia, (brother of General Howell Cobb, a member of our provisional Congress, and a man well known in the political circles of our country,) and General Maxcy Gregg, of South Carolina.

Every battle added fresh leaves to the mourning chaplet

of the South. General Gregg's name was so familiarly associated with the opening of the war, that to us in Richmond it had become a "household word." He had commanded the first regiment sent to the war in Virginia, (the 1st South Carolina Regiment.) After its term of service had expired, and it had returned to its native State, Colonel Gregg remained in Virginia, and subsequently reorganized the regiment, which after that time was constantly and conspicuously in service. He was afterwards commissioned Brigadier-General.

General Gregg was a lawyer of distinguished ability, and had for more than twenty years held a prominent position at the bar of South Carolina. He possessed, in an eminent degree, that thorough goodness of heart, that real politeness, which can emanate alone from the generous and virtuous, and the most finished eulogy on his fine character is better expressed in the remark of an humble courier, who said of him, "He was the General who always said to his.couriers, '*I thank you*' to do this and that," than in any redundant terms of measured encomium. We find that "General Gregg was remarkable for his firm and unflinching temper. In the army he had an extraordinary reputation for self-possession and *sang froid* in battle. He was never disconcerted, and had the happy faculty of inspiring the courage of his troops—not so much by words as by his cool determination and even behavior." The conduct of the women of Fredericksburg at this terrible time surpasses all expressed admiration, and the success of our engagement there is greatly attributable to their heroic courage and patriotic self-abnegation.

The writer to whom we have so frequently referred, says, " The romance of the story of Fredericksburg is written no less in the heroism of her women than in deeds of arms. The verses of the poet, rather than the cold language of the mere chronicle of events, are the most fitting to describe the beautiful courage and noble sacrifices of those brave daughters of Virginia, who preferred to see their homes reduced to ashes rather than polluted by the invader, and who in the blasts of winter, and in the fiercer storms of blood and fire went forth undismayed, encouraging our soldiers, and proclaiming their desire to suffer privation, poverty, and death, rather than the shame of a surrender, or the misfortune of a defeat. In all the terrible scenes of Fredericksburg there were no weakness and tears of woman. Mothers, exiles from their homes, met their sons in the ranks, embraced them, told them their duty, and with a self-abnegation most touching to witness, concealed from them their want, sometimes their hunger, telling their brave boys they were comfortable and happy, that they might not be troubled with domestic anxieties. At Hamilton's Crossing, (near Fredericksburg, on the Richmond, Fredericksburg, and Potomac Railroad,) "Many of the women had the opportunity of meeting their relatives in the army. In the haste of flight mothers brought a few garments, or perhaps the last loaf of bread for the soldier boy, and the lesson of duty whispered in the ear, gave to the young heart the pure and brave inspiration to sustain it in battle. No more touching and noble evidence of the heroism of the women of Fredericksburg could be offered than the gratitude of our army, for afterwards, when subscriptions for their relief came to be added up it was found that thousands of dollars had been contributed by ragged soldiers out of their pittance of pay to the fund of the refugees. There could be no more eloquent tribute than this offered to the women of Fredericksburg—a beautiful and immortal souvenir of their sufferings and virtues."

What occurred in the sacking of the town must bring a blush of shame to the cheeks of all those who were engaged in the wanton destruction and robbery of the houses of those forced to leave under such cruel circumstances. Not even the thirst for revenge, the promptings of malice against a people who had dared to raise their hands to prevent further encroachments upon principles they held as sacred,—but to which others gave the name "*treason,*"—can excuse the lawless violence and the wanton destruction of the places of abode of wandering and helpless women. "Might" can never make Right a cowardice, that takes form in deeds of ignoble revenge.

Very soon the population of Richmond was increased by hundreds of these helpless refugees, hundreds of the wounded of our army, and hundreds of the prisoners taken captive at this time. The labors of benevolence that had been for awhile suspended, or less extensively exercised, were called into full action, and the summer occupation of the inhabitants of Richmond was rehearsed in the cold of winter. There did not at this time exist so great a number of private hospitals, but the general hospitals remained in full operation, and the nursing qualifications of the women of Virginia were kept in constant practice.

Conspicuous among the ladies of the South, whose management of hospitals in Richmond was blessed to the final health or the comfortable condition of the soldier, we mention first the noble "Sisters of Charity," of the institution of St. Joseph's and St. Frances de Sales, Mrs. Judge Hopkins, of Alabama, Mrs. General Memminger, of Georgia, Mrs. Webb, Miss S. Robinson, Mrs. Judge Clapton, and Mrs. Grant, of Richmond; Miss Mason, Mrs. Rowland, Mrs. Hove, Mrs. Taylor, of Virginia; Mrs. Upham, of Louisiana, and many other ladies whose names it is unnecessary to mention, but who were angels of mercy to the sick, the wounded, and helpless sufferers from the dire misfortunes of the war. Again the cycle of time had brought to us the Christmas season. But with sadder remembrances still was the festival observed than that of one year before. Aside from the usual religious observances of the day—the joining in the chorus :

> "Shout the glad tidings, exulting sing—
> Jerusalem triumphs, Messiah is king,"

there was little to remind us of the festival of yore.

The Christmas dinner passed off gloomily. The vacant

chairs were multiplied in Southern homes, and even the children who had so curiously questioned the cause of the absence of the young soldier brother from the festive board, had heard too much, had seen too much, and knew too well why sad-colored garments were worn by the mother, and the fold of rusty crape placed around the worn hat of the father, and why the joyous mirth of the sister was restrained, and her beautiful figure draped in mourning. Congratulations were forced, and tears had taken the place of smiles on countenances where cheerfulness was wont to reign.

CHAPTER XXXIX.

RUNNING THE BLOCKADE.

AT an early period in the New Year—1863—the Confederate Congress reassembled, and our reading was varied by the daily reports from that body, and our time enlivened by mornings spent at the Capitol. Discussions in Congress were mainly carried on between Mr. Foote, on the one side, and one or another of his many incorrigible opposers on the other. He was sensibly affected with the importance of making terms with certain of the Western and Middle States, which were suffering from the effects of the war, in proportion as the New England States were gaining in wealth and importance, by tendering them the free navigation of the Mississippi River, and proposing to secure to them that right in an alliance with the Confederacy. However much these propositions, apparently submitted in good faith by the aged member, may have been for the real good of the Confederacy, they were feebly encouraged by the press, and in the army and in Congress it seemed enough that they originated with the unfortunately unpopular member.

That active measures were necessary on the part of our Congress to meet the opportunity which had arisen in the divided sentiment at the North, from the Emancipation Proclamation of Mr. Lincoln, appeared obvious; and that terms offered the States so greatly disaffected at that time to the Federal government, by internal trouble, might have resulted in good for the Confederacy is also supposable; but these opportunities for profit, if indeed they did exist, were permitted to pass by unimproved—were lost. Upon whose head must rest the consequences we know not.

The scarcity of provisions was becoming a matter of serious consideration. This is known from the fact that Congress passed laws for the impressment of food for the army. At the same time our financial troubles had grown to be alarming.

A great portion of our territory, and especially the principal grain-growing section of Virginia, was in the occupation of the enemy. All these difficulties combined to bring about the enormous prices placed on all articles of food, and to meet the excessive demands, Congress authorized a heavy increase in the circulation of the money issued by the Confederate Treasury, and every attempt made to improve our condition, under the unfortunate financial management of our Secretary of the Treasury, was from bad to worse. The depreciation of our currency was mainly attributable to the redundancy of the circulating medium, and encouraged a spirit of the wildest speculation and the most relentless extortion.

Blockade-running was extensively practiced by the Jews of Richmond, as well as by others, whose nationality, purely Southern, ought to have encouraged expectations of more decided patriotism than was exhibited by them in their insane desire to grow rich. In this unlawful business they found willing coadjutors in Baltimore and other cities, and it soon became evident that all the boxes, barrels and crates that were brought into Richmond could not contain drugs for the Confederacy. The city almost abounded in well-filled stores. The quantity, rather than the quality, was noticeable in these supplies, and for the most worthless articles we were compelled to pay the most extravagant prices.

The region of country from Richmond across the Pamunky and Mattapony Rivers, through King and Queen and Essex counties to the Rappahannock River, and thence across the northern neck of Virginia and the Potomac into Maryland, was constantly traversed by these wanderers, who took delight in a trade which, notwithstanding the dangers from capture and the confiscation of their strangely gotten merchandise, had in it a pleasurable excitement. Ports of entry were opened at different points on the route, and sometimes the unlucky blockade runner, for want of proper credentials for carrying on his trade, was unmercifully relieved of his goods by a cunning custom-house officer, and the confiscation of his effects was the consequence.

Occasionally women were found engaged in this singular business, and successfully smuggled into Richmond many articles that failed to pass the inspection of the custom-house officers, and thus made heavy profits on the goods they succeeded in taking in free of duty. A lady who had been on a visit to some friends in King and Queen County tells an amusing story of her trip to her home in Richmond, and her apprehension as a "blockade-runner." She says: "I had been mud-bound in King and Queen County from the middle of January until the beginning of March, and constantly fearful that by some movement of the enemy I might be cut off from Richmond, I was in great anxiety to return. From day to day it would rain and snow, and hail and sleet, until the roads, cut up with the heavy wagons of the army, were left in no condition for a carriage to travel even a mile in the direction of Richmond.

"At last a friend took me in a buggy as far as Frazier's Ferry, on the Mattaponi River, with the intention of going with me to the White House, on the Pamunky, there to take the cars on the York River Railroad for Richmond. When we arrived at the Ferry we met not less than a dozen wagons, filled with the goods of the blockade runners, *en route* to Richmond. But the wind was high, and the ferryman positively refused to take the boat over, as thereby he should endanger the lives of his passengers and the loss of the teams, goods, etc. I was in despair. At last two or three blockade runners, of the tribe of Israel, proposed to help me out of my difficulty by crossing in a foot-boat, and if a carriage could be procured on the opposite side of the river, to signalize me, and then I could decide whether or not I should accept their escort to Richmond. They were rather questionable looking men, and their trade being so much in disfavor, I debated in my mind whether I should go with them: but the fear of being thrown in the lines of the enemy decided me. When I caught the signal of success in procuring a carriage, I passed over the stream in a foot-boat, and on the opposite shore took leave of the kind gentleman, who regretted his inability to go on with me further.

"Our conveyance was an ambulance, and making myself as agreeable as possible to my friends, the blockade runners, I passed on safely to the ferry at the White House. When we arrived at the river, there was standing a wagon filled with trunks, barrels, boxes, kegs, carpet-bags, and articles of baggage of every conceivable description, all of which were stored around me in the ferry-boat, to the exclusion of my escorts. When I arrived on the opposite shore, pointing out my bonnet-box and carpet-sack to an officer who assisted me from the boat, I hastily purchased a ticket at the station, and had only time to take my seat in the cars before the time for them to leave.

"I confess I felt some anxiety for the welfare of my Jewish friends, but I was awakened to a sense of the suspicion my own appearance amid the piles of baggage had created, by the appearance of two villainous-looking detectives, who demanded my passports for the goods I was carrying through the blockade.

"'I have no blockade goods,' I replied, regarding this as a joke.

"'Oh,' said the detectives, 'do you pretend to tell us that a lady travelling alone can carry as much baggage as you carry, and have nothing contraband?'

"'You are indeed mistaken,' I replied; 'the baggage that came over in the boat with me is not all mine, by any means. I only have a small carpet-bag and a bonnet-box.'

"'Very strange!' continued one of the detectives; 'but have you a passport to go into Richmond?'

"'I did not know that a passport was necessary to take me into Richmond.'

"'Where is your home?' asked the detective.

"'In Richmond,' I replied.

"'Where have you been, and where are you now from?' persisted the detective.

"'I have been making a visit to some friends in King and Queen County; I am a native Virginian, and have done all I could for the success of the Confederacy. I am a lady, sir, (which remark was intended to be very comprehensive,) and would hardly engage in the questionable business of blockade-running; and from whom should I obtain a passport?'

"I was growing angry, but began to fear further trouble.

"'You should have obtained a passport from a Justice of the Peace, and then you would not have been suspected. Our orders are to put off all suspected persons.'

"'Well, do you intend to put me off here? It is almost dark, very cold, and no accommodations for the night!'

"'Our orders are peremptory,' replied the detective.

"Turning on my seat, (the trouble was growing serious, that I at first considered only a capital joke,) I caught the attention of a Confederate officer of my acquaintance, who was just then approaching me, and I implored him to help me out of my difficulty.

"He laughed heartily, and then turning to the persistent detectives, remarked : 'Be off, sirs, I can indorse this lady. She carries nothing contraband, I can assure you.'

"The dissatisfied detectives, who evidently wished to have 'a scene,' left me rather reluctantly, and soon returning, said to me : 'Will you be kind enough to go into the baggage-car and point out your baggage?'

"'No, I will not,' I replied ; 'if you are not satisfied with the identification of me by my friend, Lieutenant ———, just put me off the car, and I'll seek protection somewhere in the neighborhood, and see about this hereafter.'

"This show of courage," said she, "drove away my persecutors, but I was careful after that time not to travel over the route of the blockade-runners."

This species of trade became so objectionable, and added so greatly to the discomfort of our situation, that "running in goods" in that way was made subject to a heavy legal penalty ; but it was either impossible to hinder the underground importation, or it was winked at, for these supplies of goods continued to be brought into Richmond, and the temporary check to the trade by legal prohibition only made an excuse for the increase in price of those goods already on the shelves of the merchants.

Whether it was in the power of Congress to correct the evils entailed upon us so singularly, or whether they lacked the moral courage to pass stringent laws against such abuses, it remains for those better informed to speak.

To add to other afflictions, our city was visited by the small pox early in the winter. This disease not only prevailed among the soldiers in and around the city, but many of the inhabitants, exposed to the contagion they could not tell when, nor where, contracted the disease, and all over the city the infected houses were distinguished by the white flag of alarm from the windows. The mortality from small pox was not extensive, and considering all the circumstances of its appearance and prevalence, it existed for a very short time, and its disappearance was sudden. It is said to have been brought into Richmond by the prisoners taken at the battle of Fredericksburg; but by the spring it had entirely disappeared from the city, and only existed at the small pox hospital, more than a mile without the limits of the corporation. In connection with the small pox other violent diseases appeared, and there seemed to remain for us to endure only the last of the three great plagues—war, pestilence and famine! Some of our hopeless ones—the miserable croakers who ever look on the dark side of the picture—added to our distress by predicting that famine would certainly follow in the train of evils, and our enemies had engaged to bring it upon us as one of the means of our subjugation.

CHAPTER XL.

THE BREAD RIOT IN RICHMOND.

THESE precautions had some influence in originating in Richmond in the Spring of this year, (1863,) a most disgraceful riot, to which, in order to conceal the real designs of the lawless mob engaged in it, was given the name of the "bread riot."

The rioters were represented in a heterogeneous crowd of Dutch, Irish, and free negroes—of men, women, and children—armed with pistols, knives, hammers, hatchets, axes, and every other weapon which could be made useful in their defence, or might subserve their designs in breaking into stores for the purpose of thieving. More impudent and defiant robberies were never committed, than disgraced, in the open light of day, on a bright morning in spring, the city of Richmond. The cry for bread with which this violence commenced was soon subdued, and instead of articles of food, the rioters directed their efforts to stores containing dry-goods, shoes, etc. Women were seen bending under loads of sole-leather, or dragging after them heavy cavalry boots, brandishing their huge knives, and swearing, though apparently well fed, that they were dying from starvation— yet it was difficult to imagine how they could masticate or digest the edibles under the weight of which they were bending. Men carried immense loads of cotton cloth, woolen goods, and other articles, and but few were seen to attack the stores where flour, groceries, and other provisions were kept.

This disgraceful mob was put to flight by the military. Cannon were planted in the street, and the order to disperse or be fired upon drove the rioters from the commercial portion of the city to the Capitol Square, where they menaced the Governor, until, by the continued threatenings of the State Guards and the efforts of the police in arresting the ringleaders, a stop was put to these lawless and violent proceedings.

It cannot be denied that *want of bread* was at this time too fatally true, but the sufferers for food were not to be found in this mob of vicious men and lawless viragoes who, inhabiting quarters of the city where reigned riot and depravity, when followed to their homes after this demonstration, were discovered to be well supplied with articles of food. Some of them were the keepers of stores, to which they purposed adding the stock stolen in their raid on wholesale houses.

This demonstration was made use of by the disaffected in our midst, and by our enemies abroad, for the misrepresentation and exaggeration of our real condition. In a little while the papers of the North published the most startling and highly colored accounts of the starving situation of the inhabitants of Richmond. By the prompt preventive meaures brought into requisition this riot was effectually silenced, and no demonstration of the kind was afterwards made during the war.

The real sufferers were not of the class who would engage in acts of violence to obtain bread, but included the most worthy and highly cultivated of our citizens, who, by the suspension of the ordinary branches of business, and the extreme inflation in the prices of provisions, were often reduced to abject suffering; and helpless refugees, who, driven from comfortable homes, were compelled to seek relief in the crowded city, at the time insufficiently furnished with the means of living for the resident population, and altogether inadequate to the increased numbers thrown daily into it by the progress of events. How great their necessities must have been can be imagined from the fact that many of our women, reared in the utmost ease, delicacy and refinement, were compelled to dispose of all articles of taste and former luxury, and frequently necessary articles of clothing, to meet the everyday demands of life.

These miseries and inconveniences were submitted to in no fault-finding spirit; and although the poverty of the masses increased from day, to-day there is no doubt that the sympathies of the people were unfalteringly with the revolution in all its phases. Our sufferings were severe, and the uncomplaining temper in which they were borne was surely no evidence that there was in the Southern masses a disposition of craven submission, but rather of heroic devotion to a cause which brought into exercise the sublime power "to suffer and be strong." While our enemies in their country were fattening upon all the comforts of life, faring sumptuously every day, clothing themselves in rich garments, and enjoying all that could make existence desirable, they made merry over the miseries endured by the South, and laughed at the self-abnegation of a people who surrendered luxuries and comforts without a murmur for the cause of the revolution.

Our churches were stripped of their cushions, which furnished beds for the hospitals. Private houses were denuded of pillows to place under the heads of the sick. Carpets and curtains were cut up for blankets for the soldiers, and many a poor woman yielded up her couch to the invalid and suffering. Many times the dinner was taken from the table and distributed to soldiers in their march through our streets, when perhaps there was nothing in the larder with which to prepare another for the self-sacrificing family which had so generously disposed of the principal meal of the day. The generosity of our people was unstinted, and became more and more beautifully manifest as our poverty increased. A disposition was evinced to withhold nothing of ease or luxury which might in any way benefit a cause that called forth the most earnest devotion of patriotism.

CHAPTER XLI.

SPIES.

THE existence of spies had become more than a mere suspicion, but whether from the amiable temper and laxity of our government or the inefficiency of our military police, there were very few apprehended and brought to trial. It was during the spring of 1863 that one Webster, a clerk in the War Department, and his wife, were suspected, brought to trial, and found guilty of the charge of espionage for the Federal government.

He had undertaken the difficult and dangerous part of a double spy, and was in the pay of both governments, and had also been guilty of murder. The facts being fully made manifest, he was condemned to die upon the gallows, and his wife, not less guilty of treachery, was sent through the lines to Washington.

Since the occupation of Richmond by the Federal forces, we have been told by their officers that numerous spies were in the city during the entire existence of the Confederacy, and were in constant communication with the enemy. They were, said the officers, generally ladies who occupied enviable positions in society, and were in the regular pay of the Federal government. Suspected persons were, however, extremely rare, and we are inclined to believe the statements of these officers admit of much questioning.

A residence there during the entire period of the Confederacy, and a pretty general acquaintance with the state of feeling and society, would warrant us in allowing much latitude to remarks coming from a source which would fain establish the idea that a certain portion of our population, and a much larger portion than there is any evidence to believe, were disaffected towards the Confederate government. We shall later have occasion to notice the apprehension of a female spy; but that they existed in alarming numbers cannot have been true.

The lenity of the government towards suspected persons was one of its most remarkable features, and illustrates the confiding and unsuspecting character of the Southern people. "It is better to trust all than to suspect any of wrong," becomes not a useful maxim when circumstances arise such as have recently convulsed our common country.

It was not easy for us to accredit the tale that there were those among us who worshipped at the same altars, who knelt at the same chancel, who broke bread at our tables, who co-operated with us in works of benevolence, who bent with us over the couch of suffering, and whose words as well as actions were all in sympathy with the revolution, who could only be enacting a falsehood, and using their real endeavors to sell us into the hands of our enemies; and all for filthy lucre—bartering for it their honesty, their integrity, their reputation, their eternal salvation.

It is difficult for us to imagine that those who smiled when prosperity seemed about to shed over our cause a permanent light, and who seemed to sorrow when our troubles thickened, who joyed when we joyed, who wept when we wept, were the ones who were ready to open upon us the floodgates of destruction, and to consign us to all the horrors of betrayal. We are not willing to believe this to be true, and would let the mantle of oblivion fall over those who have proved so base.

CHAPTER XLII.

STONEMAN'S RAID—PANIC IN RICHMOND.

THE cold, stern, dreary winter, through which we had experienced so many trials and had witnessed so much suffering, had at length departed. It had lingered tardily, but the snow had melted from the hillsides, and the ice-bound streams once more gushed forth, and made merry music in the warm, genial sunshine. The meadows were green with verdure, and bright with golden dandelions and buttercups. In the gardens, fragrant exotics threw out their budding beauties, and the atmosphere was redolent with their perfume. Amid the trees, feathered songsters filled the air with melody, and trilled joyous welcome to the return of spring. All nature invited to the enjoyment of the season, yet were our hearts heavy, and these beauties sickening, since they but awakened the remembrance that they were indeed the heralds of the opening of active operations in the military campaign. The roads were becoming firm, the mud which impeded the movement of the armies was fast drying up, and we looked forward to another movement having in view the capture of Richmond.

The long season of quiet had been broken only by an engagement at Kelly's Ford, in Culpepper County, in March. Here we lost our brave young artillerist, Major Pelham. He had attracted the special attention of General Lee, and was styled by him in his report of the battle of Fredericksburg, "the gallant Pelham." His remains were brought to Richmond, and laid in our Capitol, and loving stranger hands strewed rare flowers over the young hero.

We were now awakened by threatening demonstrations at our own doors. The cavalry of the enemy were becoming troublesome. The alarm bells tolled, and there appeared the forms of our enemies, headed by General Stoneman, at the very gates of the city. It is said that some of his men slept within the intrenchments. This may not have been true; but it is true that they came near enough to create general agitation and the wildest excitement. Our forces for local defence were under arms at a few moments' notice, but the wary foes, afraid to venture upon us, though all unconscious of our danger, contented themselves with a detour around the fortifications, and passed down across the Chickahominy and Pamunky into the county of King William, where they captured a train of commissary wagons belonging to the Confederates, and frightened the inhabitants by their unexpected appearance. No greater harm was done.

How much mischief they might have wrought upon us, had they persisted in forcing their way into Richmond, we cannot tell; but unconscious as we were of the approach of danger, and equally unprepared to resist it at that time, it may not be wrong to suppose that in a rapid raid upon our city much evil might have come to it. At all such times, mingled with the tragical there was a singular blending of the ludicrous. When the news spread that the Yankees were within a few miles of the city, the most energetic preparations for flight were noticeable. Trunks, long empty on account of the security that we had for months enjoyed, were suddenly brought out, and again the panic caused by the Yankees induced the more careful of our ladies to secrete the valuables they possessed, and make ready for flight to a place of greater safety. Closets, drawers and presses were speedily stripped of their contents, and trunks quickly filled and strapped for travelling, were seen in the halls of the frightened inhabitants. The news was communicated from one to another on the street, the bells were rung frantically, and the whole place was soon thrown into the most intense alarm.

An old lady, noticing the commotion, stopped a gentleman on the street and inquired the cause of it. On being informed, she turned about to go back to her home. Another lady, perceiving her perturbation, and not having been informed of the cause of the agitation of her friend, approached quickly and asked: "What is the matter?" The old lady replied: "Why, the Yankees are within two miles of Richmond! I was just going up on Broad street to purchase a bonnet, but now I shan't go." Her friend, notwithstanding the evident cause for alarm, could not suppress a laugh at the manner and language of the old lady. "Why, will you not need a bonnet if the Yankees do come?" inquired the second lady. "No, no; I shall want no bonnet if the Yankees get here!" returned the old lady, hastening her steps in the direction of her home. "No, I shall not want a bonnet!"

The raid of General Stoneman, while it appeared so insignificant in its results, was the precursor of the great battle which occurred in the month of May, on the banks of the Rappahannock. The long delay, the "grand hesitation" of the enemy, had been the cause of much impatience at the South. We had seen one and another of the commanders of the armies of our enemies deposed, and more trustworthy men, or those who made louder pretensions to skill, elevated to the command of the Northern army, to try the mettle of the veteran "Army of Northern Virginia."

CHAPTER XLIII.

HOOKER'S CAMPAIGN—DEATH OF STONEWALL JACKSON.

TO General Hooker, whose fighting qualities had gained for him the *sobriquet* of "Fighting Joe," was committed the command of the army declared to be the "finest army on the planet," the same which had so frequently fled before the "ragged rebels" led on by General Lee. Once more these ragged rebels, these miserable troops, that were despised by the well-fed, well-clad troops of our enemies, were to meet them on the field of conflict. Once more the "On to Richmond" movement was to receive a check at the hands of our invincible Lee, and another Federal commander was destined to the place on "the shelf" occupied by so many illustrious predecessors. But we are anticipating. Hooker, following the plan of General Burnside, attempted the "On to Richmond" by the way of Fredericksburg. He was allowed by General Lee to cross the Rappahannock without opposition and without loss, and to secure a position deemed by him impregnable, where he proclaimed: "The rebels must fly ingloriously, or come out from their defences and do battle on our own ground, (the ground of the Yankees,) where certain destruction awaited them."

To secure success, nothing had been left wanting in the appointment of his army. The North had been ransacked for horses for the cavalry and for artillery purposes; the most improved arms had been placed in the hands of the troops; General Hooker had made extraordinary exertions to increase the strength of his army, and everything was done to place every department of the command upon a thorough war footing; and these labors completed, our enemies vaingloriously boasted that they only awaited the expected measurement of strength to overwhelm Lee with his army of "half-starved secesh." This spirit of confidence seems to have been shared with General Hooker by the majority of officers in his command.

Whether deceived by the false representations of spies, or whether from an overweening confidence in his own ability to succeed, the Federal commander made the loudest pretensions to wisdom in the management of an army, and represented to his government the causes for failure in his

HOOKER'S CAMPAIGN. 217

predecessors in command, and pointed out the manner in which he would steer clear of the shoals upon which they had been stranded, and moor his bark in a haven of peace, by the destruction of the army of the Confederates, under General Lee.

Wisely keeping his counsel, but keenly watching the movements of the enemy, General Lee permitted his plans of strategy to be perfected, and when all was arranged, and he had secured a position which he deemed impregnable, while congratulating himself upon his good fortune in securing the rear of the Confederate army, and finding only a small force to oppose him, and while engaging Anderson's and McLaw's divisions in the front, with the swift movements for which he was so famous, and in the mystery which he termed the "secret of success," General Jackson amazed and confounded the Federal commander by suddenly falling upon his right and rear. His assault was fierce and furious. Says a writer of the time : " In a short time he threw Sigel's corps (the Eleventh) of Dutchmen into a perfect panic, and was driving the whole right wing of the Yankee army fiercely down upon Anderson's and McLaw's sturdy veterans, who in turn hurled them back, and rendered futile their efforts to break through our lines, and made it necessary for them to give back towards the river. There was an intermission of about one hour in the firing, from three until nine o'clock. It was about this time that General Jackson received his death wound from his own men, who mistook him for the enemy."

For three days, with short intervals in which to give some attention to the dead and wounded, this bloody work continued. Time after time the enemy rallied his almost discomfited hosts, and brought them to the onset to be beaten back, to rally again, until, on the evening of the 4th of May, the signal for a general attack was given, when the Confederates rushed on the foe with the fury of a hurricane.

But little further resistance was made. The enemy were
10

driven in the wildest confusion to the banks of the river, and on that night ended his remarkable series of battles on the lines of the Rappahannock.

The courage of our troops, tested on so many fields of conflict previous to this time, had been fully maintained during this succession of bloody battles. The ragged Rebels had defeated and discomfited the well-appointed armies of the vainglorious Federal commander, who, taking advantage of the rain and darkness of the succeeding night, recrossed the Rappahannock, and on the opposite bank reorganized his shattered and disheartened forces.

But with the thanksgivings for victory that went up from our hearts; with the shouts of triumph in which, with the deeds of our brave troops, there were blended the names of Lee, Jackson, the two Hills, Wilcox, Barksdale, Stuart, Ewell, Rhodes, Pryor, Anderson, McLaws, and others holding rank in our army, (too numerous to mention,) there went up from every Southern heart a wail, so long, so loud, that in the sad sound was heard only the heart-breaking refrain, "Jackson has fallen!" It could not be, the unwelcome news could not be true! We hugged the phantom Hope from day to day, as from all who could give us information we anxiously inquired after the condition of his wounds. Anon we would hear, "He is better — his wounds, though serious, are not necessarily fatal," and buoyed up with the thought "he cannot die; he is an immortal reality," we prayed for his recovery, and very few sent up to the ear of the Almighty their petition coupled with Christian resignation to the Almighty will. Discarding the submission which should have accompanied our confidence in the wisdom of the dispensations of Providence, and not possessing the sublimity of faith, the simple, childlike trust in God, which issued from the lips of our beloved hero, in the thrilling words, "It is all right!" we felt that we could not give him up. We hoped on until hope was against hope, and then came the crushing intelligence that covered our hearts with the midnight gloom of sorrow—"Jackson is dead!" A pall of deepest mourning mantled the South, and with impious hearts we inveighed against the will of God in the destruction of our idol.

The thunderbolt was too sudden, the blow too heavy. Our uninstructed hearts were not prepared for a chastisement so severe, and in the miserable impotence of human nature we dared to question the designs of Omnipotence. What to us were the victories gained on the fields of Fredericksburg and Chancellorsville? What to us were all the spoils of conquest? What to us were the long lines of captives that were marched through our streets? What to us all the glories that perched upon the banners of the Confederacy? What to us the triumphs that proclaimed trumpet-tongued the deeds of heroes and martyrs in the cause of the South, when the tower of strength upon which we had leaned had been overthrown—the brave heart upon which we had thrown so great a portion of the dire troubles that surrounded us had been stilled in the icy calmness of death!

Were we writing alone of the soldier, we should refer with sadness to the grief which must have torn his noble soul as he listened upon his couch of suffering to the roar of battle that still raged, and reflected on the probable condition of his beloved command, that seemed dearer to him than the life that was soon to be extinct. We should refer with pride to the declaration made by him with the glow of martial ardor suffusing his countenance, and the proud smile that is said to have beamed over his face, "If I had not been wounded, or had had one hour more of daylight, I could have cut off the enemy from the road to United States Ford; we would have had them entirely surrounded, and they would have been obliged to surrender or cut their way out—they had no other alternative. My troops may sometimes fail in driving an enemy from a position, but the enemy *always* fails to drive my men from a position."

We should refer with pleasure to the fact that in his moments of suffering he remembered and kindly inquired after the officers of his command, and thoughtfully remembered the honor due General Rhodes, whose commission, said he, as Major General should date from that day, (meaning from the 2nd of May, for gallant conduct on the field of Chancellorsville,)—we should refer to the pride with which he regarded the brigade made memorable through their wonderful leader, and the smile with which he said, "The men who live through this war will be proud to say, to their children, 'I was one of the Stonewall brigade!'"

But it is not of Stonewall Jackson alone, the soldier, that we write—but of more—of Jackson the Christian! It was not alone on the battle field that traits of heroism shone out so conspicuously in his spotless character; but the patient resignation, the calm "Thy will be done, oh Lord!" with which he awaited the sure and steady coming of the "King of terrors," had more of heroism in it than the courage with which he had faced so often the mouth of the cannon. The calmness with which he could say to his stricken wife, when she informed him that his physicians thought he had not long to live, "Very good, very good; it is all right," had more of sublimity in it than the valor which dilated his figure as the battle raged, and carved his name in letters of immortality.

The Christian character which shone out in the gesture that raised his hand to heaven, at which signal the men of his command would take off their hats, and order, "Hush! old Stonewall's going to pray!" was more radiant far than the mighty deeeds which made him the idol of his men and the terror of the enemy.

The following account of the dying moments of this great and good man is taken from the authentic testimony of a religious friend and companion:

"He endeavored to cheer those who were around him.

Noticing the sadness of his beloved wife, he said to her, tenderly, 'I know you would gladly give your life for me, but I am perfectly resigned. Do not be sad; I hope I shall recover. Pray for me, but always remember to use in your prayer the petition, "Thy will be done." Those who were around him noticed a remarkable development of tenderness in his manner and feelings during his illness, that was a beautiful mellowing of that iron sternness and imperturbable calm that characterized him in his military operations. Advising his wife in the event of his death to return to her father's house, he remarked, 'You have a kind and good father, but there is none so kind and good as your Heavenly Father.' When she told him the doctors did not think he could live two hours, although he did not expect, himself, to die, he replied, 'It will be infinite gain to be translated to Heaven and be with Jesus.' He then said he had much to say to her but was too weak. He had always desired to die, if it were God's will, on the Sabbath, and seemed to greet its light that day with peculiar pleasure, saying, with evident delight, 'It is the Lord's day,' and inquired anxiously what provision had been made for preaching to the army; and having ascertained that arrangements were made he was contented. Delirium, which occasionally manifested itself during the last two days, prevented some of the utterances of faith which would otherwise have doubtless been made. His thoughts vibrated between religious subjects and the battle field; now asking some questions about the Bible or church history, and then giving an order, 'Pass the infantry to the front,' 'Tell Major Hawks to send forward provisions to the men,' 'Let us cross over the river and rest under the shade of the trees,' until at last his gallant spirit gently passed over the dark river and entered on its rest."

> "For none return from those quiet shores
>   Who cross with the boatman cold and pale;
>   We hear the dip of the golden oars,
>   And catch the gleam of the snowy sail,

> "And lo! they have passed from our yearning heart.
> They cross the stream, and are gone for aye;
> We may not sunder the veil apart
> That hides from our vision the gates of day."

With the words of cheerful resignation, "It is all right," with which he bowed to the will of God, almost the last words that fell from his lips were, "A. P. Hill, prepare for action!" and at fifteen minutes past three in the evening of the 10th of May this great spirit returned to the God who had given it to bless us only a little while here on earth.

Such was the death of Jackson, resigned, cheerful, hopeful. As his life had been a model of all that was ennobling in virtue, heroism and patriotism, his death taught the more useful lesson still—how a Christian soldier ought to die.

His body was conveyed to Richmond, where a great and solemn pageant attested the feeling of universal loss in the death of this hero-idol of the South. His body was embalmed and laid in a metallic coffin in the reception room at the Governor's House. The mourning and stricken daughters of the South congregated from all parts of the Confederacy in Richmond, wended their way to the sacred spot, and covered the star-crossed pall with floral offerings, bedewed with the tears of national grief. The coffin was draped with the snow-white banner of the Confederate States—fit emblem of his own pure spirit and the sublime courage with which he bore his Master's cross. Alas! it was the first use to which was devoted this, the new banner of his cause, under whose folds we had so hoped to see him travel until its establishment; but there rested his noble form—

> "Like one who wraps the drapery of his couch
> About him and lies down to pleasant dreams."

On the next morning at the appointed hour, the coffin was borne to the hearse, a signal gun was fired from near the equestrian statue of Washington on the Capitol Square, and the great procession began to move to the solemn strains of the Dead March in Saul. The hearse was preceded by two regiments of General Pickett's division, with arms reversed, General Pickett and staff, the Fayette Artillery, and Warren's company of cavalry. The carriage which bore the body came slowly, mournfully on, the mourning-plumes nodding dark and gloomily, and casting long shadows over the flower-covered ensign under the folds of which he would have caught that heroic inspiration that he had been wont to communicate to the Old Brigade. Then, led by a groom, came the war-horse of the dead soldier, caparisoned for battle, and bearing across the saddle the boots last worn by the rider now still in death. Then followed, with saddened mien, and hearts crushed with heavy sorrow, the staff officers of the departed hero; then, more sadly still, the remaining members of the Stonewall Brigade, invalids and wounded, with downcast looks and sad forebodings that they should never see his like again; then, a vast array of officials, President Davis, the members of his Cabinet, Generals Longstreet, Elzey, Winan, Kemper, Garnett, Corse, Commodore Forrest, and other officers of the Confederate Navy, the Mayor and city authorities of Richmond, and a long cavalcade of carriages bearing the heart-broken friends of the deceased.

The procession, nearly a mile in length, proceeded down Governor street, and thence up to the head of Main street, whence it returned to the western gate of the Capitol Square, where a dense throng, of countless numbers, awaited to see it enter.

Business had been suspended in the city, and all along the route of the procession were seen the saddened countenances of weeping friends and admirers, as they gazed on the mighty pageant that commemorated the death of Stonewall Jackson. The hearse moved on to the steps of the Capitol, the band playing a mournful dirge, and lifting the coffin, the pall-bearers, General Longstreet, General Kemper, General Elzey, and others, bore it into the Hall of the House of Representatives, where it was deposited on an altar covered with white linen, and looped with bows of crape, in front of the Speaker's chair. The crowd was then admitted. So densely were the multitude packed in the vestibule and halls that opened into the legislative chambers of the Capitol, that only one at a time could be admitted to view the remains of the man who had won so dear a place in the hearts of the people. Slowly and patiently they remained, regardless of the sweltering heat which oppressed them, until a fortunate moment placed them at the door of the hall, now sacred with the hallowed dust that in it lay, and then a moment's glance at the loved form, no more to be witnessed until the last trump shall sound the awakening note to the resurrection of the just. A momentary glance, a single tear on the lid of the coffin, and they passed away to give place to others in waiting. All day, and until a late hour of the night, this continued, and it is computed that more than twenty thousand persons came thus to gaze on the form so dear, now still in the quiet repose of death, to pay this last tribute of admiration to the body of General Stonewall Jackson, "who, though he were dead, yet shall he live!"—"that was not born to die."

When we reflect upon his stainless reputation, we feel that he was one of whom the world was not worthy,—that "he walked with God, and was not, for God took him." With us, Jackson can never die. The mouldering remains that lie where he wished them, in the beautiful village of Lexington, in the Valley of Virginia, are not all of him; there is an immortal part to which all the South, all the noble, good and true of all lands lay claim,—the spirit of patriotism in Stonewall Jackson,—that can never die! In our souls he lives; in our hearts is graven the name whose destiny is a glorious immortality. Though dead, he yet lives—shall ever live!

From the Capitol the remains of General Jackson were

conveyed to Lexington, where so many years of his life had been spent in the tranquil quiet of domestic life, according to the murmured wish of his last moments: "Bury me in Lexington, in the Valley of Virginia."

Around this unpretending little village how many tender associations now cluster! There lie the remains of the great, the good Stonewall Jackson, to whose tomb the pilgrims of the South may wend their way, if not with the idolatrous devotion of the Mussulman to the tomb of Mahomet, yet with a patriotic devotion, which would bend the knee upon the hallowed sod, and pray to the mighty God whom he served, that a double portion of the spirit that moved this wonderful man may descend upon the sons of freedom, and nerve their arm as his was nerved, to the service of their country.

The distress of General Lee, when informed of the dangerous nature of the wounds received by General Jackson, and the critical condition of his health, is said to have been of the most poignant character. The soul of the great commander, so long tutored to self-control, bursting the bonds which fettered the emotion he could no longer restrain, cried out, in the anguish of the deepest bitterness: "Jackson will not, he cannot die!" Waving his attendants from him with his hand, he repeated "he cannot, he cannot die!"

CHAPTER XLIV.

SUFFERINGS OF THE WOUNDED—LACK OF SUPPLIES.

WE had but little time to indulge the luxury of grief in quiet retirement. The mournful strains, as they grew fainter and fainter on the ear, had only died at last away, and were drowned in the sound of the shrill whistle of the cars that bore off to Lexington the remains of our departed hero; when, with hearts burdened with sorrow almost too heavy for endurance, our attention was again called to the active duties of benevolence to the mutilated beings who had again so dearly purchased for us victory on the banks of the classic Rappahannock. The busy round of hospital duties again engrossed surgeons, stewards and nurses, paid and amateur. Our stock of delicacies by this time was nearly exhausted, and it required the exercise of the greatest skill and judgment to compound appetizing food for the invalid. Very fortunately for the condition of the Confederate larder, the vigorous appetite occasioned by the constant drain on the system from the suppuration of wounds, rendered the coarse and simple diet of the hospital grateful to the ever-hungry wounded men, and we were not pained to see a delicate appetite turn with nausea from the repulsive food served on the coarse tin plate, or from the miserable tea and coffee, sweetened with coarse brown sugar, and served in the dingy tin cup.

"Never mind, this will do ; it is indeed very good," was almost constantly the grateful response to an apology for the poor and simple fare of the wounded, which our hearts were pained to be compelled to offer, and the cheerful submission to these unavoidable inconveniences was one of the most strikingly admirable traits of the Southern soldier. Not alone in the camp and on the field did his courage shine forth, but in the loathsome wards of the hospital, when under the most intense suffering, the patient endurance of racking pain and cruel privation displayed yet more actively this trait in his character.

Many a woman's heart has been filled with grateful emotions, too great for utterance, as she bent over the couch of the sufferer, when her hand was grasped by the rough, hardened hand of the soldier, and his voice, husky with feeling long suppressed, would break out with : "I thank you—I can never forget you for this kindness ;" and many a soldier has gone out from the hospital a better and braver man for the remembrance of the angel of mercy who made pleasant the couch of suffering by her gentle acts of kindness and love.

We were at this time blessed with a plentiful supply of ice, (gathered and housed with unusual care during the severe winter that had passed,) and to its use many a poor fellow owed his life.

For more than two weeks after the battles on the Rappahannock, detachments of prisoners were sent into Richmond from day to day. These men presented striking contrasts of temper and spirit, as they were marched through our streets. Many were sullen, morose, gloomy, and glanced with an angry scowl upon the spectators who assembled on the pavements, at the windows and on the porticoes to look at them. Many seemed humiliated, cowed and depressed, while others were buoyant and cheerful, and laughingly left the ranks to purchase papers, and occasionally a loaf of bread, with which to regale themselves on the march to the prison. These were frequently amused with the cry from the bystanders, "On to Richmond, boys!" to which would be replied, in the Western or Yankee dialect: "I guess we didn't think to come this route;" or, "I guess we got here sooner than we thought;" and not unfrequently we heard: "I guess I'm glad I am here, for I'm tired of fighting the Johnnies, anyhow." Their appearance was quite as dissimilar as their manner and expressions. The prisoners seemed to be gathered up from all the nations of Europe, with a very fair showing of Western men, and "a smart sprinkling" of down-easters. Some were well clad, but many were barefooted, ragged, and quite as miserable in appearance as the ragged rebels of Texas, who marched so cheerily through our streets. The most remarkable were the villainous looking Zouaves, with their fanciful costume, and countenances disfigured by long acquaintance with crime, in the reeking purlieus of New York or other cities of America or Europe.

The reputation brought with them of infamy, desperation and degradation, elicited no sympathy for them in their painful condition of captivity. Yet, as before stated, though the writer of these details has witnessed the passage of many thousands of prisoners of war through the streets of Richmond, and although the minds of the people were keenly sensible of the immense endeavor to capture their city, with the prospect of being rendered homeless, she has yet to remember a single expression of hatred or reproach against the unfortunates taken captive by Confederate arms.

With the rejoicings over victory, in which grief for the dead was mingled in the strange incongruity that so frequently brings together joy and sorrow, our minds were not relieved of the heavy load of anxiety in regard to our military situation. The victory of Chancellorsville was again a victory barren of practical results. It was remarkable that in the changing fortunes of war, there had not yet on either side been secured a success which might be considered decisive, for at that time no entire army had been captured. But our hopes were brightening. Speculation was on the decrease in Richmond, and the idea of a speedy termination of our difficulties filled the public mind for a time.

CHAPTER XLV.

THE FALL OF VICKSBURG—ITS EFFECT.

THE question of the fall of Vicksburg was now considered by our enemies only one of time. From day to day, as reports reached us of a contradictory character, our hopes would rise and fall as the mercury in a barometer, yet were kept up to a healthy standard by the thought that the garrison was supplied with provisions for six months, and although the siege was telling fearfully upon the brave men who stood in the intrenchments, yet they declared their willingness to die there rather than give up the place; and we were also buoyed up with the thought that General Johnston could finally extricate Vicksburg from the hold of the invader. This was a most unhappy delusion to the unfortunate garrison and a credulous public. With the Confederate authorities in Richmond a singular correspondence originated in regard to the situation of Vicksburg, and General Johnston was advised to movements that would have endangered his own army, which were by him left unattempted. General Kirby Smith, and General Dick Taylor, from the trans-Mississippi, sent troops to the assistance of General Pemberton, but all to no effect. The garrison was in a deplorable condition, constantly exposed to the shot and shell of the enemy, and if a man dared to raise his head above the breastworks he was immediately a target for hostile sharpshooters. Yet there is no reason to doubt that the place was provisioned sufficiently to hold out much longer, and much suspicion attaches to the loyalty of General Pemberton to the Confederate cause from the fact that he prepared himself on the third of July to surrender the city on the Fourth of July—the cherished anniversary of the declaration of American Independence—a day peculiarly glorious to our enemies.

The news to us in Richmond was astounding; it was paralyzing, and at first accredited only as a sensation rumor got up by some shrewd sugar speculator. The authorities in Richmond maintained a sullen silence. But at last the unwelcome truth came out, naked, stark, appalling, and with the surrender went a force of more than twenty-three thousand men, with three Major-Generals and nine Brigadiers, upwards of ninety pieces of artillery, and about forty thousand small arms, throwing the Confederacy back upon its road to success, giving the key to the free navigation of the Mississippi into the power of our enemies, and throwing an alarming preponderance of prisoners into their hands!

The sun of hope had receded many degrees on the good fortune of the Confederacy, and for the first time a prop was knocked from the fabric, which caused it indeed to totter.

The public indignation against Pemberton was at first fearful, yet never did Mr. Davis defer to public opinion, and his fidelity to Pemberton was never modified.

In connection with the siege of Vicksburg many incidents of thrilling interest are related. The apology given by General Pemberton to the enraged public for the surrender of Vicksburg was, "to save further effusion of blood," and the explanation of his motives for yielding up the city on the Fourth of July to General Grant was the hope of conciliating the ambition of Grant, and invoking the generosity of the Yankees. He says: "If it should be asked why the Fourth of July was selected as the day for the surrender, the answer is obvious. I believed on that day I should obtain better terms. Well aware of the vanity of our foes, I knew they attached vast importance to the entrance on the Fourth of July into the stronghold of the great river, and that to gratify their native vanity, they would yield then what could not be expected of them at any other time." This miserable excuse increased the humiliation and disgrace of the surrender of Vicksburg.

The conduct of some of the inhabitants was in many respects exceptionable. As in other cities of the South, there were those who rushed, through fear of further distress, to take the oath of allegiance, and the Jewish portion of the population, it was said, with one honorable exception, went forward and took it.

These evidences of submission were rewarded at first with some show of leniency, to be followed by a tyrannical despotism under the Dutch General Osterhaus—quite equal in its rigor to that exercised by Butler in New Orleans.

About this time, as noticed in Pollard's History of the War, a Mississippi paper declared that it had no words of excuse or charity for the men who had remained in Vicksburg under the enemy's flag. To quote their own slang dialect, 'The Confederacy was about gone up, and there was no use in following its fortunes any further.' But it repeated the characteristic stories of the conquered cities of the South. The spirit of the women of Vicksburg was unbroken, and amid all its shameful spectacles of subserviency, female courage alone redeemed the sad story of a conquered city."

From Captain W., the young Mississippian heretofore mentioned as being the soldier for whom a lady of Richmond braved the august presence of the Surgeon General to secure a furlough, we heard of many interesting circumstances connected with the siege of Vicksburg. For gallantry there he was promoted from the position of private to Captain of Cavalry, and from time to time his promotion continued until he ranked as Brigadier-General, (but subsequently to his exchange.)

He says: "I paid frequently two and a half dollars for rats for food, and was glad to get them, for I assure you they are quite as nice as squirrels; but I never could bring myself to decide to dine upon mule-meat until I was deceived at dinner with General B., by the assurance that I was dining upon beef. I ate peas-bread. Oh, we lived very hard it is true, but there was no lack of provisions such as they were, and there was no excuse in that explanation of Pemberton for surrendering Vicksburg when he did. Our men, some of them, call him 'a traitor.'" In describing the spirit of some of the troops that occupied Vicksburg, he said, "I had a friend, (a lady,) sick, and rowed out of the city to a Yankee gun-boat to procure a lemon for her. On my return I was surrounded by a squad of low fellows, who took the bridle of my horse and demanded my horse, side-arms and watch. I explained, 'I am an officer, and by the terms of the parol, I am entitled to my horse and side-arms, and I shall not surrender them.' Whereupon they cursed me furiously, and then in the vilest manner commenced abusing the women of Vicksburg, and heaping on them the most opprobrious epithets. One of them was particularly insulting. Rising in my stirrups, and drawing my revolver, I exclaimed, 'I hate to kill as mean a dog as you, but you'll have to die,' and shot him through the head. As he fell the remaining five made threatening demonstrations, and I remarked, 'you can overpower me, but some more of you will have to die before I surrender myself to you, or am killed.' Thinking it quite as well to let me pass they loosened their hold on the rein of my bridle, and I put spurs to my horse and galloped into the city." He succeeded in making his escape but a price was set on his head for his arrest, and vengeance threatened him for shooting an enemy, (a robber,) while on parole.

During the bombardment of the city many casualties are reported of citizens who ventured out of the pits dug for their safe retreat. Mrs. Reed, the wife of Major Reed, of the Confederate army, ran out of the pit in which she lived during the bombardment, to secure her little child who, tired of restraint, eluded the vigilance of the mother, and made her way into the street. Terrified, the mother went to seek her child, and had just secured the mischievous little girl, and was returning to the pit, when a shell exploded near her, a fragment of which struck her on the arm and so mangled it that amputation was deemed necessary, and she submitted to the loss of her right arm.

The injury to the city was incalculable, but scarcely to be considered in comparison with the moral effect upon the fortunes of the Confederacy. Yet the press of the South made vigorous efforts to console the people, and represented the advantage which might accrue in using the armies there in co-operation with the defence of Vicksburg more effectively elsewhere. But it was impossible to close our eyes upon the painful consequences of the downfall of this hope of the Confederacy.

The fall of Vicksburg was followed by the enemy's reoccupation of Jackson, the capitulation of Port Hudson, the evacuation of Yazoo City, and important events in Arkansas, which resulted in the retreat of our army from Little Rock and the surrender to the enemy of the important valley in which it was situated.

As was the case after the fall of New Orleans, we were in Richmond made to feel at once some of the consequences of the disaster. Fortunate speculators who had on hand a good supply of sugar saw within their grasp immediate wealth, and many of the citizens from this time, from the high price to which it was at once raised by these remorseless merchants (who might be termed "vampires,") were compelled to retrench heavily in the use of sugar, or to give it up entirely. The speculation in gold, which had been dull with the brokers, and the sale of "greenbacks," were busily resumed, and the evil to the many was made the source of riches to the few.

From this time until the end of the war it was extremely rare to see a dessert at dinner which required the use of sugar ; and all delicacies compounded with the precious article, were abandoned almost entirely except when needed for the sick. Yet for this there was never heard a murmur, and as with articles of luxury this needful condiment was used in the most sparing manner, or altogether abandoned, and still in a spirit of cheerfulness.

CHAPTER XLVI.

LEE'S INVASION OF PENNSYLVANIA—EFFECT OF THE BATTLE OF GETTYSBURG.

SIMULTANEOUSLY with the intelligence of the fall of Vicksburg, tidings reached us of a still more distressing character. We had been watching with intense solicitude the operations of the army of Northern Virginia. Unbounded confidence was felt in the skill and judgment of General Lee, yet from the time of the battle of Chancellorsville, the movements of his army awakened the keenest anxiety. Important changes had been effected in the ranking and disposition of the officers. General Ewell and General A. P. Hill had been commissioned by the President as Lieutenant Generals, the former to command the corps left without a leader by the death of General Jackson, and the fondest hopes were entertained that with his mantle a double portion of Jackson's spirit might have fallen on his successor.

Other promotions of inferior rank also took place. On the third of June General Lee began his onward movement. On the ninth occurred the cavalry fight between the Confederates under General Stuart and the Federals at Brandy Station, on the Alexandria Railroad, in which the Federals were defeated. In this engagement, the regiment under Colonel Lennox was particularly distinguished. At the same time our forces were advanced to operate in the lower portion of the Valley, and on the fourteenth of June General Rhodes drove the enemy from Martinsburg, and took possession of the town. On the same day General Ewell attacked and drove Milroy from Winchester.

The occupation of this town by the Confederates was attended with the wildest demonstrations of delight from the citizens. They had long groaned under the yoke of captivity, and the appearance of the Confederate troops was like the opening of the prison doors to the long imprisoned.

It is said that as the Confederates came into the place, at every door and window were seen the figures of the ladies with handkerchiefs waving and tears of gratitude flowing in the unrestrained excess of joy. Loud calls were made upon General Ewell from his fair friends for a speech, but the brave old man pleasantly replied to them, "I can't make a speech to ladies. Excuse me if you please, I never made a speech to but one lady in my life," and pointing to General Early, (an incorrigible old bachelor,) he continued, "My friend, General Early can speak. He will address you, ladies." But the disconcerted bachelor, who it seems never made an effective speech to one lady, was dumb before his fair and grateful admirers, and was compelled to stammer out the unfortunate remark, "I can't speak to ladies—excuse me." This was to General Early a serious misfortune, for just at that time a speech from him to some fair lady might have redeemed him from the lonely, miserable estate of a bachelor, and there is recorded against him the result of a "lost opportunity."

By a series of manœuvres General Lee succeeded in freeing that portion of Virginia from the invader. From the 24th to the 30th of June he was engaged in crossing his army over the Potomac into Maryland and Pennsylvania. His progress had been effected with trifling opposition. General Hooker, satisfied, perhaps, with his essay at Chancellorsville, and cured of his boastful spirit, declined a battle in Virginia. This hesitation cost him his command. Lee had been allowed to obtain important advantages, and had so disposed his forces as to be able to hurl them wherever he might desire. He was expected by Hooker to offer battle in Maryland, but finding himself disappointed in this, and smarting under the distrust of the authorities which had placed him in position, General Hooker in disgust relinquished his command, and was quietly "laid on the shelf" alongside of his unfortunate contemporaries who had aspired to the glory of conquering the rebel army of Northern Virginia. The command of the Federal army was now given to General George G. Meade, who, perceiving that General Lee had turned aside in his march through Pennsylvania, moved towards Chambersburg to meet him. The most intense excitement prevailed at the North. The sight of the horsemen of the Confederate cavalry who were scouring the southern region of Pennsylvania, dismayed them. Their Capitol at Harrisburg was threatened, and the sound of the trumpets of the rebels as they dashed between the Susquehanna and the Alleghanies, and along the region of the tributaries of the Potomac, awoke the most dire apprehensions in the minds of the frightened population.

At the first news of the invasion, the President at Washington called for a hundred thousand more troops. The Governor of Massachusetts tendered the services of the whole military strength of his State. Governor Seymour of New York, called into consultation General McClellan to advise in reference to measures of defence. Regiment after regiment was sent to reinforce the army of the Federals. Bells were rung in the different cities, and the alarm for the condition of Pennsylvania, and the consequent insecure condition of the States further North became universally contagious. The Dutch farmers of Pennsylvania drove their stock to the mountains, and every precaution was used which was counselled by their fears to secure their effects from capture by the foes who, were then in their midst

The contrast between our situation and that of one year previous was startlingly vivid. Then our capital was surrounded by the "Grand Army" of our enemy, knocking at our very doors, and threatening to overwhelm us. We had seen that army driven from our sight, defeated, disgraced. Another and another and still another commander had been compelled to retire before the invincible prowess of the unpretending, unostentatious leader of the "rebel forces," and now, instead of "On to Richmond," the cry was: "Washington is in danger! Philadelphia is in danger!" and it could not be conjectured what would be the consequence of the onward progress of the army that had at one time awakened only the contempt of our haughty foes.

Remembering the desolation left behind him, wrought upon the soil of his own native State, it might be supposed that a spirit of retaliation would have possessed General Lee, but he was superior to a warfare waged against non-combatants, and any depredation upon private property was expressly forbidden ; protection was given to citizens, and the destruction of subsistence never allowed. Where food was required, it was paid for in Confederate money—at first refused by the indignant inhabitants, but, to use the language of a soldier, "They were finally very careful in making the change."

We are proud to know that not the slightest stain of permitted violence to the citizens of the enemy's country, from his soldiers, can ever attach to the pure and noble reputation of our beloved Commander-in-Chief. We are proud to remember his admirable practice of the "Golden Rule" towards those whom, if they did not order, at least permitted deeds which degrade them from the high position of the soldier to the common murderer and marauder. We are glad to know that when our army left Pennsylvania, there the name of "rebel" was not coupled by its women with all that is terrible.

Whatever we may have lost by the leniency of our noble commander, we have gained the happy consciousness that no blush of shame can ever mantle the cheeks of the rebels for maltreatment of the innocent and helpless in the country they invaded. But his noble example was lost upon those with whom we were waging war, as the tales of sorrow, of horror, too well attest, when recited with trembling fearfulness by many of our Southern people, (need we say, our Southern women?)

It is said by those who disapproved of the course of leniency and politeness pursued by General Lee, that "he attempted the conciliation of a people who were little capable of it, but were always ready to take counsel of their fears." The effect of this moderate warfare on such a people was to irritate them without intimidating them—in fact, to compose their alarms and to dissuade them from what had been imagined as the horrors of invasion. In this respect his movement into Pennsylvania gave to the enemy a certain moral comfort, and encouraged the prosecution of the war." The same writer observes: "Such tenderness, the effect of a weak and strained chivalry, or more probably that of deference to European opinion, is another of the many instances which the war has furnished of the simplicity and sentimental nature of the South."

The position now occupied by General Lee had been secured with but little opposition. The rapid dispersion of the armies of the enemy on the route indicated plainly the moral reputation of the army under him. The whole of the Valley of Virginia had been in the possession of the enemy, and yet, from Culpepper Court-House, in Virginia, until he reached Gettysburg, in Pennsylvania, he had encountered only trifling opposition. He had carried his army across the mountains, along the valleys, and over the rivers, and made his way into the heart of the land of the enemy, to be confronted by General Meade at Gettysburg.

The hopes of the people of the South had risen to fever height. The thought of a speedy termination of the war was fostered, until peace seemed something tangible, and already within our grasp. To use the language of another : "In Richmond, the garish story of the newspapers had prepared the public mind for a great victory. There was the renewed and feverish anticipation of an early peace. The elated public of the Confederate capital little imagined that in a few days events were to occur to turn back the war for years." Alas! the clouds were already hovering over us, surcharged with dreadful disasters, soon to burst, only to collect again, and never more entirely to be lifted.

The action of the 1st of July was brought on by General Reynolds, who commanded the enemy's advance, and who thought himself superior in force to the Confederates. He paid the penalty of his rashness by a defeat—was overpowered and outflanked, and fell mortally wounded on the field. The battle of this day was fought on the side of the Confederates by General A. P. Hill's corps, General Ewell's and General Longstreet's, and resulted in the repulse of the Federals. They were driven back through the town of Gettysburg, to a mountain, at the distance of half a mile, where they gained a commanding position, and there fortified.

The fighting on Thursday, the 2d, was not resumed until late in the afternoon, after which time it is said to have been of the most stubborn and desperate character. The conflict was indecisive, but in the fight the Confederates lost a number of officers, among whom fell the brave and gallant Barksdale, from Mississippi. He perished where he had most anxiously desired to die—on the ensanguined field —declaring with his last breath that he was proud of the cause for which he was fighting, proud of the manner in which he received his death, and "confident that he believed his countrymen invincible."

In the account of the death of this brave man by our enemies, he was styled this "haughty rebel," and seemingly with fiendish satisfaction they related his pleading for a cup of cold water, as a dying boon, and a stretcher from an ambulance boy.

The fighting of Friday, the 3d of July, was more fierce and bloody than on the preceding two days. The Federals occupied the heights, and from every crest cannon were planted, frowning down in grim array on the assailants. The charge of the Confederates upon these heights is said to have been of the most determined and irresistible character; but in the attempt they were cut down like grass before the reaper. In describing this scene, a Southern historian says: "But there was now to occur a scene of moral sublimity and heroism unequalled in the war. The storming party was moved up, Pickett's division in advance, supported on the right by Wilcox's brigade, and on the left by Heth's division, commanded by Pettigrew. With steady, measured tread the division of Pickett advanced upon the foe. Never did troops enter a fight in such splendid order. Their banners floated defiantly on the breeze as they passed across the plain. The flags which had waved amid the wild tempest of battle at Gaines's Mill, Frazer's Farm and Manassas, never rose more proudly. Kemper, with his gallant men, leads the right; Garnett brings up the left; and the veteran Armistead, with his brave troops, moves forward in support. The distance is more than half a mile. As they advance, the enemy fire with great rapidity; shell and solid shot give place to grape and canister; the very earth quivers beneath the heavy roar; wide gaps are made in this regiment and that brigade. The line moves onward, cannons roaring, grape and canister plunging and plowing through the ranks, bullets whizzing as thick as hail-stones in winter, and men falling as leaves fall in the blasts of autumn.

"As Pickett got well under the enemy's fire, our batteries ceased firing, for want, it is said, of ammunition. It was a fearful moment, and one in which was to be tested the pride and mettle of glorious Virginia. In the sheets of artillery fire advanced the unbroken lines of Pickett's brave Virginians. They have reached the Emmettsburg road, and here they meet a severe fire from heavy masses of the enemy's infantry, posted behind the stone fence, while their artillery, now free from the annoyance of our artillery, turn their whole fire upon this devoted band. Still they remain firm. Now again they advance. They reach the works; the contest rages with intense fury; men fight almost hand to hand; the "Red Cross" and the "Stars and Stripes" wave defiantly in close proximity. A Federal officer dashes forward in front of his shrinking column, and with flashing sword urges them to stand. General Pickett, seeing the splendid valor of his troops, moves among them as if courting death. The noble Garnett is dead, Armistead wounded, and the brave Kemper, hat in hand, still cheering on his men, falls from his horse. But Kemper and Armistead have already planted their banners in the enemy's works. The glad shout of victory is already heard.

"But where is Pettigrew's division—where are the supports? The raw troops had faltered, and the gallant Pettigrew himself had been wounded in vain attempts to rally them. Alas! the victory was to be relinquished again. Pickett is left alone to contend with the masses of the enemy now pouring in upon him on every side. Now the enemy moved around strong flanking bodies of infantry, and are rapidly gaining Pickett's rear. The order is given to fall back, and our men commence the movement, doggedly contesting every inch of ground. The enemy press heavily on our retreating line, and many noble spirits, who had passed safely through the fiery ordeal of the advance and charge, now fell on the right and on the left.

"This division of Virginia troops, small at first, with ranks now torn and shattered, most of the officers killed or wounded, no valor able to rescue victory from such a grasp, annihilation or capture inevitable, slowly, reluctantly fell back. It was not given to these few remaining brave men to accomplish human impossibilities. The enemy dared not follow them beyond their works. But the day was already lost."

Washington—and his recrossing the Potomac into Virginia still remains unexplained, and the Confederate authorities are strongly suspected of directing it. Yet the hearts of great numbers were gladdened when the safe passage of the Potomac had been effected, and once more on our own soil we welcomed the army of Northern Virginia.

While our losses were severe and the gains by no means commensurate with them, yet the invasion of Maryland and Pennsylvania was not without advantages to the army and the State of Virginia. It withdrew the invading army from our soil for a time, and we were freed from depredations of and the constant drain upon our resources in feeding not only our own army but the foraging parties of the enemy.

Our cavalry supplied their worn-out horses with the horses of the well-to-do Dutchmen that inhabited the regions scoured by them as they dashed through the country of the enemy, and the fat beeves, mutton and pork of the settlers of Pennsylvania were taken as pay for the losses sustained for more than two years in the stock of the farmers of Virginia. It gave us an opportunity to harvest our wheat crop, and all things considered we consoled ourselves with the gains of the invasion, with all the philosophy we could bring to our aid, yet we could not suppress the heart-sickening effect of the dire calamities which overtook us so suddenly and unexpectedly.

On the same day that we received intelligence of the fall of Vicksburg, arrived the still more distressing tidings of the defeat of the army of Virginia at Gettysburg. "In twenty-four hours the two calamities had changed the entire aspect of the war, and had thrown the South from the exultation of hope to the brink of despair."

The invasion of Maryland and Pennsylvania was the fruitful source of much amusing anecdote. Attached to the army of Northern Virginia were two ministers of the Methodist persuasion, one of whom doffed his clerical habits, donned the soldier's uniform and commanded a battalion to fight the battles of the Confederacy. His brother accompanied a regiment as chaplain. These two men, than whom there were not more ardent adherents to the cause of the Confederacy in the South, were Pennsylvanians by birth, natives of Greencastle, a town through which our armies passed on their way to and from Gettysburg. The chaplain, in speaking of the invasion of his native State, was asked how he felt when passing through the village of his birthplace, and the scene of his boyhood and youth. He replied:

"I felt that I was engaged in a holy cause, and that I was doing right; but," said he, "when we passed through on the advance of our army, I saw no one I had ever known. The doors and windows of the houses were closed against us, and no sign of notice was perceptible except from a few of the curious who wished to know what a 'rebel' looked like. But on the retreat of our army the village was alive with the curious and triumphant spectators to witness the flight of the rebels. Now and then I would see an old acquaintance, perhaps a schoolfellow, who would lift his hands in astonishment and exclaim, 'Great God,* Charley B.! I never expected to see you in the rebel army!' 'In the rebel army? Why, man, every gentleman on this continent is in the rebel army,' I would reply. Amazement met me at every turn. My former friends had lost the history of me after the commencement of the war, and were under the impression I was pursuing the duties of the ministry quietly, and were not therefore prepared to see me in the Confederate uniform and doing battle against the place of my birth. I had an old aunt in the village, of whom I cherished the most tender memories, but rather feared the kind of reception I might meet, if I attempted to make myself known to her; but I determined to run the risk. I rode up to her house. Remembrances of other days came over me, and my heart was heavy with strange forebodings as I crossed the threshold so familiar in the days of my boyhood. When

---

* The identical language.

announced, my old aunt met me, embraced me tenderly, and led me into her own apartment, where she very soon spread before me a collation of what appeared to my inexperienced appetite, accustomed only to soldiers' fare, the most choice dainties. The cause of my singular appearance there at the time was not mentioned until I was about to depart, when my kind old aunt embraced me again, and said, 'God bless you, my boy, and God bless the cause for which you are fighting! I pray for your success! This is an unholy war waged against the South, and my heart has never favored coercion.'

"I was much surprised, and thanked my kind relative for her generosity, and much overcome with emotion, I said good-bye to her. But a young lady, a cousin of mine, who lived with my aunt, followed me to the gate, and as she bade me good-bye and I mounted my horse, she said, 'C——, I can ask the blessing of God on you individually, but cannot, like my aunt, ask for success on the cause in which you are engaged, for I do not consider it right.'

"'It is immaterial,' I replied, 'that you do not wish us success; we'll have it at any rate.' I kissed my pretty cousin, and rode on to rejoin my regiment."

He told of riding with a party of Confederate cavalry, to the farm-yard of a rich old Dutchman, who had in his stable one horse alone, but as fine an animal as he ever looked upon. A cavalryman dismounted from his worn-out steed, and taking off his saddle and bridle levied an attachment on the splendid horse of the old Dutchman. He had only put on the saddle, and was about to mount the captured animal when the owner came out in the greatest agitation and distress, exclaiming, "Mein Gott! mein Gott! don't take mein horse, don't take mein horse! Take anything else I've got, but leave me mein horse!" And with tears in his eyes he implored thus piteously.

The rebel cavalryman replied, coolly, "Must take him, old fellow; military necessity, military necessity. See my worn-out nag. You shall have that!" Finding his enemy unmoved by his distress, the poor old Dutchman cried, "Vell, vait! vell, vait!" and running into his house he brought a bag of gold, counted out three hundred dollars in the bright yellow metal, and handing it to the rebel, he said, "Vell, take dish, but leave mein horse." "Oh, yes, I'll do that," replied the incorrigible rebel, and pocketing the gold, he transferred the saddle to his miserable hack, and left the farm-yard of the old Dutchman to seek a steed elsewhere.

We were congratulating the good old Dutchman on the security of his favorite nag, and found our sympathies already warmly enlisted in behalf of the old man, when the chaplain continued, "But the old Dutchman lost his horse at last. Another detachment of cavalry coming on, and seeing the horse, which the old man had not time to secrete, laid violent hands on the animal, and that night it was tethered in our camp."

"Too bad! too bad!" we exclaimed. "An exchange is no robbery," persisted the chaplain. "For more than two years we have had to submit to such depredations, and they are the very least of what we have endured."

He also told of compelling a native of that section to pilot our forces to certain ravines in the mountains, to which the horses and cattle had been carried for security, and "where we captured more than a thousand horses, and an immense number of beeves and other stock."

Our soldiers told amusing stories of the temper of the women in the section of country through which they passed. At first they were defiant, abusive and denunciatory, but grew amazingly polite to the "Rebs," who paid little attention to the angry clamor of their female enemies.

In the diary of an English officer in the Confederate army we notice: "I entered Chambersburg at 6 P. M. (on the 27th of July.) This is a town of some size and importance; all its houses were shut up, but the natives were in the streets or at the upper windows, looking in a scowling and bewildered manner on the Confederate troops who were marching gaily past to the tune of Dixie's Land.

"The women (many of whom were pretty and well dressed) were particularly sour and disagreeable in their looks and remarks. I heard one of them say: 'Look at Pharaoh's army going to the Red Sea.' Others were pointing and laughing at Hood's ragged Jacks, who were passing at the time."

He speaks frequently of a genial son of Israel, who was a most efficient commissary. His name was Moses, and Major Moses retaliated with much apparent delight upon the well-stocked farm-yards of the enemy through whose country he passed, for the depredations committed upon Virginians. On his route, he says: "Our bivouac being near a large tavern, General Longstreet had ordered supper there for himself and staff, but when we went to devour it, we discovered General McLaws and his officers rapidly finishing it. We, however, soon got more, the Pennsylvania proprietors being particularly anxious to propitiate the General, in hope that he would spare the live stock which had been condemned to death by the ruthless Moses.

"During supper, women came rushing in at intervals, saying: "Oh, good heavens! now they are killing our fat hogs. Which is the General—which is the great officer? Our milch cows are now going.' To all of which expressions Longstreet replied, shaking his head in a melancholy manner : 'Yes, madam, it's very sad, very sad, and this sort of thing has been going on in Virginia for more than two years—very sad!'"

But the saddest of all reflections is that it should ever become necessary to settle disputes in a manner that brings in its train the multiform evils of war. All the glory which attaches to it seems but insignificant when brought into comparison with the miseries it entails. Yet, strange paradox! in the history of nations no people have ever yet attained enviable greatness who have not passed through the fiery yet purifying ordeal to national greatness and national purity.

CHAPTER XLVII.

THE SUMMER OF 1863—A WOMAN ARRESTED FOR TREASON.

THE spirits of the people were deeply bowed down by defeat ; but terrible as were the disasters at Vicksburg and Gettysburg, they were not sufficiently appalling to subdue the courage and hope of the South. With a resilience as astonishing as admirable, rising superior to these depressing influences, a stronger spirit of resistance was manifested, and a more ardent determination to be free at any cost. This result of misfortune must have disabused the mind of the North of the idea that there remained in the South an element of Union sentiment sufficiently powerful to defeat the cause of the rebellion. There were murmurs against the administration, but as these complaints grew louder, more ardent devotion to the Confederacy was manifested, and an increase of the persevering self-sacrifice and admirable self-abnegation which from the first had characterized the masses of the people.

Doubtless many of these complaints had their origin in imaginations painfully sensitive or preternaturally vivid ; but it is true the public anger was not appeased by the continued fidelity and devotion of Mr. Davis to his special favorites. Pemberton had fallen under well-merited censure, and the patronage of our President was put in mortifying contrast to his depreciation of General Price and others, who unfortunately lacked the valuable prestige of training at West Point. To the graduates of that truly admirable institution Mr. Davis was thought to accord special attention.

When the relative position of the Confederate President is rightly considered, we cannot conceive of one less desirable, one of heavier responsibility, one in which an Executive would be as little likely to be justly or gratefully appreciated, and while we concede the most indubitable faith in his patriotism, his loyalty to the cause for which he had made stupendous sacrifices, and had brought into exercise the most remarkable and conscientious efforts of his life, while we accord the most unfeigned admiration for the virtue and purity of his morals, and the sublime and beautiful simplicity of his manner of life, we must also concede the right of a free people to demand of their Executive deference to their wishes in acts of administrative character. Man, at best, is fallible.

Whether Mr. Davis's disregard of the public wish was the result of the ordinary weaknesses of humanity, fostered by the flattery of those in temporary power, or of an obstinate confidence in his own judgment, in defiance of the cries of the multitude for the displacement of certain officers of the army and government, must be decided by the judgments and sympathies of the disinterested.

The summer of 1863 in Richmond was made memorable by the apprehension and arrest of the wife of a wealthy and respectable citizen, for treasonable correspondence with enemies of the Confederacy. The circumstances were of an aggravating character. She was the confidential friend and at that time the guest of the wife of a prominent Presbyterian minister, who was then absent in Europe on a benevolent mission for the Confederacy. Having the unsuspecting confidence of the family under his roof, she acquired the information disclosed in the intercepted correspondence, and basely suggested the plans and time for his arrest, as a person who, from his talents and influence, was dangerous to the Union, and particularly useful to the Confederate cause. At the same time, a child of the minister was dying in the absence of his father, and in simulated sympathy with them in affliction the family were deceived, and unsuspectingly harbored an enemy whose treachery to them was more fiendish than that to the government which she had affected to sustain by her sympathy, her wealth and her influence. The indignation against her was universal, and Mr. Seddon, the Secretary of War, was made to share it, for the special direction given by him against her imprisonment in an ordinary prison. She was sent to an agreeable and romantic confinement at the Infirmary of St. Francis de Sales. Her trial was postponed for six months, and her imprisonment in an institution of mercy was the polite invention of the Confederate Secretary of War.

This course was by no means popular among the women of the South when they remembered the treatment to which Mrs. Greenhow, Mrs. Baxley, Mrs. Phillips, and her daughters, and numerous other females, (for the open and conscientious avowal of principles held and expressed at the cost of their personal freedom,) had been subjected. Their unwarrantable and lawless imprisonment by our enemies was not forgotten. The *lex talionis* was very rarely enforced in the generous dealing of the Confederate authorities. It was something of which we heard much, but saw little in practice.

CHAPTER XLVIII.

POVERTY IN RICHMOND.

AT this time our Richmond workshops were turning out large supplies of valuable arms and weapons of warfare, and our Nitre Bureau was made effective in contributions of valuable ammunition. While our financial interests were going to ruin, and our navy doing comparatively nothing for our assistance, our people were striving, by their own energies, and by the development of their personal resources, to neutralize, as far as possible, the maladministration of certain departments of the government, which, properly conducted, might have remedied many of the evils and inconveniences entailed upon us. While the men were in the field branches of female industry were faithfully attended to. We were carried back to the times of our grandmothers.

POVERTY IN RICHMOND. 255

now, though so late our experience, the reality seems almost incomprehensible. That "necessity is the mother of invention," was fully exemplified in the South, in the exigencies which brought into use the most valuable of all inventive faculties—"How to live!" To exist in any sort of ease or comfort, no calculation could be made upon the amount of income in the continually and fearfully depreciating Confederate currency.

For more than a year previous to this peculiar period, there had not been any perceptible increase of crime. We heard of fewer instances of midnight villainies, our citizens walked the streets at night with less fear of garrotting and robbery, but gambling-houses abounded, and wickedness in a shape less evident—less palpable—but not the less unquestionable, existed in defiance of the rigor of military rule, and all law, civil and religious.

We have in our possession an article taken from a Richmond newspaper about this time, which may serve to illustrate to a certain extent, the contrast to the patriotic and self-sacrificing spirit that characterized the majority of the inhabitants. It is entitled the "Stranger's Guide," and contains the following :

1. The very large number of houses on Main, and other streets, which have numbers painted in large gilt figures over the door, and illuminated at night, are *Faro Banks*. The fact is not known to the public.

2. The very large numbers of flashily-dressed young men, with villainous faces, who hang about the street corners in the day time, are not gamblers, garrotters and plugs, but young men studying for the ministry, and therefore exempt from militia duty. This fact is not known to General Winder.

3. The very large number of able-bodied, red-faced, beefy, brawny individuals, who are engaged in mixing very bad liquors in the very large number of bar-rooms in the city, are not, as they appear to be, able to do military duty. They are consumptive invalids from the other side of the Potomac, who are recommended by the Surgeon General to keep in cheerful company, and take gentle exercise. For this reason only, they have gone into the liquor business.

4. The very large number of men who frequent the very large number

of bar-rooms in the city, and pay from one to two dollars for drinks of very bad liquor, are not men of very large fortunes, but out-of-door patients of the hospitals, who are allowed so much a day for stimulants, or else they belong to that very common class of people who live noboby knows how. None of them are government clerks on small salaries with large board to pay. This fact is not known to the heads of departments.

5. The people of Richmond have little or nothing to do with the government of the city. Early in the war it was, for some reason, handed over to Maryland refugees, who were not thought fit for the army. Strangers stabbed, robbed, garrotted or drugged in Richmond will not charge these little accidents to the people of Richmond, but to the city of Baltimore.

The keen irony in these notes presents an inside view of Richmond on which a woman could not be permitted to look; but from many things that were whispered in the social circle, and from the very broad hints dropped in the newspapers, our imaginations were left to conceive that there were more things of daily occurrence in the Confederate metropolis, than were "dreamt of in our philosophy."

But all must be happy to know that the classes so strongly hinted at in these notes, did not represent the ruling class of the Richmond public. As intimated, they were generally found in the cosmopolitan population that crowded into the city during the war.

It is rather unfair, however, to charge upon Baltimore exclusively, the grave sins hinted at in these sarcastic strictures. There was a lamentable importation of the rowdies of Baltimore; but willing coadjutors in vice are easily found, and Richmond was not entirely exempt from facile material.

Congress passed an act, imposing a heavy fine and imprisonment on the keepers of gambling establishments, and yet in the search for the missing Federal Colonel Streight, who had escaped from the Libby Prison, the military police are said to have surprised certain persons of high positions, and in the attempt to escape, these gentlemen made exit through the trap-door of a gambling den, and took an airing on the roof of the building; greatly to the interest and amusement of the crowd assembled to witness the arrest of the escaped prisoner. This was a sad and singular commentary on the non-enforcement of law, and the demoralization of men in high places. However, with us, it rendered more brilliantly conspicuous the numerous exceptional cases, the high and virtuous morality of those who, in the furnace of four years' bitter trial, passed through the fire unharmed, with not even the smell upon their garments.

CHAPTER XLIX.

BRAGG'S CAMPAIGN—THE BATTLE OF CHICKAMAUGA.

THE month of September, 1863, was full of painful interest to the cause of the Confederacy. While we congratulated ourselves on the gallant defence of Charleston, our minds were directed with no less interest to the theatre of war in Tennessee, upon the ill-starred soil of which the Confederate cause was ever destined to disaster. With the most intense anxiety we watched for the news from the Confederate army under General Bragg, which was opposed by General Rosecrans, who had made in the commencement of the war a great reputation from his successes over General Lee, in the campaign in Western Virginia. This general was now to be tested in his generalship by one of the most extensive movements in the West—the occupation of East Tennessee, and a movement into the heart of the cotton States.

We have before noticed that General Bragg's army had been weakened by the withdrawal of a portion of his forces to Mississippi to sustain General Pemberton at Vicksburg. The movement against Chattanooga, the principal point of strategic importance in this section of the Confederacy, was made by the enemy in two columns; Rosecrans advancing on Chattanooga, and Burnside on Knoxville.

The first engagement with the enemy in this campaign, occurred on the 9th of September, with Frazier's command of Buckner's Division, (at Cumberland Gap, in the mountains of East Tennessee,) which resulted in the disgraceful surrender of that important point, without the firing of a shot, at the demand of General Burnside. In his message to Congress, President Davis remarked of this, the most disgraceful occurrence of the war: "The country was painfully surprised by the intelligence that the officer in command of Cumberland Gap had surrendered that important and easily defensible pass, without firing a shot, upon the summons of a force still believed to have been inadequate to its reduction, and when reinforcements were within supporting distance, and had been ordered to his aid. The entire garrison, including the commander, being still held prisoners by the enemy, I am unable to suggest any explanation of this disaster, which laid open Eastern Tennessee and Southwestern Virginia to hostile operations, and broke the line of communication between the seat of government and Middle Tennessee."

Various reports were in circulation explanatory of this affair, some of which reflected on the bravery and loyalty of the men, and some gave the want of provisions as the apology; all of which were disproven by the correspondence of Major McDowell, of Frazier's command, with a newspaper of Richmond, for he declared that he never saw men in better spirits nor more anxious for a fight, and that when surrendered they had provisions sufficient for thirty days. This disgraceful episode in the war was the subject of a "nine days' wonder" in the Confederate capital. We were not willing to accredit the fact that without a single shot a place of importance had been given up. A feeling of intense disgust and indignation was expressed, and our hearing was sharpened for other tidings from the same section of the Confederacy.

A few days brought us news of a victory gained by General Bragg, at Chickamauga. These battles occurred on the

19th and 20th of September. The Federal General Rosecrans, who was considered one of the most distinguished graduates of the West Point Military Academy, was defeated, with the loss of eight thousand prisoners, fifty-one cannon, and fifteen thousand stand of small arms, abundant supplies of ammunition, wagons, ambulances, teams, medicines, hospital stores, etc., in large quantities, and then driven back to Chattanooga.

The victory, though a brilliant one, was purchased at a fearful price to the Confederates. Bragg, in his official report of these engagements, makes the confession that on this "River of Death" he lost "two-fifths" of his troops. Our loss in general officers was conspicuous. Brigadier-Generals B. H. Helm, of Kentucky, Preston Smith and James Deshler had died on the field. General Hood, of Texas, whose bravery from the commencement of the war had been distinguished, was wounded so dangerously that he was compelled to submit to amputation of the thigh. His extraordinary gallantry on this occasion was made the subject of special notice by General Longstreet, in a letter to the government, characterized by a noble and generous ardor of praise, which obtained for the youthful General the commission of Lieutenant-General, and ranged him with the heroes of the war.

But our success was only half accomplished by the victory at Chickamauga, so long as the enemy held possession of Chattanooga. The awkward pause of General Bragg is still unsatisfactorily explained to the public at the South, and his attempt to mend the matter by avowing his intention to invest Chattanooga and starve the enemy out is considered a lame apology for the unprecedented halt on the road to brilliant success, when his troops were flushed with victory and ready for deeds of courage that might have immortalized their commander.

Among the general officers of Bragg's army there was a galaxy of the brightest names of the South. Generals Longstreet, Buckner, D. H. Hill, Polk, Hood, Breckinridge,

Hardee, Hindman, Walker, Preston, Cleburne, Helm, Deshler, Pegram, Cheatham, Wheeler, Forrest, Kershaw, Robertson and Humphreys were some of the men upon whom General Bragg could rely for successfully carrying forward the campaign of East Tennessee; and when we are assured that the pause made after the victory of Chickamauga was with the disapproval and in defiance of the convictions of a majority of his officers, we are not at a loss to account for the rapidly waning popularity of the General in command.

The story of Chickamauga was burdened by much recrimination between General Bragg and his officers, yet in the public mind there is no doubt upon whom rests the blame for the fruitless victory.

The grave mistake here made, says another, "must stand, conspicuous among the fruitless victories gained by the Confederates, amid the least pardonable blunders and shortcomings of history." It must even take precedence in magnitude of that at the famous battle of Bull Run, when the pursuit of the routed enemy might have gained for the Confederates the coveted possession of the Federal seat of government, and would doubtless have changed the entire face of the war. Here again, at Chickamauga, by the failure of a proper and vigorous pursuit of the enemy, were neutralized the most brilliant successes that ever crowned Confederate arms.

As a disciplinarian, General Bragg is thought not to have had a superior, if he had his equal, in the armies of the Confederacy; but this fundamental element of skillful generalship and soldierly character seems to have been indulged by General Bragg until it assumed the more rigorous form of tyranny over the troops in his command. With them he was unpopular. He is said to have required the strictest obedience to orders, and to have carried this principle so far that a soldier was condemned to be shot for killing a chicken, in disobedience to a command forbidding the disturbance of private property. While in the main, under the rigid requirements of military law, it would seem right to enforce such an order, it reflected unhappily upon the character of the Confederate commander, and presented him in an unfavorable contrast to the mild and magnanimous policy pursued by General Lee, General Beauregard and others in our service.

In reference to the military prestige of General Bragg, we had long been accustomed to listen to stories of the war with Mexico, in which names that have become brighter still, from great and glorious deeds, were interwoven, until imagination elevated our heroes into something more than mortal, and alongside of the mighty dead of our own and foreign countries we would place those made famous on the blood-stained soil of the rich country of the Montezumas. Among the number was that of Captain Bragg, invested with the glory which ever attaches to the hero of battle. "A little more grape, Captain Bragg," has grown to a proverb in military parlance, attesting his skill as an artillerist. At the commencement of the late war our thoughts turned upon him as one on whom we might rely with the utmost certainty; but as our troubles progressed, instead of the prompt and ready fighter, the active and brilliant strategist which his reputation gained in Mexico warranted us in expecting, we heard much more of him as the rigid disciplinarian, punishing his men for offences in themselves venial, and gaining for himself an unenviable reputation among a people who delight in being generous, and would gladly have been indebted to him in the obligations of grateful hearts. However, ill luck in such a position as that filled by General Bragg does much towards revealing unfortunate disagreements of character and disposition.

CHAPTER L.

TROUBLE WITH THE NEGROES.

FROM pictures of battles and sieges, of carnage and strife, of victories and defeats, which make memorable the history of the autumn of 1863, we return to our capital to note the effect of good fortunes and misfortunes, as taken collectively, upon the spirit and temper of the people.

The idea of the final defeat of the cause for which we fought had not then possessed us, even in the faintest degree; yet gloom pervaded our hearts.

The fine weather, the bracing atmosphere, the delicious, dreamy influence of the beautiful Indian summer could not chase from our doors the dread phantom that lurked on the threshold—could not drive from the dark closet the skeleton of the house. We felt, though we might not see the ghastly sight, nor stir the curtain folds to hear the awful rattling of the dry bones. Our spirits were heavy. The trail of war had drawn its red lines around our hearts, had made huge gaps in our home circles, had multiplied the vacant chairs around our hearthstones, had draped our forms in the solemn livery of the mourner, and had bowed us with anguish as we counted here and there one or more gone of those who had made life to us a long holiday. But our spirits were untamed; the fierce trials to which we had been subjected served not to subdue, but to strengthen in us the desire and the determination to be free.

On our streets the trickeries of trade, the unremittent pursuit of bargain and sale, were vigorously enacted. The red flag of the auctioneer hung out, and the exciting and fashionable scenes of the vendue entertained those whose selfish and avaricious propensities rendered them more intent upon the accumulation of wealth than upon the greater interests and good of the country. But in the quiet of home, in the private sanctuary, in the seclusion of retirement, in every place where the mind was given to thought and contemplation, the dread of the future presented itself in characters unmistakable.

Winter was approaching, our currency was frightfully depreciating, (an old story) we were wholly at the mercy of avaricious speculators, (a story quite as old,) food was scarce, fuel was scarce, articles of clothing, run in through the blockade, were held at a figure that prevented many from obtaining such as would shield them from the severity of winter, and we saw no means of relief in the power of those in authority over us.

Our soldiers in the field were insufficiently supplied with shoes and blankets, subsisting on the meanest and most scanty fare, and the prospect of peace was so far away in the dim future that in bitterness of anguish we turned our stricken hearts to God, and cried out again in the accents of woe, "Oh, Lord, how long, how long?"

Our Congress met in December. In his message, President Davis said: "We know that the only reliable hope for peace is in the vigor of our resistance." We stifled our complaints, we whispered to our fears the comforting tales of hope, and nerving our souls afresh for the contest of trial, suffering and death, we unflinchingly trod the bloody track, and looked to the inestimable prize of Liberty, the goal of Peace, conquered alone through our own endeavors.

About this time we were entertained with the proceedings of the trial for treason of the lady before mentioned. Much interest was manifested, summary punishment was spoken of by some, to be discountenanced by the majority, who only wished to see her placed beyond the reach of further mischief to the Confederacy. The evidence in the case was such as to divide the opinion of the jury, though amply sufficient to convict her in public opinion. She was held to bail for her reappearance at some future time, and retired to her luxurious home on James River, above Richmond. After the evacuation of the city by the Confederate forces, Mrs. —— again appeared on the streets. Guilty or not guilty, let God alone judge. No one should be willing to be an executioner on circumstantial evidence, yet against her, it appeared to admit of no doubt. She is said to have suffered much. The question is whether her suffering was from conscious guilt, or from unjust suspicions; if the former, the punishment could not well be too severe, if the latter, she was only treading the path of a martyr, and the consciousness of innocence must have converted her anguish into peace. Her reappearance in so short a time after the occupation of the city by Federal troops, was at least untimely, and argued but little for the native sensibility of a woman, or of gratitude for a people who had regarded with clemency an offence of so foul a character as that with which she was charged.

Domestic troubles of an irritating nature now arose to vex and annoy us. There was unquestionably an underground agency to decoy away our negro servants, or to assist any who meditated flight from their owners. Thefts of the most provoking character were everywhere perpetrated, usually under circumstances which pointed to family domestics as the perpetrators. For everything stolen purchasers could be found among the low and depraved in questionable quarters of the city, and the extraordinary amount of money obtained in Confederate figures was a temptation to dishonesty, with those who did not understand the real value of the money in circulation. The storeroom or pantry of a citizen, or a gentleman's or lady's wardrobe, would be plundered and the articles mysteriously disappear and all efforts of the police to discover the thief, or the destination of the missing goods, would generally prove unavailing, to be followed in a short time, by the singular disappearance of one or more of the domestics of the robbed establishment, to be heard of no more in Richmond.

A lady who lived on Franklin Street, in one of the most fashionable and respectable quarters of the city, left her house to attend an early prayer-meeting at the church to which she was attached, and returned about eight o'clock

A. M. to find two of her maids, reared, trained, and belonging to her, missing. Inquiries were made, detectives employed, advertisements issued, rewards offered for their return or apprehension, but no clue to the whereabouts of the absconding parties could ever be discovered. Nor was the loss of the negroes the only misfortune sustained by her. Upon a thorough examination into her wardrobe, linen closet, etc., she ascertained that she had been robbed of ladies' clothing of every quality and description, bed-clothes to a large amount, upwards of sixty dollars in gold, as much perhaps in silver coin, and with these things had disappeared several trunks which had been empty, without doubt used by the cunning thieves for packing their stolen goods. Her losses were estimated at several thousand dollars, and many of the articles were of a description that could not be replaced in the Confederacy. These were confidential servants, brought up in the house of their mistress, and well acquainted with the depositories of everything valuable that pertained to the establishment, and with the usual trustfulness and want of suspicion of Southern character, it was an easy matter for them to hide away from time to time their petty thefts until the moment arrived for their escape, when they disappeared with their booty.

The more effectually to carry out their plan of deception, they had professed to be seriously exercised on the vital subject of religion, and the unsuspecting mistress, much gratified at the disposition evinced by her maids, permitted them from day to day to go out, ostensibly to attend religious meetings of the friends of their own race, but she had afterwards abundant reason to believe that these were only subterfuges invented by them and their guilty coadjutors, the better to carry out their nefarious intentions.

Instances of this kind were, at the time, of constant occurrence. A lady accepted an invitation to dinner with a friend, and returned in a few hours to find her chamber robbed to the amount of several thousand dollars, in money, jewelry and clothing, by her body servant, to whom she had intrusted the management of her room. But so soon was the theft discovered, that the maid had not time to escape with her plunder, and a portion of it was discovered. As she was amenable to punishment, the mistress was compelled to give her up into the hands of the law, by which she was punished for the crime, and her escape thus prevented.

We will mention one more incident in this connection. A member of Congress from Tennessee—a man of wealth—brought his family with him to the capital. His wife, one of the most elegant and accomplished of the ladies of the South, owned a servant in whom she placed implicit confidence, whose honesty and fidelity had been tested by years of trial, and on whom the mistress relied perfectly. She had been but a few weeks in Richmond, when her servant disappeared, and at the same time elegant and costly articles belonging to her wardrobe, and diamonds valued at thirty thousand dollars! Detectives were employed to arrest her, advertisements and descriptions multiplied, but no tidings of the fugitive ever reached her quondam owners.

It appeared to be an easy matter to elude the vigilance of the police, to flank the pickets on the outworks of Richmond, and when once at the pontoon bridge, or when a convenient boat was found at hand to convey them across to the Peninsula, then in the occupation of our enemies, all attempts to arrest these fugitives were in vain.

We were compelled to keep up a rigid practice of barring and bolting and locking; yet all precautions proved ineffectual to prevent the thievish depredations of the negroes, demoralized by the various contending influences which served to develop such propensities in them.

However, when all things relative to our peculiar situation are considered, our troubles from the demoralization of the negroes were of a character less remarkable, and by far less annoying than could have been reasonably expected.

CHAPTER L.

CHRISTMAS, 1864—OPENING OF THE NEW YEAR.

ANOTHER annual revolution in the cycle of time brought us again to the Christmas season, the third since the bloody circle of war had been drawn round our hearts and homes. For days preceding the festival the anxious little ones, who had learned to share the cares and troubles of their elders, peered curiously into the countenances of mothers and fathers, for an intimation that good old Santa Klaus had not lost his bravery, and that ·despite the long continued storm of war, he would make his way through the fleet at Charleston or the blockading squadron at Wilmington, and from foreign countries, or perchance across the country from Baltimore, he would pick his way, flank the numerous pickets on the lines, and bring *something* to drop in their new stockings, knitted by mother herself. Sometimes the simple present that brought happiness to the child was purchased at the expense of some retrenchment in the table-fare for a week, or with the loss of some needed article of comfort in clothing. But the influence of childhood is magical. The children find their way to our hearts, and unloose the purse-strings when all other inducements fail.

The Christmas-box for the soldier in the field was not forgotten; but it was less bountifully supplied than when first the Christmas dinner was despatched to him to be shared with his comrades in his soldier's tent. Santa Klaus once more generously disposed of socks and scarfs and visors, to the husbands, brothers, sons, and lovers in the army.

In the Confederate Capital, the churches were always filled on this particular festival. On this day not the knee alone, but the heart was bowed, and fervent prayers were offered that no more should the Christmas sun dawn on our land deluged in blood, but that when Christmas came next the sun of peace might shed its light on hearts now breaking under the cruel oppression of remorseless war. The exercises at church were all that was left to remind us of Christmas as of yore.

Could the vail have been uplifted that hid the privacy of home, and the Christmas dinner of Richmond on this day have been exposed, we should have seen here and there, the fat turkey, the mince pie, the bowl of egg-nog and other creature comforts, which ordinarily abound on the tables of Virginia on this occasion; but generally, (and particularly among those who were reduced to keeping-rooms) if from the accumulating expenses of the times, the turkey could be afforded it was accompanied simply with potatoes and corn-bread, and this was the dinner for Christmas on the tables of many, with whom all the luxuries of our own and foreign climes had been in every-day use. But this could all have been borne bravely, cheerfully, heroically —it is almost too trifling to notice, had not the vacant place recalled the memory of one or more, whose bones were bleaching somewhere on the field made red with the mingled blood of friend and foe. It was not the want of delicacies and luxuries that brought the tear to the eye of the mother, or heaved the father's bosom in a long-drawn sigh.

When such a multitude of striking events are compressed into a brief space, time appears much longer, and of more importance than in the ordinary routine of every-day existence. The years seemed now very long to us, and not the less that our hearts were burdened with present and prospective sorrows consequent upon the time and place of our existence, and upon the mighty events which were daily occurring before our eyes—the most mighty, the most remarkable in the history of our country. We stood once more upon the threshold of a new year, and as the mind is prone to run forward, and wonder, and anticipate, and peer into the misty mazes of dim futurity, and longs to draw aside the veil that hides coming events from present scrutiny, more than ever at this time, when the future held within its remorseless grasp, the destiny of our infant nation, our spirits grew restive and impatient, and we would fain have spurred on the fiery coursers that drew the chariot of time, to take us to the goal more speedily.

The New Year with us was celebrated by the inauguration of another incumbent of the gubernatorial chair.

Governor Letcher—Honest John—whose courage, whose patriotism, whose loyalty had stood the test of fiery trial, and whose integrity had been weighed in the balances and not found wanting, resigned the helm of state to another. The gubernatorial mantle fell on the shoulders of an old and tried friend of Virginia, an old "war-horse" of the South, who, in the field as well as in the forum, in the chair of state as well as in the councils of the nation, had proved himself worthy of the honor conferred upon him by his fellow citizens of the commonwealth of the dear Old Dominion. General and Ex-Governor Smith, who had obtained in early life the sobriquet of Extra Billy, was again inaugurated Governor of Virginia. He had the confidence of the people, which was increased by the brave and patriotic addresses delivered on this occasion. In Virginia the people were not divided by party spirit, and happily demagogueism was almost wholly unknown. The best man for the position the one who would most truly and impartially support and sustain the cause of the South, was the one who secured the suffrages of the people.

The terms Whig and Democrat, Federalist and Republican were almost unheard; but the terms Unionist and Secessionist were those that came into competition, where there was any competition at the South; but with us a Unionist was a comparative nonentity, and in the undivided feeling there were no bickerings of politics or party strife.

We had still very few places of public amusement. The Richmond Theatre had been rebuilt, and the indefatigable manager, Mr. Ogden, used praiseworthy exertions to render it attractive. The stock company, however, ranked in talent below mediocrity. No stars of brilliant histrionic lustre loomed out on the Confederate firmament, and none were imported.

Our social gatherings during this winter were much more frequent than those of the two previous winters. They were, however, distinguished for their extreme simplicity. There existed in Richmond, among the young people of the best class of society, a club known as the "Starvation Club," which weekly, or semi-weekly, assembled at different houses in the city for social enjoyment. Money was contributed amongst them in payment for the music required for dancing; but all refreshments were strictly forbidden, and the only expense to the generous host, whose house might be impressed for the novel reception of the "Starvation Club," was an extra fire in the rear parlor, then not in every-day use, from the scarcity and high price of fuel. These entertainments were varied occasionally by the performance of plays and tableaux vivants, in which considerable talent was exhibited in the histrionic art by some of the quickly created actors and actresses. This introduction of plays and tableaux added an exquisitely charming variety to the winter's social enjoyment in the rebel capital. Mrs. De S——, Mrs. C. and Miss C——, (the latter a charming little belle,) were particularly distinguished for the ready talent displayed by them.*

---

* Miss C. is well known in the literary circles of Richmond as Refugita, and over this nom de plume has written some very touching and beautiful romances, some of which found publication in The Richmond Illustrated News and in the Magnolia, the principal mediums in Richmond for the publication of such literary efforts.

CHAPTER LII.

CONDFEDERATE CURRENCY—FABULOUS PRICES IN RICHMOND.

OUR chief interest was now centred on the promised redemption of the currency, which had accumulated and depreciated pntil its nominal value was not more than four cents in the dollar. We were told of various schemes to bring our paper money up to a specie value, all of which fell through, and the redemption of the currency at last resulted in the repudiation of one-third of the money in circulation, the remaining two-thirds to be secured in Confederate bonds bearing four per cent. interest; the old issue to be withdrawn by the 1st of April in the parts of the Confederacy east of the Mississippi, and by the 1st of June in the Trans-Mississippi department. This extended to all notes over the denomination of five dollars until the 1st of May, and to all five-dollar bills after that time, subjecting all Confederate bills from five dollars and upwards to a discount of thirty-three and one-third cents.

This law increased instead of relieving us from the oppression under which we were already groaning. Confidence in the circulating medium, was weakened. For articles of food, medicines, and all needful clothing, our money was taken at the prescribed discount, and the prices increased in this manner continued, nevertheless, to increase after the new issue of the Confederate Treasury was in circulation. It seemed to drive from us many of the tribe of Israel, who had battened and fattened upon speculation to the misery of the population of Richmond generally. They sold out their wares, converted their money into gold, and left for parts unknown, some of them to be arrested by the pickets on the lines of one or the other army in their attempts to run the blockade, to be fleeced of their gold, and sent on their way, not rejoicing but miserable.

There was one who had kept a jewelry store, in which he displayed goods of the finest order—diamonds and rubies, pearls and precious stones of rare value, gold watches of splendid workmanship, and other equally rich and valuable articles. But finding it prudent to husband his riches while he had time for it, he advertised his goods and sold them. He had, for more than two weeks previously, advertised his household furniture, (which was of a style and richness that was altogether creditable to his taste,) in a manner that was peculiarly noticeable from its imposing length and style, in a city where rich furniture was at the time rarely or never offered for sale. His house was quite low down on Main street. For several days before the sale took place, it was thronged with visitors to examine the elegant furniture, and on the day of the auction a crowd filled the rooms. The most ridiculous, the most fabulous prices were paid for certain articles, and the scenes of this sale reminded one of the Toodles, said a Richmond paper. But some of our people had superfluous amounts of Confederate money, and they were glad to invest it in his curtains, sofas, plate, etc.

To elude suspicion, these ancient people usually pretended they were going to Europe—back again to Germany—where they figured as alien friends, and not as alien enemies, and thus prevented the confiscation of property left behind in the Confederacy. But generally they found Germany, on this side of the water, for New York became a "city of refuge" for the Jews from the South while the war lasted. These poor wanderers, claiming no distinctive nationality, finding nowhere rest for the soles of their feet, seem happy and contented at any place where they can accumulate riches, and show singular talent and wisdom in amassing of wealth even under the most discouraging circumstances. In Richmond the road to its accomplishment appeared easy to some, while others, were suffering from extreme penury.

We sometimes hear of those who did not "feel the war." Situated as we were, we could not exactly understand what the idea imported. If not in fortune at least, in the more delicate and refined sensibilities of our nature, in the loss and absence of dear friends, in the constant anxiety for the probable fate of our country, surely every Southern person must have "felt the war." There was no one so obscure or humble, so far remote in the wilds and mountain fastnesses of our country, but that he shared in the common distress, and there was no table so bountifully supplied, no wardrobe so faultlessly elegant in its appointments, that did not show the effect of the war. If within our homes we had comforts and elegances, we had only to step out on our streets to meet here a soldier with one leg, there one with one arm, another who had lost an eye, another with horrid scar, that told a tale of battle; or on our passage through a certain quarter of our city where government work was given out to the indigent, we would see hundreds of poor women in waiting for the coarse sewing from which they earned the pittance that saved them from hunger; or we might pass government offices and see numbers of the most refined and elegant daughters of former ease and luxury, accustomed from their birth to seek only their own enjoyment, in daily toil at the desk of clerk, by which they earned a livelihood.

If feeling was not dead within the soul, if the sensibilities were not benumbed by extraneous influences, there was no one in our Southern land who did not "feel the war." And while this was our situation, while an air of the deepest seriousness pervaded our capital, while with every breath we inhaled the vapors of war—in the news that came to us through the blockade from the seat of the rival government we heard of balls and brilliant receptions, of fashion and show, extravagance and plenty; and we took these things to heart, and pondered and meditated, and eagerly looked forward to the end which should decide whether the greater strength lay in moral courage—the force of human will and virtuous endeavor—or in the mere majority of numbers. We lifted our hearts to God, and prayed in the depths of our spirit, and asked His all-powerful help in our weakness; but we rarely said: "Thy will, not ours, oh Lord, be done!" Perhaps therein lay our fault.

CHAPTER LIII.

THE CONFEDERATE CONGRESS IN THE WINTER OF 1863-4.

DURING the winter of 1863-4, the military operations of the Confederates were eminently successful. On the 30th of January an expedition undertaken by General Rosser, in the Valley of Virginia, was brilliantly successful. The details are full of interesting incident, but cannot here be noticed.

On the 1st of February General Pickett undertook an expedition against Newbern, North Carolina, which resulted in the destruction of the "Underwriter," one of the largest and best of the Federal gunboats in the Sounds.

On the 11th occurred the affair at Johns Island, in the vicinity of Charleston, disturbing the monotony of the attempts on that city. On the same day the Federals were repulsed by the Confederates under General Wise—breaking in confusion and leaving some of their dead. But the most important of the active engagements of the winter was at Ocean Pond, in Florida, where the Federals, under General Seymour, were dispersed and badly defeated by the Confederates, under General Finnegan.

General Sherman's expedition in the Southwest—a part of the grand combination of Grant in the West, in co-operation with a naval expedition from New Orleans against Mobile—was a stupendous failure. Thomas's advance on Atlanta was suddenly checked, and he was compelled to fall back upon his base at Chickamauga. As says another: "The 'On to Atlanta' was a programme, all parts of which had been disconcerted, and to amend which the campaign in the West had to be put over until the fighting month of May."

With this digression we return to Richmond, to give a passing notice to the actions of the Confederate Congress during the session of this winter. In the early part of the session, the Senate was interested in discussing the right of the President to remove or appoint certain officers pertaining to the military department of the government. This arose from the removal of Quartermaster-General Myers, who had been considered one of the most prudent, sagacious and efficient officers under the government, and the appointment of General Lawton, to whom no objection could be urged, save that he was used to supersede Colonel Myers, whose conduct of the affairs under his supervision had been singularly free from mistakes. The discussion was excited, and often bitterly acrimonious, and gave rise to some unpleasant *on dits* of a personal character. In his action, however, the President was sustained, and the gossip circulated in the capital was silenced, unequivocally, by the Senatorial voice.

The effort of Congress to increase the conscription met with the hearty approval of the public, and was by no means considered unjust or oppressive, as it served to keep in course of instruction an army of reserves, of youths from sixteen to eighteen years of age, which could be sent in to reinforce the army depleted by death, or to meet the demands for more troops, occasioned by the continual and heavy reinforcement of the army of the enemy. But the suspension of the writ of *habeas corpus*, as passed under an enactment of our Congress, was considered unjustifiable, intolerable and tyrannical, though its enforcement was qualified by a stringent bill of particulars. A writer says: "But what can be most said to wipe from the record of the Confederacy the stain of this infamous act is, that it was never put into practice. It was not put into practice for the simple reason that there was no occasion for it. No one doubted the integrity and patriotism of our judiciary; that branch of the government was practically permitted to continue its dispensations of law and justice, and the worst that can be said of the law suspending the *habeas corpus* was that it was a stain upon our political history. It was an uncalled-for libel on the Confederacy; but although it might blacken our reputation, yet it is a satisfaction to know that it did not practically affect our system of liberties." The writer proceeds: "In contrasting the political systems of the North and South in this war, we find an invariable superiority in the latter with respect to all questions of civil liberty. This, indeed, is to be taken as the most striking and significant moral phenomenon of the war." These questions, together with the more important and absorbing matters of finance, were the burden of Congressional duties for this session.

The winter was waning. The increased depression and anxiety consequent upon the increase of suffering and privation from the severe cold and dreariness of the season, were lightened in a measure in prospect of the bright, warm weather which would soon mantle the earth with the beauty and fragrance of spring. Our military successes, also, served to lift the gloom that rested on our hearts in the early days of winter. But we were on the eve of being victimized by a fiendish attempt at the destruction of our city, that must vie, in the horror of its details, with the most cruel arts of warfare practiced in the darkest ages.

CHAPTER LIV.

DAHLGREN'S RAID AROUND RICHMOND.

ON the 28th of February, a raid was undertaken towards Richmond by the Federal cavalry under General Kilpatrick, seconded in command by Colonel Ulric Dahlgren, a son of Admiral Dahlgren, of Charleston notoriety.

After reaching Beaver Dam, a station on the Virginia Central Railroad, in Hanover County, the force divided, Kilpatrick with his command passing through the upper part of Hanover and Louisa, where he took a road that led to the Brooke turnpike, leading immediately into Richmond. Dahlgren's command proceeded at once to Frederick Hall, in Louisa County, where they captured several of our officers, who were engaged in holding a Court Martial, among whom was Captain Dement, of a Baltimore battery, whom they compelled to follow the expedition.

After tearing up the railroad for some distance, Dahlgren proceeded towards James River, which he struck in Goochland County. Here he burnt a grist-mill, some barns, some locks on the canal, and did other trifling damage. His men, in the meantime, were allowed to amuse themselves by destroying furniture, pilfering plate, and doing other mischief to the farm-houses in the vicinity. His purpose was to cross the James River, and get into Richmond by the south side; and to accomplish this he employed a negro to guide him to a ford in the river, and for this service paid him what the black supposed to be a five-dollar note, but which in fact proved to be only a barber's advertisement, gotten up in the ingenious fashion common at the North. The negro conducted Dahlgren to a ford, but finding the water too high to cross, he turned upon the helpless guide and ordered him to be instantly hanged, and to expedite this horrible deed he furnished a rein from his own bridle for the purpose.

Finding that he could not cross, he sought to make a junction with Kilpatrick, but in the meantime all other parts of the expedition had failed. The part under the command of General Custer, which had moved towards Charlottesville, intended merely to distract attention, had suffered disaster. A portion of Stuart's horse artillery, under Colonel Beckham, stationed at Rio Mills, in Albemarle County, opened upon the advancing column, and drove them into rapid retreat, which was not abandoned until they reached their infantry supports at Madison Court House.

A cowardice not less ridiculous was manifested by Kilpatrick in the part of the expedition intrusted to, or assumed by him. He had reached the outer line of the fortifications around Richmond a little after ten o'clock on the morning of the first of March. A desultory fire was kept up for several hours, in which the enemy, who had set out with the intention of making a desperate inroad into Richmond, never got within sight of the artillery of the Confederates, and, contented to boast of having got within sight of the spires of the rebel capital, they retired in the direction of the Peninsula.

Unapprised of the cowardly flight of his coadjutor, on the night of the 1st of March, Dahlgren, with some seven or eight hundred horsemen, pursued his way towards Richmond, following the Westham plank road until within a few miles of the city. But a still greater exhibition of cowardice was reserved for him than had been manifested even by Custer or Kilpatrick.

All that intervened in the darkness of the night between Dahlgren and Richmond, between the remorseless enemy and the revenge he had threatened to visit with dire destruction, fire and blood, upon the devoted capital of the Southern Confederacy, was a force of Local Defence, composed of artisans from the Richmond armory, and a battalion of clerks from the different government departments, many of whom were young boys. But this was the force to give Dahlgren's "braves" a lesson for their temerity.

The Armory battalion were on the enemy's flank, and are reported to have been surprised. But when they came in contact with Henly's battalion, (the clerks,) the well-appointed cavalry of the enemy, which had started with such grand expectations, broke at the first fire. A single volley of musketry seems to have been quite sufficient for the completion of all the disaster that occurred, and to have finished the business. Eleven of Dahlgren's Yankees were killed, and thirty or forty wounded, while the rest scattered in shameful flight.

Some prisoners were then captured, from the persons of

whom, when brought into Richmond, were taken silver egg-cups, spoons, forks, and other articles of plate marked with the initials of families whose houses, they had robbed in Goochland County.

After his disgraceful defeat, Dahlgren appeared only intent upon his retreat. He divided his forces so as to facilitate their escape, and the command of which he took charge moved down the south bank of the Pamunky River, and proceeded by the most direct route through King William County to Aylett on the Mattaponi, watched at every turn by scouts detached from Lee's Rangers.

Lieutenant James Pollard, of this command, who had chanced to notice on a newspaper bulletin the direction of Dahlgren's retreat, declared that he would make him "pay toll" on the route, and hastened to intercept him.

While Dahlgren and his party of fugitives, with sinking spirits and cowardly caution proceeded on the road to Walkerton in King and Queen County, Lieutenant Pollard, with reinforcements from Captain Fox, of the Fifth Virginia cavalry of Lee's Rangers, and some members of Lieutenant-Colonel Robins's cavalry, continued to press them in the front and rear, and by a rapid circuit they succeeded, when the night came on, in getting ahead of him, and awaited his approach in the darkness. To insure his position, Dahlgren required Captain Dement, the Confederate officer taken at Frederick's Hall, to ride by his side. Seeing in the darkness some figures ahead of him, and supposing they were rebel scouts, he shouted, "Surrender!" It was a fatal moment for him. "Fire!" was returned, and the darkness was lighted by a volley of Confederate musketry. It was enough. Dahlgren fell, pierced by two bullets in the head, two through the body, and one through the hand. The woods were filled with the fugitives, who implored the Confederates to accept their surrender. Captain Dement was miraculously preserved. His horse was shot under him, but he himself escaped unhurt. The remnant of Dahlgren's force taken at this time was one hundred and fifty negroes and Yankees. Thus ended Dahlgren's raid around Richmond.

On the body of this leader was found remarkable documentary evidence, proving the intention of the expedition and the horrors from which we had been so providentially preserved—escape from which was made the subject of public thanksgiving in our churches.

The following address to the officers and men of the command was written on a sheet of paper, having in printed letters on the upper corner, " Head-Quarters Third Division Cavalry Corps, ——, 1864;"

"OFFICERS AND MEN:

" You have been selected from brigades and regiments as a picked command to attempt a desperate undertaking—an undertaking which if successful will write your names on the hearts of your countrymen in letters that can never be erased, and which will cause the prayers of your fellow soldiers, now confined in loathsome prisons, to follow you and yours wherever you may go.

" We hope to release the prisoners from Belle Island first, and having seen them fairly started, we will cross James River into Richmond, destroying the bridges after us, and exhorting the released prisoners to destroy and burn the hateful city; and do not allow the rebel leader, Davis, and his traitorous crew to escape. The prisoners must render great assistance, as you cannot leave your ranks too far, or become too much scattered, or you will be lost.

" Do not allow any personal gain to lead you off, which would only bring you to an ignominious death at the hands of citizens. Keep well together and obey orders strictly, and all will be well; and on no account scatter too far, for in union there is strength.

"With strict obedience to orders, and fearlessness in the execution, you will be sure to succeed.

" We will join the main force on the other side of the city, or perhaps meet them inside.

" Many of you will fall, but if there is any man here not willing to sacrifice his life in such a great and glorious undertaking, or who does not feel capable of meeting the enemy in such a desperate fight as will follow, let him step out, and he may go hence to the arms of his sweetheart and read of the braves who swept through the city of Richmond.

" We want no man who cannot feel sure of success in such a cause.

" We will have a desperate fight, but stand up to it when it does come, and all will be well.

" Ask the blessing of the Almighty, and do not fear the enemy.

U. DAHLGREN,
Colonel Commanding."

The following special orders, written on detached slips of paper, disclosed the plans of the leaders of this murderous expedition.

"Guides, Pioneers, (with oakum, turpentine and torpedoes;) Signal Officers, Quarter-master, Commissary, Scout and Pickets, men in rebel uniform:

These will remain on the north bank, and move down with the force on the south bank, not getting ahead of them; and if the communication can be kept up without giving alarm, it must be done; but everything depends upon a SURPRISE, and NO ONE must be allowed to pass ahead of the column. Information must be gathered in regard to the crossings of the river, so that should we be repulsed on the south side, we will know where to recross at the nearest point. All *mills* must be burned and the *canal* destroyed, and also everything which can be used by the rebels, must be destroyed, including the boats on the river. Should a ferry-boat be seized and can be worked have it moved down. Keep the force on the south side posted of any important movements of the enemy, and in case of danger, some of the scouts must swim the river, and bring us information. As we approach the city the party must take great care that they do not go ahead of the other party on the south side, and must conceal themselves and watch our movements. We will try and secure the bridge to the city, (one mile below Belle Isle) and release the prisoners at the same time. If we do not succeed, they must then dash down and we will try and carry the bridge from each side.

When necessary the men must be filed through the woods and along the river bank. The bridge once secured, and the prisoners loose and over the river, the bridge will be secured and the city destroyed. The men must keep together and well in hand, and once in the city, it must be destroyed, and *Jeff Davis and his cabinet killed.*

Pioneers will go along with combustible materials. The officer must use his discretion about the time of assisting us. Horses and cattle which we do not need immediately must be shot rather than left. Everything on the canal and elsewhere, of service to the rebels, must be destroyed. As General Custer may follow me, be careful not to give a false alarm.

The signal officer must be prepared to communicate at night by rockets, and in other things pertaining to this department.

The quartermasters and commissaries must be on the lookout for their departments, and see that there are no delays on their account.

The engineer officers will follow to survey the road as we pass over it, etc.

The pioneers must be prepared to construct a bridge or to destroy one. They must have plenty of oakum and turpentine for burning, which will be rolled in soaked balls, and given to the men to burn when we get into the city. Torpedoes will only be used by the pioneers for destroying the main bridges, etc. They must be prepared to destroy railroads. Men will branch off to the right, with a few pioneers, and destroy the bridges and railroads south of Richmond, and then join us at the city. They must be prepared with torpedoes, etc. The line of Falling Creek is probably the best to work along—or, as they approach the city, the line of Goody's Creek, so that no reinforcement can come up on any cars. No one must be allowed to pass ahead, for fear of communicating news. Rejoin the command with all haste, and if cut off, cross the river above Richmond, and rejoin us. Men will stop at Bellona Arsenal, and totally destroy it, and anything else but hospitals; then follow on and rejoin the command at Richmond with all haste, and if cut off, cross the river, and rejoin us. As General Custer may follow me, be careful and not give a false alarm."

These documents developed a plot so murderous in intention, that many persons in the Confederacy thought the prisoners taken in this adventure should not be accorded the usual privileges of prisoners of war, but should be turned over to the State authorities to be dealt with as thieves and murderers, and subjected to the usual punishment of felons. Again we heard the old talk of retaliation, and to give the show of reality to the threat, the Libby Prison was undermined as a miserable warning against attempting another such demonstration, but no one for a moment believed that the threat of blowing it up would ever be carried into effect.

Dahlgren's body was buried out of sight, mysteriously concealed from all but the prying, curious eyes of a negro, who for a heavy bribe disclosed the place to parties who exhumed it, and since have returned it to his friends.

There is one revolting circumstance in connection with the termination of this raid of Dahlgren, and the capture and death of that officer, which we regret exceedingly to record, and would if possible forget—that his finger was cut off at the joint to secure a handsome diamond ring, worn by him. But if anything so revolting to the nobler instincts of humanity must be excused on any ground, it should be in the general and disgusting practice permitted on both sides, of stripping dead bodies on the battle field.

There was very little excitement in Richmond. So suddenly and unexpectedly did this adventure occur, that we were scarcely aware of our danger until it was over. What "might have been," was so terrible to reflect upon, that it awakened grateful prayers to a merciful and protecting Providence. The ease with which the invading force was scattered and repulsed, the signal failure of every part of the combination, give evidence of the cowardly fear which must always possess those whose purposes are guilty, and the strength which nerves the arm when the design is founded in right. The moral of this story is pointed in the memorable language in Hamlet's eulogy:

> "Thus, conscience doth make cowards of us all,
> And thus the native hue of resolution
> Is sicklied o'er with the pale cast of thought;
> And enterprises of great pith and moment
> With this regard, their currents turn awry
> And lose the name of action."

It may or it may not be surprising to the people of the South to learn that the papers found on the person of Colonel Dahlgren are said by our enemies to have been forged, or interpolated so as to present the aspect in which they were made public. It is a grave charge, and reflects heavily on those who intercepted the raiders and brought the evidences of their guilt into Richmond—a charge which we feel prepared to resent with sincere indignation, as Lieutenant Pollard, a man as much distinguished for his nice sense of honor as for his bravery, would be altogether incapable of an act that would so compromise his character as a gentleman and a soldier. To all, it must appear patent as a flimsy subterfuge, by which to palliate or extenuate the dire offence against a comparatively defenceless, and unsuspecting people.

All other evidence wanting, the headings of the orders in print are in themselves sufficient, and magnanimity would suggest that it were, perhaps, more honorable to permit the mantle of oblivion to fall over the ill-starred leader of this unfortunate expedition, which, if not devised by him, was one in which he himself became a victim to the diabolical machinations of the projectors of the plot, than to attempt to fasten upon the innocent the base charge of forgery. And here it may be asked, whether if it had been successful, and the capture and killing of the much-hated Davis the result, any extenuating apology would be brought forward, for the means by which it was accomplished? It failed, and the indubitable evidences of murderous purposes are pronounced counterfeit!

CHAPTER LV.

THE SPRING OF 1864—MORGAN'S RETURN TO RICHMOND.

THE spring of 1864 set in hopefully for the cause of the South. Our successes during the winter had been of the most encouraging character. The spirit of the army was buoyant and determined—that of the people elastic and cheerful. A generous disposition was shown by them in the supply of means to support the war. The agricultural interests of the country were attended to with redoubled energy, and the impressment of supplies for the use of the army was regarded with entire satisfaction by those who, engaged in agricultural pursuits, were expected to furnish them. In Virginia this was peculiarly evident. From her moral and geographical position, her responsibilities and sufferings were heavier than those of any other State. Her statistics are full of glory, and history must hand down her record so nearly stainless, that despite the contemptible weakness accredited to the claims of the F. F. V.'s, her children will be pardoned a noble pride in the confession : "My mother State is Virginia!" More than ever before a nativity on her soil is to be envied, if the place of birth can lend, as it assuredly does, anything of interest to the individual.

From advantages gained in excess of prisoners taken at Vicksburg, the conduct of the exchange was almost wholly under the power of the Federals. A refusal to accord terms such as could honorably be acceded to by the Confederate government, gave rise to anxious doubts and fears that an exchange would not occur at all, or at least until some unprecedented success placed it in the power of our government to dictate terms. After many disappointments, and after tiresome negotiation, the disagreements on this question were so reconciled that the much-desired business of exchange was resumed. With the most grateful pleasure it was announced to us in Richmond that certain numbers were to be taken from our prisoners, and in return we were once more to welcome to Dixie's Land the defenders of the soil. This occurred early in the spring. It was announced from the different pulpits of our churches on a Sabbath morning that a boat load of returned prisoners was expected on that day, and the citizens were requested to send to the Capitol Square provisions for their refreshment. The occasion called forth thousands to the square to welcome their appearance. Refreshments were lavishly provided, of the best that could be afforded from the impoverished larder of the city of Richmond, and after waiting in intense anxiety for a sight of our returned friends, after several hours, from afar off, down the main street, were heard the strains of "Dixie," and the cheers of the multitude that assembled all along the route to greet the soldiers so long imprisoned in a hostile land. Finally the strains, so faint at first, grew louder and louder, and at last a body of nondescript looking men filed into the Capitol Square ; but there were enough of them clad in the Confederate grey to announce our returning braves. Hats were all off on the instant ; cheer after cheer rent the air ; the strains of music were drowned in the loud acclamations of delight, and as these sounds subsided, enthusiastic boys in the crowd raised another shout : " Hurrah for the greybacks," which was warmly responded to, and resounded in volumes of heartfelt congratulation over the hills of Richmond.

The soldiers were met and addressed by the President in a stirring speech of welcome, praise and encouragement; then followed a short and cheerful address from the Governor of Virginia, and again the welkin reverberated the loud acclaim for President Davis and Governor Smith. Refreshments were distributed, hands shaken, congratulations exchanged, and tears of joy glistened on countenances radiant with welcome to the captives.

The scenes of this occasion can never be forgotten by those who witnessed them. Mr. Davis evinced the calm dignity for which he is distinguished, presenting a vivid contrast to the exuberant spirit and mercurial youthfulness of Governor Smith. On this afternoon, with as much apparent pleasure as a young gallant of twenty-five, the latter triumphantly exhibited a superb bouquet, the gift of some fair friend and admirer.

Of these festive scenes there was a quiet and unobtrusive spectator, then the most distinguished guest in the capital. He, too, had been a captive—not formally exchanged by the provisions of the cartel, not accorded the usual privileges of a prisoner of war; but his escape had been from the convicts' cell, the home of the felon—from the gloomy, thick, impenetrable walls of the Ohio Penitentiary; and on the Capitol Square of the seat of government of his own country, with the brazen statue of Washington looking down upon the scene, General John Morgan greeted the return of his fellow captives. This was not, however, his first appearance in Richmond after his escape from his disgraceful incarceration. There was nothing needed in the manner of his reception to testify the grateful appreciation of his fellow citizens of the South. A brilliant welcome was accorded him. A splendid banquet was served in his honor at the Ballard House, and the President and Vice-President, and officers of the government, army and navy, the State of Virginia and the members of Congress attended, in testimony of their admiration and appreciation. He was the hero of the hour. But General Morgan was far too modest, too noble, too sensible, to be affected only in the deep gratitude of his brave soul by these manifest declarations of his worth by grateful countrymen.

On this afternoon, as he passed through the crowd, accompanied by his young and beautiful wife, save for the stars on the collar of his plain grey coat, and his military cap, a stranger would have discovered about him none of the insignia of rank, and from his modest bearing no one would have supposed him to be the Marion of Kentucky. Of rarely precious materials are heroes made.

For awhile the business of exchange was again conducted regularly, and as the spring advanced fresh successes gilded Confederate arms. Our hopes brightened and our faith increased, yet were our hearts heavy with the dread of the coming events which must mark their records again in blood upon our soil, already glutted with the crimson stream which for three long years had been poured in fury upon our devoted land. Our souls were sick of carnage, but the remorseless maw of War, like the daughter of the horseleech, cried Give! give! And the gentle image of Peace was thrust aside, and with horent front that of War obtruded. But there appeared another,—a mediator who, capturing the olive branch of peace, waved it temptingly before us, and whispered "Reconstruction!" and vaguely hinted at conquest over foreign nations, in which were strangely blended the words Mexico, France and England. But thrusting aside a friend who came to us in such questionable guise, and refusing an alliance purchased at the price of our national honor, we reached forth our hands, and over the heads of fathers, brothers, sons and friends in the field, grasping once more the bloody hand of War, we resolved to dare the worst rather than be a party to ignoble submission.

CHAPTER LVI.

PROPOSED EVACUATION OF RICHMOND—REMOVAL OF THE TREASURY NOTE BUREAU.

THE month of April, 1864, had chronicled a succession of good fortunes to our cause, but the "river of death" was ahead of us, and friend looked into the face of friend to read a tale of anxiety and sorrow, while sighs usurped the place of smiles as the names of friends were mentioned. Ever busy Rumor circulated stories from her "thousand tongues" in the Confederate Capital, and again we heard the ominous word, "Evacuation!" It was reported that the government had appropriated a sum for the removal of the non-combatants from the city, in order to allow a more thorough opportunity for its defence in the event of assault.

To give this story the semblance of truth, Mr. Memminger had ordered the removal of the Treasury Note Bureau, (in which women principally were employed,) to Columbia, South Carolina, ostensibly to prevent the transportation of unsigned notes to the Capital, (as the printing operations of the Treasury were conducted in that city,) but the credulous and the suspicious drew a different augury. The greatest dissatisfaction at the prospect was manifested by the ladies, and a petition was presented to Mr. Memminger, signed almost unanimously by them, praying him to rescind the objectionable edict; but whether from prudential motives, or otherwise, the Secretary of the Treasury was inexorable, and gave his fair operatives their choice, to go to Columbia or to resign their places in the department. Deriving, many of them, their daily support from their clerkships, they felt compelled to remain in the employment of government, and in sorrow and in tears they bade adieu to Richmond, and took up their departure for the capital of the Palmetto State.

The excitement occasioned by this gave rise to reports that the archives of the government were all to be removed, and the time and place designated. Every day the teeming population of women and children, and the infirm and aged, expected to be sent forth as wanderers, they knew not whither, over the wasted territory of the Southern Confederacy.

In a few days, corrected reports and satisfactory explanations sufficed to silence these rumors, and to restore confidence. Yet nought could lift from our hearts the heavy gloom of impending terror in the immense preparations made by the enemy for our destruction. The monster "Anaconda," of which we had been hearing from the commencement of the war, which was to crush us in its fatal coil, was reported by our enemies to be in a fair way to have his "tail in his mouth." Once surrounded in his murderous embrace, there was little chance for our freedom; the death throes of the Confederacy would then tell the agony of the final struggle.

But we listened to these ominous warnings as we listened to the whisperings of the wind; they came to us from the North to dampen our ardor, to discourage our fortitude, to dismay our souls, but they failed of effect. Defeat was nowhere written on our future prospects. Discouragement might be, but defeat nowhere! And we once more hugged to our bosoms the phantom of hope, and it sang a lullaby to our fears, and the Confederate metropolis pursued its usual busy routine, and contented itself with the thought that "the end is not!" But the bright genial airs of Spring, the perfume of the flowers, the carolling of the feathered musicians, awoke in our hearts little feeling of pleasure, when we drew in at every breath the fiery vapors of war, and our ears were quickened to hear once more the awful music of artillery.

CHAPTER LVII.

THE SUMMER CAMPAIGN OF 1864—THE BATTLES OF THE WILDERNESS.

THE summer campaign of 1864 against the South was devised upon a plan of enormous magnitude. General Grant, whose former successes had raised him to the highest popularity, and gained for him the willing confidence of the North, had been commissioned Lieutenant-General, and immediately transferred his personal presence to the army of the Potomac, leaving General Sherman as his vicegerent to carry out his campaign in the West. Never, since the commencement of the war, had there been made such magnificent preparations in the "On to Richmond" design. Warren, Sedgwick, and Hancock had been made corps commanders of General Grant's army, and to Burnside had been assigned a separate corps. Butler, at Fortress Monroe, was reinforced by Gillmore's corps from Charleston, and by Baldy Smith's corps from the west. To the hero of New Orleans was allotted the task of cutting off the city of Richmond from its southern lines of communication, while Sigel, operating in the Shenandoah Valley, was to cut the railroad which by way of Gordonsville connected the army of General Lee with its principal base of supplies at Lynchburg.

These preparations completed for the most important campaign in the history of our country, on Wednesday, the 4th of May, just eight weeks after Lieutenant-General Grant had received his commission, his two grand columns were ready to move—the one from the north on the line of the Rapidan, and the other from Fortress Monroe, one day's sail from Richmond.

On the 5th and 6th days of May was fought the Battle of the Wilderness. How well the Confederates sustained themselves during the first fight may be inferred from an account by a Northern correspondent, who says, "No cheer of victory swelled through the Wilderness that night."

The results of the second day's fight were eminently successful to the Confederates, but it seems they were not aware of the magnitude of their victory, and failed to press the advantage gained by them. Generals Seymour and Shaler, of the Federal army, with the greater portion of their commands, were captured. Being confessedly outgeneralled, Grant was compelled to change his front, which required a change of line for General Lee. This change was given by the enemy the name of "retreat," and it was heralded in the press of the North as a "Waterloo defeat of the Confederates," and "The retreat of Lee to Richmond." But very soon these mendacious reports were corrected by subsequent developments, as had been many of a similar character in the preceding history of the war. In this engagement General Longstreet was severely wounded, and General Jenkins, of South Carolina, lost his life.

On the 8th of May two engagements were fought at Spotsylvania Court-House, in which the enemy were repulsed. On the 9th, which was marked by some skirmishing, General Sedgwick, one of the corps commanders of General Grant's army, and reported to be a valuable and gallant officer, was killed (probably by a stray bullet.) It is said he had just at that moment been bantering his men about dodging and ducking their heads at the whistle of the Confederate bullets in the distance. "Why," said he, "they couldn't hit an elephant at this distance," when in a moment a ball entered his face, just below the eye, penetrated his brain, and caused his death instantly.

But on the 12th of May occurred what is entitled the great battle of Spotsylvania Court-house. In this engagement the Confederate Major-General Johnston, with almost his entire division, and a brigade or two of other troops, under command of Brigadier-General George H. Stuart, were captured; but the result of the battle was that the enemy were repulsed with tremendous loss. The ground in front of the Confederate lines was piled with his slain.

The fighting had now continued during six days, and had been of the most obstinate and desperate character.

An intelligent critic says of this period: "It would not be impossible to match the results of any one day's battle with stories from the wars of the old world; but never, we should think, in the history of man, were five such battles as these compressed into six days."

Grant had been foiled, but his obstinacy had not been subdued. He telegraphed to Washington: "I propose to fight it out on this line, if it takes all summer."

While Grant was engaged on the Rapidan, a cavalry expedition, under the command of General Sheridan, moved around on the right flank of General Lee, to North Anna River, committed some damage at Beaver Dam Station, on the Virginia Central Railroad, proceeded thence to the South Anna River and Ashland Station, on the Richmond, Fredericksburg and Potomac Railroad, destroyed a portion of the road at that point, and made its way round to the James River at Turkey Island, where its forces joined those of Butler. The damage inflicted in this raid was not considerable, but a severe fight occurred at Yellow Tavern, on the direct road to Richmond, on the 10th of May, where a Confederate force of cavalry, under our gallant General J. E. B. Stuart, encountered that of Sheridan. In this engagement our illustrious cavalry commander, who had for so long a time made Virginia the theatre of brilliant and chivalrous exploits, which in feudal times would have made all Europe ring with the praise of so gallant a knight, was killed.

It seemed indeed very difficult to realize that General Jeb. Stuart, late so full of life, so bright, so gay, so brave, could be cut down in a moment; but soon the mournful strains of the Dead March, the solemn procession of military mourners, the funeral carriage, the coffin draped with the Confederate banner, the saddened citizens who with tearful eyes gazed upon the melancholy pageant, told but too truly the story of the departure of another hero of the South. The laurel and the cypress strangely intertwined in the wreath of the South, and the mourning chaplet was growing almost too heavy to be borne on her brow.

In the meantime, Butler's column, intended to operate against us on the south side, in co-operation with Grant on the north of Richmond, had commenced its movement.

On the 5th of May he proceeded with his fleet of gunboats and transports up the James River, landing at Wilson's Wharf a regiment of Wild's negro troops, two brigades of negroes at Fort Powhatan, thence up to City Point, where he landed Hinks's division, and at Bermuda Hundred he disembarked his whole army. On the 7th of May a portion of his command struck for the Richmond and Petersburg Railroad, and succeeded in destroying a bridge seven miles north of Petersburg. His intention was, and he boasted that he could carry the defences of Drewry's Bluff, the main barrier of approach to the Confederate capital, by the route of the James River, and it had been stated in the papers at the North that he had succeeded in cutting the army of Beauregard in twain, and "held the keys to the back door of Richmond." But this consummation, so "devoutly to be wished" by the redoubtable hero of New Orleans was altogether in anticipation. We read: " On the 16th of May General Beauregard fell upon the insolent enemy, in a fog, drove Butler from his advanced positions back to his original earth-works, and inflicted upon him a loss of five thousand men in killed, wounded and captured. He had fallen upon the right of the Yankee line of battle with the force of an avalanche, completely crushing it backward and turning Butler's flank. The action was decisive. The day's operation resulted in Butler's entire army being ordered to return from its advanced position within ten miles of Richmond, to the line of defence known as Bermuda Hundred, between the James and Appomatox Rivers."

The expedition of Sigel in the Valley had also come to grief. On the 15th of May his column was encountered by the Confederate General Breckinridge, near New Market, who drove it across the Shenandoah, captured six pieces of artillery, nearly one thousand stand of small arms, and inflicted upon it heavy loss in men. Sigel was forced to abandon his hospitals and to destroy the larger portion of his train.

In the meantime a new movement was undertaken by General Grant, to pass his army from the line of the Po, (which had been occupied by him since the battle of Spotsylvania Court-House,) down the valley of the Rappahannock, which compelled General Lee to evacuate a strong position occupied by him on the line of the Po, and by admirable strategy he succeeded again in intercepting Grant, and planted himself between Grant and Richmond, near Hanover Junction. We find : " On the 23d and 25th of May General Grant made attempts on the Confederate lines, that were repulsed, and left him to the last alternative. Another flanking operation remained for him, by which "he swung his army from the North Anna around and across the Pamunky. On the 27th Hanovertown was reported to be occupied by the Yankee advance under General Sheridan, and on the 28th Grant's entire army was across the Pamunky."

" General Lee also reformed his line of battle north and south, directly in front of the Virginia Central Railroad, and extending from Atler's Station south to Shady Grove, ten miles north of Richmond. In this position he covered both the Virginia Central and the Fredericksburg and Richmond Railroads, leading to Richmond, west of and including the Mechanicsville pike. The favorite tactics of Grant appear to have been to develop the left flank ; and by this characteristic manœuvre he moved down the Hanover Court-House road, and on the first day of June he took a position near Cold Harbor."

He was now within a few miles of Richmond. The Northern mind was buoyed up with the report of the certainty of the capture of the "rebel capital" within the usual time— "ten days." But it was altogether too fast. The circumstance of the close proximity to the city, the view of the spires of the churches and domes of prominent edifices in Richmond, did not mean that the army of the enemy were quite in occupation, as was proven by the defeat of General McClellan, when so near that he might almost, with good glasses, have looked in upon our breakfast tables; and the "retreat of Lee," as usually understood by the Federals, was simply to counteract and check every movement attempted by General Grant, from the time of his advance at the battle of the Wilderness up to the time that he essayed the passage of the Chickahominy and succeeded in establishing himself at Cold Harbor, a strategic point of great importance to him, as it furnished him an easy communication with his base of supplies at the White House, on the Pamunky River. But the attainment of this point had not been at slight cost, but with the loss of more than two thousand men in killed and wounded.

There is abundant evidence to infer that General Grant intended to make the conflict at Cold Harbor the decisive battle of the campaign. One who was well-informed, and and who closely watched the progress of these events, writes: "The movements of the preceding days, culminating in the possession of Cold Harbor—an important strategic point—had drawn the enemy's lines close in front of the Chickahominy, and reduced the military problem to the forcing of the passage of that river; a problem which, if solved in Grant's favor, would decide whether Richmond could be carried by a *coup de main*, if a decisive victory should attend his arms, or whether he should betake himself to siege operations, or some other course.

Early on the morning of the 3d of June the assault was made. The first line of the Confederates held by General Breckinridge was carried—but the reverse was only momentary—for the troops of Millegan's Brigade and the Maryland battalion dashed forward, and retrieved the honors temporarily gathered by the enemy.

The account before referred to proceeds: "On every part of the line, the enemy was repulsed by the quick and decisive blows of the Confederates. Hancock's corps, the only portion of the Yankee army that had come in contact with the Confederate works, had been hurled back in a storm of fire; the Sixth corps had not been able to get up further than within two hundred and fifty yards of the main works; while Warren and Burnside, or the enemy's right and right centre were staggered on the lines of our rifle-pits. The decisive work of the day was done in ten minutes. Never were there such signal strokes of valor, such despatch of victory. It was stated in the accounts of the Confederates, that fourteen distinct assaults of the enemy were repulsed, and that his loss was from six to seven thousand. No wonder that the assurance of the capture of Richmond was displaced in the newspapers of the North, by the ominous calculation that Grant could not afford many such experiments on the intrenched line of the Chickahominy, and would have to make some other resort to victory."

The battle of Cold Harbor forever removed the impression of the demoralization of General Lee's army, and ended the attempt to take Richmond from the north side. The barefooted, ragged, ill-fed rebel army, which had been under fire for more than a month, had achieved a succession of victories unparalleled in the history of modern warfare. General Grant and his friends were alike astonished. The latter insisted he should have half a million of men to enable him to accomplish his work, and a Boston paper said, "We should have a vigorous and overwhelming war, or else peace without further effusion of blood."

We had witnessed the failure of the seventh expedition sent out for the capture of Richmond. We had seen, one after another, six of the defeated candidates for that honor, relieved of command, and quietly consigned to his place on the shelf. We had watched with the most curious interest the rivalry in the different routes to the desired end. We had seen General McClellan in his Peninsular rout driven from our walls, and taking refuge on board his gunboats; we had seen McDowell and Pope from the North, driven back, routed and dismayed, under cover of the guns of Alexandria and Washington. Burnside and Hooker had been driven back across the Rappahannock, and now General Grant from his eccentric route through the tangled roads of the Wilderness, and by Spotsylvania Court House, dismayed, disconcerted with his stock of expedients well nigh exhausted, had been compelled to transfer his army to the south side of the James, and was driven to resort to the capture of Richmond by siege operations.

Notwithstanding, his avowal to "fight it out on this line" if it took all summer, Grant found himself most unwillingly transferred to a new base of operations.

The most striking feature in the character of this distinguished commander of the Federal army, seems to be quiet determination, and indomitable perseverance and energy. Under similar disappointment, another would have had his courage so shaken that he would gladly have foregone an undertaking that promised so little fulfillment in success. The saving of his army appeared not to have been with him an object, if by it he should lose an advantage. He had received, from the battle of the Wilderness to that of Cold Harbor, repeated and powerful repulses; his losses in men were unparalleled in the whole history of the struggle, but his perseverance was undisturbed, and the intention to bear him out is evidenced by the immense reinforcements with which he was continually supplied.

From the Wilderness to Richmond he is reported to have lost from sixty to one hundred thousand men—some accounts place his figures still higher, but from the teeming multitudes of the North, it was an easy matter to fill up the gaps in his ranks—while for a Confederate soldier killed, the question began to be one of importance, "Where shall one be found to fill his place in the ranks?"

A Confederate officer, in speaking of one of these battles, remarked, "I never witnessed such destruction of life. One day after a battle," said he, "my own horse being exhausted, I borrowed one to ride to a position of the field, a mile or two distant. On passing a company of soldiers, I asked, 'Are there any Yankees in this direction?' they replied,

'Yes; thousands, and in line of battle.' 'Well, then,' I rejoined, 'I must retreat, this horse is a borrowed one, and however little I may care for my own capture, I do not wish my friend to lose his horse.' I had turned my horse to ride back, when they shouted, 'Halloo, soldier, but they are all dead!' I then pursued my way to that portion of the field, and such a sight met my gaze as I had never before witnessed, and pray never to see again! In a direct line for more than two miles, in every attitude of death, it seemed to me there was not a foot of earth uncovered by a human figure. In some places they lay in heaps of two, three and four, which proved that a whole line of the enemy must have been cut down by our fire, and there they lay unburied, their ghastly features distorted in the terrible repose of an agonizing death."

It has been said, (but denied by certain Federal officers with whom we have conversed) that at the battle of Cold Harbor Grant's men were furnished with extra rations of whiskey, to sustain their sinking courage; but it is a fact that many of them were said to have been partially intoxicated when taken prisoners, and to have marched up to the breastworks of the Confederates and voluntarily surrendered themselves, and those who resisted were knocked down by clubbed muskets. These things were stated to us by more than one Confederate officer, of whose veracity there is not the slightest question.

From the difference also evinced in the temper and disposition of the prisoners taken during this series of battles may be gathered the impression made upon the mind of the army of General Grant, by the repeated reverses experienced in his attempt to take Richmond, in the spring of 1864. At first those taken seemed defiant and revengeful, spoke freely of a speedy rescue, and the certainty of the capture of the rebel capital, and of the success of Grant's campaign; those captured at the later battles were despondent, discouraged, hopeless, and heaped unmeasured blame upon their government for continuing a war that appeared to them unlikely to end successfully for their cause; and applied to General Grant an unenviable *sobriquet*, for the unparalleled sacrifice of human life in an undertaking that promised so little hope of accomplishing the end desired.

CHAPTER LVIII.

PETERSBURG.

PETERSBURG had already sustained a heavy attack. On the 9th of June an expedition under Butler, had essayed the capture of the "Cockade City." The approach was made with nine regiments of infantry and cavalry, and at least four pieces of artillery, with which the enemy searched the Confederate lines for a distance of nearly six miles. They were opposed by Hood's and Battle's battalions, the forty-sixth Virginia, one company of the twenty-third South Carolina, with Sturdevant's battery, and a few guns in position, and Taliaferro's cavalry. The enemy were twice repulsed, but succeeded finally in penetrating the line of the Confederates, when the timely appearance of reinforcements to the Rebels, the most of whom were raw troops and militia, enabled them to drive back the greatly superior numbers that opposed them. The successful repulse of the first attack upon the "Cockade City" greatly encouraged the forces for its local defence. General Wise delivered an address to the troops under his command with his peculiarly thrilling eloquence, telling them that "Petersburg is to be and shall be defended on her outer walls, on her inner lines, at her corporation bounds, in every street, and around every temple of God, and every altar of man."

However, the resolution of this gallant little city was to be tested by a more severe trial, and to stand the shock of battle from the bulk of Grant's army. General Beauregard was transferred with his army to command and operate in the defence. On the 14th June an assault was made on the line of the Confederates which covered the northeastern approach to the city, and resulted in the capture of that line of works. On the evening of the 16th an attack was ordered on the Confederate works in front of Petersburg, resulting not only in a repulse at every point, but, the rebel troops, assuming the aggressive, drove the enemy from their breastworks at the Howlett House, and opened upon them an enfilading fire under which they fled with the utmost precipitation. Particularly noticeable in this defence was the action of General Hoke's division, which successfully repulsed three different charges of the enemy. In the final repulse a large portion of a brigade of the foe, being exposed to a heavy fire from the Confederate artillery, sought shelter in a ravine, and surrendered to the Sixty-fourth Georgia regiment.

On the 17th, the fighting was renewed without result. On the 18th, it was resolved by the enemy to make an assault along the whole line for the purpose of carrying the town, and evidently intended to be decisive. Three different assaults were made during the day, each to be repulsed. After severe losses on the part of each corps of the enemy engaged in the assault, at night the Confederates were still in possession of their works covering Petersburg, and General Grant was driven to the necessity of making still another change in his operations. The series of engagements around Petersburg had cost him not less than ten thousand men in killed and wounded, and had culminated in another decisive defeat.

Pickett's division at the same time taught the enemy another severe lesson at Port Walthall Junction. It was here that the heroes of Gettysburg engaged and repulsed a force under General Gillmore, (of Charleston notoriety,) who were employed in the destruction of the railroad, took two lines of his breastworks, and put him to the most disastrous flight.

Another portion of the combination, designed as an auxiliary to the general plan of Grant, had also failed of success. General Sheridan, in his advance on Charlottesville, had, on the 10th of June, been intercepted by the Confederate cavalry under General Wade Hampton, disastrously defeated in an engagement at Trevillian's Station on the Central Railroad, and compelled to withdraw his command across the North Anna River.

General Hunter's expedition had also failed. On the 18th of June he made an attack upon Lynchburg, and was repulsed by the Confederates from General Lee's lines under General Jubal Early. On the next day, more reinforcements having arrived, General Early prepared to attack the enemy, when he retreated in great confusion. An account says, "We took thirteen of his guns, and pursued him to Salem, in Roanoke County, and forced him into a line of retreat into the mountains of western Virginia." Strange to say, General Hunter officially announced to his government that his expedition had been "extremely successful;" that he only left Lynchburg because his ammunition was running short, and that as to the eccentric line he had taken up, he "now was ready to move in any direction."

But the measure of the misfortunes of this campaign was not yet full. On the 22d of June, Grant made an attempt to get possession of the Weldon Railroad, which resulted in disaster, the Confederates under General Anderson capturing four guns and one entire brigade of prisoners, and a portion of another brigade from the Second and Sixth corps of the army of Grant. And yet another expedition was destined to failure. Another raid on the railroad was attempted in the neighborhood of the Spotswood River, on the 28th of June, by Wilson's and Kautz's divisions of cavalry. Here they encountered the Confederate cavalry under Hampton, and the infantry brigades of Mahone and Finnegan, and the results of the engagements were in loss to the enemy of one thousand prisoners, thirteen pieces of artillery, thirty wagons and ambulances, and many small arms.

With this may be said to have ended this long-protracted

and remarkable campaign. It had been distinguished, from the beginning, by a series of disasters, and would have effectually discouraged one less intrepid and persevering than General Grant. From all indications it appeared to us evident that the North was beginning to stagger under the accumulation of disaster. Gold had already touched nearly three hundred. There were ominous whispers in Washington of the necessity for another draft, and the discontent at the North was growing strong. The disposition at the South to continue the war at all hazards, had been combated by the Confederate Congress in a published deprecatory address. One account says: "These declarations were eagerly seized upon by Northern journals, who insisted that no time should be lost in determining whether they might not possibly signify a willingness on the part of the South to make peace on the basis of new constitutional guaranties." The financial condition of the Federal Treasury was growing desperate. Mr. Chase, the Secretary of the Treasury, had peremptorily resigned, and had declared that nothing could prevent the financial ruin of the country but a series of the most unqualified successes.

In the temper of the masses at the South there was still no perceptible change. They seemed more than ever before determined on the prosecution of the war, and desired peace only upon the recognition of their independence. It is true in the last elections to the Confederate Congress there were several members elect known as "Union Men," but they only held those principles under certain guaranties to the South, and these men represented a very small portion of one of the States of the Confederacy, and their influence was almost unappreciable in that body.

CHAPTER LIX.

STARVATION IN RICHMOND.

IN Richmond we had never known such a scarcity of food —such absolute want of the necessaries of life. The constant interruption to our means of transportation prevented the importation of the usual supplies, and the hucksters from the adjoining counties dared not attempt to bring in their products to Richmond, for fear of capture or other misfortune. Our markets presented a most impoverished aspect. A few stalls at which was sold poor beef, and some at which a few potatoes and other vegetables were placed for sale, were about all that were opened in the Richmond markets. Our usual supplies of fish were cut off by the lines occupied by the enemy, and as a general rule a Richmond dinner at this time consisted of dried Indian peas, rice and salt bacon, and corn bread. A servant sent to market would be likely to return with an empty basket, or something of so miserable an appearance that the stomach revolted, probably, at the sight, and we very gratefully partook of our salt meat and dried peas, varied sometimes with a dessert of sorghum sirup. Yet the spirits of the people were unconquered. Despondency was unknown. A cheerful submission to these increased inconveniences was everywhere visible, and a more certain hope of prosperity in the Confederate cause indicated by all. The want of necessary food, the inflated prices of provisions, the constant depreciation of the Confederate money, were all reconciliable in the cheerful confidence of final success. The safety of Richmond we began to regard as incontestable. We had witnessed too many attempts and too many failures in the attempts at its capture to believe it would ever be abandoned to our enemies. We had begun to regard it as invulnerable.

In illustration of this belief a lady says : "I was one afternoon, accompanied by a young officer of the Confederate army, returning from a visit to a wounded friend, then at Howard's Grove Hospital, a mile and a half from Richmond. On passing the Capitol Square we were attracted by the music of a brass band. We turned into the grounds, and there we witnessed the review of the Corps of Cadets from the Virginia Military Institute, by Governor Smith. It was an interesting affair. These young soldiers had acquired an honorable prestige in the war, and were addressed with very happy effect by the Governor, who complimented them as they so well deserved on their services in the cause of the Confederacy. His speech over, there were loud calls for an address from a prominent officer then present, who was distinguished for his eloquence as well as his patriotism. His remarks were beautiful and encouraging. This corps carried a banner, on one side of which was the coat of arms and motto of Virginia, and on the other was the portrait of Washington. In one corner of the banner was a miniature representation of the "old flag"—the Stars and Stripes. It was an old banner and had been borne by these youthful soldiers on many a hotly contested field. The orator alluded, in beautiful and glowing language, to the gallant action of this youthful band of soldiers, and pointing to their banner, happily alluded to the fact that, though riddled all around by the balls of the enemy, the portrait of Washington still remained untouched. There on the canvas it remained intact, while the miniature flag in the corner was riddled with bullets. He alluded to the protracted and bloody campaign through which we had passed, and to the many futile attempts to capture our capital—and then pointing to the equestrian statue of Washington, he declared that until we gained our independence, 'On that statue no Yankee shall ever look, unless he comes as a captive.'

"Standing on the outskirts of the crowd, I was led by these remarks to approach near enough to examine the ensign borne by the cadets. Sure enough, the image, like the living body of the immortal Father of his Country, seemed not made to be pierced by a ball; and, strange to say, the miniature Stars and Stripes was very nearly cut out, and I laid this by in my heart as an omen of good for our cause."

Alas for the wisdom of human calculations, for the prescience which is uttered with all the assurance of prophecy! Twelve months had not passed and the beautiful month of May had not returned to chronicle the records of another bloody campaign, ere, underneath the shadow of that same equestrian statue, on which our distinguished orator had told his youthful fellow soldiers "no Yankee shall ever look, unless he comes as a captive," there were seen thousands, not as captives, but as the conquering hosts, to whom our devoted city was at last compelled to surrender. When they once more planted the "Stars and Stripes" over the building where once sat in council our National Legislators, —our prophetic orator was a fugitive; and the cause that gave inspiration to his eloquence was ruined!

CHAPTER LX.

DESTRUCTION OF THE ALABAMA—SHERMAN'S MARCH.

CLOUDS and sunshine, light and darkness, alternately shed their brightness or their gloom upon the firmament of the Confederate capital, as day by day we heard tidings of success or failure in our cause. While our hearts were filled with congratulation at the success of the campaign in Virginia for the Confederates, from the high seas was borne to us the intelligence of the loss of our most efficient privateer, the "Alabama." Having so little of a navy with which to compete with the powerful and well-appointed fleets of the enemy, and fully appreciating the value of the "Alabama," her loss to us was a severe infliction, a heavy blow to the privateering interests of the South.

When we compare the glory which might have attached to Confederate arms in the event of his success, with the more powerful interests imperilled by defeat, we cannot forbear to censure Captain Semmes for the risk he ran in the naval engagement which, although it might have been victorious, could but very little have damaged the cause of the enemy, while his own defeat and the loss of the "Alabama" threw a heavy shadow over the fortunes of the Confederacy. This engagement occurred near the French port of Cherbourg. Whether through the persuasion of others, or because Captain Semmes felt persuaded that victory would settle on the Confederate flag in this naval duel, it seems he had not the moral courage to resist the temptation when placed in his way in a form so alluring. An hour's fight decided the fate of the "Alabama." So seriously had she suffered that she was found to be sinking, and when the "Kearsarge" was within four hundred yards of him, Captain Semmes hauled down his colors; yet was the "Alabama" fired upon five times after her colors were struck. Captain Semmes said : "It is charitable to suppose that a ship of war of a Christian nation could not have done this intentionally."

We find that : "As the Alabama was on the point of settling, every man, in obedience to a previous order which had been given to the crew, jumped overboard and endeavored to save himself. There was no appearance of any boat coming from the enemy after the Alabama went down. Fortunately, however, the steam yacht "Deerhound," owned by a gentleman of Lancashire, England—Mr. John Lancaster—who was himself on board, steamed up in the midst of the drowning men, and rescued a number of both officers and men from the water, among them Semmes himself.

The loss of the Alabama, in killed and wounded, was thirty. There was no life lost on the Kearsarge, and but little damage done to the vessel. In his official report of the fight, Captain Semmes said, "At the end of the engagement it was discovered by those of our officers who went alongside the enemy's ship with the wounded, that her midship section on both sides was thoroughly iron-coated, this having been done with chain constructed for the purpose, placed perpendicularly from the rail to the water's edge, the whole covered with a thin outer planking, which gave no indication of the armor beneath. The planking had been ripped off in every direction by our shot and shell, the chain broken and indented in many places, and forced partly into the ship's side. She was most effectually guarded, however, in this section, from penetration."

Such had been the terror inspired by the Confederate privateers, (of which the Alabama was the most formidable,) so great the damage done to American shipping, that it was officially reported in Washington that 478,665 tons of American shipping were flying other flags. That service had caused nearly a thousand Yankee vessels to be sold to foreign shipping merchants. The Alabama alone had accomplished a work of destruction estimated at from eight to ten millions of dollars. It is not, therefore, to be wondered at that the news of her loss was received with the most intense delight on the Exchanges of New York and Boston—in the language of another, "with a joy far livelier than would have been conceived by these commercial patriots if they had heard of a great victory over Lee's army in Virginia."

Simultaneously with Grant's movement against Richmond was the parallel movement of General Sherman against Atlanta. It appears from the official report of General Sherman's operations that he estimated the force required to reach Atlanta at one hundred thousand men and two hundred and fifty pieces of artillery. He started with ninety-eight thousand seven hundred and ninety-seven men and two hundred and fifty-four guns. He was opposed by the Confederates under General Joseph E. Johnston, who, with his force all told, of infantry, cavalry, and artillery, had not more than forty-five thousand men. Seeing himself confronted by more than twice his number, General Johnston had no other prospect of success than in the exercise of superior skill and strategy. 'From the very superior numerical strength of the enemy, it became evident to General Johnston that it would be expedient in him to risk the chances of battle only when some unfortunate blunder of the enemy might place him in such a position as to give him counterbalancing advantages. He therefore fell slowly back, but kept sufficiently near the Yankee army to prevent its sending reinforcements to General Grant, hoping by successfully manœuvering, and by taking advantage of positions as they opportunely appeared, to weaken the force of the enemy, and reduce the enormous odds against which he was contending.

He also expected Sherman's force to be materially reduced before the end of June by the expiration of the terms of service of many of the regiments which had not re-enlisted. He therefore fell back to Cassville in two marches. Here, expecting to be attacked, he made a stand. He had secured a position which he considered highly advantageous to him, but deferring to the opinion of Lieutenant-General Hardee, he decided to abandon this position and fall back across the Etowah. In his official report of this movement he says of this dilemma : " The other two officers, however, were so earnest and unwilling to depend on the ability of their corps to defend the ground, that I yielded, and the army crossed the Etowah on the 20th of May, a step which I have regretted ever since."

From the 25th to the 27th of May occurred the engagements at the New Hope Church, which resulted favorably for the Confederates. Thus far the retrograde movement of General Johnston was regarded as successful, and the victories achieved at Resaca and New Hope, very considerable.

A writer says of the strategy of General Johnston: " It had been executed deliberately, being scarcely ever under the immediate presence of the enemy's advance, and it had now nearly approached the decisive line of the Chattahoochee, or whatever other line he who was supposed to be greatest strategist of the Confederacy should select for the cover of Atlanta." On the 1st of June he telegraphed to Richmond with his usual modesty, "In the partial engagements," (referring to his army,) "it has had great advantages, and the sum of all the combats amounts to a battle." The two armies continued to manœuvre for position. From the 4th of June, from point to point, the skirmishing continued at intervals until the 27th of June. General Johnston was attacked by Sherman on his position on the Kenesaw Mountain, which, by Sherman's frank admission, was to him a failure. He again resorted to manœuvering, until finally General Johnston fell back upon Atlanta, and there commenced intrenching himself. This retreat of Johnston was variously received the Confederate public. To many it was a sore disappointment. It had abandoned to the enemy more than half of Georgia, one of the finest wheat districts of the Confederacy, then ripe for the harvest, and at Rome and on the Etowah River had surrendered to the enemy iron rolling-mills and government works of immense value. In other respects it was considered a masterpiece of strategy, and a solid as well as a splendid success. General Johnston possessed in an eminent degree the confidence of his army, and the people of the Confederacy, and although there was evinced sincere disappointment in the conduct of the campaign, yet so well satisfied were the public generally of the superior military wisdom and tact of General Johnston that few were really disposed to complain of a strategy, which was not altogether at that time understood.

The advantages secured by him were indisputable. In explanation, Johnston writes: " At Dalton the great numerical superiority of the enemy made the chances of battle much against us; and, even if beaten, they had a safe refuge behind the fortified pass of Ringgold and in the fortress of Chattanooga. Our refuge in case of defeat was in Atlanta, one hundred miles off, with three rivers intervening. Therefore victory for us could not have been decisive, while defeat would have been utterly disastrous. Between Dalton and the Chattahoochee we could have given battle only by attacking the enemy intrenched, or so near intrenchments, that the only result of success to us would have been his falling back into them, while defeat would have been our ruin.

"In the course pursued our troops, always fighting under cover, had very trifling losses compared with those they inflicted, so that the enemy's numerical superiority was reduced daily and rapidly, and we could reasonably have expected to cope with the Federal army on equal ground by the time the Chattahoochee was passed. Defeat on this side of the river would have been its destruction. We, if beaten, had a refuge in Atlanta, too strong to be assaulted, and too extensive to be invested.

When midsummer came on, it was obvious that an unmistakable check had been given to the concurrent operations intended for the destruction of the Southern Confederacy. General Grant had been brought to a "stand still" before Petersburg, and General Sherman before Atlanta, and the rebellion, which in its inception its enemies vainly thought to crush in the space of three months, was then, in the fourth year of its existence, even more formidable than before and awakened in the mind of the North more serious doubt of its power to destroy it than when it first reared its head in support of rights claimed by the South.

It was a curious question then to contemplate, and now a curious one upon which to reflect. And if in the cause that animated the South, that prompted devotion and self-sacrifice unparalleled in history, there were no elements of right, it was most unmercifully given over to a delusion to work its ruin. Can a believer in a God of justice accredit this?

We hardly dare to refer to the sufferings endured by the people of that section of the South over which General Sherman drew the trail of war. Enough to say that desolation was written on almost every foot of ground, misery on almost every human heart. Let a pen more eloquent describe all except the fierce spirit of revenge that reared its hydra head in every bosom, and quenched effectually the latent fires of love that once glowed in devotion to the Union. The heart of woman is rarely broken by oppression, but it is sometimes turned to stone!

At the same time the vandalism of Hunter in Virginia awoke a similar spirit, and even drew upon him the censure, in no measured terms, of certain journals of the North. After his defeat at Lynchburg by General Early, on the 18th of June, he found no way of escape but through the Blue Ridge to the Gauley River. His footprints were marked by desolation, devastation, misery. He was distinguished in Virginia for the lawless execution of Dr. Creigh, of Greenbrier County, the burning of the Virginia Military Institute and the house of Ex-Governor Letcher, whose family were allowed only ten minutes to secure a few articles of clothing. These are prominent acts. On the fair face of the country over which he travelled, unmistakable marks of ruin spell the name of "Hunter!"

Yet no craven spirit of fear, no miserable spirit of submission took possession of the souls of the people, but a more defiant resistance, a more stubborn resolution to oppose to the bitter end the lawless mob who came armed to commit outrages under the plea of "military necessity." It is deeply painful to refer to phases of the late war that reveal only the dark shades of demoralization and brutality. We generally prefer to contemplate beautiful instances of humanity with which our recollection is furnished; but truths are stubborn — they are irresistible; and in defence of the women of the South we may say, the wonder is not that in many instances they are fierce, revengeful and vindictive, but that in them there is left any of the woman's heart — any quality to redeem them from the character of fiends incarnate. Alas! too many of them have stories to tell — not mere figments, painted in the glowing imagination of the sensitive, excited brain, but truth, "stranger than fiction"—substantiated by the bare chimneys, the charred and blackened walls, the ruin and desolation of homes that were domestic Edens until the fierce blast of cruel war awoke them from their dream of happiness. And more. Their tales of sorrow are verified in the green hillocks that cover the remains of their hearts' treasures—the dear ones, not sent thither by powder and ball, but who found in the friendly bosom of "mother earth" the only refuge from the dire miseries entailed upon them by the invader. Over these things we would fain throw the mantle of oblivion; but the wounds are too deep for the friendly covering to hide from view the ugly scars left by them.

CHAPTER LXI.

EARLY'S CAMPAIGN—WASHINGTON THREATENED.

TO further their summer campaign, the Confederates planned a series of offensive operations, the object of which was to frustrate the main campaigns of the enemy in the East and West. They were, however, on a small scale, comprehending the invasion of Maryland and Pennsylvania by General Early, the invasion of Kentucky by General Morgan, and the invasion of Missouri by General Price. Their results were in the main small, weak and unimportant, and productive of but little sensible good to the Confederacy.

General Early penetrated as far as Hagerstown and Greencastle, dislodging the enemy on the route, and capturing valuable stores. On the 9th of July he disappeared from the vicinity of Hagerstown, Greencastle and other points threatened, for the purpose of concentrating his forces. In the meanwhile the Yankee forces, who had held Frederick City, fell back four miles, to Monocacy bridge. At this point they were engaged by the Confederates, which resulted in their dislodgment, and with considerable loss they fled in the direction of Gettysburg. In this action, which lasted only about two hours, General Early lost, in killed and wounded, between five and six hundred men and some valuable officers. He did not pursue the flying enemy, but pressed on directly towards Washington and Baltimore, making rapid marches, but valuable collections of cattle and horses all along the route.

Washington was in imminent peril. The Confederate army was within sight of the city. Whispers of alarm ran through the North. The garrison defending the city was comparatively weak, and there are reasons to believe the Federal capital might have been taken by assault. But the opportunity was lost. General Early reconnoitred the defences, scattered his forces into expeditions to intercept trains and destroy telegraphs, but could not decide to attack the capital of the enemy

The hopes and expectations of the South, which had been elevated to fever height, were doomed again to disappointment. We were mortified to contemplate another half-finished victory, and public censure bore heavily upon General Early. But for his indecision, it was said, he might have achieved for the Confederacy the most brilliant success that ever adorned her arms.

But this expedition of Early was not barren of practical results. About the middle of July he recrossed the Potomac, laden with the rich spoils of the enemy. It was reported that he brought with him five thousand horses and twenty-five hundred beef cattle. He also created a useful diversion, and compelled General Grant to weaken his army materially before Petersburg. Though he accomplished all this, he was not forgiven at the South for the opportunity lost for an assault upon Washington.

After crossing the Potomac he gave the enemy another severe lesson. He was pursued by the Federal General Crook, with about fifteen thousand infantry and cavalry. At a short distance from Winchester Early turned upon him, drove him twelve miles beyond Winchester, and thoroughly routed him. His entire loss was sixty men.

Crook confessed to a loss of one thousand killed and wounded.

After this there ensued a pause of some weeks in the valley campaign, broken only by a raid of Confederate cavalry to Chambersburg, Pennsylvania, in which, for a refusal of supplies to the invader, McCausland's brigade burned a considerable portion of the town. Although retaliation is understood as an equivalent in warfare, this act, though considered justifiable, gave little pleasure to the Southern people. By it the North was horrified, and loud and revengeful were the cries. "Tit for tat" is not always regarded as a good rule.

CHAPTER LXII.

LIFE IN RICHMOND IN 1864.

BOSTON has been facetiously termed the "Hub of the Universe." Richmond, without undue assumption, could style itself the "Hub of the Confederacy." Never was her spirit more buoyant than over the results of the various campaigns of the summer of 1864. Peace and independence seemed dependent only on the endurance of the Southern people. Of that they had already given the most indubitable evidence.

So long had the camp-fires glowed around Richmond—so long had we breathed the sulphurous vapors of battle—so accustomed had our ears become to the dread music of artillery—so signal had been our deliverance from the most elaborate combinations for the capture of our city, that more surely than ever before we felt at this time that our Confederate house was built "upon a rock."

We were practically solving a curious question, and one which most nearly involved the vital interests of the population of the city of Richmond. So enormous had become the expenses of living that the question had grown to be one of moment: "On what can we subsist that will furnish the greatest amount of nutriment for the least amount of money?" In our social gatherings the war topic was most frequently varied in the discussion of rich dishes, and the luxurious tables of days of yore. Sometimes would arise the question: "I wonder if we shall ever see the like again?" Often were we forcibly reminded of our former discontent and dissatisfaction with the luxuries under which our tables then groaned, when we contrasted them with the severe and simple style to which we were now compelled to submit. Yet we sipped our Confederate tea, swallowed quickly our confederate coffee, (frequently without sugar,) dined on fat bacon and Indian peas, and took our dessert of sorghum-syrup and corn bread, with as much cheerfulness and apparent relish as we formerly discussed the rich viands on the well-filled boards of the old Virginia housewives.

Richmond was growing rusty, dilapidated, and began to assume a war-worn appearance. Very few of the buildings had been brightened by a fresh application of paint since the commencement of hostilities, and where a plank fell off or a screw got loose, or a gate fell from its hinges, or a bolt gave way, or a lock was broken, it was most likely to remain for a time unrepaired; for the majority of our mechanics were in the field, and those left in the city were generally in the employment of the government, and we were forced to wait for a needful job, until patience would become almost exhausted.

The fashion for dress would have seemed absurdly simple to the fashionable belle of New York, yet despite the rigor of the blockade, the latest mode would now and then struggle through in *Godey's Lady's Book*, or *Frank Leslie's Magazine*, or *Le Bon Ton*, and when Richmond was disclosed to the gaze of the outer world it was found that even the "waterfall" had worked its way through the "lines" to the heads of the fair ladies of the rebel capital. We were not so much behind the times as might have been supposed from the sympathetic article that appeared in one of the journals of our Northern friends, which stated that the women of Richmond flaunted in the rich but well-worn silks in use before the war, but that they were minus shoes and hose, and perambulated the streets with their feet "wrapped in rags!" We were never barefooted, although at this time a pair of ladies' boots could not be purchased for less than one hundred and twenty-five dollars, and this price at a later period was thought to be very moderate. When we consider the times, we may say our stores were pretty well stocked with goods, such as they were, but at prices marvellous to contemplate, even in Confederate money.

The summer's work at the hospitals in the year 1864 commenced in all its fullness early in May, after the battles of the Wilderness. It was attended with multiplied disadvantages, owing to the increased scarcity of provisions. The sick, mutilated and miserable, as ever before, uttered warm expressions of gratitude. This last remark is hazarded, though a matron in a Confederate hospital has written as follows: "There is little gratitude felt in a hospital, and none expressed. The mass of patients are uneducated men who have lived by the sweat of their brow, and gratitude is an exotic planted in a refined atmosphere, kept free from coarse contact, and nourished by unselfishness. Common natures look only with astonishment at great sacrifices, and cunningly avail themselves of them, and give nothing in return, not even the satisfaction of allowing one to suppose that the care exerted has been beneficial;—*that* would entail compensation of some kind, and in their ignorance they fear the nature of the equivalent which might be demanded."

Without desiring to create an issue with the excellent and accomplished matron, pardon may be craved for venturing a most unqualified dissent from her views. Gratitude cannot truly be said to be an exotic, needing the nourishment of refinement and cultivation. It is indigenous, rooted in all the nobler instincts of humanity, a growth directly emanating from the goodness and purity of God, illustrating and embellishing the heart, despite adventurous or fortuitous circumstances. Moreover there is understood in the remark a direct reflection upon the rank and file of our army—the usual class of patients in Confederate hospitals. This every woman of the South should feel prepared to resent, when it is remembered that these helpless unfortunates were her defenders, her protectors, the slender thread upon which her hopes were hanging, and that the few attentions bestowed on them in hospitals were a very meagre and dissatisfying equivalent for the sacrifices, the miseries, the wretchedness endured by them.

Oh, no! we cannot forget the rough grasp of the horny hand, the eye brightened by the glistening tear, the manly lip quivering with emotions which surcharged the noble soul, or the feeble voice whispering "God bless you!" for simple acts of attention that duty dignified into pleasure, and that pleasure exalted into duty. If ingratitude was ever evinced, let sensitive and exacting natures admit the instances were not general, but exceptional and individual.

Early in June, the officers' hospital in the Baptist Female College buildings was infected with pyæmia—the most malignant disease which can attack the wounded—a malady for which no specific has ever yet been found, and from which many more died than from the wound itself. In this disease the virus that should be discharged by suppuration is disseminated through the circulatory system, causing chills, and soon death supervenes. For awhile this hospital was a charnel house, and it was found necessary to remove the patients to the city alms-house, after which the disease disappeared, and our hearts were more rarely sickened by the sight of military funerals through our streets. Still death did not cease its revels in our hospitals. This was evidenced by the continually enlarging dimensions of our cemeteries, and the multiplication of mounds that marked the soldiers' graves.

It is generally conceded that the medical interests of the Confederacy were judiciously managed. Our Surgeon-General, Dr. Moore, as heretofore remarked, was an exacting and conscientious officer, and few men who passed the Confederate ordeal came out so nearly blameless. In the examining Board of Surgeons he was assisted by the most eminent and accomplished medical men of the South, and no applicant for commission as surgeon was permitted to receive it until after passing a thorough examination, and had thus proven to the Board his qualification for office.

Prominent, we may say at the head of this Board, was the lamented Dr. Charles Bell Gibson, whose skill in his profession was rarely equalled in this country, and whose broad benevolence and thorough penetration admirably fitted him for his position. We may also notice as belonging to the Examining Board, Dr. Peticolas, of the Richmond Medical College, acknowledged to be of superior skill and talent in his profession; while all attached to this responsible body were men of undoubted integrity, and pre-eminent medical information.

The most efficient coadjutors of the surgeons, and those to whom next the gratitude of the soldiers was justly due, were the noble matrons and nurses of the Richmond hospitals. Yet, strange to say, some of the surgeons seemed envious of, or impatient towards them. However, from the testimony of the poor sufferers themselves, we may with propriety assert where one owes his life to a skillful surgical operation, or judicious medical treatment, a dozen owe their lives to the patient and careful nursing of woman.*

Nor in this connection must we omit to notice the noble body of chaplains who followed the army on its marches and countermarches, and ministered to the spiritual wants of the soldiers. The camp and the hospital were frequently the scenes of sublimely touching religious exercises. Doffing the clerical vestments, many of the chaplains donned the uniform of the soldier, and were distinguished only by the

---

* We have before noticed the names of some women illustrious for their deeds of charity, and to this list we will respectfully add that of the accomplished and gifted Mrs. Pember, who long presided as chief-matron at Chimborazo Hospital.

LIFE IN RICHMOND IN 1864. 319

simple cross of "gold lace" on the sleeve of the coat or jacket. Conspicuous among them, though not strictly occupying the position of a chaplain, was the Reverend General Pendleton, who at the commencement of the war was rector of a parish in Lexington, Virginia. In Richmond, prominent in their efforts for the spiritual good of the soldier, we may name the Reverend Doctor M. D. Hoge, Reverend Mr. Peterson, and Reverend Mr. Duncan, Christian ministers.

The inhabitants of Richmond were very closely confined to the city, not only by the active duties of benevolence, which absorbed so much of their time, means, and talents, but frequently by the actual impossibility of travel. When we summoned the courage to run the risks that a passage upon our insecure railroads involved, the trip was usually accomplished between the raids in which tracks were torn up, bridges burned, and other damage done as a means of capturing the city.

Our delightful watering-places, which had formerly been favorite resorts of the Southern people, for health or pleasure, were most of them closed up, or occupied as hospitals, or otherwise, for war purposes. However much the system, relaxed or depressed by long confinement to the hot impure atmosphere of the city, needed the bracing and healthy influence of the mountain air, and the healing waters, our situation was such that if we dared to travel fifty or a hundred miles, we might be cut off, and subjected to nameless inconveniences and troubles in getting back to our homes. While the war lasted, the most of us were fixtures in Richmond. We ventured outside the city limits only when the skillful manœuvring of our army made it possible to go with a certainty of being able to return when we desired. The fresh fruits and vegetables, pure milk and butter, and the various other luxuries and comforts to be found in the country served to tempt us, who subsisted on the meagre supplies of our markets; and when an opportunity offered, we gladly availed ourselves of the chance for rusticating in the quiet, delightful country.

The tide of exiles and refugees which set toward Richmond from the commencement of the war, continued until its close. Notwithstanding the repeated attempts to capture it, those driven from their homes crowded into the capital. Their stories of terror and distress were generally concluded with the exclamation, "Oh, we are too happy in getting to Richmond! It is after all the safest place in the Confederacy!"

Where to quarter the refugees, had long been a question of serious importance. From the second year of the war, the floating population quite equalled, if it did not exceed in numbers the resident inhabitants. Every influx of these unhappy wanderers occasioned grave consideration as to where they might find resting places, and the means of livelihood. There were few hotels, and boarding-houses might then have been counted on the fingers. The Spotswood Hotel, the American and the Powhatan, were all of the larger hotels then open for public accommodation; and so enormous were expenses at those places, that very few of the miserable refugees, who had been compelled to fly from their homes of ease and comfort, could afford the luxury of living in them. Lodgings were hired which seemed of india-rubber capacity, from the numbers frequently packed in them, and to tell of the contingent expenses of housekeeping at this time would sound like stories of wildest fable.

We were frequently awakened from a temporary dream of quiet and security, by the sudden ringing of alarm bells, occasioned often by only a reconnoissance of the enemy, but of a character sufficiently threatening to call out our forces for local defence, which consisted mainly of the battalion of government clerks under Major Henly, and the battalion of armorers and artisans from the government work-shops. After several days of absence, they would be ordered to return to the city, generally without having participated in any engagement.

After the explosion of the mine at Petersburg, there was

quiet on the Richmond lines during the remainder of the summer, broken only by a demonstration at Bottom's Bridge, in August, which, in practical results, was scarcely of sufficient importance at that period of the war to deserve notice. But our trials were becoming daily more and more severe, and we looked forward with shuddering apprehensions to the aproaching winter.

CHAPTER LXIII.

BOTH SECTIONS TIRED OF WAR—THE NEGOTIATION AT NIAGARA FALLS—VISIT OF COLONEL JACQUES TO RICHMOND—THE CHICAGO CONVENTION.

THE failure of General Grant's campaign in Virginia, and the stand-still of General Sherman had awakened in the North the most clamorous demands for peace. These desires, cherished in the public heart, found expression through the press. Peace was the ultimatum of the wishes of the South. The last Confederate Congress had published a manifesto that asked only immunity from interference. "Let them forbear aggressions upon us and the war is at an end. If there be questions which require adjustment by negotiation, we have ever been willing, and are still willing to enter into communication with our adversaries in a spirit of peace, of equity and manly frankness."

In the month of July some attempts at negotiation were undertaken by Messrs. C. C. Clay and Jacob Thompson, who, associating with them Mr. George Sanders, suddenly appeared as Southern commissioners at Niagara Falls. There they obtained the intermediate assistance of Mr. Horace Greeley, to negotiate for an interview with Mr. Lincoln in order to ascertain on what common ground they could possibly treat for the much desired end. It ended futilely, like all similar attempts. Mr. Lincoln did not appear; but dispatched a reply addressed "To whom it may concern," and signified unequivocally, that the Union with the positive and unconditional abandonment of slavery were indispensable conditions of peace.

In striking contrast was the notice bestowed on the envoys dispatched by General Grant, with permission of the Confederate authorities, to meet Colonel Ould, the Confederate Commissioner of Exchange. These two, Colonel Jacques, of the 73d Illinois Infantry, and J. R. Gillmore, were brought, by Colonel Ould, into the presence of Mr. Davis. They were treated by him with marked courtesy and respect, and he discussed with them frankly and politely, the leading questions of political dissension. It is said Colonel Jacques arrived in Richmond attired in a large linen duster, but he had no sooner confronted the President of the Confederacy, than he threw off the garment and disclosed his rank, and insignia in the Federal army.

It seemed that these persons had not a single proposition to offer, but they succeeded in adroitly and insidiously obtaining from Mr. Davis a thorough exposition of his views and designs, of which, says an account, "They carried back a long story to the Yankee newspapers, and made no little capital out of their visit to Richmond by sensations in the Northern periodicals, and itinerant lectures at twenty-five cents a head."

It was mortifying to the Southern people to contrast the difference between the unmerciful snubbing received by their commissioners from President Lincoln with the courtesy and distinction with which Mr. Davis received the envoys extraordinary of General Grant. Its influence on the public mind, the compromise of dignity which it comprehended, can well be understood in the language of another, who thus notices it: "The more intelligent and worthy portion of the Confederate public, were greatly wounded in their pride by the behavior of their authorities on the peace question. Many of these persons had, since the very commencement of the war, insisted on the futility and impropriety of essaying to open any special negotiations with the enemy on peace. There were the many distinct avowals of the purpose of the war on our side, in the declarations and acts of the government, invariably protesting our simple desire to be let alone, which were already a clear and standing tender of peace. The issues could not be made more distinct or more urgent than in the official record. Why, they argued, should we go beyond it, by attempts at kitchen conferences, which might not only be insolently rebuffed by the enemy, to the damage of our self-respect, but which, as experience had so far shown, were invariably misinterpreted, and not without plausibility, as signs of decadence and weakness in our military affairs. True, proud and intelligent persons in the Confederacy were as anxious for peace as those who were constantly professing their devotion to this end. But they considered that the honor and self-respect of their countrymen, had been lowered by devious and unworthy attempts at negotiation. Having once announced the terms of peace sufficiently, they judged they would do right, while awaiting the overtures of the enemy, not to betray their anxiety, or open any unnecessary discussions on the subject. And there could be no doubt of the sufficiency of those announcements."

While the North cried "peace!" peace was echoed at the South, but when the North proclaimed "Union," the heart of the South replied·" Independence!"

In reply to a letter from Goverrner Vance of North Carolina, alluding to the political discontent in that state, and suggesting an effort at negotiation with the enemy, which might appease the malcontents, and if unsuccessful intensify the war feeling—as early as January, 1864, Mr. Davis wrote:

"We have made three distinct efforts to communicate with the authorities at Washington, and have been invariably unsuccessful. Commissioners were sent before hostilities were begun, and the Washington government refused to receive them or hear what they had to say. A second time I sent a military officer with a communication addressed by myself to President Lincoln. The letter was received by General Scott, who did not permit the officer to see Mr. Lincoln, but promised that an answer would be sent. No answer has ever been received. The third time, a few months ago, a gentleman was sent, whose position, character, and reputation were such as to insure his reception, if the enemy were not determined to receive no proposals whatever from the government. Vice President Stephens made a patriotic tender of his services, in the hope of being able to promote the cause of humanity; and although little hope was entertained of his success, I cheerfully yielded to his suggestion that the experiment should be tried. The enemy refused to to let him pass through their lines or to hold any conference with them. He was stopped before he reached Fortress Monroe, on his way to Washington. To attempt again (in the face of these repeated rejections of all conferences with us) to send commissioners or agents to propose peace, is to invite insult and contumely, and to subject ourselves to indignity, without the slightest chance of being listened to.

"I cannot recall at this time one instance in which I have failed to announce that our only desire was peace, and the only terms which offered a *sine qua non*, were precisely those which you suggested, namely, 'A demand only to be let alone.' But suppose it were practicable to obtain a conference through commissioners with the Government of President Lincoln, is it at this moment that we are to consider it desirable, or even at all admissible. Have we not just been apprised, that we can only expect his gracious pardon by emancipating all our slaves, swearing allegiance and obedience to him and his proclamation, and becoming in point of fact, the slave of our own negroes."

The Niagara Falls negotiation, and the Jacques-Gillmore embassy served to sensibly weaken the confidence of the Southern people in the strength of their government. We were at this time, watching, with the most anxious solicitude, the movements of the Democratic party at the North, in reference to the peace question. They were expected to be developed in a more practical direction in view of the approaching Presidential election.

The Democratic National Convention met at Chicago, Illinois, on the 29th of August. In the platform there adopted, notwithstanding its protestations of attachment to the Union, the South understood an evident acknowledgment of the independence of the Confederate States. General George B. McClellan was the nominee for President, upon the Chicago platform. In an eminent degree, General McClellan commanded the confidence and respect of the

Southern people; and had men alone, and not measures, been involved in the election, there is not doubt the voice of the South would have been substantially in favor of his election to office, inasmuch as the party represented by him were the avowed friends of the South, in her most vital interests.

With the majority, the desire for McClellan's election was intense, although in comparing the two adverse wings of the Democratic party, known as the "War Democrats" and the "Peace Democrats," the Republicans were considered by many to be more certainly friends of the South, than the Democrats, who advocated the prosecution of the war.

In reference to the final acknowledgment of Confederate independence, as understood in the platform of the Chicago Convention, an intelligent and sagacious Southern author says: "It was proposed perhaps to get to this conclusion by distinct and successive steps, so as not to alarm too much the Union sentiment of the country. The first step was to be the proposition of the 'Union as it was' in a convention of the States; if that was voted down, then the proposition of a new principle of federation, limited to the foreign relations and to the revenue; if that was rejected, then the proposition of an inter-confederate Union to preserve as far as possible, by an extraordinary league, the American prestige; and, if all these propositions, intended as tests of the spirit of the South, were to fail, then, at least, the independence of the Confederate States, under the *sine qua non*, was to be conceded by the Democratic party of the North, as the last resort of pacification, and one of the two alternatives where their choice could no longer hesitate. In short it appeared to be the design of the Democratic party to get the North, on the naked issue of the war and separation. * * * Why the programme broke down is explained almost in a word. The military events which took place between the date of the Chicago Convention and election day, put upon the war a more encouraging aspect for the North, and with these changes the Democratic party abandoned ground which they took professedly on principle, but really on the mean considerations of expediency and time-serving. The fact was, that all party changes in the North since the war, might be said to be constantly accommodating themselves to the course of military events. After the Chicago Convention, the peace party moved inversely with the scale of military success, and as that mounted in Northern opinion, it fell, until, as we shall see months later, it almost approached zero."

But at this period we of the Confederacy dreamed not that we were on the very eve of disasters which would so effectually neutralize the successes of the summer campaigns as to work the change of sentiment understood in the remarks we have quoted. We little thought that the friendly intentions of the Democratic party of the North, which advocated the independence of the South, were on the point of being overthrown by the mismanagement or misfortune of the military operations of the Confederates. But it was even so.

CHAPTER LXIV.

THE CAPTURE OF MOBILE—THE FALL OF ATLANTA—THE FALL CAMPAIGN AROUND RICHMOND.

MOBILE was valuable to the Confederacy as one of the principal ports for the blockade-running business. It was also a nursery of the Confederate navy, where vessels were built for the purpose of raising the blockade. Hence it became an object of extreme desire on the part of our enemies to get possession of Mobile Bay. As soon as operations on the Mississippi permitted the detachment of a sufficient co-operating military force, an expedition for this purpose was fitted out, and on the 5th of August Admiral Farragut passed the forts and closed the harbor of Mobile.

But in the meantime we had experienced a reverse, beside

which the affair in Mobile Bay was almost forgotten or overlooked. The events of the Georgia campaign were indeed "to put a new aspect on the war; to annihilate the peace party in the North, to give a new hope and impetus to the enemy, and to date the serious and rapid decline of the fortunes of the Confederacy."

General Johnston's position at Atlanta was as secure as that of General Lee at Petersburg, and judging by the superior skill and energy he had displayed in the conduct of the forces under his command, from the beginning of the war, we were led to expect that he would at least effectually hold Sherman in check, as General Lee was holding Grant. He could easily have done that, and if he had succeeded in destroying Sherman's communications he might have compelled a disastrous retreat to Tennessee.

At midsummer we beheld both campaigns of the enemy essentially failures. Could the military situation which then existed have been preserved, the election of McClellan to the Presidency of the United States would have been secured, and a peace negotiation, that would have placed the South in a different *status*, might have been effected.

But these bright prospects were changed in a day. Whether from a desire to gratify popular clamor, or other causes at best imperfectly understood, General Johnston, who was then executing the masterpiece of strategy of the war, with a perfection of design and detail which delighted his own troops and challenged the admiration of his enemy —who had performed the prodigy of conducting an army in • retreat over three hundred miles of intricate country without loss in prisoners or material, was removed. It was a dark day for the Confederacy, and the public hardly regarded this act with leniency. But it is undeniable there were some insane enough to inveigh against the strategy of General Johnston, and to cry continually for a "fighting man"—one not given so entirely to "brilliant retreats." Well, indeed, might General Scott's remark have been heeded: "Beware of Lee's advances and Johnston's retreats!"

After General Hood was placed in command of the army, there were a number of engagements, from the 20th of July until the 1st of September. On that day the struggle for the "Gate City" came to an end. Atlanta fell into the hands of the enemy, and the Confederacy took the first signal step in its downward road to ruin.

Shortly after the fall of Atlanta it was declared that certain leading men of Georgia, among whom were included Governor Brown and Vice-President Stephens, were in favor of the withdrawal of the State from the Confederacy, and that negotiations to that effect had been opened with General Sherman. This report arose from the fact that a Mr. King had brought to Governor Brown a message to the effect that he would be pleased to confer with him and others upon the state of the country, with a view to the settlement of the difficulties, and would give him a pass through the Federal lines, going and returning, for that purpose. To this the Governor replied that he, as Governor of a State, and General Sherman, as commander of an army in the field, had no authority to enter upon negotiations for peace. Georgia might, perhaps, be overrun, but could not be subjugated, and would never treat with a conqueror upon her soil. That while Georgia possessed the sovereign power to act separately, her faith had been pledged by implication to her Southern sisters, and she would not exercise this power without their consent and co-operation. She had entered into the contest knowing all the responsibilities which it involved, and would never withdraw from it with dishonor. "She will never," he said, "make separate terms with the enemy which may free her territory from invasion and leave her confederates in the lurch. Whatever may be the opinion of the people as to the injustice done her by the Confederate administration, she will triumph with her Confederate sisters or she will sink with them in common ruin. The independent expression of condemnation is one thing, and disloyalty to our common cause is another and quite a different thing. If Mr. Lincoln would stop the war, let him recognize the sovereignty of the States, and leave each to determine for herself whether she will return to the old Union or remain in her present league."

Vice-President Stephens defined his position in an elaborate letter, in which he declared that the only solution for our present and future troubles was "the simple recognition of the fundamental principle and truth upon which all American constitutional liberty is founded, and upon the maintenance of which alone it can be preserved—that is, the sovereignty—the ultimate sovereignty—of the States." In conclusion he wrote : "All questions of boundaries, confederacies, and union or unions, would naturally and easily adjust themselves according to the interests of parties and the exigencies of the times. Herein lies the true law of the balance of power and the harmony of States."

The fall of Atlanta was a severe blow to the Confederacy, and was received in Richmond with unconcealed distress. Mr. Davis was sensibly affected by this misfortune. Toward the close of September he made a visit to Georgia, and delivered a remarkable speech at Macon. He told the people that it grieved him to meet them in adversity, but that he considered the cause not lost—that sooner or later Sherman must retreat, and then would he meet the fate that befell Napoleon in his retreat from Moscow.

The reinforcement of Hood's army was a question of the utmost importance ; but where the reinforcements were to be obtained was another question of equal significance. From the army of General Lee none could be sent, for in Virginia the disparity in numbers was as frightful as in Georgia. The army of Early, that guarded the Valley, was absolutely necessary to prevent the enemy from gaining possession of Lynchburg. After a consultation with General Lee on all these points, Mr. Davis's conclusion was : "If one half of the men now absent from the field would return to duty, we can defeat the enemy. With that hope I am now going to the front. I may not realize this hope, but I know that there are men who have looked death too often in the face to despond now."

The spirit and temper of Mr. Davis was encouraging, and served in a great measure to restore confidence. We looked forward with the greatest anxiety for the fruits of the coming campaign, which we were promised would repair our recent disasters. Even then, in Richmond there were those of superior prescience who openly predicted the end as it came. We would not listen to them; we flouted the idea of downfall; we called them "croakers." Our vain-glorious confidence had not yet received a check so signal as to destroy all hope.

The fall campaign of the enemy was unusually active. On the 28th of September a demonstration was made on the Richmond lines, against the works on Chaffin's farm, in sufficient force to awaken the deepest interest. On the 29th it was evident to us that a most terrific battle was raging. We had never heard peals of artillery in more rapid succession, or more continuously for hours. The flashes from the pieces were plainly distinguishable from exposed points in the city. The evening brought to us the intelligence of the capture of Fort Harrison, which commanded a position below Drewry's Bluff, and constituted the main defence at that point.

The enemy then attempted the capture of Fort Gilmer, but were fearfully repulsed. General Field, who arrived with his division just prior to the attack upon Fort Gilmer, favored an attempt to retake Fort Harrison that evening, before the enemy could have time to strengthen his position, but being overruled in his opinion, the attack was deferred until the succeeding day, the 30th, when the main attack failed, but the Confederates succeeded in retaking a redan in the left of the fort, which so protected their left flank as to neutralize the loss of the main defence.

On the 6th of October a desperate engagement occurred on the Charles City road. It resulted in the repulse of the enemy; but in it the Confederates lost the brave and chivalrous General Gregg, of Texas, who fell at the head of his troops, pierced through the neck by a Minnie ball.

Thus one by one our bravest and best were falling, like stars from the Confederate firmament. Whenever tidings came of the clash of arms in sanguinary conflict, we laid our hands upon our hearts until we could hear, "Who is dead?"

After an interval of a month from the time of the capture of Fort Harrison, another engagement occurred, on the 27th of October, on the Williamsburg and Boydton roads, which led into Richmond. The Federals were repulsed at all points, and it was the last demonstration made by them on the lines south of Richmond before the re-election of Mr. Lincoln, which it was doubtless designed to facilitate.

CHAPTER LXV.

SHERIDAN'S CAMPAIGN IN THE VALLEY—NAVAL LOSSES—RE-ELECTION OF MR. LINCOLN—ARMING OF SLAVES.

IN the meantime, success had crowned the Federal arms in a quarter heretofore unknown to us, and where it was least expected. In the Valley of Virginia, General Early was in command of the Confederate army. His first battle with General Sheridan occurred on the 18th of September, at Opequan Creek, of the result of which the latter telegraphed to Secretary Stanton as follows: "I have captured one entire regiment, officers included."

On the 19th, an engagement occurred near Winchester. It was a fiercely contested battle, and was lost to the Confederates by the unaccountable misbehavior of their cavalry when victory seemed ready to perch upon the Confederate banners.

In our losses was numbered the intrepid General Rhodes,

than whom no young officer in the Confederate army had won a more enviable reputation.

The disaster of this defeat, unexpected as it was, was sensibly felt and painfully acknowledged by the Conferate public. General Early fell back to Fisher's Hill, eighteen miles from Winchester and seventy-two from Staunton. This position is considered by military men the strongest in the Valley of Virginia. On the 22d of September, Sheridan brought up his entire force to assault him in his position at Fisher's Hill. An account of this battle says: "The works were too formidable to be carried by an attack on the front alone, and therefore while keeping up a feint of a front attack, the Eighth Corps was sent far to the right, and sweeping about Early's left, flanked him and attacked him in the rear, driving him out of his intrenchments, while the Sixth Corps attacked him at the same time in the centre front, and the Nineteenth Corps on the left. Confused and disorganized by attacks at so many different points, the Confederates broke at the centre and fled in disorganization towards Woodstock. Artillery, horses, wagons, rifles, knapsacks, and canteens were abandoned and strewn along the road. Several hundred prisoners and twelve pieces of artillery were captured. The pursuit was continued until the 25th, and did not conclude until Early had been driven below Port Republic."

This second reverse, the news of which was entirely unexpected and surprising, caused increased despondency in Richmond. Though not so serious nor so extensive as accounts from the enemy indicated, it was quite sufficient to awaken alarm and misgiving. The harvests of the Shenandoah Valley had been lost, and the most productive districts of Virginia opened to the waste and desolation of the enemy.

It is said that General Sheridan was either ordered or avowed his intention to so devastate this section of Virginia that, "The crows in flying over should be compelled to carry their own rations." How nearly this was fulfilled is shown by the charred ruins visible at every step over this beautiful region.

This success at Fisher's Hill involved the capture of Staunton, with the loss of all the storehouses, workshops, and other buildings there connected with the Confederate government.

After devastating the Valley, General Sheridan retired northward to Woodstock, where he made his headquarters. On the 9th of October he had an affair with Rosser's cavalry, which had hung on his rear. In this engagement Sheridan claimed to have taken eleven pieces of artillery and over three hundred prisoners. His dispatch to the War Department in Washington was that he had "finished the savior of the Valley, and had pursued the worsted Confederates on the jump for twenty-six miles."*

Still another disaster was to be the crowning misfortune of this ill-starred campaign. General Early again advanced to Fisher's Hill. On the 18th of October he came out of his intrenchments and attacked the enemy at Cedar Creek. So completely were they taken unawares, that at ten o'clock on the morning of the 19th two-thirds of Sheridan's army were routed, and nothing was left them but to cover their disorderly retreat. But, as a published account says, "there our troops stopped. There was no more rushing, no more charging. They had betaken themselves to plundering the enemy's camp; demoralization was fast ensuing, the fire and flush of their victorious charge was quenched, the fighting was now at long range, the infantry was pushed forward at a snail's pace, then there was no longer ardor or enthusiasm." †

In the meantime the enemy were not idle. General Sheridan slept at Winchester the preceding night, and on hearing of the disaster to his forces at Cedar Creek, mounted

---

* A young officer of the Confederate Army, a correspondent of the author, wrote in reference to the retreat from Fisher's Hill: "Compared with our flight from Fisher's Hill, the Yankees at Bull Run didn't run at all."

† Our correspondent before alluded to says: "We lost the day by the insane search for plunder. Some of our men seemed to forget their honor as soldiers in the mad hunt for Yankee gimcracks and the spoils of the enemy's camp."

his horse, and pushed to the scene at full gallop. He immediately ordered a new line of battle. At three o'clock he assumed the offensive. Attacking our plundering and demoralized forces, they were soon shamefully routed. Never before had our troops behaved so badly. An account of it says, "Our loss in killed, and wounded, and prisoners, was perhaps not greater than three thousand, but the route of the retreat was strewn with abandoned wagons, ambulances, and small arms, thrown away by the panic-stricken fugitives."

General Early lost nearly all his artillery, and indeed received so stunning a defeat that his army never recovered from it, and the Valley campaign ere long ceased to absorb so great a portion of public interest. It was not, however, abandoned, but the engagements after that time deserved only the name of skirmishes, through a course of some weeks, until late in the winter, when the affair at Waynesboro assumed the proportions of a battle.

"Troubles never come alone, but in battalions." The truth of this proverb was experienced by us in our Confederate history. While we were mourning our reverses on land, misfortune settled on our naval interests. If these were not of such importance as to awaken serious apprehension, they were at least of sufficient magnitude to afford exultation to our enemies.

On the 7th of October the Confederate privateer, "Florida," while at anchor in the port of San Salvador, on the coast of Brazil, was attacked by the Federal steamer "Wachusett," and captured. So unexpectedly did this occur, that at the time the commander and a portion of the crew were on shore, little dreaming that in this manner the laws of neutrality would be so violated.

A few weeks after this, the formidable ram "Albemarle" was destroyed in the Roanoke River. This was accomplished by running a torpedo boat upon the ram at her wharf, and sinking her by the explosion of a torpedo, in the darkness of the night, on the 27th of October.

The destruction of the "Albemarle" left Plymouth defenceless. On the 31st that place was taken by the Federals, and they succeeded in re-establishing their supremacy in the Sounds of North Carolina.

The military successes of our enemies in the last two months had decided the Presidential election, and wrought a second triumph for the Republican party. The hopes of peace that animated the Democrats at the North went down in darkness, and the South was forced to look only to an indefinite prolongation of hostilities, and to further revolve the question of endurance. Early in November the Confederate Congress reassembled in Richmond. Mr. Davis's message was hopeful and encouraging. He deemed that the clouds which then dimmed the Confederate skies might and would be dispelled, in the spirit of patriotic determination that had all along sustained the people of the South. He declared the Confederacy had no "vital points," that though our principal strongholds might be captured, no peace would be made which did not recognize our independence. He recommended the repeal of all laws granting exemption from military service, and appealing to the patriotism and just sense of duty in the people, he said: "No position or pursuit should relieve any one who is able to do active duty from enrollment in the army." Upon the question of arming the slaves of the South, after carefully noting its relative bearings, he remarked : " The subject is to be viewed solely in the light of policy and of our political economy. Should the alternative ever be presented of subjugation or the employment of the slave as a soldier, there seems to be no reason to doubt what then should be the decision."

CHAPTER LXVI.

HOOD'S CAMPAIGN IN TENNESSEE — SHERMAN'S MARCH THROUGH GEORGIA — CONFEDERATE DESERTIONS.

WHILE reflecting minds at the North were calculating how long the South could withstand the gigantic forces prepared for its subjugation, the people of the South expected to retrieve their disasters in the projected campaign of Hood. We had not long to wait.

On the 18th of September Mr. Davis arrived at the headquarters of General Hood, and in the evening delivered to the troops an encouraging address. To General Cheatham's Tennesseans he said: "Be of good cheer, for in a short time your faces will be turned homeward, and your feet pressing Tennessee soil." General Hood was enthusiastically called for. He said: "Soldiers, it is not my province to make speeches. I was not born for such work; that I leave to other men. Within a few days I expect to give the command 'Forward!' and I believe you are, like myself, willing to go forward, even if we live on parched corn and beef. I am ready to give the command forward this very night. Good night."

On the 29th of September Hood commenced his march. We cannot follow him through his course of strategy against Sherman, but will notice him next on the 29th of November, after two months, with thousands of his men within sight of their own homes, on the soil of their native State, driving the enemy before him into their intrenchments at Franklin, Tennessee. On the succeeding day, without giving them time to strengthen their works, he attacked them. General Thomas commanded the Federal army at this point. Hood knew that Thomas would endeavor to hold the old line of Nashville, Murfreesboro' and Franklin, and he felt that if he could fight the battle of Nashville at Franklin with success, Nashville would once more be surrendered to the Confederates, Tennessee be given up, and the war transferred to the Ohio. The fighting was fierce and terrible. Our troops behaved with a gallantry unsurpassed in any former engagements. Never before had our officers displayed more courage or determination. With reckless gallantry they exposed themselves, and the loss in general officers was unequalled in any battle of the war.

General Pat. Cleburne, who has been styled the "Stonewall Jackson of the West," fell pierced through the head by four bullets, and died on the ramparts. A description of this battle says: "General Gist, previously wounded in the leg, had refused to leave the field, limping along on foot, cheering his men, and finally received a ball through the breast, killing him instantly. Brown, Manigault, Johnston and Stahl, and scores of field and staff officers, who had exposed themselves at the head of their troops, were either killed or wounded. Still our men faltered not."

The resistance was stubborn, but finally the enemy were forced to retreat into Nashville, and General Hood proceeded to invest the city. On the 2d of December he laid siege to Nashville. While Hood was intrenching himself, Thomas was largely reinforced, and on the 15th of December (after several consultations with his officers) he determined to attack both flanks of Hood's army.

The results of the first day's engagement were not such as to dispirit the Confederate troops. On the following day the attack was renewed. All assaults of the enemy were repulsed up to three o'clock in the afternoon; when General Hood thought he had already his grasp on a splendid victory, a sudden stampede took place in one of his divisions, and the day was lost in a moment.

It was considered a most disgraceful retreat. Hood lost fifty pieces of artillery and all of his ordnance wagons, and the utter demolition of his army, shattered and demoralized by the panic, was prevented only by the want of vigor displayed by Thomas, in his failure to pursue them.

Hood finally made his escape across the Tennessee River at Florence with the remnant of his army, having lost, from various causes, more than ten thousand men, half of his generals, and nearly all his artillery. He was at Tupelo on the 6th of January 1865; and on the 23d resigned the command of his army to General Joseph E. Johnston, whose reinstatement was demanded by the Confederate Congress and by public clamor.

The news of the failure of this campaign filled Richmond with despondency, and was unmercifully commented upon by the Richmond press.

But other, and more serious trials awaited us. While the Tennessee campaign had resulted in defeat, we were destined to experience disasters in Georgia, more fatal to the Confederacy than any previous misfortune.

Before undertaking his great campaign, Sherman ordered the destruction of the most inhabited portion of Atlanta, and left behind him a picture of ruin and desolation, such as is seldom found in the ravages of war. On the 15th of November he began his march to the sea. This he accomplished leisurely and almost unimpeded. With the exception of one or two small conflicts with Wheeler's cavalry, and some few militia men and conscripts, he was unopposed until, within ten miles of Savannah, he encountered a force of skirmishers which indicated for the first time the presence of the Confederate forces under Hardee.

On the 10th of December he lay in line of battle, confronting the outer works of Savannah, about five miles distant from the city. Seeing that it was necessary for him to open communication with the fleet, he attacked Fort McAllister, the most formidable earthwork which guarded the entrance to the city. So formidable was the attack that resistance was useless and the fort was surrendered.

The surrender of the city was now only a question of time. From the 10th to the 16th of December heavy artillery firing and skirmishing went on along the lines, but no regular engagement occurred. On the 16th Sherman demanded a surrender of the city, from its commander, General Hardee, who declined on the next day to accede to the demand. Sherman then hurried more heavy siege guns upon the lines, and on the 20th was prepared to bombard the city and assault its works. But Hardee had taken the alarm, and resolved to evacuate Savannah. On the afternoon of the 20th he opened a tremendous fire from his batteries and iron-clads, and under cover of this demonstration, he marched his army from the city and secured his little band of fifteen thousand men from capture.

On the morning of the 21st of December, it was formally surrendered by its mayor, to General Geary of Sherman's command. The Confederate troops were gone. The navy-yard, two iron-clads, many smaller vessels, and a vast amount of ammunition, ordnance stores, and supplies had been destroyed before the evacuation, but all the rest of the city fell uninjured in to the hands of the enemy. Sherman sent a characteristic dispatch to Washington, and to President Lincoln he wrote:

"I beg to present you as a *Christmas gift*, the city of Savannah, with one hundred and fifty guns and plenty of ammunition, and also about twenty-five thousand bales of cotton."

The fall of Savannah greatly increased the despondency in the Confederacy. Calculations of failure now took the place of calculations of success in the minds of many. The morale of the Georgia troops in the army of Northern Virginia was unhappily affected by it, and desertions became frequent among them. They seemed unable to endure separation from their families, placed in such cruel distress by the devastations of the enemy that ravaged the territory of Georgia. The people began to count the cost of the sacrifices of the war and to estimate the terrible depletion that had taken place in the armies of the Confederacy during the campaign of 1864. The causes of this extraordinary depletion can easily be made apparent. During the year that was fast drawing to a close, the prosecution of the war against us had been more vigorous, a greater number of severe battles had been fought; and consequently the casualties had been more numerous. There were in our armies, as in all large armies, a great number of stragglers; and as our situation grew more unhappy, and provisions for the sustenance of soldiers more scarce, desertion was most unworthily encouraged by our enemies. But a reason more powerful still, may be found in the persistent refusal of the enemy's government to exchange prisoners.

Simultaneously with the fall of Savannah the intelligence was received that the salt-works at Saltville in the Kenawha Valley, had been recaptured, and other misfortunes had attended the small but not unimportant campaign in Southwestern Virginia.

Ill-tidings had now been borne to us in long-continued, and rapid succession. Sorrow had deepened its shadows in our hearts. But our faith in the justice of our cause, sustained us in the belief that these were no more than passing clouds, to be dispelled ere long by the sunshine of success.

CHAPTER LXVII.

THE WINTER OF 1864-5—WANT OF FUEL AND PROVISIONS—ROMANCE—PRICES.

WE were now in the midst of winter—the cheerless season to which we had looked forward with dread. It was the fourth year of the war. The festivities of Christmas were rendered mournful by the fall of Savannah, and the demolition of hopes which had trusted in that city, as a stronghold which could not be taken. With saddened mien we turned our steps towards the sanctuaries of God. On this occasion our praise and thanksgiving were blended with fasting and prayer, with deep humiliation and earnest contrition.

We left the temples of the Most High, and wended our

way back, many of us, not to the luxurious homes, where once the festival was gladdened by the reunion of loved ones, but to the humble, contracted lodgings which were all that remained to us, to call "home." Instead of the sumptuous banquet, around which we were wont to gather, we sat down to the poverty-stricken board. We counted again the vacant chairs, and glanced with eyes blinded by tears, upon the sombre living of woe, that indicated whither had been borne our domestic idols.

With a brave attempt at cheerfulness, we decked our dwellings with the evergreen, cedar, arbor-vitae, and holly, and here and there, under the magical influence of the kind old patron saint of the holiday, the Christmas tree once more reared its cheery head, laden with a precious and incongruous burden of bon-bons and simple toys.

The New Year was ushered in with no better prospects. If there was no foreboding of the coming wreck of our coveted independence, we could at best only look forward to an indefinite continuation of the dire evils which had shrouded our land in sorrow and misery. Day by day our wants and privations increased. The supply of provisions in the city of Richmond was altogether inadequate to the demand, and generally of a quality that would have been altogether unappetizing in seasons of plenty. Every fresh encroachment of the enemy increased this scarcity, and in a proportionate ratio, the prices at which articles of food were held. There was also a great want of fuel. Those formerly accustomed to well-heated houses, where comfort and luxury presided, now parsimoniously economized with a single ton of coal, or a single cord of wood to insure its lasting as long as possible, lest, when the last lump, or the last stick was consumed, no more could be obtained at any price.

In addition to our other miseries, robberies were fearfully on the increase. The fortunate possessor of a well-stocked larder or coal house was in constant danger from burglary. It finally became an almost universal fashion in Richmond to permit "every day to take care of itself." It was useless to lay up for the morrow, or to anticipate the rise in prices and provide against it, for the cunning house-breakers were still better at calculation, and would ever upset the best laid schemes by their successful midnight depredations.

During the war the "rebel capital" became famous for the large number of beautiful ladies who belonged to the city, or who found within its friendly walls refuge and security. While the god of war thundered from its ramparts, not less busy was the artful boy-god. As usual, the gossips thoroughly acquainted themselves with Cupid's victories. Ever and anon these *quid nuncs* whispered of interesting *affaires de cœur*, in which were associated the names of gallant officers and soldiers of our army and of the fair and beautiful belles of the capital. That they reckoned not without their host was made evident from the unusual number of weddings that were celebrated during this winter. St. Paul's seemed to be the fashionable church for the solemnization of these happy bridals. It appeared indeed that many a fair young girl was only

> "Doffing her maiden joyousness,
> For a name and for a ring."

ere long to cherish the memory of the early loved and the early lost in the grave of the soldier. But the true sentiment of the heart of Southern women found expression in the language of a noble daughter of Virginia, who, when she buckled the armor on her patriot husband, remarked, "I had rather be the widow of a brave man than the wife of a coward."

Of the numerous marriages which served as fruitful digressions from the war topic, and brightened the usual gloom that hung over the social circles of Richmond, we will mention particularly only one, rendered of thrilling interest from all the associations connected with it. In January, the brave, gallant, and chivalrous young Major-General Pegram, of Richmond, led to the altar the fairest

of the fair—the universally acknowledged queen of society—
the beautiful and accomplished Miss C. A dense throng
crowded the church to witness the nuptials of the popular
young officer and his magnificent bride. Sincere congratulations were pressed upon them, and they set forth on their
matrimonial route with the brightest prospects for happiness, and sustained by the prayers and best wishes of numberless friends.

Three weeks had only passed when on the field of Hatcher's Run this young officer—this happy young husband—
was cut down. Death, remorseless, cruel Death, claimed the
warrior bridegroom, and the snowy robe of the bride, the
orange wreath, and the misty veil, which had shaded, yet
heightened her splendid beauty, were exchanged for the weeds
of the widow, the sable robe of the heart's deepest affliction.

It is noticeable in connection with the scarcity of food and
the high prices, that the class usually know as the poor,
was not the class which experienced the most serious inconvenience, and was reduced to the most dreadful misery.
They were provided by the Common Council of the city with
such staple articles of food as could be obtained, and in a
quantity sufficient to secure them from suffering. They had
furnished to them rations of corn-meal, sorghum syrup, and
small quantities of bacon and flour. Starvation to them was
not imminent, and the pauper class were indeed in more comfortable circumstances than persons who lived on salaries, or
depended upon a moderate income for support.*

Salaried officers with families dependent upon them found
it extremely difficult, with the constantly increasing prices,
and the depreciation of the currency, to bring their expenses

---

* In a conversation with a distinguished Southern divine, the rector of a once wealthy parish, he said, "Butter is a luxury in which we rarely ever indulge, and frequently we are without sugar; and if there is not sickness in our family we manage to get on quite comfortably without the use of many things once considered necessary." This system of philosophizing became a part of our war educa-
tion.

within the limits of their income. In some instances we heard of those who subsisted solely on bread, and not enough of that to satisfy the cravings of hunger. But all this did not subdue the indomitable spirit of the people generally. The disaffected, if any such were discovered by signs of weakness and a failing spirit, were not of those whose bodily sufferings were greatest, but were found among unwise financiers, who began to tremble for their own selfish interests in the fear that Confederate investments might not in the end pay very liberally. Sherman's operations in the South, and Sheridan's successes in the Valley of Virginia, began to arouse the apprehensions of extensive holders of Confederate bonds, lest they had miscalculated and overshot the mark.

"Croakers" now began to multiply, and murmurs of dissatisfaction, deep but not loud, and mutterings of vexation and disapproval were sometimes heard from a certain class of malcontents, who, when the light of prosperity shone on our arms, were the first to hail the Confederacy, but who, like the fickle and inconstant people of France, in the time of the revolution, were ready to veer with every change of the political weathercock, and possessed not moral courage enough to sustain them under the dark clouds and beating winds of adversity. Like individuals, governments have their summer friends; and though we are proud to know that these exceptions in the Confederacy were exceedingly rare, still we are forced to admit, and mourn that we are compelled to admit, they did indeed exist.

Another and very obvious sign of weakness was the growing want of confidence in our currency. The necessity for final repudiation was currently entertained; and those who looked with certainty to the establishment of the independence of the Confederacy, looked with equal certainty to the great financial crisis which must follow. Ruin, bankruptcy, and the multitudinous evils which follow in the train of all great political convulsions, were predicted. These "birds of ill omen " gave us to understand that though we might safely steer the Confederate vessel through Charybdis, danger equally imminent threatened to leave her stranded on Scylla. But there were brave hearts that gave little heed to these warnings, and clung to the phantom of Hope that lured them, like the *ignis fatuus*, to the bogs and morasses of final and crushing disappointment.

There was, however, a marked change visible in the general disrespect of the people for the circulating medium. This was evident in a reckless expenditure of money, and a disposition to indulge in extravagances, at whatever cost. The *trousseau* of a bride, which might formerly have been procured at an expense of a few hundred dollars, could now only be purchased at the expenditure of as many thousands; yet there was no hesitancy manifested at this time to indulge in what a year before we might have considered reprehensible extravagance. As the result proved, if wanton expenditure is, under any circumstances, to be tolerated, there was evinced much real wisdom in what might have seemed folly to the prudent economist. It was simply a good investment.

The simplest wardrobe of a lady at this time was enormously expensive. For an ordinary calico, for which we formerly paid twelve and a half cents per yard, (a New York shilling,) we were forced to pay from thirty to thirty-five dollars. For an English or French chintz, the price was fifty dollars per yard. A nice French merino or mohair dress cost from eight hundred to a thousand dollars. A cloak of fine cloth was worth from a thousand to fifteen hundred dollars. A pair of balmoral boots for ladies brought two hundred to two hundred and fifty dollars. French kid gloves sold at from one hundred and twenty-five to one hundred and seventy-five dollars per pair. Irish linens commanded from fifty to one hundred dollars per yard, and cotton cloth, of inferior quality, varied from thirty to fifty dollars per yard. We hardly dare trust ourselves to give the price of ladies' hats, but they varied, from the difference in quality and material, from six hundred to fifteen hundred dollars; and all things else pertaining to a simple outfit commanded proportionate prices.

While the industry and benevolence of our ladies were in no wise relaxed, there was a sensible disposition to a greater indulgence in dress. This may be accounted for, in many instances, by the threadbare condition of wardrobes, which had been made to suffice through the wear and tear of four years of privation and self-sacrifice, and could no longer resist the necessity for replenishment.

Similar figures ruled the market for gentlemen's goods. We cannot pretend to give the price of broadcloth or cassimere, or boots or gloves, etc., of a gentleman's wardrobe. Our men, however, (especially those connected with the army,) were relieved of a very heavy expense by being able to purchase of government stores at government prices, such articles as were absolutely necessary for them. A suit of new broadcloth, or a new hat, or other article of dress of extraordinary neatness, would be sure to subject the fortunate wearer to the annoyances of the boys or soldiers on the street, who were wont to accost them in the slang of the army, with : "Come out of that broadcloth! Come out of that hat!" etc.

Our dry goods were now principally obtained through the blockade from Nassau. A very large capital was invested in this trade, and it was carried on successfully and at comparatively little risk. The most important port to the Richmond market was Wilmington, North Carolina. But at the period which we are now noticing, (having in our narrative gone ahead of our military history,) this port was in the hands of the enemy ; and as the circle of our advantages gradually narrowed, the price of gold became higher and higher, and all articles of trade advanced in undue proportion. Day by day we congratulated ourselves on what we were fortunate enough to have, and were not forced to purchase of the remorseless tradesmen, who exhibited a provoking indifference to the sale of their wares, in striking contrast to the patronizing anxiety with which they had formerly courted custom.

"Except wind stands as never it stood,
It is an ill wind turns none to good."

In the month of February occurred one of the most awful casualties which had been remembered in Richmond since the burning of the Richmond Theatre in 1811. During the night a fire originated in a block of buildings on Main Street, between Thirteenth and Fourteenth, the lower stories of which were occupied for store-rooms, and the upper stories for private dwellings. This fire, it seems, broke out in the lower story of the block, in the store of a Jew, who very soon succeeded in getting his goods safely out of reach of the flames. After the fire had progressed to an alarming extent, it was ascertained that a family just above the store were still in the burning building. They appeared at the windows, and the most extraordinary efforts were made for their rescue, but the sad story may be told in the heart-broken shout of the unhappy mother: "Too late!" In this awful manner six persons met death. They consisted of a father, a mother, a young and beautiful girl, who had just attained the age of womanhood, two young boys, and one negro servant. Their charred and half destroyed bodies were secured from the wreck of the burnt buildings on the following morning, and deposited in Hollywood Cemetery. A young soldier son, then in the field, is all that is left of the Stebbins family. This awful catastrophe sent a thrill of horror over Richmond.

CHAPTER LXVIII.

CAPTURE OF FORT FISHER—OCCUPATION OF WILMINGTON AND CHARLESTON—END OF SHERMAN'S MARCH.

IN December an expedition had been fitted out to operate against Fort Fisher, which guarded the entrance to the harbor of Wilmington. The principal attack occurred on the 24th of the month, and was completely and successfully resisted by the Confederates. A second expedition was undertaken in January, 1865, and resulted in the capture of the fort by the Federals. In a few days Wilmington was occupied without resistance, and General Bragg retired with his army of eight or ten thousand troops to the principal theatre of war in the interior of the Carolinas.

Knowing that it would be useless, with his comparatively small forces, to attempt to hold Charleston, General Beauregard prepared to evacuate that city. Before retreating, General Hardee made the destruction of all property belonging to the government as complete as time and opportunity would allow. On the morning of the 18th of February the enemy made a triumphal entrée into the city. Charred and blackened monuments of the ravages of fire, scarred and mutilated buildings showing the work of shot and shell, and the rude and terrible marks of war greeted the beholder at every turn.

On the same day Columbia, the capital of the State of South Carolina, was occupied by General Sherman. After leaving Columbia, Sherman proceeded on his march northward. By the 11th of March he had reached and occupied Fayetteville, North Carolina, not, however, without a serious conflict of his cavalry forces under Kilpatrick with the Confederate cavalry under General Wade Hampton. His onward advance was again checked by a small detachment of the Confederates under Hardee, at Averysboro', on the Cape Fear River, about midway between Raleigh and Fayetteville. In this engagement General Johnston telegraphed to Richmond that the total Confederate loss was four hundred and fifty; that of the Federals, thirty-three hundred. On the 19th of March occurred the engagement at Boltonville, by which General Johnston designed to prevent the junction of Schofield with Sherman. Though gaining, as he conceived, an advantage, he found it impossible to accomplish his purpose, and drew off his forces in the direction of Raleigh. On the night of the 20th the enemy abandoned their works and moved on towards Goldsboro'.

On the 22d of March Sherman published in Goldsboro' a congratulatory address to his troops, in which he said: "After a march of the most extraordinary character, nearly five hundred miles over swamps and rivers deemed impassable to others, at the most inclement season of the year and drawing our chief supplies from a poor and wasted country, we reach our destination in good health and condition."

After disposing of his army in his camp at Goldsboro', Sherman hastened to City Point for an interview with General Grant and President Lincoln, which gave rise in Richmond to talks of a "peace negotiation," but, as the result proved, was for anything else.

CHAPTER LXIX.

MORE PEACE NEGOTIATIONS—GOVERNMENT APPEAL FOR FOOD.

WHILE Sherman was prosecuting his triumphal march through a portion of our territory, the minds of the people of Richmond were encouraged to hope from certain demonstrations, that, like ourselves, our enemies were growing heartily tired of the war, and were willing to make overtures for an honorable and peaceable adjustment of the difficulties which distracted, and had already brought such ruin on the country.

In January, Mr. Francis P. Blair of Maryland made several visits to Richmond, which occasioned much curiosity and speculation in the public mind. He came with a pass from Mr. Lincoln, but the objects of his mission were not committed to paper. They were, however, soon developed. After some preliminaries, in which a short correspondence was entered into, by the rival presidents, it was decided that the Confederate Government should. send commissioners to confer with Mr. Lincoln, as to what terms could be expected from him, and what agreement might be entered into, to effect a peaceable adjustment of existing difficulties. Mr. Lincoln signified his willingness to receive ambassadors regularly authorized to negotiate for the restoration of peace to the people of our "common country." In consequence of this notification Mr. Davis requested Vice President Stephens, Senator R. M. T. Hunter and Judge Campbell to pass through the lines and hold a conference with Mr. Lincoln, or such individuals as he might depute to represent him.

They met at Fortress Monroe. The result of the interview was that no terms were agreed upon. President Lincoln positively refused to listen to any proposal that had in view a suspension of hostilities, unless based upon the disbandment of the Confederate forces. He refused to enter into any negotiation on any other basis than "unconditional surrender."

The hopes of peace that had been for a long time entertained were thus effectually crushed. The expectations of the majority, as to what would be the result of this conference, were fully realized.

Every avenue of peace now being closed, except such as might be conquered by our arms, a fresh attempt was made to rally the people to a determined war feeling. A mass-meeting of the citizens was called at the African Church. Business was suspended, stores were closed, and thorough interest in the action of the hour was manifested. Eloquent addresses were delivered; patriotic appeals were made; a spasmodic enthusiasm was enkindled. But despondency rested too heavily on the hearts of many to permit more than a momentary and convulsive effort to shake off the incubus. Strange terms now began to be in use. With "evacuation," to which we had listened as a vague probability, for four years, were intermingled the words, "submission, surrender, subjugation, reconstruction," indicating ideas hitherto unknown in the Confederacy, or if entertained, certainly not bruited abroad.

To those who reflected on our situation in all its bearings, though it was evidently desperate and discouraging, there seemed no necessity for subjugation. We earnestly looked forward to the spring campaign. We relied on the grand old Army of Northern Virginia to retrieve the reverses of the last few months, and to lift the Confederacy from the "Slough of Despond."

The Confederate Congress had passed a bill extending the conscription to slaves. It was a desperate measure, and was vigorously combated. It was a question which involved intricate and subtle interests, and was made the subject of careful and laborious legislation. Doubts entertained as to whether the negro could be made efficient as a soldier, were silenced by the use made of him in the Federal army. General Lee favored the employment of negroes in the service; the Richmond press had recommended it since the fall of 1864; and the majority of intelligent and patriotic minds at the South inclined to believe in the usefulness of the measure. Almost at the eleventh hour of its session, Congress passed the bill, hedged by certain limitations, and made dependent to a certain extent on the will of the master, authorizing the employment of slaves in the military service.

Recruiting offices were opened in Richmond, and soon a goodly number of sable patriots appeared on the streets, clad in the grey uniform of the Confederate soldier. Their dress-parades on the Capitol Square attracted large crowds of all colors to witness them, and infused a spirit of enthusiasm among those of their own race, that served daily to increase the numbers of those who were willing to fight.*

---

* An enthusiastic female slave one day said to her master, "The very next time I meet General Lee on the street, I mean to shake hands with him."

"You had better be careful," replied the master, "you might find a place in Castle Thunder for your presumption."

"No, oh no; he won't send me there," she answered, "for when I do shake hands

By examination of a secret committee of the Confederate Congress, the Confederate Commissariat was discovered to be in a shamefully low condition, and under the supervision of Commissary General Northrop, celebrated as much for his want of judgment as for his contempt of advice, there seemed little prospect for its improvement. Various schemes were devised for procuring supplies for the army, with but slender probability of accomplishment, under the obstinate control of Commissary Northrop.

Richmond was now almost destitute of provisions. Northrop was removed, and St. John appointed Commissary General, and the following appeal "To the people of Virginia" was put forth :

RICHMOND, February 22d, 1865.

FELLOW CITIZENS: Commissary General St. John, at his recent entrance upon the duties of his bureau, invited several gentlemen of this city, including a number of clergymen, to a conference as to the best means of increasing the supplies of food necessary for the subsistence of the Army of Northern Virginia. At this conference, the undersigned were appointed as a committee to prepare and issue an address to the loyal people of the State, for the purpose of placing before them such facts, and of making such suggestions as will, it is confidently believed, ensure a general and hearty co-operation in this great and necessary work.

You are aware, fellow-citizens, that the movements of the enemy in South Carolina and Georgia have interrupted our communications with the Southern States, and seriously embarrassed the operations of the Subsistence Department, so that immediate and energetic action on the part of the Government and the people is demanded for the support of the army.

It is ascertained that the supply of food in the accessible counties of North Carolina and Virginia is ample for the subsistence both of soldiers and citizens. Of the four modes of obtaining it for the use of the army, viz.: by impressment, purchase, loan, and voluntary contribution, it is

---

with him, I am going to tell him that all I'm sorry for is, that I have not got ten sons to give him to fight for the Confederacy."

Her master, amused, commended her for her patriotism. The same negress, at the time of the occupation of Richmond by the Federal troops, secured from the wreck of some of the dry-goods stores a lot of gentlemen's collars, which she carefully preserved, to send, as she said, —"Just as soon as I get a chance"—as a present to President Davis. Even to this day, this poor woman avows the most unqualified devotion to the memory of the Southern Confederacy.

believed that when the exigency, now existing, is clearly understood, the last mentioned method will be the one most approved by the people, and therefore the one which will command the most cheerful, immediate, and generous aid on their part.

The resources of the people have already been severely taxed. Vast quantities of food have already been obtained by impressments, loans, and voluntary contributions. But for these extraordinary efforts our armies would have long since been disbanded, and without a continuation of these efforts, our soldiers cannot accomplish the task yet before them. Apart from all those considerations of honor and duty, which most constrain high-toned and patriotic men, these liberal contributions on the part of citizens are necessary to the preservation of their own rights of property and personal safety. Interest itself demands any and every sacrifice necessary to prevent subjugation.

On this point, one testimony will be sufficient. Virginians and patriots all over the Confederacy will regard with explicit belief and profoundest respect any statement on such a subject emanating from our beloved General-in-chief, Robert E. Lee. In reference to the very appeal we are now making, he writes;

"I cannot permit myself to doubt that our people will respond to it, when they reflect on the alternative presented to them. They have simply to choose whether they will contribute such commissary and quartermaster stores as they can possibly spare to support an army which has already borne and done so much in their behalf, or retaining their stores, maintain the army of the enemy engaged in their subjugation. I am aware that a general obligation of this nature rests lightly on most men—each being disposed to leave its discharge to his neighbor—but I am confident that our citizens will appreciate their responsibility in the case, and will not permit an army which, by God's blessing and their patriotic support, has hitherto resisted the efforts of the enemy, to suffer now through their neglect."

Such being the emergency, and the corresponding obligation, it only remains now to consider the best practicable means of attaining the end in view.

There is in every county accessible to us in the State an officer or agent of the Bureau of Subsistence, charged with the duty of collecting, by purchase or otherwise, army subsistence, and forwarding the same to this city. It is also proposed to appoint two or more gentlemen of influence, energy and intelligence, in each county, (who shall appoint others in each magisterial district,) to call the attention of every family to the wants of the army, and to urge them to contribute in some way as large a portion of their supplies as can possibly be spared. These contributions can be made as DONATIONS, SALES or LOANS, at the option of the owner, and the supplies so obtained, will be sent to some convenient point to be indicated by the local officer, where he will receive and receipt the same, and give the parties, when required, an obligation in kind or in currency.

But, as already intimated, there are difficulties in the way of obtaining supplies either by purchase or by loan, which can be best overcome by the spontaneous and free-will offerings of the people, generously contributing of their substance for the support of the army now battling and suffering in their behalf.

For the information of those who desire to aid the cause by voluntary contributions, we beg leave to state that the following plan has been considered and approved by the authorities;

1. Let every citizen who can, pledge himself to furnish the rations of one soldier for six months, without designating any particular soldier as the recipient of the contribution.

2. Let those thus pledging themselves furnish, say 80 pounds of bacon and 180 pounds of flour, or their equivalent in beef and meal, to be delivered to the nearest commissary agent.

3. Let the donor bind himself to deliver one half of the amount above stated, viz.; 40 pounds of bacon and 90 pounds of flour (or its equivalent) IMMEDIATELY, and the remainder at the end of three months, unless he prefers to adopt the better plan of advancing the whole amount pledged at once.

4. Let the pledge of each individual subscribing and furnishing the rations of one soldier for six months be made the basis of larger subscriptions. Those whose generosity and whose means will enable them to do so, may obligate themselves to provide the rations of five, ten, twenty, or any other number of soldiers for six months; while even the poor, who could not afford to supply the rations of one man, by uniting their contributions may authorize one of the number, so combining, to make the designated subscription of at least one ration for one man for six months.

We trust that this plan, so intelligible and so easily put in execution, will commend itself to thousands of our patriotic people who, by reason of age, sex, or infirmity, cannot serve in the field, will yet take pride and pleasure in being represented in the field in the persons of soldiers whose rations they themselves furnish.

On this subject, General Lee expresses the opinion that almost every one who has a family, especially among our farmers, could afford to support one more in addition to his present number, and that this plan will not require a man to do more than to send to a soldier what he would always be able to give in the way of hospitality to such soldier, were he an inmate of his house.

The scheme thus explained presents a system which may be contracted or expanded according to the ability of the contributor—not excluding the poor, and giving scope to the largest liberality of the rich; and in fact, presents a plan for securing all the food in the country which can be obtained by voluntary contribution.

And now in order to carry it into immediate execution, the co-operation of the legislators, magistrates, ministers of the gospel, and all persons of influence and standing in every county is earnestly invoked. The cause is one which makes its own appeal to fathers and mothers who have sons in the army; to men of wealth who have large possessions to protect; to men in humble circumstances, to whom the liberties of their country are equally dear; to all classes in the community, whose security and happiness are involved in the issue of this struggle for the right of self-government. Every right-minded, and right-hearted man must feel that citizens in their comfortable homes, exempt from the privations and perils of the field, should be willing to exercise the severest self-denial, if necessary, that the army to which, under God, we are indebted for our present safety, and to whom we must owe our final deliverance from the presence and the power of the enemy, should at least be supplied with the food which is essential to the vigorous health and comfort of its soldiers. A claim so reasonable and just MUST and WILL be satisfied.

And now, in concluding our appeal to you, fellow-citizens, we do not forget that Virginia has already suffered sorely in this struggle to obtain all that is dearest to the patriot's heart. The bloody tide of battle has swept over almost every portion of her territory; the sacrifices, as well as the services of her sons have been great; yet the spirit of her people has never flagged, nor are her resources exhausted. She has hitherto responded nobly to every call the Confederate Government has made upon her: and it is not doubted that now, when made aware of its present wants, her people will prove themselves both able and willing to relieve them.

    MOSES D. HOGE,
    JOHN E. EDWARDS,
    M. J. MICHELBACHER,
    THOS. W. McCANCE,
    SAMUEL J. HARRISON,

    J. L. BURROWS,
    CHAS. MINNIGERODE,
    W. J. PETTIGREW,
    R. EDMOND.

The harmony of this session of the Confederate Congress was disturbed by unfortunate recrimination between that body and Mr. Davis. The latter was accused of being self-willed and intractable; the Confederate Legislature evinced a spirit of captiousness and impatience.

It was during this session that a member of this body attempted to escape to Washington. The excitement produced by his flight did not assume the character of a "nine days' wonder" in Richmond, and was the occasion of ridicule rather than indignation. Before its adjournment the Confederate Congress published an address, which served in a measure to inspirit the despairing, and to confirm the hopeful, although there is abundant reason to believe that they considered the reassembling of their body in Richmond in the light of a bare possibility.

An important change had taken place in the Cabinet. Under the pressure of strong outside disapprobation, and against the remonstrances of Mr. Davis, Mr. Seddon, the Secretary of War, had resigned, and General Breckinridge had been appointed to the position. This appointment was popular, and from the character of the new Secretary, the people were induced to hope for and expect a more judicious management of the War Department than had been exercised by his predecessor.

We had now passed through the winter. The first month of spring had been ushered in. We felt that the approaching campaign, which was expected to open very early in the season, whether it terminated in favor of or against us, would conclude the war. This opinion, which was freely expressed, seemed rather the result of intuitive conviction than of extraneous evidence.

The exalted moral and religious character of our men in authority served greatly to encourage our belief in the countenance of the all-wise Ruler of human affairs. Not a few of us love to recall the scenes at St. Paul's Church on the first Sabbath day in March, when the monthly celebration of the Lord's Supper was observed. The communicants had generally approached, partaken of the sacred symbols, and retired from the chancel, when President Davis, General Lee, and Secretary Trenholm came forward and knelt before the sacramental table. The house was solemnly quiet. Not a sound was heard save the low, sweet voices of the priests. All hearts were impressed, and silently called down benedictions on the heads of the kneeling men. They retired from the chancel. In a few moments the sublime strains of *Glo-*

ria in Excelsis floated up from heart and lip, from choir and organ. It seemed indeed as if that house of God was the very gate of Heaven. Many of us left the holy place with impressions time can never efface, and in the fullness of trust, asked, "Can the Almighty forsake a people whose God is the Lord?" Alas! in one short month our idols of hope were shattered by the rude iconoclasm of despair.

CHAPTER LXX.

FOREBODINGS OF DISASTER—SHERIDAN'S GREAT RAID AND HIS JUNCTION WITH GRANT.

VARIOUS rumors were now afloat in Richmond which should have convinced any people that "evacuation" was not improbable. Yet there were no more definite indications of such an event than had existed frequently before. We had long been under depressing influences, and we felt that the spirits of the people were gradually bending to the stern destiny of defeat. But the fire of resistance was not yet extinguished. We were not blind to a certain weakness that had developed itself; still we trusted to the latent spirit which, though we mourned that it slumbered, was not dead. We did not feel that it would require an Herculean effort to shake off our lethargy. We had seen how much had been done; we believed there was in us the power to do much more.

Towards the latter part of February, Sheridan again proceeded up the Valley of the Shenandoah. As we have before noticed, in advance of our narrative, a battle occurred at Waynesboro' between his forces and those of General Early, resulting in the rout of the Confederates; Early himself barely escaping capture. Sheridan then crossed the Blue Ridge, and occupied Charlottesville. This village is the seat of the Virginia University, the principal institution of learning in the South, and for the ability of its corps of instructors, and for educational advantages, ranks below none in this country. From the imposing and peculiar style of its architecture, this cherished pet of Mr. Jefferson's later years, situated in the midst of the most beautiful and romantic scenery, as it bursts first upon the vision of the beholder, presents a picture of enchanting loveliness.

A memorable remark is quoted of General Sheridan in reference to this institution. He is said to have been asked why he did not destroy the University of Virginia, and was reminded that such had been the intention of Hunter, had he succeeded in capturing Charlottesville. "I wish to live on the pages of history," replied this illustrious officer. This is not given as indisputably authentic, and it must be hoped that a nobler principle and motive actuated him than merely a weak desire for posthumous notoriety; and, *en passant*, it may not be amiss to regret that he seems lately to have strangely forgotten the promptings of that nobler inner heart, in his ungenerous treatment of the unconscious remains of a distinguished enemy, in those of General Albert Sidney Johnston.

After the capture of Charlottesville, Sheridan divided his forces and proceeded on a gigantic and destructive raid * in two different directions, and finally brought his forces into junction with the Army of the James. While no one can be

---

* The writer of these sketches acknowledges her indebtedness to General Sheridan for the last letter that reached her hand in the Southern Confederacy. It was an object to overhaul the mails in these predatory incursions. In the one that fell under hostile examination at Frederickshall, in Louisa County, Virginia, there was a billet-doux addressed to her by a young Mississippian who had only very lately been released from captivity at Point Lookout. It detailed a touching story of disappointment in an *affaire de cœur*, for which he pleadingly asked the sympathy of his friend, saying: "To you alone I commit this record of my troubles—for your eyes alone this missive is intended." It reached her "Read, approved, and respectfully forwarded to ——— by Colonel Sherman, by order of General Sheridan." She does not confess to great gratitude to General Sheridan, however, as it is peculiarly disagreeable to have one's correspondence subjected to inquisition. It may not be uninteresting to learn that this young son of Mars was finally consoled by the hand of his lady-love.

so prejudiced as to willingly withhold from General Sheridan the meed of praise for skillful and brilliant generalship, for perseverance and success, which his superior, General Grant, generously avows was a powerful auxiliary to his own success, it is equally true that the Confederate forces in the Valley were destined to encounter numbers so greatly superior that the principal element of success in the operations of Sheridan in that section of Virginia, may without doubt be found in the numerical weakness of the enemy that opposed him. As General Early has since declared : " I was leading a forlorn hope, and the people can appreciate the character of the victories won by Sheridan over me."

CHAPTER LXXI.

OPERATIONS OF GRANT AND LEE—FALL OF PETERSBURG.

ON the 6th of February an attack was made upon the lines of General Lee at Hatcher's Run, which resulted in a repulse of the assailants. After this, quiet supervened, unbroken by any remarkable incident for several weeks. A history of our experience during this interval may be expressed in the words, " We were only waiting." The monotony was now and then broken by the passage of troops through Richmond. Many of them, from their rags and tatters, would have made admirable scare-crows had they made their appearance in the spring in our corn-fields; but their faces were radiant with courage and hope, and they cheerily, even at that time, carried forward the colors under which they had gained immortal renown.

Our infantry troops, however, did not present such an aspect of misery as the cavalry. Among the latter we saw our tatterdemalions mounted on poor, weak, miserable animals, scarcely more than moving skeletons.

On the 25th of March, the quiet was broken. General Lee

made a sudden attack on Grant's lines south of the Appomattox, at Hare's Hill. It was a surprise, and at first signally successful; but when thoroughly aroused to their danger, the enemy made a determined resistance, and under the pressure of superior numbers, General Gordon, who directed the attack, was compelled to retire.

Grant speedily retaliated for Lee's attempt to break his lines. In order to give an authentic account of the events which brought upon us a sudden and unexpected calamity that shocked our reason and unsettled memory, subjoined, from a history of the times, is a sketch of the battles around Petersburg:

"On the 29th of March, Grant began a heavy movement towards the Southside Railroad. The cavalry command, consisting of General Davison's and Sheridan's cavalry, moved out on the Jerusalem Plank Road about three and a half miles from Hancock Station, where they took the County road leading across the Weldon Railroad at Ream's Station, and into the Vaughan road one mile from Dinwiddie Court House, General Crook's division going in advance. They reached Dinwiddie Court House about four o'clock in the evening.

"In the meantime, the Fifth and Sixth Corps of Infantry had been moving in a parallel line on the Vaughan Road. General Grant's headquarters on the night of the 29th were on the Boydtown plank road in the neighborhood of Gravelly Run.

"The next day heavy rains impeded operations; but the force of the enemy pressed on towards the Five Forks, the extreme right of Lee's line on the Southside Railroad. General Lee had not been idle in meeting this movement. On the 31st of March, the enemy found on his front, prepared to contest the prize of the railroad, Pickett's Division of infantry, General Fitzhugh Lee's and General William H. F. Lee's divisions of cavalry. In the afternoon of the day the Confederates made a determined and gallant charge upon the whole cavalry line of the Yankees; forced it back, and drove the enemy to a point within two miles of Dinwiddie Court House.

"But the news of Sheridan's repulse had no sooner reached General Grant, than the Fifth Corps was moved rapidly to his relief. The reinforcement arrived in time to retrieve the fortunes of the enemy. The next day, April 1st, the combined forces of the Yankee cavalry and Warren's Infantry, advanced against the Confederates. Overpowered by numbers the Confederates retreat d to Five Forks, where they were flanked by a part of the Fifth Corps, which had moved down the White Oak Road. It was here that several thousand prisoners were taken.

"On the night of Saturday, April 1st, the prospect was a most discouraging one for General Lee. Grant had held all his lines in front of Petersburg, had manœuvred troops far to his left, had turned Lee's right, and was now evidently prepared to strike a blow upon the lines in front of Petersburg.

"By daylight on Sunday, April 2d, these lines were assaulted in three different places, by as many different Yankee corps. They were pierced in every place. The Sixth Corps went through first, at a point about opposite the western extremity of Petersburg; the Twenty-fourth, a little way further west; and the Ninth Corps further east, near the Jerusalem plank road, capturing Fort Mahone, one of the largest forts in the Petersburg defences. The Confederates made a desperate struggle for Fort Mahone, which was protracted through the day, but without success. At dark the position of the contending parties was the same as during the day.

"The Yankees had congratulated themselves that by the success of the Sixth Corps, they had cut Lee's Army in two, cutting off the troops that were not in Petersburg. As that place was supposed to be the Confederate point of manœuvre, as it was supposed that troops could not cross the Appomatox except through the city, their capture was taken as certain by the enemy, since they were hemmed in between Sheridan, the Sixth Corps and the river. But in this they were mistaken. The Confederates easily forced the river; and the close of the day found Lee's army brought together within the inner line of the Petersburg defences.

"But the disasters which had already occurred were in General Lee's opinion irretrievable. In killed and wounded his loss had been small — two thousand would probably cover it in the entire series of engagements; but he had lost an entire line of defence around Petersburg, and with it the Southside railroad, so important to Richmond as an avenue of supply.

Among the Confederate dead was the brave General A. P. Hill, whose name is reckoned amongst the most illustrious of the many heroes of the war. All through the long series of battles, for four years, it had been untarnished by a single accident or misfortune, or reproach, to dim the well-deserved brilliancy of its lustre, made memorable by deeds of heroism.

The news came to us in Richmond in fragmentary parcels; General Hill's death produced a profound sensation and unfeigned grief. But we dreamed not, as night brought the time for rest on the 1st of April, of the sad morrow in reserve for us. The whole truth had not reached us. We slept, as it were, over the heaving crater of a volcano. Destruction hovered over our fair city, yet happily we knew it not, and dreamed on in blissful unconsciousness of impending danger.

CHAPTER LXXII.

EVACUATION OF RICHMOND—BURNING OF THE CITY.

THE morning of the 2d of April, 1865, dawned brightly over the capital of the Southern Confederacy. A soft haze rested over the city, but above that, the sun shone with the warm pleasant radiance of early spring. The sky was cloudless. No sound disturbed the stillness of the Sabbath morn, save the subdued murmur of the river, and the cheerful music of the church bells. The long familiar tumult of war broke not upon the sacred calmness of the day. Around the War Department, and the Post Office, news gatherers were assembled for the latest tidings, but nothing was bruited that deterred the masses from seeking their accustomed places in the temples of the living God. At St. Paul's church the usual congregation was in attendance. President Davis occupied his pew.

It was again the regular monthly return for the celebration of the sacrament of the Lord's Supper. The services were progressing as usual, no agitation nor disturbance withdrew the thoughts from holy contemplation, when a messenger was observed to make his way up the aisle, and to place in the hands of the President a sealed package. Mr. Davis arose, and was noticed to walk rather unsteadily out of the church. An uneasy whisper ran through the congregation, and intuitively they seemed possessed of the dreadful secret of the sealed dispatch—the unhappy condition of General Lee's army and the necessity for evacuating Richmond. The dispatch stated that this was inevitable unless his lines could be reformed before eight o'clock that evening.

At the Second Presbyterian Church, Dr. Hoge, who had received information of the dire calamity impending over us, told his congregation of our situation, and the probability that never again would they meet there for worship, and in the thrilling eloquence of which he is so truly the master, bade them farewell.

The direful tidings spread with the swiftness of electricity. From lip to lip, from men, women, children and servants, the news was bandied, but many received it at first, as only a "Sunday sensation rumor." Friend looked into the face of friend to meet only an expression of incredulity; but later in the day, as the truth, stark and appalling, confronted us, the answering look was that of stony, calm despair. Late in the afternoon the signs of evacuation became obvious to even the most incredulous. Wagons were driven furiously through the streets, to the different departments, where they received as freight, the archives of the government, and carried them to the Danville Depot, to be there conveyed away by railroad.

Thousands of the citizens determined to evacuate the city with the government. Vehicles commanded any price in any currency possessed by the individual desiring to escape from the doomed capital. The streets were filled with excited crowds hurrying to the different avenues for transportation, intermingled with porters carrying huge loads, and wagons piled up with incongruous heaps of baggage, of all sorts and descriptions. The banks were all open, and depositors were busily and anxiously collecting their specie deposits, and directors were as busily engaged in getting off their bullion. Millions of dollars of paper money, both State and Confederate, were carried to the Capitol Square and buried.

Night came on, but with it no sleep for human eyes in

Richmond. Confusion worse confounded reigned, and grim terror spread in wild contagion. The City Council met, and ordered the destruction of all spirituous liquors, fearing lest, in the excitement, there would be temptation to drink, and thus render our situation still more terrible. In the gutters ran a stream of whiskey, and its fumes filled and impregnated the air. After night-fall Richmond was ruled by the mob. In the principal business section of the city they surged in one black mass from store to store, breaking them open, robbing them, and in some instances (it is said) applying the torch to them.

In the alarm and terror, the guards of the State Penitentiary fled from their posts, and numbers of the lawless and desperate villains incarcerated there, for crimes of every grade and hue, after setting fire to the workshops, made good the opportunity for escape, and donning garments stolen wherever they could get them, in exchange for their prison livery, roamed over the city like fierce, ferocious beasts. No human tongue, no pen, however gifted, can give an adequate description of the events of that awful night.

While these fearful scenes were being enacted on the streets, in-doors there was scarcely less excitement and confusion. Into every house terror penetrated. Ladies were busily engaged in collecting and secreting all the valuables possessed by them, together with cherished correspondence, yet they found time and presence of mind to prepare a few comforts for friends forced to depart with the army or the government. Few tears were shed; there was no time for weakness or sentiment. The grief was too deep, the agony too terrible to find vent through the ordinary channels of distress. Fathers, husbands, brothers and friends clasped their loved ones to their bosoms in convulsive and agonized embraces, and bade an adieu, oh, how heart-rending!*— perhaps, thought many of them, forever.

---

* At eleven o'clock on that night, Colonel ——, on General ——'s staff, came into the city and was married. In a few moments he left his bride, in the terrible uncertainty of ever again meeting.

At midnight the train on the Danville Railroad bore off the officers of the Government, and at the same hour many persons made their escape on the canal packets, and fled in the direction of Lynchburg.

But a still more terrible element was destined to appear and add to the horrors of the scene. From some authority —it seems uncertain what—an order had been issued to fire the four principal tobacco warehouses. They were so situated as to jeopardize the entire commercial portion of Richmond. At a late hour of the night, Mayor Mayo had dispatched, by a committee of citizens, a remonstrance against this reckless military order. But in the mad excitement of the moment the protest was unheeded. The torch was applied, and the helpless citizens were left to witness the destruction of their property. The rams in the James River were blown up. The "Richmond," the "Virginia" No. 2 and the "Beaufort" were all scattered in fiery fragments to the four winds of heaven. The noise of these explosions, which occurred as the first grey streaks of dawn broke over Richmond, was like that of a hundred cannon at one time. The very foundations of the city were shaken; windows were shattered more than two miles from where these gunboats were exploded, and the frightened inhabitants imagined that the place was being furiously bombarded. The "Patrick Henry," a receiving-ship, was scuttled, and all the shipping at the wharves was fired except the flag-of-truce steamer "Allison."

As the sun rose on Richmond, such a spectacle was presented as can never be forgotten by those who witnessed it. To speed destruction, some malicious and foolish individuals had cut the hose in the city. The fire was progressing with fearful rapidity. The roaring, the hissing, and the crackling of the flames were heard above the shouting and confusion of the immense crowd of plunderers who were moving amid the dense smoke like demons, pushing, rioting and swaying with their burdens to make a passage to the open air. From the lower portion of the city, near the river, dense black clouds of smoke arose as a pall of crape to hide the ravages of the devouring flames, which lifted their red tongues and leaped from building to building as if possessed of demoniac instinct, and intent upon wholesale destruction. All the railroad bridges, and Mayo's Bridge, that crossed the James River and connected with Manchester, on the opposite side, were in flames.

The most remarkable scenes, however, were said to have occurred at the commissary depot. Hundreds of Government wagons were loaded with bacon, flour and whiskey, and driven off in hot haste to join the retreating army. In a dense throng around the depot stood hundreds of men, women and children, black and white, provided with anything in which they could carry away provisions, awaiting the opening of the doors to rush in and help themselves. A cascade of whiskey streamed from the windows. About sunrise the doors were thrown open to the populace, and with a rush that seemed almost sufficient to bear off the building itself, they soon swept away all that remained of the Confederate commissariat of Richmond.

By this time the flames had been applied to or had reached the arsenal, in which several hundred car loads of loaded shell were left. At every moment the most terrific explosions were sending forth their awful reverberations, and gave us the idea of a general bombardment. All the horrors of the final conflagration, when the earth shall be wrapped in flames and melt with fervent heat, were, it seemed to us, prefigured in our capital.

At an early hour in the morning, the Mayor of the city, to whom it had been resigned by the military commander, proceeded to the lines of the enemy and surrendered it to General Godfrey Weitzel, who had been left by General Ord, when he withdrew one-half of his division to the lines investing Petersburg, to receive the surrender of Richmond.

As early as eight o'clock in the morning, while the mob held possession of Main street, and were busily helping themselves to the contents of the dry goods stores and other shops in that portion of the city, and while a few of our cavalry were still to be seen here and there in the upper portions, a cry was raised: "The Yankees! The Yankees are coming!" Major A. H. Stevens, of the Fourth Massachusetts Cavalry, and Major E. E. Graves, of his staff, with forty cavalry, rode steadily into the city, proceeded directly to the Capitol, and planted once more the "Stars and Stripes"—the ensign of our subjugation—on that ancient edifice. As its folds were given to the breeze, while still we heard the roaring, hissing, crackling flames, the explosions of the shells and the shouting of the multitude, the strains of an old, familiar tune floated upon the air—a tune that, in days gone by, was wont to awaken a thrill of patriotism. But now only the most bitter and crushing recollections awoke within us, as upon our quickened hearing fell the strains of "The Star Spangled Banner." For us it was a requiem for buried hopes.

As the day advanced, Weitzel's troops poured through the city. Long lines of negro calvary swept by the Exchange Hotel, brandishing their swords and uttering savage cheers, replied to by the shouts of those of their own color, who were trudging along under loads of plunder, laughing and exulting over the prizes they had secured from the wreck of the stores, rather than rejoicing at the more precious prize of freedom which had been won for them. On passed the colored troops, singing, "John Brown's body is mouldering in the grave," etc.

By one o'clock in the day, the confusion reached its height. As soon as the Federal troops reached the city they were set to work by the officers to arrest the progress of the fire. By this time a wind had risen from the south, and seemed likely to carry the surging flames all over the northwestern portion of the city. The most strenuous efforts were made to prevent this, and the grateful thanks of the people of Richmond are due to General Weitzel and other officers for their energetic measures to save the city from entire destruction.

The Capitol Square now presented a novel appearance. On the south, east, and west of its lower half, it was bounded by burning buildings. The flames bursting from the windows, and rising from the roofs, were proclaiming in one wild roar their work of destruction. Myriads of sparks, borne upward by the current of hot air, were brightening and breaking in the dense smoke above. On the sward of the Square, fresh with the emerald green of early spring, thousands of wretched creatures, who had been driven from their dwellings by the devouring flames, were congregated. Fathers and mothers, and weeping, frightened children sought this open space for a breath of fresh air. But here, even, it was almost as hot as a furnace. Intermingled with these miserable beings were the Federal troops in their garish uniform, representing almost every nation on the continent of Europe, and thousands of the *Corps d'Afrique*. All along on the north side of the Square were tethered the horses of the Federal cavalry, while, dotted about, were seen the white tents of the sutlers, in which there were temptingly displayed canned fruits and meats, crackers, cheese, etc.

The roaring, crackling and hissing of the flames, the bursting of shells at the Confederate Arsenal, the sounds of instruments of martial music, the neighing of the horses, the shoutings of the multitude, in which could be distinctly distinguished the coarse, wild voices of the negroes, gave an idea of all the horrors of Pandemonium. Above all this scene of terror, hung a black shroud of smoke through which the sun shone with a lurid angry glare like an immense ball of blood that emitted sullen rays of light, as if loth to shine over a scene so appalling.

Remembering the unhappy fate of the citizens of Columbia and other cities of the South, and momentarily expecting pillage, and other evils incidental to the sacking of a city, great numbers of ladies sought the proper military authorities and were furnished with safeguards for the protection of themselves and their homes. These were willingly and generously furnished, and no scene of violence is remembered to have been committed by the troops which occupied Richmond. Throughout the entire day, those who had enriched themselves by plundering the stores were busy in conveying off their goods. Laughing and jesting negroes tugged along with every conceivable description of merchandise, and many an astute shopkeeper from questionable quarters of Richmond thus added greatly to his former stock.

The sun had set upon this terrible day before the awful reverberations of exploding shells at the arsenal ceased to be heard over Richmond: The evening came on. A deathlike quiet pervaded the late heaving and tumultuous city, broken only by the murmuring waters of the river. Night drew her sable mantle over the mutilated remains of our beautiful capital, and we locked, and bolted, and barred our doors; but sleep had fled our eyelids. All night long we kept a fearful vigil, and listened with beating heart and quickened ears for the faintest sound that might indicate the development of other and more terrible phases of horror. But from all these we were mercifully and providentially spared.

We will just here notice the range and extent of the fire which had in the afternoon literally burned itself out. From an authentic account we copy at length:

"It had consumed the very heart of the city. A surveyor could scarcely have designated the business portion of the city more exactly than did the boundaries of the fire. Commencing at the Shockoe warehouse the fire radiated front and rear, and on two wings, burning down to, but not destroying, the store No. 77 Main street, south side, halfway between Fourteenth and Fifteenth Streets, and back to the river through Cary and all the intermediate streets. Westward on Main the fire was stayed on Ninth Street, sweeping back to the river. On the north side of Main, the flames were stayed between Thirteenth and Fourteenth streets. From this point the flames raged on the north side of Main up to Eighth Street, and back to Bank Street.

"Among some of the most prominent of the buildings destroyed were the Bank of Richmond, Traders' Bank, Bank of the Commonwealth, Bank of Virginia, Farmers' Bank, all of the banking houses, the American Hotel, the Columbian Hotel, the Enquirer building, on

Twelfth Street, the Dispatch office and job-rooms, corner of Thirteenth and Main Streets, all that block of buildings known as Belvin's Block, the Examiner office, engine and machinery rooms, the Confederate Post Office Department building, the State Court House, a fine old building on the Capitol Square at its Franklin Street entrance, the Mechanics' Institute, vacated by the Confederate War Department, and all the buildings on that Square up to Eighth Street, and back to Main Street, the Confederate Arsenal, and the Laboratory on Seventh Street.

"The streets were crowded with furniture and every description of wares, dashed down and trampled in the mud, or burned where it lay. All the government stores were thrown open, and what could not be gotten off by the government was left to the people.

"Next to the river the destruction of property was fearfully complete. The Danville and Petersburg Railroad depots, and the buildings and shedding attached, for the distance of half-a-mile from the north side of Main Street to the river, and between Eighth and Fifteenth Streets, embracing upwards of twenty blocks, presented one waste of smoking ruins, blackened walls, and solitary chimneys."

Except the great fire in New York, in 1837, there is said never to have been so extensive a conflagration on this continent as the burning of Richmond on that memorable day.

Upon reaching the city, General Weitzel established his headquarters in the Hall of the State Capitol, previously occupied by the Virginia House of Delegates. He immediately issued an order for the restoration of quiet, and intended to allay the fears and restore confidence and tranquillity to the minds of the inhabitants. General Shepley was appointed Military Commander of Richmond, and Lieutenant-Colonel Fred L. Manning was made acting Provost Marshal.

General Shepley issued an order which protected the citizens from insult and depredation by the Federal soldiers, and which also included a morbidly sensitive clause in deprecation of insult to the "flag," calculated rather to excite the derision than the indignation of the conquered inhabitants.

The scenes of this day give rise to many reflections, the most of which are too deeply painful to dwell upon. The spirit of extortion, the wicked and inordinate greed of mammon which sometimes overclouds and overrules all the nobler instincts of humanity, are strikingly illustrated by a single incident in this connection. A lady passed up Franklin Street early on the morning of the 3d of April, and held in her hand a small phial in which there was about a table spoonful of paregoric. "This," said she, "I have just purchased on Main Street, at ——'s drug store. Richmond is in flames, and yet for this spoonful of medicine for a sick servant I had to pay five dollars."

An hour had not passed when the fire consumed the establishment of the extortionate vender of drugs. This incident points a moral which all can apply. Riches take to themselves wings, and in a moment least expected elude our grasp. Many who shirked the conscription, who made unworthy use of exemption bills, for the purpose of heaping up and watching their ill-gotten treasures, saw them in a single hour reduced to ashes and made the sport of the winds of heaven. Truly man knoweth not what a day may bring forth.

CHAPTER LXXIII.

VISIT OF PRESIDENT LINCOLN TO RICHMOND—THE FEDERAL GOVERNMENT FEEDING THE PEOPLE.

THE principal pillar that sustained the Confederate fabric had been overthrown, the chief corner-stone had been loosened and pushed from its place, and the crumbling of the entire edifice to a ruined and shapeless mass, seemed to us but a question of time.

On the morning of the 4th of April, the people of Richmond were aroused from the partial paralysis that succeeded the terrors of the previous day, by loud shouting and cheering on the streets. As they very readily conjectured, it was occasioned by the presence of his Excellency the President of the United States. Mr. Lincoln came up as far as Varina in the steamer "River Queen," and was thence drawn over in an ambulance to Richmond, where he met Admiral Porter, who had by that time reached the wharf in the Malvern. About eleven o'clock he walked up the streets of the half-burned city. He was accompanied by a young son, and escorted only by Admiral Porter, Captain Bell, a few marines and some of the citizens who had already declared Union sentiments, and had been apprised of his approach. Hundreds of the colored population thronged about him, to get a look at him, to shake his hand, to hear the tones of his voice, or otherwise to testify their admiration or secure his notice. He made his way to the Capitol. On the Square a superb carriage was in readiness for him, in which he was conveyed through the principal streets of the city. In the carriage were seated his son, Admiral Porter, and Captain Bell, while in attendance was an escort of negro cavalry. All along his triumphal passage, sable multitudes of both sexes and every age gathered and pressed around the vehicle to press or kiss his hand, or to get a word or look from him. As the carriage rolled up the streets they ran after it in furious excitement, and made the welkin ring with the loud and continuous cheering peculiar to their race. Mr. Lincoln visited the late residence of Mr. Davis, and the principal places of interest in Richmond, and as night approached returned to the steamer that had conveyed him thither, and departed forever from the conquered capital of the rival government.

A tissue of unhappy events had thrown the people of Richmond into the most painful and positive destitution. We have before mentioned the universal circulation of Confederate money. We have noticed the scarcity of provisions and the usual manner of living. The evacuation of the city found great numbers of the inhabitants totally without food, and entirely destitute of means by which it might be procured. The distress was wide spread, and to prevent the horrors of starvation immediate relief was demanded. In a very few days liberal assistance was extended through the Relief Association of the United States and the Christian

Commission of the Federal army, and the United States Sanitary Commission dispensed suitable delicacies, and what, indeed, in many instances, seemed luxuries to the sick and enfeebled.

To give an adequate idea of the extent of the destitution, we notice, from the Richmond *Whig*, that Mr. J. L. Apperson, Secretary of the Relief Committee, reported that from the 8th to the 15th of April, inclusive, 17,367 tickets were issued, calling for 86,555 rations. When the number of inhabitants in the city of Richmond is taken into the account, it will be seen that at least one-third of the entire population remaining in the city (and thousands had fled when it was surrendered) were driven to the humiliation of subsisting alone on supplies of food furnished them by the conquerors. The supplies consisted of the coarsest and most substantial quality of edibles, yet they were not ungratefully, though with sickened hearts, received by the miserable people who depended upon them to prevent hunger or starvation.

The miseries of our situation, which would have been incalculable at best, were inconceivably enhanced by the disastrous burning of the business portion of the city. Nearly all the supplies of food were kept in the stores which were consumed by the fire, and our poor people were almost totally dependent upon the mercy of the captors. For several months no remunerative employment could be obtained by the masses, and they were compelled to live by charity. The humiliation to many of this means of livelihood cannot be estimated. Commissary stores, where rations were dispensed, presented a novel aspect. Intermingled in a strange, incongruous and hitherto unacquainted throng, might be seen some of the most refined and delicately-nurtured of the women of Virginia, (who were driven by cruel want to seek such subsistence,) with the coarse, rude and vulgar of questionable parts of the city, and frequently with negroes who had left their former homes, and who thus took their first step in freedom.

The wretchedness of our people was sometimes made the subject of ridicule in certain of the illustrated periodicals of the North. One, which seems to find special delight (or perhaps profit) in delineations of the horrible, flourished an extensive illustration of "The Aristocratic Ladies of Richmond drawing Rations." For the sake of decency and humanity, and all the nobler instincts which must underlie the promptings of revenge or triumph in souls not deadened by vice to all fellow-feeling, we hope and must believe that the only pleasure experienced in representations holding up to ridicule the want, misery and humiliation of starving, helpless women, found lodgment only in the breasts of ambitious special artists and speculative picture-mongers.

CHAPTER LXIV.

THE SURRENDER OF LEE.

AFTER the occupation of Richmond by the Federal forces, all tidings from our friends in the Confederate army were as entirely cut off as though an ocean rolled between us and them. Nearly a week had passed, when, an hour or two after sunset, reports of cannon disturbed the stillness of the evening.

It boded no good to us, and we immediately connected it with a victory over our war-worn and retreating army. It was the Sabbath evening of the 9th of April. Soon from lip to lip ran the dreadful intelligence: "General Lee has surrendered!" Our fears had boded but too truly! Victory had perched triumphantly on the banners of our enemies, and our own cause, which had cost us four long and weary years of prayers and tears, of sacrifice, pain and woe and blood, was lost! "Our cause is lost!" How dreadfully, even at this moment, sounds the re-echo of those words, as we remember the crushing of our hopes at the tidings of

General Lee's surrender. At the dawn of the following morning, we were awakened by the reverberations of cannon, that confirmed the news of the evening previous. On the streets, gathered here and there at the corners, small squads of citizens discussed the sad event. Upon every countenance rested the shadow of gloom, and on every heart the paralyzing torpor of despair. There was only one whisper of consolation left to comfort us in our misery; and that was, "At least, then, the tide of blood is stayed." No tears were shed. In the speechless agony of woe, in the mute eloquence of despair, we moved about, little more than breathing automatons, and were slow to receive all the dreadful truth, and slower still to say: "Thy will be done, oh Lord!"

In accordance with the opinion of Virginians generally, and of great numbers of the people of the South from other States, the *Richmond Examiner*, several weeks before the fall of the city, had used the following language:

"The evacuation of Richmond would be the loss of all respect and authority towards the Confederate Government, the disintegration of the army, and the abandonment of the scheme of an independent Southern confederation. Each contestant in the war has made Richmond the central object of all its plans and all its exertions. It has become the symbol of the Confederacy. Its loss would be material ruin to the cause, and in a moral point of view, absolutely destructive, crushing the heart and extinguishing the last hope of the country. Our armies would lose the incentive inspired by a great and worthy object of defence. Our military policy would be totally at sea; we should be without hope or an object; without civil or military organization; without a treasury or commissariat; without the means of keeping alive wholesome, and active public sentiment; without any of the appliances for supporting a cause depending upon popular faith and enthusiasm; without the emblems or semblance of nationality."

After the withdrawal of General Lee's army, a very few days sufficed to prove the wisdom of this prophecy. As the retreat progressed, day by day, the situation became more and more desperate. Thoroughly demoralized, and seeing the necessity of surrender inevitable, thousands threw away their arms, and wishing to avoid what they supposed might be the conditions of surrender, went to their homes.

The meeting between General Lee and General Grant, to arrange terms of capitulation, took place at the house of Mr. Wilmer McLean. General Lee was attended only by Colonel Marshal, one of his aids, while with General Grant there were several of his staff officers, and a number of Federal generals are said to have entered the room during the interview.

The two commanders greeted each other with courtesy, and without delay proceeded to the business that had convened them. General Lee alluded at once to the conditions of surrender, expressed his satisfaction as to their leniency, and left the details to General Grant's own discretion. General Grant repeated the terms of the parole; that the arms should be stacked, the artillery parked and the supplies and munitions turned over to him, the officers to be allowed to retain their horses, side-arms and personal effects. General Lee promptly assented to the conditions, and the agreement of surrender was signed by him at half-past three o'clock in the afternoon.

General Lee's appearance on this memorable interview is thus described by a northern correspondent:—"General Lee looked very much jaded and worn, but nevertheless presented the same magnificent *physique* for which he had always been noted. He was neatly dressed in grey cloth, without embroidery or any insignia of rank except three stars worn on the turned portion of his coat collar. His cheeks were very much bronzed by exposure, but still shone ruddy underneath it all. He is growing quite bald, and wears the side-locks of his hair thrown across the upper portion of his forehead, which is white and fair as a woman's. He stands fully six feet one inch in height, and weighs something over two hundred pounds, without being burdened with a pound of superfluous flesh. During the whole interview he was retired and dignified to a degree bordering on taciturnity, but was free from all exhibition of temper or mortification. His demeanor was that of a thoroughly possessed gentleman who had a very disagreeable duty to perform, and was determined to get through with it as well and as soon as he could."

General Grant's conduct on this occasion was in the highest degree magnanimous. The affair was conducted simply and quietly, and with no effort or desire on his part to make a sensation. He exhibited no triumphant exultation, and avoided everything which might serve to wound the feelings of his vanquished foe. His whole deportment indicated the possession of a great mind, and the nobility of a great heart. Before the surrender, General Grant had declared to his own officers, his intention not to require of General Lee, the same formalities as are required in a surrender of the forces between two foreign nations or belligerent powers, and to exact no terms for the mere purpose of humiliation.

While this interview between the commanders of the two armies was taking place, an informal conference of the general officers, occupied the period of the armistice. They met in the streets of Appomattox Court House. On the Federal side were Generals Ord, Sheridan, Crook, Gibbon, Griffin, Merritt, Ayers, Bartlett, Chamberlain, Forsyth and Michie. The Confederate army was represented by Generals Longstreet, Heath, Gordon, Wilcox and others. None but general officers were allowed to pass through the skirmish line. Mutual introductions were given, healths were drank in whiskey, and there was a cordial interchange of fraternal feelings. This singular conference, from which was banished all restraint, lasted for more than an hour, when these officers returned to their respective armies, to learn the result of the important interview between the commanders.

Both armies awaited in the most anxious suspense for the word that was to signalize the resumption of hostilities, or the prospect of peace which would terminate the dreadful work of war. Anon, there was heard the clatter of hoofs, a flag of truce appeared, and an order from General Grant for a suspension of hostilities until further orders.

After the interview with General Grant, General Lee returned to his own camp, where his leading officers awaited him. He made known to them the result and the conditions. They then approached him in the order of their rank, shook hands, expressed satisfaction at the course he had taken, and regret at parting, all shedding tears. When General Lee appeared among his troops, after the surrender had been announced to them, he was loudly cheered.

At four o'clock, when it was proclaimed to General Grant's army that the surrender had been comsummated, and the articles signed, the enthusiasm which had been restrained by uncertainty—broke loose. The brigade commanders announced to their commands the joyful news, and cheer after cheer of the most excititing description rent the air.

On the day after the surrender, General Lee bade adieu to his troops in the following simple, manly and characteristic address:

GENERAL ORDER, No. 9.

HEADQUARTERS, ARMY OF NORTHERN VIRGINIA,
April 10th, 1865.

After four years of arduous service, marked by unsurpassed courage and fortitude, the Army of Northern Virginia has been compelled to yield to overwhelming numbers and resources.

I need not tell the survivors of so many hard-fought battles, who have remained steadfast to the last, that I have consented to this result from no distrust of them; but feeling that valor and devotion could accomplish nothing that would compensate for the loss that would have attended the continuation of the contest, I have determined to avoid the useless sacrifice of those whose past services have endeared them to their countrymen.

By the terms of agreement, officers and men can return to their homes and remain there until exchanged.

You will take with you the satisfaction that proceeds from the consciousness of duty faithfully performed, and I earnestly pray that a merciful God will extend to you his blessing and protection.

With an unceasing admiration for your constancy and devotion to your country, and a grateful remembrance of your kind and generous consideration of myself—I bid you an affectionate farewell.

R. E. LEE, General."

With heavy hearts our soldiers now turned their steps

homeward. Sad were the parting scenes as the veterans of the Army of Northern Virginia bade each other adieu. The ties of friendship which had sprung up in the field, on the march, and in the camp were cemented by mutual glory, mutual toil, privation and suffering; and in the common cause, all were brethren. They returned to their homes, not to contemplate the independence they had struggled so bravely to win, but cruel, crushing, bitter disappointment. They accepted the decision with the fortitude of veteran soldiers. They acknowledged their defeat as indeed accomplished. But the fire of patriotism can never be quenched on the altar of such hearts as theirs.

Among the missing from Richmond, who returned not to their homes with their comrades after the surrender, were two noble young men whose deeds of courage and bravery were the theme of universal admiration. Our youthful, noble Colonel Willie Pegram, (whose brother fell at Hatcher's Run) was killed in the very last engagement of the Army of Northern Virginia. His conduct at the time, is said to have been unsurpassed. He seemed to court death, and death accepted him! For days we mourned, also, the death of young C. M——, the son of the beloved pastor of St. Paul's Church; but finally our hearts were relieved when the news came, "he is not dead." However, a wound of the most painful character kept him hovering between life and death, for many days, and left him, as we then feared, a hopeless cripple.

A few days after the surrender, General Lee, accompanied by five members of his staff, rode into Richmond. He had hoped to reach his home unnoticed, but the fact of his presence spreading quickly through the city, crowds gathered around his door to receive him, and cheered him loudly as he approached. As he dismounted from his horse, large numbers pressed around him, and shook his hand warmly and sympathetically. Disengaging himself, in a few moments he passed into his house, and thus withdrew from public observation.

CHAPTER LXXV.

THE ASSASSINATION—CAPTURE OF JEFFERSON DAVIS—CONCLUDING EVENTS OF THE WAR.

THE news of the surrender of Lee's army had not been carried to remote distances in the South, nor even to all parts of the State of Virginia, nor had the people of Richmond more than begun to digest the unwelcome truth, when there came another startling piece of information to disturb the public mind.

It was the Sabbath afternoon of the 16th of April. The city was quiet. No sound arose to disturb the serenity of the holy day. The church bells were calling the people to vesper service. But here and there, groups collected; and as they discussed the astounding intelligence which spread like electricity from one to another, doubt, amazement, awe and incredulity, found expression on their countenances. Passers by heard the ominous exclamation, "The President is killed!"

It was whispered with bated breath, yet even a whisper is sometimes trumpet-tongued. "The President killed, Mr. Seward and his sons killed; the lives of the entire Cabinet attempted; the Vice-President escaping death only by a fortunate providence;" this was the appalling description of the Washington tragedy, as we received it in Richmond on that Sabbath afternoon.

The steps of many were arrested in their progress to church. They returned to their homes, or sought the houses of friends to inquire into the truth of the startling report. Many doubted it, and some accepted it, with the usual qualification of "A Sabbath day rumor." On the following morning, a glance at the newspapers, with their columns divided by the broad black lines adopted by the press in mourning, indicated that this was no mere fictitious report, gotten up for effect; no figment of morbidly excited imaginations. Though not so extensive and terrible as rumor had at first declared, it was substantially true. The head of the nation had fallen. The man who so short a time before had made our city a visit, who had trodden the streets of our subjugated capital a conqueror, had been cut down by the hand of violence! Reflection was terrible! The judgments of God were abroad in the land! In sections where late there were exultation and universal acclamations of delight there was one long, loud wail of sorrow. The country was called to question where these judgments would stop? With reason overwhelmed by the sudden, awful and signal dispensations of the Providence which distinguished this peculiar period in the history of our country, we laid our mouths in the dust, and were dumb before the awful majesty of the Eternal!

Vague conjectures succeeded surprise at the appalling news. With folded hands we watched the turn of the wheel of public events, and acknowledging the impotence of man to fathom the mind of the mighty God, with anxious hearts inquired, "What next?"

In the wonderful charity which buries all quarrels in the grave, Mr. Lincoln, dead, was no longer regarded in the character of an enemy; for with the generosity native to Southern character, all resentment was hidden in his tomb at Springfield. We were satisfied to let the "dead Past bury its dead."

To finish the story of the war but little more remains to be told. The surrender of the Army of Northern Virginia, was "the beginning of the end," and in effect terminated the contest.

Contending against the most enormous odds, and without the necessary means for its longer prosecution, all attempts to continue the war successfully appeared to General Johnston as utterly futile. Under these circumstances, he announced his conclusion to the governors of the States within his department in the following address:

"The disaster in Virginia, the capture by the enemy of all workshops for the preparation of ammunition and repairing of arms, the impossibility of recruiting our little army, opposed by more than ten times its number, or supporting it except by robbing our own citizens, destroyed all hope of successful war. I have therefore made a military convention with Major General Sherman to terminate hostilities in North and South Carolina, Georgia and Florida. I made this convention to spare the blood of this little army, to prevent further suffering of our people by the devastation and ruin inevitable from the marches of invading armies, and to avoid the crime of waging a hopeless war."

The terms agreed upon between General Sherman and General Johnston, which were intended to insure protection to the citizens as well as to soldiers of the South, but which were understood to concede certain privileges and prerogatives to the States, raised against the Federal Commander such a storm of indignation in Washington, and called down upon him such undeserved censure as required all his military reputation to withstand. The President repudiated them, the War Department prohibited them, and General Grant, although an ardent personal friend of General Sherman, censured them.

So decided was the dissatisfaction at the conduct of General Sherman, that Grant was ordered to proceed at once to North Carolina, to take control of Sherman's army, and to compel Johnston at once to unconditional surrender.

Here again General Grant exhibited the magnanimity of character shown so signally and grandly in his hour of triumph. Truly, as says a distinguished Southern author, "in the most fortunate period in the life of any living man in America, Grant was not intoxicated by vanity or conceit. He was incapable of an attempt upon the reputation of a rival."

General Grant, obedient to instructions, went to North Carolina, but he kept the military operations in the hands of Sherman, and insisted on giving him the honor of concluding the negotiations with General Johnston, and of receiving the surrender of his army, which was finally effected upon such terms as had been conceded to General Lee.

On the 4th of May, General Dick Taylor surrendered to General Canby all the forces, munitions of war, etc., in the

END OF THE WAR. 383

department of Alabama, Mississippi, and East Louisiana. The negotiations for this surrender were concluded at Citronville, Alabama, and were essentially the same as those entered into with Generals Lee and Johnston.

Of the Confederate forces in Virginia, the last to lay down their arms were the brave band of dashing and valorous spirits that had rallied around our gallant young partisan leader, Colonel Jack Mosby. This remarkable young man left his law office in Bristol, on the western border of Virginia, and gathering up a band of chosen men, made his name one of dread to the enemy and a pillar of reliance to the South. It is now a household word. Jack Mosby— the Albemarle boy—the youthful, unpretending lawyer of a Western Virginia village, is known among our enemies as, "Mosby, the guerrilla," a name inspiring terror from unpleasant remembrances of bitter retaliation, but in the South he is known as "Mosby, the young partisan warrior —Mosby, the hero." Being an independent organization, his force was not regarded as included in the surrender of the Army of Northern Virginia. Some weeks subsequent to that event, he formally surrendered his command upon terms similar to those accorded his illustrious companions in arms.

By the first days of May, all the Confederate forces east of the Mississippi had been surrendered. There only remained of the Southern armies in the field, the command of General Kirby Smith, west of the Mississippi. With the struggling faith of a "drowning man that will catch at a straw" for safety, the hopes of some clung to the idea that Southern independence might at last be secured through the little army that still carried its colors in the far Southwest. General Smith endeavored to infuse into his troops a spirit of confidence, a determination still to resist invasion, and predicted help from sympathetic foreign nations. He said to them: "The great resources of the Department, its vast extent, the numbers, discipline and efficiency of the army, will secure to our country terms that a proud people can with honor accept; and may, under the providence of God, be the means of checking the triumph of our enemy, and securing the final success of our cause." War meetings were held in different parts of Texas. At Houston, General Magruder addressed the citizens, and told them he was not discouraged by the turn of events; and ended by protesting he had rather be a "Camanche Indian, than submit to the Yankees."

The excitement and enthusiasm thus awakened, was however momentary. When the extent of the disasters east of the Mississippi became fully known, symptoms of demoralization impossible to counteract speedily possessed the army of General Smith. On the 21st of May, he sent officers to Baton Rouge, where General Canby was then stationed, to negotiate with him terms of surrender. These were concluded on the 21st of May, and were such as had been accorded to other Confederate forces.

This was the last act in the Confederate War for Independence. But all was not yet accomplished. We had to turn another leaf to look upon the epilogue of sorrow. With heart-sickening anxiety, with forebodings too dreadful to be whispered, we listened for tidings from our beloved, our unhappy and fugitive President. We were painfully aware that his enemies were in pursuit of him. Various rumors were in circulation. His escape across the Mississippi was reported; and the doors of Mexico were said to have opened to him.

On a bright Sabbath morning, after the middle of May, the voices of news-boys in the familiar cry, "Extra! Extra!" drew us to the doors and windows; and our hearts were chilled, and our complexions paled, as in trembling agony, we heard proclaimed, "The capture of Jeff. Davis!"

Thus was announced the fate of the unfortunate chief representative of our lost cause. What Southern heart cannot recall the sickening, the palsying weakness of that moment? Our chastisement seemed heavier than weak human nature could endure.

END OF THE WAR. 385

Our President a captive, the members of his Council fugitives or prisoners, our cause perished, our country ruined, our land desolated, our armies overpowered! We were left to muse on the mutability of human events, to glance mournfully backward on the Past, and to gaze with steady, cold, dead calmness on the altered Present. We were driven to reflect on the strange and mysterious dealings of the wonder-working hand of God, and wiping the film from the eyes of faith, to steer clear of the wrecking reefs of infidelity. Should these pages fall under the eye of one disposed to censure, we ask that the tones of human sympathy may not fall on deadened ears, that the heart may not be steeled against the divine accents of tender mercy.

It may be inquired how we fared under the regime of our conquerors, in the quondam capital of what has been derisively termed the "so-called Southern Confederacy."

The psalmist of Israel tells us when the ancient people were carried into Babylonish captivity:

"By the rivers of Babylon we sat down, yea we wept when we remembered Zion."

"We hanged our harps upon the willows in the midst thereof."

"For there they that carried us away captive required of us a song: and they that wasted us, required of us mirth."

It cannot be denied that to some extent we experienced the bitter fruits of subjugation, so graphically described by David. The burden of our agony was thus expressed: "If I forget thee, oh Jerusalem, let my right hand forget her cunning." The occupation of Richmond by our enemies occurred at a peculiarly interesting period in the ecclesiastical division of the year. It was the last week of the Lental season, the week which commemorates the passion of our Saviour.

In the diocese of Virginia, the clause in the prayer for the "President of the United States, and all others in authority," had been altered by order of the Bishop, to correspond to our status under the Confederacy. The Bishop being absent, it could not then be conveniently changed,

17

and owing, as they felt they then owed, political allegiance only to the President of the Confederate States, and with no instruction at that time from their diocesan, to make use of the prayer differently, the Protestant Episcopal ministers of Richmond could not conscientiously use the unamended prayer of the Prayer-book. They were therefore required by the military authorities of the city to close their churches. It was the most rigorous and aggravating feature of our peculiar situation, and was felt to be a direct blow upon the very root of the tree of religious liberty. In a few weeks these unhappy disagreements were reconciled, and the Bishop directed the use of the unamended prayer in the churches.

There would be a failure in simple justice, and a compromise of conscientious generosity, did we refuse to accord to those placed in temporary authority over us as military rulers of Richmond, the offering of sincere gratitude, for the respect, the kindness, the lenity with which the citizens were treated. For a conquered people, the lines had fallen to us in pleasant places. The names of Ord, Weitzel, Patrick, Dent, Manning, Mulford and others, cannot be remembered with unkindness. They softened greatly the first bitter experiences of our subjugation.

The vast armies of our conquerors, on their homeward march, now began to pour through the streets of Richmond. Day after day, as we witnessed the passage of the countless, and as they seemed to us interminable legions of the enemy, against which our comparatively little army had so obstinately, and all but successfully held out for four years, the question that arose in our minds, was not why we were conquered at last, but "how we could have so long resisted the mighty appliances which operated against us." Our pride, our glory in our countrymen was heightened, and we felt indeed, "the South is the land for soldiers," and though our enemies triumphed, it was at a price that was felt by them.

As General Meade's corps passed through Richmond, a singular acquaintance was revived with a lady, by one of his men. Going accidentally to the front door of her house a soldier in a Federal uniform sprang up from the steps, and offered her his hand. She recoiled instantly, but overcome by the deprecating expression on the face of the man, she reluctantly extended her hand.

"Do you not know me?" inquired the soldier.

"Your face is altogether familiar," replied the lady, "but you must pardon me for not knowing you under your blue jacket."

"Don't you remember that you were kind to me in ——— Hospital?"

"Yes, I remember; I was attentive to you, when you were helpless, and needed attention and sympathy, and I should have done the same for any honorable soldier in the Union Army, had he been a sufferer and thrown under my notice—but then you were in the Confederate army, and how did it happen that you were so base as to be a deserter from our cause—the cause in which you then professed to find such glory?"

"Did you never hear?" returned the crest-fallen, guilty-looking man, who now cowered before the calm, steady gaze of the woman, "did you never hear that when I left Richmond, I went to Fairfax County on some business for Major ———, when I was taken prisoner? I was then carried to Washington, and granted a parole. I then went to Philadelphia; there I made some unfortunate acquaintances, who invited me to a saloon to drink. I went with them—drank with them, and knew no more, until I found myself in a Yankee camp, with the bounty-money in my pocket."

"No;" replied the lady, listening incredulously to the cunning story of the deserter, "I heard nothing whatever from you after your mysterious disappearance from Richmond."

The deserter winced under the keen reproof he well understood. As if to palliate his unprincipled conduct, he remarked: "I never raised a gun against a Confederate soldier; I could not do it. This is my instrument, (holding up a bugle.) And I could not pass your house without coming to thank you for your great kindness to me when I was wounded and helpless."

"I see, I see," replied the lady, sarcastically. "It has been returned most gratefully. I have no sympathy, sir, with *deserters.*"

While this conversation was going on, several Federal officers, attracted by the singular interview, gathered around, and smiled and bowed their admiration of the lady's remarks.

As she looked upon the disconcerted, miserable wretch before her, pity took the place of contempt; she regretted that the dormant spirit that rested in her bosom, should have been fanned into a blaze of such severity. Kindly extending her hand to him, and modulating her voice to a softer key, she continued: "Listen to the voice of conscience, unless that in your bosom has become deadened by disuse, and I shall hope to hear better things of you hereafter."

CHAPTER LXXVI.

LIFE IN THE OLD LAND YET!

FOR Richmond—the still fair and beautiful "seven hilled" city of the South—there is a great destiny in reserve. Earthly malice would be powerless to prevent it. Her climate invites it, her geographical position courts it, the intelligence, enterprise, and industry of her inhabitants will compel it; by her side the flowing waters of the classic stream upon which she proudly looks, send up a never ceasing cry to expend our might in works for her prosperity. We long to see the dust and rubbish removed, the city thoroughly rebuilt and enlarged, her wharves multiplied, the waters of the James turning hundreds of mills, and Richmond what Nature designed her to be, the great manufacturing metropolis of the Western Continent.

The restoration of the railroad lines, now making good

progress, will again bring into her marts the varied productions of her naturally generous soil. The farmer already carries on his arm the basket containing the seed of the rich and rare vegetable products which must once more deck her fields in loveliness, and bid her "deserts rejoice and blossom as the rose." The miner, even now, holds the pick which shall compel the jealous earth to disgorge her mineral treasures for the use of her master—MAN!

The rising generation pray their native mother to forget not her ancient prestige, they plead for still greater light, they call for an increase of educational resources, for academies and colleges, and with this cry is mingled the plaintive voice of the orphan. They conjure up the spirit of her statesmen, and whispering her honored and honorable names in their nation's history, pray her to remember:—

> "Beneath the rule of men entirely great,
> The pen is mightier than the sword!"

The energy, the enterprise, the almost universal self-abnegation, and complete devotion, with which the people of the South entered into and sustained the cause of the war, to all but a successful termination, prove that they are capable of still grander, and higher, and nobler enterprises. The world must expect it, and they be held responsible if those expectations fail of reality. Disappointment does not comprehend a folding of the hands in sleep, nor defeat, death!

From the Potomac to the Rio Grande, from the grass-covered prairies of the West to the Atlantic shores, over every desolate hill and valley, on every wasted homestead, upon every ruined hearthstone, is written as with an angel's pen, in letters of fire, the magic word RESURGAM!

"There is LIFE in the OLD LAND yet!"

THE END.

NEW BOOKS
And New Editions Recently Published by
G. W. CARLETON & CO.,
NEW YORK.

GEORGE W. CARLETON.   HENRY S. ALLEN.

N.B.—THE PUBLISHER, upon receipt of the price in advance, will send any of the following Books by mail, POSTAGE FREE, to any part of the United States. This convenient and very safe mode may be adopted when the neighboring Booksellers are not supplied with the desired work. State name and address in full.

Victor Hugo.
LES MISÉRABLES.—*The best edition*, two elegant 8vo. vols., beautifully bound in cloth, $5.50 ; half calf, $10.00
LES MISÉRABLES.—*The popular edition*, one large octavo volume, paper covers, $2.00 ; cloth bound, $2.50
LES MISÉRABLES.—In the Spanish language. Fine 8vo. edition, two vols., paper covers, $4.00 ; cloth bound, $5.00
JARGAL.—A new novel. Illustrated. . 12mo. cloth, $1.75
THE LIFE OF VICTOR HUGO.—By himself. 8vo. cloth, $1.75

Miss Muloch.
JOHN HALIFAX.—A novel. With illustration. 12mo. cloth, $1.75
A LIFE FOR A LIFE.—   .   do.   do. $1.75

Charlotte Bronte (Currer Bell).
JANE EYRE.—A novel. With illustration. 12mo., cloth, $1.75
THE PROFESSOR. —do.   .   do.   .   do. $1.75
SHIRLEY.—   . do.   . do.   :   do. $1.75
VILLETTE.—   . do.   . do.   .   do. $1.75

Hand-Books of Society.
THE HABITS OF GOOD SOCIETY; with thoughts, hints, and anecdotes, concerning nice points of taste, good manners, and the art of making oneself agreeable. The most entertaining work of the kind ever published. 12mo. cloth, $1.75
THE ART OF CONVERSATION.—With directions for self-culture. A sensible and instructive work, that ought to be in the hands of every one who wishes to be either an agreeable talker or listener.   .   .   .   . 12mo. cloth, $1.50
THE ART OF AMUSING.—A collection of graceful arts, games, tricks, puzzles, and charades, intended to amuse everybody, and enable all to amuse everybody else. With suggestions for private theatricals, tableaux, parlor and family amusements, etc. With nearly 150 illustrative pictures. 12mo. cloth, $2.00

LIST OF BOOKS PUBLISHED

Mrs. Mary J. Holmes' Works.

'LENA RIVERS.— . . . A novel. 12mo. cloth, $1.50
DARKNESS AND DAYLIGHT.— . do. do. $1.50
TEMPEST AND SUNSHINE.— . do. do. $1.50
MARIAN GREY.— . . . do. do. $1.50
MEADOW BROOK.— . . . do. do. $1.50
ENGLISH ORPHANS.— . . . do. do. $1.5
DORA DEANE.—. . . . do. do. $1.5
COUSIN MAUDE.— . . . do. do. $1.50
HOMESTEAD ON THE HILLSIDE.— do. do. $1.50
HUGH WORTHINGTON.— . . do. do. $1.50
THE CAMERON PRIDE.—*Just published.* . do. $1.50

Artemus Ward.

HIS BOOK.—The first collection of humorous writings by A. Ward. Full of comic illustrations. 12mo. cloth, $1.50
HIS TRAVELS.—A comic volume of Indian and Mormon adventures. With laughable illustrations. 12mo. cloth, $1.50
IN LONDON.—A new book containing Ward's comic *Punch* letters, and other papers. Illustrated. 12mo. cloth, $1.50

Miss Augusta J. Evans.

BEULAH.—A novel of great power. . 12mo. cloth, $1.75
MACARIA.— do. do. . do. $1.75
ST. ELMO.— do. do. *Just published.* do. $2.00

By the Author of "Rutledge."

RUTLEDGE.—A deeply interesting novel. 12mo. cloth, $1.75
THE SUTHERLANDS.— do. . . do. $1.75
FRANK WARRINGTON.— do. . . do. $1.75
ST. PHILIP'S.— . do. . . do. $1.75
LOUIE'S LAST TERM AT ST. MARY'S. . . do. $1.75
ROUNDHEARTS AND OTHER STORIES.—For children. do. $1.75
A ROSARY FOR LENT.—Devotional readings. do. $1.75

Mrs. Ritchie (Anna Cora Mowatt).

FAIRY FINGERS.—A capital new novel. . 12mo. cloth, $1.75
THE MUTE SINGER.— do. . . . do. $1.75
THE CLERGYMAN'S WIFE—and other stories. do. $1.75

New English Novels.

DEYMINSTRE.—A very interesting novel. 12mo. cloth, $1.75
RECOMMENDED TO MERCY.— do. . . do. $1.75
AKEN UPON TRUST.— do. . . do. $1.7

Geo. W. Carleton.

OUR ARTIST IN CUBA.—A humorous volume of travels; with fifty comic illustrations by the author. 12mo. cloth, $1.50
OUR ARTIST IN PERU.— $1.50

A. S. Roe's Works.

A LONG LOOK AHEAD.—	A novel.	12mo. cloth,	$1.50
TO LOVE AND TO BE LOVED.—	do.	do.	$1.50
TIME AND TIDE.—	do.	do.	$1.50
I'VE BEEN THINKING.—	do.	do.	$1.50
THE STAR AND THE CLOUD.—	do.	do.	$1.50
TRUE TO THE LAST.—	do.	do.	$1.50
HOW COULD HE HELP IT?—	do.	do.	$1.50
LIKE AND UNLIKE.—	do.	do.	$1.50
LOOKING AROUND.—	do.	do.	$1.50
WOMAN, OUR ANGEL.—*Just published.*		do.	$1.50

Richard B. Kimball.

WAS HE SUCCESSFUL.—	A novel.	12mo. cloth,	$1.75
UNDERCURRENTS.—	do.	do.	$1.75
SAINT LEGER.—	do.	do.	$1.75
ROMANCE OF STUDENT LIFE.—	do.	do.	$1.75
IN THE TROPICS.—	do.	do.	$1.75
THE PRINCE OF KASHNA.—	do.	do.	$1.75
EMILIE.—A sequel to "St. Leger."	*In press.*	do.	$1.75

Orpheus C. Kerr.

THE ORPHEUS C. KERR PAPERS.—Comic letters and humorous military criticisms. Three series. . 12mo. cloth, $1.50
AVERY GLIBUN.—A powerful new novel.—*In press.*

Josh Billings.

HIS BOOK.—Rich comic sayings. Illustrated. 12mo. clo., $1.50

Thos. A. Davies.

HOW TO MAKE MONEY, and how to keep it.—A practical and valuable book that every one should have. 12mo. clo., $1.50

T. S. Arthur's New Works.

LIGHT ON SHADOWED PATHS.—A novel.		12mo. cloth,	$1.50
OUT IN THE WORLD.—	do.	do.	$1.50
NOTHING BUT MONEY.—	do.	do.	$1.50
WHAT CAME AFTERWARDS.—	do.	do.	$1.50
OUR NEIGHBORS.—*Just published.*		do.	$1.50

Robinson Crusoe.

A handsome illustrated edition, complete. 12mo. cloth, $1.50

Joseph Rodman Drake.

THE CULPRIT FAY.—A faery poem . . 12mo. cloth, $1.25
AN ILLUSTRATED EDITION.—With 100 exquisite illustrations on wood. . . Quarto, beautifully printed and bound, $5.00

Algernon Charles Swinburne.

LAUS VENERIS—and other Poems and Ballads. 12mo. cloth, $1.75

LIST OF BOOKS PUBLISHED

Cuthbert Bede.
VERDANT GREEN.—A rollicking, humorous novel of English student life; with 200 comic illustrations.   12mo. cloth, $1.50

Private Miles O'Reilly.
BAKED MEATS OF THE FUNERAL.—A comic book. 12mo. cloth, $1.75
LIFE AND ADVENTURES—with comic illustrations.   do. $1.50

M. Michelet's Remarkable Works.
LOVE (L'AMOUR).—From the French. .   . 12mo. cloth, $1.50
WOMAN (LA FEMME).—   do. . . .   do. $1.50

J. Sheridan Le Fanu.
WYLDER'S HAND.—A powerful new novel.   12mo. cloth, $1.75
THE HOUSE BY THE CHURCHYARD.— do.   do. $1.75

Rev. John Cumming, D.D., of London.
THE GREAT TRIBULATION.—Two series.   12mo. cloth, $1.50
THE GREAT PREPARATION.—   do.   .   do. $1.50
THE GREAT CONSUMMATION.—   do.   .   do. $1.50
THE LAST WARNING CRY.—   ,.   .   do. $1.50

Ernest Renan.
THE LIFE OF JESUS.—From the French work. 12mo. cloth, $1.75
THE APOSTLES.—   . do.   . do. $1.75

Popular Italian Novels.
DOCTOR ANTONIO.—A love story. By Ruffini. 12mo. cloth, $1.75
VINCENZO.—   do.   do.   do. $1.75
BEATRICE CENCI.—By Guerrazzi, with portrait.   do. $1.75

Charles Reade.
THE CLOISTER AND THE HEARTH.—A magnificent new novel—the best this author ever wrote.   .   . 8vo. cloth, $2.00

The Opera.
TALES FROM THE OPERAS.—A collection of clever stories, based upon the plots of all the famous operas. 12mo. cloth, $1.50

Robert B. Roosevelt.
THE GAME-FISH OF THE NORTH.—Illustrated. 12mo. cloth, $2.00
SUPERIOR FISHING.—   do.   do. $2.00
THE GAME-BIRDS OF THE NORTH.—   do. $2.00

John Phœnix.
THE SQUIBOB PAPERS.—A new humorous volume, filled with comic illustrations by the author.   12mo. cloth, $1.50

Matthew Hale Smith.
MOUNT CALVARY.—Meditations in sacred places. 12mo. $2.00

P. T. Barnum.
THE HUMBUGS OF THE WORLD.—Two series. 12mo. cloth, $1.75

Alice Carey.
THE BISHOP'S SON.—A new American novel. 12mo. cloth, $1.75
Edmund Kirke.
AMONG THE PINES.—Or Life in the South.   12mo. cloth, $1.50
MY SOUTHERN FRIENDS.—   do.   .   .   do. $1.50
DOWN IN TENNESSEE.—   do.   .   .   do. $1.50
ADRIFT IN DIXIE.—   do.   .   .   do. $1.50
AMONG THE GUERILLAS.—   do.   .   .   do. $1.50
Mrs. C. A. Warfield.
BEAUSEINCOURT.—A deeply interesting novel. 12mo. cloth, $1.75
HOUSEHOLD OF BOUVERIE.—   do.   do. $2.00
Mrs. Whitcher.
WIDOW SPRIGGINS.—A comic work, author "Widow Bedott," $1.75
F. Bret Harte.
CONDENSED NOVELS—and other comic papers. 12mo. cloth, $1.50
Dr. J. J. Craven.
THE PRISON-LIFE OF JEFFERSON DAVIS.—Incidents and conversations connected with his captivity. 12mo. cloth, $2.00
Captain Raphael Semmes.
THE CRUISE OF THE ALABAMA AND SUMTER.—12mo. cloth, $2.00
Walter Barrett, Clerk.
THE OLD MERCHANTS OF NEW YORK.—Personal incidents, sketches, bits of biography, and events in the life of leading merchants in New York. Four series.   .   .   12mo. cloth, $1.75
Madame Octavia Walton Le Vert.
SOUVENIRS OF TRAVEL.—New edition. Large 12mo. cloth, $2.00
Junius Brutus Booth.
MEMORIALS OF THE "ELDER BOOTH."—The actor. 12mo. cloth, $1.50
H. T. Sperry.
COUNTRY LOVE vs. CITY FLIRTATION.—A capital new Society tale, with 20 superb illustrations by Hoppin.   12mo. cloth, $2.00
Epes Sargent.
PECULIAR.—A remarkable new novel.   .   .   12mo. cloth, $1.75
Cuyler Pine.
MARY BRANDEGEE.—A very powerful novel. 12mo. cloth, $1.75
RENSHAWE.—   do.   do. $1.75
Elisha Kent Kane.
LOVE-LIFE OF DR. KANE and Margaret Fox. 12mo. cloth, $1.75
Mother Goose for Grown Folks.
HUMOROUS RHYMES for grown people.   .   .   12mo. cloth, $1.25

Miscellaneous Works.

JOHN S. MOSBY.—His Life and Exploits, portraits. 12mo.		$1.75
THE SHENANDOAH.—History of the Conf. steamer.	do.	$1.50
HELEN COURTENAY.—Author "Vernon Grove."	do.	$1.75
BALLADS.—By Amelia B. Edwards.	do.	$1.50
STORMCLIFF.—A novel by M. T. Walworth.	do.	$1.75
MAN, and the Conditions that Surround Him.	do.	$1.75
PROMETHEUS IN ATLANTIS.—A prophecy.	do.	$2.00
THE PAPACY EXPOSED.—Introduction by Bishop Coxe.	do.	$1.75
PULPIT PUNGENCIES.—A rich comic book.	do.	$1.75
CHOLERA.—A Handbook on its treatment and cure.	do.	$1.00
KATE MARSTONE.—An American story.	do.	$1.50
WHO GOES THERE?—By "Sentinel."	do.	$1.50
ALICE OF MONMOUTH.—By Edmund C. Stedman.	do.	$1.25
LYRICS AND IDYLLS.— do. do.	do.	$1.25
NOTES ON SHAKSPEARE.—By Jas. H. Hackett. 12mo. cloth,		$1.50
THE MONTANAS.—A novel by Mrs. S. J. Hancock.	do.	$1.75
PASTIMES WITH LITTLE FRIENDS.—Martha H. Butt.	do.	$1.50
A SPINSTER'S STORY.—A new novel.	do.	$1.75
A LIFE OF JAMES STEPHENS.—Fenian Head-Centre.	do.	$1.00
FREE GOVERNMENT IN ENGLAND AND AMERICA.—	do.	$3.00
AUTOBIOGRAPHY OF A NEW ENGLAND FARM-HOUSE.—	do.	$1.75
NEPENTHE.—A new novel.	do.	$1.50
TOGETHER.— do.	do.	$1.50
POEMS.—By Gay H. Naramore.	do.	$1.50
GOMERY OF MONTGOMERY.—By C. A. Washburn.	do.	$2.00
VICTOIRE.—A new novel.	do.	$1.75
POEMS.—By Mrs. Sarah T. Bolton.	do.	$1.50
JOHN GUILDERSTRING'S SIN.—A novel.	do.	$1.50
CENTEOLA.—By author "Green Mountain Boys."	do.	$1.50
RED TAPE AND PIGEON-HOLE GENERALS.—	do.	$1.50
TREATISE ON DEAFNESS.—By Dr. E. B. Lighthill.	do.	$1.50
AROUND THE PYRAMIDS.—By Gen. Aaron Ward.	do.	$1.50
CHINA AND THE CHINESE.—By W. L. G. Smith.	do.	$1.50
EDGAR POE AND HIS CRITICS.—By Mrs. Whitman.	do.	$1.00
MARRIED OFF.—Illustrated Satirical Poem.	do.	50 cts.
THE RUSSIAN BALL.—Illustrated satirical poem.	do.	50 cts.
THE SNOBLACE BALL.— do. do. do.	do.	50 cts.
AN ANSWER TO HUGH MILLER.—By T. A. Davies.	do.	$1.50
COSMOGONY.—By Thomas A. Davies.	8vo. cloth,	$2.00
TWENTY YEARS around the world.—J. Guy Vassar.	do.	$3.75
RURAL ARCHITECTURE.—By M. Field. Illustrated.	do.	$2.00

www.ingramcontent.com/pod-product-compliance
Lightning Source LLC
Chambersburg PA
CBHW032033220426
43664CB00006B/463